Rise of the Spanish-American Republics

WILLIAM SPENCE ROBERTSON

Rise of the

Spanish-American

Republics

As Told in the Lives of
Their Liberators

THE FREE PRESS, _New York_
COLLIER-MACMILLAN LIMITED, _London_

Collier-Macmillan Canada, Ltd., Toronto, Ontario

FIRST FREE PRESS PAPERBACK EDITION 1965
by arrangement with Appleton-Century-Crofts, Inc.

Second printing, March 1966

TO MY
HISPANIC-AMERICAN FRIENDS

Preface

YEARS AGO, while an undergraduate at the University of Wisconsin, I was seized with a desire to study the history and politics of Hispanic America, the vast region inhabited by the wayward children of Spain and Portugal. The first fruit of this desire was an essay upon that knight-errant of Venezuela, Francisco de Miranda, who championed the independence of the Spanish colonies from the motherland. My study of Miranda's romantic career naturally aroused within me an interest in the lives of his South-American compatriots, Bolívar and San Martin. One day, while browsing in the library of Yale University, I stumbled across some musty and forgotten manuscripts pertaining to Augustín de Iturbide: that incident stimulated my interest in the movement which separated New Spain from Old Spain. From time to time other influences have aided me to form the mold of the present volume, which, in a series of lives, tells the story of the movements that separated most of the Spanish colonies in America—the Spanish-American colonies as I have uniformly designated them—from the motherland. For criticisms concerning these biographies I am indebted to Professor W. F. Dodd, now of the University of Chicago, and Professor E. B. Greene, of the University of Illinois, both of whom read the entire manuscript.

The collecting of source material for these biographical studies has been attended by no small difficulty. Although in recent years a number of libraries in the United States have been purchasing books upon Hispanic-American history, yet in few, if any, cases have complete collections been made of the learned publications, books, and pamphlets concerning any special epoch of Spanish-American history. In the preparation of this volume, it has consequently been necessary for me to use many libraries. For courtesies extended to me I am especially indebted to the University of Illinois Library, the British Museum, the National Library of Spain, and the National Libraries of Mexico, Venezuela, Colombia, Chile, Paraguay, and Argentina, as well as the Mitre Museum at Buenos Aires. In various ways my labors have been aided by scholars in America and Europe. In North America my labors

7

were aided by Mr. Gaillard Hunt of the Division of Manuscripts of the Library of Congress. Certain investigations in
Spain were facilitated by Professor Rafael Altamira of the
University of Madrid, and by Sr. D. Pedro Torres Lanzas,
chief of the Spanish archives at Seville. My investigations in
England were assisted by Hubert Hall, Esq., long connected
with the Public Record Office. Among Mexican scholars, I
mention with appreciation Sr. Genaro García, formerly director of the National Museum of Mexico, and Sr. Luis Gon-
zález Obregón, formerly director of the General Archives of
Mexico. Among South-American scholars, I must mention
with gratitude Sr. Rómulo Zabala of the Mitre Museum, and
Srs. Diego L. Molinari and Carlos I. Salas of Buenos Aires;
Professors Domingo Amunátegui Solar and Samuel Lillo of
the University of Chile; Sr. Isidro López, Sr. Diego Mendoza
and Sr. Antonio Gómez Restrepo of Bogotá; Sr. Manuel
Segundo Sánchez, director of the National Library at Caracas,
and Sr. Vicente Lecuna, president of the bank of Venezuela,
who has charge of the archives of Simón de Bolivar.

My aim throughout has been to base this volume upon the
sources. I have profited, however, by the use of many secondary accounts, largely beause of the source material which
they contain. If indeed it had not been for the numerous
contributions—bibliographies, documentary collections, and
secondary accounts—of Spanish-American scholars to the
knowledge of the revolutionary period, *par excellence,* of
their history, this book could not appear in its present form.
Fortunately for my literary plans, that period has occupied
the attention of many prominent scholars of Spanish America.
Among these scholars three great writers, who have passed
away, linked their names forever with the literary history of
the revolution, José María Restrepo of Colombia, Diego Barros Arana of Chile, and Bartolomé Mitre of Argentina. While
preparing this book I have become acutely aware of the different opinions of Spanish-Americans in regard to the respective merits of their national heroes of the revolutionary age.
Mexican writers have generally been inclined to overestimate
the historical significance of Hidalgo. South-American historical writers who live in Bogotá do not always agree concerning the respective merits of Bolívar the liberator and Santander, "the organizer of victory." Even at the present day the
scholars of Argentina and Uruguay are at variance in regard

to the historical import of the career of Artigas. The historical scholars of Buenos Aires are loath to accept the views of scholars in Caracas respecting the rôles of San Martín and Bolívar. As one who, so to speak, lives in a realm apart, I have viewed the various revolutionary heroes with sympathy and without any conscious *parti pris:* it is believed that, in contrast with many other volumes which deal with the heroic age of Spanish-American history, this volume is subjective.

I brought my labors upon this volume to a close after more than a year spent in South America during which I revised my views concerning the liberators by the use of rare material which reposes in the libraries of certain South-American capitals. From a veritable legion of books and pamphlets and studies which I have consulted during my investigations I have carefully selected the most useful works and included them in an annotated bibliography. As some of the problems which confronted me were partly solved by the use of manuscripts that repose in certain archives of America and Europe, I have included in the select bibliography a brief list of important manuscript collections which will suggest the wealth of archival material that concerns my theme.

Certain difficulties inherent in the complexity of the theme, which deals with the emergence of eleven republics, have, in my judgment, been lessened by the use of what may be styled the biographical method. I firmly believe that the history of the Spanish-American revolution can be clearly told in the lives of its notable men. This method of narration has enabled me more easily to handle, and will, I trust, aid the reader more readily to comprehend, the details of that far-reaching movement, or rather that series of movements. For, during the Spanish-American revolutionary epoch, as rarely in history, certain figures occupied the foreground of the stage. From those figures I selected certain leaders for detailed consideration and other leaders for subordinate treatment. Another writer might perhaps have employed a different emphasis; some other writer might indeed have made a somewhat different selection. My choice of salient personalities has had special regard to the rôle which they played in the origin and progress of the revolution in certain sections of Spanish America. In general, each chapter of this volume is not so much devoted to a single individual or to a single rising state, as to a revolutionary movement in which a commanding personage played the most important rôle. Rightly to portray these personages, other figures have of necessity been sketched more lightly. Among the minor characters of the great revolutionary drama—as Artigas, Francia, Santander—Bernardo O'Higgins, in particular, was an attractive figure, who appeared more significant, however, in his relations to the early revolt in Chile and to the establishment of an independent government there, than to the broad sweep of the South-American revolutionary movement.

To me a significant figure was Francisco de Miranda, often styled "the great precursor" of the Spanish-American revolution. In Mexico there were two personages of paramount importance: Miguel Hidalgo y Costilla "the father of Mexican independence," and Agustin de Iturbide, who should be styled the liberator of Mexico. In southern South America, the career of Mariano Moreno, the democrat and scholar, furnished an introduction to the troubled politics of the viceroyalty of la Plata. The struggle for Argentine independence was logically continued in the life-story of José de San Martín, a founder of Argentina, Chile, and Peru. And the fight for the establishment of Peruvian independence was ultimately crowned with success largely through the achievements of two Venezuelans, Simón de Bolívar and Antonio José de Sucre, who, after their native state had been liberated from the Spanish yoke, coöperated in the founding of independent republics in Peru and Bolivia. There were some queries which arose in my mind regarding the exact order in which the lives of these so-called liberators should be presented to the reader. Should the order be topical, or chronological, or geographical? At last, I decided upon a sequence which, with advantages that seemed to outweigh its disadvantages, in reality constituted a compromise: a sequence which began with the great precursor and permitted me to consider consecutively the two most important leaders of Mexico,—a sequence which made it possible for me to treat successively four great personages of the South-American revolution.

The *Rise of the Spanish-American Republics* aims to furnish to English readers an outline of the movement which culminated in the establishment of independent states in the Spanish Indies, as traced in the biographies of notable leaders. While considerable attention has necessarily been

devoted to campaigns, battles, and capitulations, yet a deliberate and sustained attempt has been made to present the
poltical ideals of Spanish-American leaders, as expressed in
their declarations of independence, important constitutions,
and speeches. Accordingly frequent quotations—generally
my own translations—have been made from the literary
productions of the liberators. In particular, are there many
quotations from the significant productions of Simón de Bolívar, the most formidable military and political giant of Hispanic America. Whenever it seemed advisable to make a
rather free translation, I have adopted the practice of enclosing the excerpts in single quotation marks: otherwise, I
have followed the American custom of using double quotation marks. This book deals witth a distinct period in the
history of Spanish America, the transitional epoch from
1808 to 1831, which may be said to lie between the colonial
period proper and the distinctly national period. It is an introduction to a dramatic period which furnishes a background
for the national history of the Spanish-American republics.

WILLIAM SPENCE ROBERTSON.

Urbana, Illinois.

Contents

List of Maps

Rise of the Spanish-American Republics

Chapter 1

The Historical Background

DURING THE first quarter of the nineteenth century the vast empire of Spain in America broke into fragments. In various parts of the Indies the people proclaimed their independence of the motherland. The protracted drama which transformed the Spanish colonies upon the American continent into free, sovereign, and independent states, was started by the usurpations of Napoleon in the Iberian peninsula. Here and there in Spanish America, with loud protests of loyalty to their king, some colonists asserted the right to manage their own affairs. That this dissident movement developed into a far-reaching rebellion was due in no small measure to the activities of certain leaders who played important rôles in the revolution—leaders who may be styled the liberators of Spanish America. The fortunes of the Spanish-American revolution were also affected by the economic and political conditions which prevailed throughout Spain's dominions. It is the purpose of this chapter to sketch the background of the great revolution in the Spanish Indies.

On the eve of the revolution the king of Spain claimed title to territory in the New World which stretched from the sources of the Mississippi River to Cape Horn. That territory included about seven million square miles,—almost one-half of the area of the Three Americas. "Within this vast region," said Henry Clay, "we behold the most sublime and interesting objects of creation: the loftiest mountains, the most majestic rivers in the world; the richest mines of the precious metals, and the choicest productions of the earth." It was while musing over that magnificent domain which Spain had irretrievably lost, that the exiled minister, Manuel de Godoy, the Prince of the Peace, spoke of Spain under Charles IV. as the Queen of the Two Worlds.

In the reign of Charles IV., 1788-1808, Manuel de Godoy, the secretary of state and the voluptuous favorite of Queen María Teresa, exercised a baneful influence at the Spanish court. For many years Charles IV., good-natured, fond of the chase, with small political ability, allowed the Prince of the Peace to govern Spain and to confer favors upon fawning politicians. Selfish reasons induced Godoy sedulously to foster an estrangement between the royal couple and their eldest son, Ferdinand, Prince of Asturias,—a prince who was portrayed by contemporaries as a superstitious, self-willed youth, with a poor intellect. This heir to the crown of Spain and the Indies was given no opportunity to learn the art of government; and, when at a delicate crisis in the fortunes of the Spanish people, Ferdinand became king, events demonstrated that he was neither gifted with political talent nor animated by a liberal spirit.

Under Charles IV. the administration of the government was entrusted to the secretaries of state, justice, war, marine, and finance, who managed the affairs of the Indies as well as of Spain. By virtue of their offices those secretaries were members of the royal council of state in which important matters of policy were discussed. Over that council—which other governmental officials were at times invited to attend —the king presided. In the administration of the Indies, Charles IV. was aided by special institutions in the peninsula and in America. The most important institution in the peninsula was the "Royal and Supreme Council of the Indies."

The council of the Indies was composed of fourteen members selected by the king from persons who had held office in America. That council had administrative, legislative, and judicial powers. It advised the king on commercial and political affairs relating to the colonies. It promulgated decrees which served as laws for the Indies. It was the tribunal of last resort for cases appealed from the highest courts in Spanish America, the *audiencias*. The council met regularly at the capital; the king might preside over its sessions. Evidently this council possessed a more extensive authority over the Spanish Indies than the board of trade possessed over the English colonies in America. In the eighteenth century a minister of the Indies was created, who assumed some of the functions of the council of the Indies, and who managed the voluminous correspondence between Spain and Spanish America.

Legally the title to the Indies was not vested in the Spanish people; for that glorious heritage was viewed as the property of the Spanish monarch. Spain and her American colonies were not joined in an organic union but in a personal union. His Catholic Majesty was the connecting link. With more justification than the dissatisfied subjects of England in the thirteen colonies did some Spanish colonists later contend that they owed allegiance only to the King.

In America the most important agents of the Spanish monarch were the viceroys who ordinarily held office at his pleasure. The first viceroy appointed to rule over the Spanish dominions in North America was sent to the region which had been won by the sword of Hernando Cortés. In 1535 Antonio de Mendoza became the viceroy of New Spain; he established his capital at Mexico City, upon the site of the ancient capital of the Aztecs. The viceroy of New Spain, or Mexico, was orignally considered to have jurisdiction over the Spanish possessions in North and Central America. The earliest viceroy who was sent to South America represented the Spanish monarch in the region which had been conquered by Francisco Pizarro and his followers. In 1543 a viceroy was appointed for Peru; his capital was established at Lima, the city founded by Pizarro. Originally the viceroy of Peru was granted jurisdiction throughout Spanish South-America. But in 1718 the northern part of South America was erected into a separate administrative division, the viceroyalty of New Granada, with its capital at Santa Fé de Bogotá,—a viceroyalty which was abolished in 1723 but reëstablished in 1739. It stretched along the Pacific coast from the Isthmus of Panama to Tumbez, a short distance south of the equator. The royal *cédula* which delimited the viceroyalty of New Granada declared that its provinces should be subordinated to the viceroy just as the provinces of Mexico and Peru were subordinated to their respective viceroys. In 1776 another administrative division was carved out of the region which had originally been assigned to the Peruvian viceroy: that division constituted the viceroyalty of la Plata, which had its capital at Buenos Aires. The western boundary of the Platean viceroyalty was the Andean range; on the northwest it included an extensive region known as Upper Peru. Thus the viceroyalty of la Plata stretched from the mouth of the Río de la Plata to the Pacific Ocean. On the east the viceroyalties of la Plata, Peru, and New Granada were skirted by the Portuguese colony of Brazil.

Originally a viceroy was vested with regal authority. In the vast region entrusted to his care he was the civil and military commander, the secular head of the Church and its patron, and the superintendent of finance. From time to time instructions and orders were sent to the viceroy which he was expected to observe. Each viceroy was supposed to keep the Spanish government informed in regard to the condition of his viceroyalty. Early in the nineteenth century provision was made that, in case of the disability of a viceroy, his successor should be the person who had been named as substitute by the government. By that time, however, the viceroy had ceased to be a vice-king. There is, perhaps, no better way to illustrate the position of the viceroy in Spanish America at the end of the colonial régime than to consider the commission which was given to the viceroy of New Spain on March 16, 1816. By this commission King Ferdinand VII. conferred upon Juan Ruíz Apodaca the post of viceroy, governor, and captain general of New Spain during his pleasure. It stated that the viceroy should consider God's service as well as the king's, promoting the settlement and civilization of the region under his control. The viceroy was to provide that the Indians should be well treated, taught the mysteries of the Catholic faith, and ensured justice, The members of the royal *audiencia* of Mexico City were to receive from the viceroy the accustomed oath that he would faithfully perform his duties. The officials of the *audiencias* of Mexico City and Guadalajara, the members of *cabildos,* noblemen, gentlemen, and all other inhabitants of the viceroyalty were commanded to obey Apodaca, just as they would obey the Spanish monarch. This instrument suggests the extensive powers over the people of New Spain which the viceroy retained in 1816; it indicates his threefold position as governor, captain general, and viceroy. As governor, he was the chief magistrate of the provinces under his control. As captain general, he was the commander in chief of the military and naval forces of these provinces. As viceroy, he was vested with a supervisory authority over the other adminstrative officials within his jurisdiction. In particular, was he the presiding officer of the royal *audiencia* at Mexico City.

The authority of the American viceroys was gradually curtailed by the appointment of captain generals who were placed in charge of subdivisions known as captaincies general. Although at first in some particulars a captain general was ordinarily subordinated to the viceroy from whose dominions his captaincy general had been carved, yet in other respects he was a viceroy in miniature. In fact, a captain general controlled many affairs of an extensive district which was located at a considerable distance from the capital of the respective viceroyalty. In the reign of Charles IV. there were four captaincies general in the Spanish Indies: Cuba, Guatemala, Venezuela, and Chile. Toward the end of the colonial régime, the power of the captain generals in Spanish America increased. Although the relations between the viceroys and the captain generals have not yet been studied in detail, still it appears that on the eve of the revolution the captain general of Guatemala was practically independent of the viceroy of New Spain. A royal order of 1742 relieved the captain general of Venezuela of any dependence upon the neighboring viceroy. Before the end of the eighteenth century the Spanish government had declared that the captain general of Chile was completely independent of the viceroy of Peru. While the authority of a viceroy ordinarily extended over a region in which there were two *audiencias,* the power of a captain general was confined to a district assigned to one *audiencia.* Thus the captain general of Chile exercised authority over the territory under the control of the *audiencia* of Chile, which had its seat at Santiago de Chile; and the viceroy of Peru controlled the provinces which were under the jurisdiction of the *audiencias* located at Cuzco and Lima.

The administrative and judicial institution known as the *audiencia* had been transplanted from Spain to certain colonies during the age of the *conquistadores.* Gradually that institution had been established in important cities throughout the Indies. At the opening of the nineteenth century there were twelve *audiencias* in Spanish America. The *audiencia* of Cuba was at Havana. In the viceroyalty of New Spain there were two *audiencias*: one was located at Guadalajara, and the other at Mexico City. The *audiencia* of Guatemala had its seat at Santiago de Guatemala. The *audiencia* of Venezuela was located at Caracas; the *audiencia* of New Granada was at Bogotá, while the *audiencia* of Quito was in the city of that name. As has been mentioned, there were two *audiencias* in the viceroyalty of Peru, and one in the captaincy general of Chile. In the viceroyalty of la Plata there were two *audiencias*: one was located at the city of la Plata —commonly called Chuquisaca—in the province of Charcas in Upper Peru; and the other was in the city of Buenos Aires.

An *audiencia*, which was composed of magistrates selected by the king, acted as a court of appeal within a district which had been roughly delimited by the council of the Indies. It also served as an advisory council to the personage, ordinarily a captain general or a viceroy, who presided over its meetings. In a district where a viceroy or a captain general did not reside, the *audiencia* also exercised some poltical authority. For example, the *audiencia* which was located in the city of Quito, although subject to the viceroy of New Granada, was nevertheless vested with governmental authority in certain affairs. The *audiencias* located at Guadalajara, Quito, Cuzco, and Chuquisaca—in districts where a captain general or a viceroy did not reside—were in a sense governments within governments. As the circumjacent areas were under control of the jurists who presided over the meetings of the *audiencias,* officials known as presidents, these regions were specifically designated as presidencies.

The presidency which was located at Chuquisaca in the viceroyalty of la Plata—sometimes designated as the presidency of Charcas—has a peculiar interest. For the region under the jurisdiction of the *audiencia* of Charcas, known as Upper Peru, was nominally subject to the viceroy of Buenos Aires. At the beginning of the nineteenth century there regularly belonged to that *audiencia,* besides the president who was lieutenant general of the royal forces within its jurisdiction, five *oidores,* or judges, an attorney, and some minor officials. When the office of president fell vacant, the *audiencia* temporarily assumed governmental control of the presidency. In the important capitals of Spanish America there were more judges in the *audiencias.*

Vested as the *audiencias* were with the right to correspond directly with the Spanish monarch, they served as a check upon the powers of both viceroys and captain generals. A more efficacious check upon these officials, however, were the intendants, who near the end of the eighteenth century were placed in important towns and cities throughout the Spanish Indies. In other words, the viceroyalties and captaincies general were divided into districts called intendancies which were placed in control of officials known as intendants. In 1782 intendants were introduced into the viceroyalty of la Plata, and soon they were introduced into Peru and Chile. According to the ordinance of intendants promulgated for New Spain in 1786, that viceroyalty was carved into twelve districts. Each district was entrusted to an intendant who was given charge of matters relating to justice, war, police, and finance within his district. The Mexican intendants were also given authority over certain officers in the cities, towns, and villages of their respective intendancies. That intendant who resided in the city of Mexico exercised a supervisory authority over other intendants of the viceroyalty of New Spain. It will accordingly be seen that the establishment of the system of intendants in the Indies restricted the judicial authority of the *audiencias* and reapportioned the governmental power in the captaincies general as well as in the viceroyalties. There is no doubt that in some parts of Spanish America—as in New France—there were conflicts of authority between the intendants and the other governmental officials.

In 1776 the Spanish government took measures which aimed to curtail greatly the power of the viceroy of New Spain. By a decree of August 22, 1776, a new division was carved out of Spain's over-sea dominions. That decree provided that provinces of northern New Spain should be placed under the military and political control of a commandant-general, who was declared to be absolutely independent of the viceroy of New Spain. As arranged in 1804 those provinces were to be divided into two districts: the interior provinces of the east, and the interior provinces of the west. The provisions of the Spanish government concerning the administrative organization of the interior provinces indicate that that government realized the need of a better system of colonial control; but the reform was not completely carried out. In fact, before the interior provinces were placed under commandants, the revolution against Spanish authority had begun.

Although the institutions of colonial control located in the Spanish peninsula presented a semblance of unity that was markedly absent from English colonial institutions, yet the series of conflicting or overlapping jurisdictions which existed in Spanish America made it difficult to fix responsibility.

Those diverse jurisdictions fostered discord among officials. Perhaps the most important political difference between the English colonies in America and the Spanish colonies in the middle of the eighteenth century, was the absence in the latter of any institutions comparable to the colonial legislatures of North America. In the early nineteenth century, there was only one institution existing throughout Spanish America which bore any resemblance to the self-governing institutions of an Anglo-Saxon community,—that was the *cabildo*.

The *cabildo*, or *ayuntamiento*, was the council of a city, or of a town. The most important officials composing the *cabildo* were the *alcaldes*, or justices, and the *regidores*, who may be styled aldermen. The laws of the Indies contained a provision that there should be no more than two *alcades* in a *cabildo*; that in the chief cities there should be twelve *regidores*; and that in other cities and towns there should be no more than six *regidores*. In the early nineteenth century there *belonged* to the *cabildo* of the city of Caracas two *alcaldes* who were elected annually by the *regidores*, twelve *regidores* who had secured their offices by purchase from the king, and four *regidores*—natives of Spain—who held their positions by royal appointment. At rare intervals certain American *cabildos* had revived the mediæval Spanish custom of holding a *cabildo abierto* (open council),—a meeting which prominent citizens who did not have seats in the *cabildo* were invited to attend. But a *cabildo abierto*, which by a flight of the imagination may be compared with a New England town meeting, could not be summoned without the consent of a representative of the king. According to the laws of the Indies, the meetings of a *cabildo* could only be held in the *casa de ayuntamiento*, or town hall. It was only natural that, when circumstances appeared auspicious, the *cabildo*, and especially the *cabildo abierto*, should have been used as an instrument by those colonists who dreamed of separation from Spain.

The laws of the Indies were composed of the *cédulas*, instructions, and ordinances which the Spanish government had from time to time promulgated concerning its colonies in America. In 1680 a digest of those laws was published in a code called the *Recopilación de Leyes de los Reinos de las Indias*. These laws necessarily dealt with a vast variety of subjects, such as the Church, universities, the council of the

Indies, viceroys, fortifications, public works, mines, fisheries, Indians, negroes, and taxes. There was a clause in the code which declared that, as the kingdoms of Spain and the Indies belonged to the same monarch, their laws should be as much alike as possible. Another elastic clause provided that the code was to be supplemented by the laws of Castile. This meant, after 1805, that the laws of the Indies should be supplemented by the Spanish laws which had been codified by order of Charles IV., the *Novísima Recopilación de las Leyes de España.* That revised code contained only those laws of Spain which were actually in force,—the legislative institution known as the *cortes* was not even mentioned. There is no doubt that in certain sections of the Indies some of the humane provisions in the Spanish laws relating to America were habitually ignored by agents of the crown.

The number of people who were under the jurisdiction of the laws of the Indies, it is impossible to determine with exactness. According to the estimated of Alexander von Humboldt, in the early nineteenth century there were in Spanish America about seventeen million inhabitants. He calculated that of those people about seven and one-half million were Indians, three and a quarter million were whites, three-quarters of a million were negroes, and more than five and one-quarter million were of mixed race. In general the population in the American colonies of Spain was composed of two distinct classes, freemen and slaves. Whites and Indians, or their descendants, were usually considered free; negroes and their descendants, unless they had been emancipated, were slaves. The negro slaves occupied a subordinate position: they were often ignorant, superstitious, and licentious, while the negroes who had been set free did not always enjoy the rights of colonial Spaniards. The Indians were composed of two somewhat distinct classes: those Indians called civilized, and those considered independent. In certain parts of Spanish America, as in the viceroyalty of Mexico, the Indians were a special menace to the rule of Spain.

In various sections of Spanish America, there had been much mingling of Indian, negro, and white blood. As examples of the resulting blends may be mentioned the mestizos, the offspring of Indians and Spaniards; the mulattoes, descendants of whites and negroes; the sambos, descendants of

Indians and negroes; and the pardos, descendants of whites and mulattoes. From the intermixture of those groups there sprang a large number of ethnic types. In general the mixed classes, the colored people, and the Indians were densely ignorant. Although in some parts of Spanish America the various classes had not hardened into castes, yet these classes often furnished a basis for the formation of factions. The white inhabitants of Spanish America belonged to two distinct groups: the Spaniards who had been born in the peninsula; and the so-called creoles, persons of Spanish descent who had been born in the Indies. The policy which Spain pursued toward her colonies often illustrated the maxim *divide et impera,* for the European Spaniards—in Mexico vulgarly called the *Gachupines*—although relatively small in numbers, were appointed to most of the important offices in Church and state. In consequence the proud creoles viewed the peninsular Spaniards with jealousy:—indeed, the preference accorded the peninsular Spaniard over the creole was often considered by the colonists as a crying grievance.

The aristocracy of the Spanish colonies in America was largely composed of creoles. Some of the leading creole families indeed traced their descent from the followers of the *conquistadores.* The laws of the Indies declared that the descendants of the conquerors and the founders of cities and towns were to be considered as *hijosdalgo* and as persons of noble descent with all the privileges of nobles of a similar class in the kingdom of Castile. Some wealthy descendants of later colonists anxiously sought titles of nobility despite the fact that sometimes they were not of pure Spanish blood. In the words of the Mexican historian and publicist, Lucas Alamán, "A title of count or marquis, a cross of Santiago or Calatrava . . . was an object of ambition for the person who had become rich by commerce, or who had found a bonanza in the mines." There was a tendency to consider the descendants of Spaniards as entitled to special privileges with regard to the learned professions: a royal *cédula* sent to the viceroy of Peru on July 14, 1758, declared that "sambos, mulattoes, and other low castes" should be prohibited from practicing the legal profession. The members of the social or intellectual aristocracy of the Spanish Indies resided mostly in the capitals of viceroyalties and captaincies general: this aristocracy was composed largely of the lower clergy, landowners, merchants, and local office-holders. From that self-conscious group of the creole aristocracy there sprang many partisans of the Spanish-American revolution. Each one of the seven salient leaders considered in this book was a creole.

A certain feature of Spain's colonial policy affected even the barbarous Indians,—that is, the complicated system of taxation. Some of the most important sources of the king's revenue were: the *alcabala,* or the tax upon the sale of articles according to their price; the king's share of the tithes, the duty upon the product of the silver, quicksilver, and gold mines, the income arising from governmental monopolies, the tribute levied upon the Indians, the excise duties upon the manufacture of intoxicating liquors, and the duties upon imports and exports. In many particulars the system of taxation was merely an application of the Spanish commercial policy.

The commercial policy which Spain followed toward her colonies resembled the colonial policy of France. It was animated by a spirit of monopoly and paternalism. Here, again, a few illustrations must suffice. At various times the viceroys were instructed to promote the cultivation by the Indians of hemp and flax. In 1595 the extension of grape culture was prohibited in the Indies. Further, the Peruvian viceroy was not to allow the vineyards within his jurisdiction to be replanted, while the owners of these grapevines were to pay a tax of two per cent annually upon the products. In the early seventeenth century Peruvian viniculturists were further hampered by a prohibition which was laid upon the exportation of their wines. Obviously the government of Spain thus aimed to prevent Peruvian wines from competing with Spanish wines in certain colonial markets. Another illustration of the spirit of Spain's colonial system may be found in a decree of 1595 which instructed the viceroys of Peru that neither merchandise nor slaves from any part of the Portuguese dominions should be allowed to enter Peru by la Plata River. A decree of 1614 provided that tobacco might be freely sown in Spanish America, on the condition that the tobacco which was not consumed in the colonies should straightway be transported to Seville. Early in the nineteenth century the wool produced in the colonies was allowed to enter Spain free of duty, but a heavy tax was laid upon its exportation to foreign countries.

At first the privilege to trade with the Spanish colonies in America had been restricted to the merchants of Seville. At a later date the merchants of Cadiz had the preference. By various regulations Spain attempted to prevent foreigners from engaging in commerce with her colonies. In general no commerce whatever was permitted from other than Spanish ports. For a long period there were only a few ports in Spanish America which enjoyed the privilege of trading directly with Spain. On October 12, 1778, however, a law was promulgated which modified the regulations concerning commerce between Spain and the Indies. The law opened several Spanish ports to American trade; it also opened a number of ports in Spanish America to Spanish trade. That reform law still aimed to encourage Spanish shipbuilders and shipowners, for it provided that vessels used in the commerce with America should be Spanish-built and Spanish-owned. But in consequence of this reform goods could be carried in Spanish vessels directly between a number of ports in Spain and ports in various sections of the Indies. In important cities of Spain the commercial activities were managed by local organizations which were called consulates. Those organizations were regulated by ordinances of the Spanish monarchs which contained provisions regarding such matters as the trial of commercial disputes. Among these ordinances the most important were the *Ordenanzas de la villa Bilbao* issued by King Philip V. in 1737. This institution of consulate was also established in important cities in the Indies, where the ordinances of Bilbao often served as a species of commercial code.

The tariff policy of Spain in the early nineteenth century considered the financial needs of the government, the necessities of Spanish America, and the protection of Spain's industries. Depons, an observant Frenchman who resided for some time at Caracas, divided the goods entering Venezuela into three classes. The first class included those products raised or manufactured in Spain: such products were designated as "free articles," because the duties levied upon them appeared insignificant in comparison with the duties which were laid upon other classes of goods. The duties upon articles of this class on leaving Spain and entering America amounted to about nine and one-half per cent. The second class included articles which were produced abroad, but finished in Spain: such articles paid duties amounting to about twelve and one-half per cent on leaving Spain and entering America. The third class included all goods of foreign manufacture, which paid duties on entering Spain that amounted to fifteen per cent, on departing for America seven per cent, and on arriving there seven per cent, besides various port duties which "increased the price of all foreign merchandise, imported from the mother country, about forty-three per cent." With the exception of cacao, colonial productions paid only "inconsequential duties" on leaving America, and on entering Spain; and they were generally exempt from duty when exported from Spain for foreign markets; but all "unwrought materials" that went to supply foreign manufacturers, "paid heavy duties on their exportation" which gave the Spanish manufacturers an advantage.

Accordingly it is clear that although in the beginning of the nineteenth century Spain's commercial policy had been considerably modified, yet the faith of her statesmen in the mercantile policy had not been destroyed: the Spanish colonies were still considered as estates which should be exploited for the benefit of the mother country. In certain parts of the Indies the monopolistic policy of Spain was sometimes rudely disturbed by smugglers. In 1797 a merchant of Caracas alleged that every man in that city from the captain general down to the humblest citizen was clad in contraband clothing.

The financial burdens which Spain imposed upon her colonists were made heavier by the venality of her officials. In consequence there were many Spanish-Americans who felt that the fiscal policy of Spain was oppressive. That policy was largely responsible for several uprisings against Spanish rule. In 1780, alleging that the taxes were oppressive and that the misgovernment by Spain's officials was unendurable, Tupac Amaru, a lineal descendant of the Incas, led a formidable insurrection of the Indians against Spanish rule in Peru. In a manifesto attributed to Tupac Amaru, which was widely distributed in South America, that chieftain apparently proclaimed himself "Don José I., by the grace of God, King of Peru, Quito, Chile, Buenos Aires, and the continents of the South Sea." This rebellion caused much consternation among the Spaniards, but it was suppressed, and its leader was condemned to a horrible death. Again, in April, 1781, the inhabitants of certain towns, or *comunes,* in New Granada rose in revolt against the Spanish officials. Those revolutionists declared that the main reason for their discontent was the grievous burden imposed upon them by the tobacco monopoly, the *alcabala,* and other taxes. In June, 1781, certain representatives of the Spanish government agreed to the requests of the rebels for economic and financial reforms and the tumult was stilled. But the pledges of reform were not kept. Consequently fresh signs of discontent were soon manifested; in January, 1782, the *audiencia* of New Granada condemned a number of the conspirators to an ignominious death. The revolt of the *comuneros,* as well as other revolts which may not be mentioned here, left embers of discontent smouldering in northern South America. In 1783 certain conspirators in that region actually dispatched an emissary who had laid their revolutionary projects before the government of England.

The dissatisfaction of some Spanish colonists with the fiscal policy of the motherland was occasionally fomented by English officials in America. A striking illustration of that influence is found in the action of Governor Picton of Trinidad. In June, 1797, when England was at war with Spain, Picton spread broadcast upon the adjacent coast of South America a proclamation which assured the inhabitants that they would find in the island of Trinidad a commercial emporium. He also assured the Spanish colonists that, whenever they were disposed to resist the authority of Spain, they would receive succor from the English government. This incendiary manifesto undoubtedly fomented a revolutionary spirit among the Venezuelan colonists.

It was probably a desire for commercial conquest which, in 1806, prompted the English captain, Sir Home Popham, with a few vessels bearing a small force of soldiers under General Beresford to sail from his station on the Cape of Good Hope for South America. In the end of June the small fleet sailed up la Plata River. The terrified viceroy, the Marquis of Sobremonte, offered only a weak resistance to Beresford's spirited attack. On June 27 British redcoats entered the gates of Buenos Aires. The conquerors soon announced that Buenos Aires would enjoy the same freedom in regard to export trade as the English West India colonies; and they reduced the duties on imports about twenty per cent. While Beresford was waiting for reënforcements, the citizens of Buenos Aires took steps to expel the invaders. Juan Martín de Pueyrredón, the son of a Frenchman who had settled in Buenos Aires, organized a squadron of huzzars. Cornelio de Saavedra, a prominent creole, was made the commander of a volunteer company of infantry. On August 12 the colonial soldiers commanded by Santiago de Liniers, a French officer who had fought under the Spanish banner in North Africa, forced General Beresford to surrender. A *cabildo abierto* soon selected De Liniers to be the military commander of Buenos Aires in place of the recreant viceroy. About two months later by a royal order De Liniers was appointed the viceroy of la Plata. On July 5, 1807, under the direction of De Liniers, the citizen soldiery repulsed a fresh attack of the English under the command of General Whitelocke. Although the English failed in their attempts to conquer the southern part of South America, yet their attacks upon the viceroyalty of la Plata were not without influence; for they broke down the commercial barriers which surrounded that colony, and furnished some colonists a training in the art of war. A Spanish-English journal, the *Star of the South,* which was founded in Montevideo during the English occupation, stimulated a spirit of hostility to the Spanish régime.

Many laws of Spain and the Indies contained provisions in regard to the colonial Church. Since the age of Charles I., the Spanish monarchs had acted as the spiritual lords of America. The Pope could not communicate directly with the faithful in the Spanish colonies: bulls could only be circulated in Spanish America after having been approved by the council of the Indies. As the Catholic faith progressed, Spanish America had been carved into bishoprics which were not always coterminous with the secular subdivisions. American archbishops and bishops were appointed by the king; and the problems that arose respecting the patronage were decided in the council of the Indies. The ordinances of American church councils could only be published after being approved by the omniscient council at Madrid. In Spanish America members of the secular clergy were found in those towns where Spaniards constituted a large part of the population. Among the Indians on the frontiers, Dominican and Franciscan friars often served as missionaries. Throughout the Indies an enormous amount of property had fallen into the hands of the Church: thus the influence of the clergy was steadily augmented. Largely because of the intimate relations which existed between the colonial clergy and the king, in many sections of Spanish America the Church was a great buttress of royal power. Nevertheless, some creoles who belonged to the lower clergy were animated by liberal ideas.

The conservative influence of the clergy in Spanish America was sometimes reënforced by the inquisition. Tribunals of the holy office were located at Carthagena, Lima, and Mexico City. Those tribunals strove to suppress witchcraft, blasphemy, and heresy, as well as to prevent the circulation of prohibited books. In a list of more than five thousand volumes which Depons mentioned as being prohibited in South America at the opening of the nineteenth century, there are found works of Rousseau, Montesquieu, Diderot, Helvetius, Hume, Addison, and De Foe. Although at the end of the colonial régime edicts were still published and officials of the inquisition still acted as censors, yet the holy office in Spanish America was in a decadent condition. Count Ségur, a French military officer who visited Venezuela early in 1783, quoted a Spanish officer as saying:

Here the Inquisition does not . . . order any *auto-de-fé*, nor light any fires, but it endeavors to extinguish every ray of light. I, as well as several of my friends, burn to read the works of the celebrated writers of France; but the intendant forbids their importation under the severest penalties, as if they were infected with the plague.

An illustration of the attitude of the Spanish authorities toward the publication of books may be had from the annals of the viceroyalty of Peru. In an official report which Teodoro de Croix, viceroy of Peru, wrote for his successor in 1790, he said that certain prohibited books had been seized and burned.

A proclamation has been published declaring that no printer shall publish any paper whatsoever without a license under penalty of severe punishments. An order has been sent to the royal university that neither the disputations customarily held on the arrival of the viceroys, nor the panegyrics ordinarily delivered before those officials, nor the Latin orations with which the university is annually opened, nor any paper whatsoever, can be printed without the examination and the license of this viceregal government.

In spite of the efforts of the inquisition, which were supported by the secular authorities, prohibited books circulated secretly in the viceroyalty of Peru. In the viceroyalty of la Plata certain colonists were influenced by the Declaration of Independence of July 4, 1776. Some Spanish-American colonists considered the Constitution of the United States as a grand exemplar. Further, the political opinions of the intellectual aristocracy were greatly influenced by the revolutionary philosophy of France. The "pestiferous" *Encyclopédie* was smuggled into Peru. Jean Jacques Rousseau's *Le Contrat Social* was read by the enterprising colonists in Mexico, Venezuela, and la Plata. Count Ségur stated that in Venezuela a physician led him to the most secluded part of his house, where he showed him "with infinite satisfaction the works of J. J. Rousseau and Raynal, which he kept concealed as his most precious treasure in a beam scooped out for that purpose." The *Déclaration des Droits de l'Homme,* translated into Spanish and printed by Antonio Nariño, an enterprising creole of New Granada, was clandestinely circulated in Peru, New Granada, and Venezuela. Copies of French revolutionary documents were found among the papers of Manuel Gual, a leader of the insurrection against Spanish rule which broke out in Venezuela in 1797. But although the French philosophy, in particular, became a source of inspiration for conspirators who dreamed of revolutionizing Spanish America, yet it is only reasonable to suppose that a large majority of the inhabitants of the Spanish Indies remained entirely unaffected by the revolutionary leaven.

For to them the educational facilities furnished by printing presses and schools and colleges remained more or less unknown. Although printing presses were set up in Mexico and Peru during the sixteenth century, yet, as has been shown, books and pamphlets could not be printed openly without the sanction of the civil and ecclesiastical authorities. A few books were printed surreptitiously by Jesuit fathers in South America. About 1780 a printing press was brought to the city of Buenos Aires from the dismantled Jesuit college at Córdoba. The first capital of Spanish America in which a periodical regularly appeared was Mexico City, where the *Gaceto de México* was published during a large part of the eighteenth century. In 1785 there was published at the capital of the viceroyalty of New Granada the first number of *la Gaceta de Santa Fé*. In 1790 there appeared the first number of *El Diario erudito, económico, y comercial de Lima*. The *Gaceta de Caracas*, which began to appear in 1808, was evidently printed upon a small press which Francisco de Miranda had left in the West Indies after his unsuccessful attempt to revolutionize Venezuela. A notable colonial periodical was the *Mercurio Peruano de historia, literatura, y noticias públicas*, which was founded at Lima in 1791. Such periodicals ordinarily contained only a small amount of news, besides the reports of governmental activities. While they helped to prepare the minds of certain intellectual leaders for a new order, they did not reach the common people, because elementary education was much neglected. For example, in Venezuela the creole boys of the better class were taught to read miraculous tales and instructed in the rudiments of Latin grammar. A well-informed Venezuelan said of his educated fellow-countrymen: "They fancy that all the sciences are contained in the Latin grammar of Nebrija, the philosophy of Aristotle, the institutes of Justinian, the *Curia Philippica*, and the theological writings of Gonet and Larraga. If they can make extracts from these works, say mass, display the doctor's badge, or appear in the dress of a priest or a monk, they consider that they are sufficiently accomplished."

In the sixteenth century universities were founded in the viceroyalties of Mexico and Peru. As early as 1551 Charles I. issued a *cédula* which provided for the establishment of universities at Lima and Mexico City. The chief subjects of study in the University of San Marcos at Lima were theology, civil and canon law, and certain sciences. Perhaps the most famous of the colonial institutions of learning was the "Royal and Pontifical University of Mexico." The prologue of its constitution, as printed in 1775, declared that it had granted about thirty thousand degrees. According to this constitution, the admiration of the university was vested in a rector, who was elected annually by a board of councilors. At that university, in addition to the subjects which have been mentioned as being studied at the University of San Marcos, some attention was given to Indian dialects. In the constitution of the University of Mexico there were many interesting provisions concerning matriculation, prerequisites for certain courses, student lodging-houses, and methods of teaching. The teachers were to spend one-half of each hour in dictating to the students; and the other half in making explanations in Latin: if the subject was very difficult, the teachers were to elucidate the matter in Spanish. On the roll of its graduates this university numbered many men who had acquired distinction in public life and in professional employment. Besides the universities at Lima and Mexico City, universities, or colleges, were founded by decrees of Spanish monarchs, or by the action of beneficent ecclesiastics, at many other points in the Indies, notably at Buenos Aires, Córdoba, Chuquisaca, and Caracas. At some of these colleges, as Córdoba, the teachers for a time were Jesuit padres. It was at the universities and colleges which sprang up in important cities of Spanish America that the favored sons of the colonial aristocrats—the counts, marquises, officeholders, and landowners—were mostly educated.

The policy which the government of Spain adopted in regard to the Jesuit order injured the cause of learning in the New World and lowered the prestige of the crown. The indefatigable disciples of Ignatius Loyola had established missions and planted colleges in various sections of Spanish America. Although the members of the Society of Jesus kept the Indian neophytes in a state of subordination which resembled serfdom, yet in many other respects their influence was beneficial. But in the course of generations, a considerable amount of property passed into their possession, and they incurred the jealousy of other religious orders. Worst of all, they were suspected of being disloyal to the king of Spain. Hence, early in 1767, the Spanish council of state decided that the Jesuits should be expelled from the dominions of Spain in both hemispheres. On February 27, 1767, Charles III. signed an order providing that the members of the Society of Jesus should be expelled from his possessions in Spain, the Indies, and the Philippines, and that the property of the society should be sequestrated. A short time afterwards it was provided that the Jesuits should be deported from the Indies to Europe. Governors, or other civil magistrates, were to be given command over the Jesuit provinces in America, while the missions were to be placed under the care of the members of other religious orders. A royal decere dated April 5, 1787, provided that the income accruing from the confiscated property should be used to pension the exiled Jesuits. It has been estimated that in consequence of those decrees, about five thousand Jesuit fathers were transported from the Indies to Italy. After the expulsion of the Jesuits the missions decayed, and the neophytes relapsed into barbarism. Further, some colonists resented the harsh measures which had been adopted by the Spanish government. In the viceroyalty of Mexico the disaffection which was produced by the expulsion of the Jesuit fathers stimulated thoughts of separation from Spain.

In the Papal states some of the embittered Jesuit exiles dreamed of subverting the royal authority in Spanish America. Father Juan Pablo Viscardo y Guzmán wrote a stirring pamphlet entitled *Lettre aux Espagnols américains par un de leur compatriots*. In the pamphlet the exile declared that the history of Spanish rule in America could be epitomized in four words, "ingratitude, injustice, slavery, and desolation." He likened the title which the Spanish colonists had acquired to America during the era of conquest to the title which the Goths had acquired to Spain by the conquest of the Iberian peninsula. In a scathing denunciation of the colonial policy of Spain, he affirmed that, even in times of peace, wine was so scarce in the city of Carthagena that mass could be celebrated only in one church. The spirit and the argument of this remarkable pamphlet will be suggested by the following excerpts:

The pretension of Spain to blind obedience to her arbitrary laws is based mainly upon the ignorance which she has permitted and encouraged, especially in regard to the inalienable rights of man and the imprescriptible duties of every government. Spain has attempted to persuade the common people that it is a crime to reason upon matters of the greatest importance to every individual; and consequently that it is always a duty to extinguish the precious flame which the Creator gave us for enlightenment and guidance. But despite the dissemination of such fatal doctrines, the entire history of Spain bears witness against their truth and legitimacy. . . . Nature has separated us from Spain by immense seas. A son who found himself at such a distance from his father would doubtless be a fool, if, in the management of his own affairs, he constantly awaited the decision of his father. The son is emancipated by natural law. In a parallel case should a numerous people, who are not dependent upon another nation whom they do not need, remain subject to it like the vilest slave?

Our distance from Spain, which proclaims our independence is, however, less significant than the difference in interests. We imperatively need a government in our midst for the distribution of benefits, the object of the socal union. To depend upon a government two or three thousand leagues distant, is to renounce these benefits; for such is the policy of the court of Spain, that it aspires only to give us laws which monopolize our commerce, our industry, our property, and our persons, and which sacrifice them to her ambition, her pride, and her avarice. . . .

In fine, in whatever aspect our dependence upon Spain is considered, one will see that every obligation impels us to terminate it. We ought to do so because of gratitude towards our ancestors who did not waste their sweat and their blood in order that the theater of their labors and their glory should become the scene of our miserable servitude. We owe that to ourselves because of the indispensable obligation to preserve the natural rights granted by our Creator—precious rights which we cannot alienate—rights which no one can wrest from us without committing a crime. Can man renounce his reason, or can this be taken from him by force? Personal liberty is not less essentially his property than reason. The free enjoyment of these natural rights is the inestimable heritage which we ought to transmit to our posterity. . . . The valor with which the English colonists in America fought for the liberty that they gloriously enjoy shames our indolence. . . . There is no longer any pretext to excuse our resignation; and, if we longer endure the vexations which overwhelm us, people will truthfully declare that our laziness has merited them: our descendants will burden us with imprecations, when, champing the bit of slavery,—a slavery which they inherited —they remember the moment in which . . . we did not wish to become free.

The writer can think of no expression of colonial grievances with which this document can be more aptly compared than Thomas Jefferson's *Summary View of the Rights of British America*. The Jesuit's pamphlet was an exceptional expression of sentiment, which was indubitably intended to serve as an appeal to the inhabitants of Spanish America to cast off the Spanish yoke. It was composed in Europe about 1790, and published posthumously at Philadelphia in 1799. In some manner a copy of this pamphlet fell into the hands of Francisco de Miranda. When, in 1806, that expatriated Venezuelan led a filibustering expedition against the coast of South America, he printed Viscardo y Guzmán's pamphlet in Spanish and distributed it among his fellow-countrymen. A biographical sketch of Francisco de Miranda will furnish an outline of the early revolution against Spain in the captaincy general of Venezuela. His career will also show clearly the attitude of the English government toward the Spanish empire in America during the epoch which preceded the usurpations of Napoleon in the Iberian peninsula.

Chapter 2

Francisco de Miranda

A VAST HIVE of revolution, the captaincy general of Venezuela extended along the Atlantic coast of South America from the gulf of Maracaibo on the northwest to the Essequibo River on the southeast. That administrative division was bounded on the south and west by Dutch and Portuguese Guiana and by the viceroyalty of New Granada. Near the center of the captaincy general was the province of Caracas which was under the immediate control of the captain general who acted as the governor of the province. The capital of the province of Caracas, and also of the captaincy general, was the city of Caracas: when our story begins it was the seat of an *audiencia* and of a consulate, as well as the residence of an archbishop and an intendant.

Francisco de Miranda, the promoter of Spanish-American independence, was born in the city of Caracas on March 28, 1750. His mother was Francisca de Espiñoza, who, in 1749, had married Sebastian de Miranda. In an autobiographical sketch written in early manhood, Francisco declared that his ancestors were men of pure descent and orthodox faith, who had often held honorable offices in Spain. On his father's side, Francisco de Miranda was apparently a descendant of the noble family of Miranda, which had its ancestral home in Asturias. According to the mediæval Spanish chronicler, in the ninth century Alvaro Fernandez de Miranda, the founder of the Miranda family, rescued five Christian maidens from the Moors—this adventure was commemorated by granting to him a coat of arms which bore heraldic symbols of his chivalrous deed. In the last half of the eighteenth century, Sebastian de Miranda, who had emigrated from the Canary Islands to South America, was a thriving merchant of Caracas, who had won the esteem of the captain general of Venezuela by faithful service as the captain of a volunteer militia company.

The education of Francisco de Miranda began in the schools of his native city. Whether or not he graduated from

41

the College of Santa Rosa at Caracas, Miranda evidently acquired some knowledge of Latin, philosophy, and law. When
a mere lad, Francisco showed a fondness for the profession
of arms; for he sailed from Venezuela for Spain, where, in
1772, he secured by purchase a commission as captain in the
Spanish infantry company of the Princes. The young captain received his baptism of fire while fighting the Moors on
the coast of northern Africa. He then spent many months in
dull Spanish garrisons, where he employed part of his leisure
in study. According to his own story, the officials of the inquisition threw some of his favorite books in to the flames.
It is certain that the high-spirited youth had an acrimonious
dispute with one of his superior officers. Incidents in Miranda's career in Spain indeed suggest that he became dissatisfied with his employment and pined for other scenes of
activity.

The French alliance with the revolting colonists of England in North America opened to Miranda the door of opportunity. This alliance drew Spain into the American revolution,
for that nation was bound to France by the treaty known as
the family compact. An expedition was accordingly prepared
in Spain to coöperate with the French in an attack upon the
English dominions in America. Captain Miranda, who had
been transferred to the company of Aragon, returned to the
New World with that expedition in 1780. Soon after arriving
in the West Indies, he was made the aide-de-camp of General
Juan de Cagigal, the governor of Cuba. With this general,
Miranda participated in the capture of Pensacola, West
Florida, and of Providence, the capital of the Bahama Islands.
He won the confidence of Governor Cagigal, who breveted
him colonel and urged the minister of the Indies, José de
Gálvez, to promote him. Other Spanish officials in the West
Indies, however, disliked and distrusted Miranda; and, when
occasion offered, they sent to Madrid venomous complaints
against him.

Those complaints centered around a trip which Colonel
Miranda made from Cuba to Jamaica in 1781. He was commissioned by Cagigal to arrange for an exchange of prisoners
between the Spanish and the English forces in the West Indies.
While on this errand, Miranda quietly gathered information
in regard to the military condition of Jamaica: in fact, he
acted as a spy. At the same time, he gave to Governor Dalling

of Jamaica a detailed description of the various expeditions which the Spaniards had fitted out against Pensacola. Further, on returning to Cuba, Miranda brought back a quantity of merchandise. He was soon denounced to the government of Spain because of the arrangement which he had made for the exchange of prisoners with the English, even though that agreement had been approved by Governor Cagigal. He was accused of having connived at the covert inspection of the fortifications of Havana by the English general, John Campbell, who visited Cuba while on a voyage from Pensacola to New York. He was also accused of having smuggled goods into Cuba. Accordingly, in March, 1782, a royal commissioner, Juan Antonio de Vrunela, was sent to Cuba to investigate Colonel Miranda's conduct.

In December, 1783, Vrunela pronounced judgment against Miranda. He declared that even the carts, the oxen, and the horses which had conveyed the contraband goods from Guantánamo to Havana were to be confiscated. Colonel Miranda was to be heavily fined, deprived of his military commission, and banished for ten years. A strange light is cast upon this judgment by the fact that the council of the Indies afterwards fully exonerated the disgraced officer. Even before Vrunuela's judgment was pronounced, that officer had closed ten years of service under the Spanish banner by a secret and hasty flight. When departing from the West Indies, Miranda wrote to his true friend, Governor Cagagil, to inform him that he intended to appeal to King Charles II. for justice. Further, he declared that he wished to improve his education by a tour of the United States and Europe. He said that "the only way in which he might complete the great work of making himself a sound and useful man was to study carefully the laws, government, agriculture, military condition, navigation, sciences, and arts of the most wise and virtuous societies in the universe."

The ten years spent as a Spanish military officer constituted a formative period in Miranda's life. He gained some knowledge of the art of war, and became aware of the crying evils of Spain's colonial system. In 1772 he was a loyal youth. By 1783 he had become a resentful man. Whether Miranda was deliberately disloyal to his king or not, it is clear that the Spanish government viewed him as a dangerous conspirator. Several years later he asserted that it was during his sojourn in the West Indies that he first received representations from certain discontented inhabitants of northern South America. According to his own statements, at least as early as 1783 he possessed a collection of papers, maps, and plans concerning the Spanish colonies. It was probably during his military service in the West Indies—when he was fighting for the independence of England's revolted colonists—that Miranda first harbored the thought which was to dominate his life. As was suggested by a writer in the *Edinburgh Review*—who evidently secured his information from Miranda himself—in a scene where the cause of liberty was the object of men's desires, and in a country which somewhat resembled South America, it was only natural that a design to liberate his native land should have been suggested to Miranda's mind.

After the treaty of peace had been signed between England and the United States, Miranda visited that country. In a vain-glorious autobiographical sketch written in 1785, he declared that, while traveling through the United States, he visited the scenes "of the most important operations of the revolutionary war, and conversed at length with the heroes and sages who had promoted that immortal work." It is certain that the fugitive from Spanish justice visited Charleston, Philadelphia, New York, and Boston. In June, 1784, Miranda was in New Haven, Connecticut, where he called on President Stiles of Yale College, and visited some of the college classes. The South American described to President Stiles the educational system of Mexico, and characterized Mexican learning as "inferior, trifling, and contemptible." Miranda not only impressed Stiles as being too free-spoken and too liberal-minded to live in either Old or New Spain, but he also convinced the latter that he had "a perfect acquaintance with the policy and history of all Spanish America." Of the bustling, self-important South American, President Stiles wrote in his diary that he was "a learned Man and a flaming Son of Liberty."

Colonel Miranda doubtless became acquainted with many other citizens of the United States. Among them were Thomas Paine, the ardent lover of liberty, Stephen Sayre, who soon took a keen interest in Spanish America, and Rufus King, who became an enthusiastic champion of Miranda's revolutionary schemes. Possibly the South American also met

General Washington; he certainly became acquainted with Alexander Hamilton and Henry Knox. About twenty years later, Miranda apparently asserted that those three generals had promised to coöperate with him in the revolutionizing of Spanish America,—an assertion that is not supported by the evidence which is available. Nothing has been found to show that Miranda even discussed this topic with General Washington. There is no doubt, however, that the ardent South American talked to both Hamilton and Knox regarding the liberation of America from Spanish rule, and that, for the time being, they were interested. To judge by letters which Miranda sent to Knox, these two men held several symposiums in regard to the liberation of Spanish America: and, when Miranda left Boston, he entrusted Knox with the key to a secret cipher. But in later years, when Miranda tried to get Generals Hamilton and Knox to coöperate in his revolutionary designs, their interest in Spanish America had cooled.

In February, 1785, Miranda had reached the British Isles. He soon visited the Spanish Ambassador in London, Bernardo del Campo, and tried to get an honorable dismissal from Spain's military service. To promote that object, on April 10, 1785, Colonel Miranda addressed to King Charles III. a long petition, which was accompanied by justificatory documents. In this petition that officer spoke of his long service to the Spanish king. The petitioner attributed the shabby treatment which he had been given in the West Indies to the undermining influence of jealous enemies. He gave his version of the events which had caused his flight from Cuba, alleging that false accusations had been brought against him. He declared that he labored under the disadvantage of being a creole:

I am tired of struggling with powerful enemies, inveterate prepossessions, and the jealousies of all classes; for the triumphs of a creole, however complete they may be in theory, can never repay him for the injuries which they cause him in honor, in estate, and in time—the most precious of all—from which inestimable advantages may be drawn if it is dedicated to the solid studies and useful occupations which are most suitable to his genius. I humbly beseech your Majesty to dismiss me from the office which I enjoy in the army by your royal bounty,—an office which, by this petition, I lay at your royal feet. I merely desire your Majesty to know that, in the matters entrusted to me,

I have always proceeded with purity and have always been animated by the lofty desire to promote the service and glory of my king, without allowing jealousies, persecutions, or the threats of commanders and ministers to alter my intentions, or to incline my spirit to indecorous submission. I also desire, if it please your Majesty, to be reimbursed the amount of eight thousand pesos, the price of the office of captain in which I began to serve in the army; so that I may be recompensed for the serious injuries which I have recently suffered.

But the court of Madrid did not accept Miranda's version of the suspicious events in the West Indies. Although Bernardo del Campo told Miranda that his petition might be granted, yet that ambassador tried to spy upon Miranda's movements and to seize his precious papers. In fact, the Spanish government would doubtless have made a formal demand upon the government of England for the person of Miranda, if the laws of that country and the attitude of her cabinet had promised success. Although the quick-witted creole soon suspected that the Spanish ambassador was trying to hoodwink him, yet it is unlikely that he laid any plans for the liberation of Spanish America before the English cabinet at this juncture. Nevertheless, Miranda must have aired his views concerning the Indies in the English metropolis; for, in the summer of 1785, the *Political Herald and Review* declared that there was then in London a Spanish-American of "great consequence and possessed of the confidence of his fellow-citizens," who aspired "to the glory of being the deliverer of his country." The review declared that that "distinguished character" had spent many years in the study of politics and government, and that he was a man of sublime views and penetrating understanding, skilled in the ancient and modern languages, conversant with books and acquainted with the World." That personage had proceeded from North America to England, which he regarded as "the mother country of liberty, and the school for political knowledge." There is no doubt that Francisco de Miranda had posed for this flattering portrait.

In August, 1785, Miranda proceeded from London to Harwich. He then traversed the continent from the meadows of Holland to the Russian steppes, visiting Prussia, Austria, Italy, Turkey, Russia, and Sweden. Possibly he also visited Egypt and Asia Minor. While in Italy he met some of the Jesuits who had been exiled from South America and conceived the idea of using those embittered exiles to promote his revolutionary projects. It is likely that Miranda communicated his views concerning the liberation of Spanish America to Empress Catherine II. He returned safely to London in June, 1789, having cleverly outwitted various agents of Spain who had tried to ensnare him.

The observant tourist profited greatly by his trip through the United States and Europe. He had acquired a better knowledge of the English and French languages; he had become acquainted with adventurers and statesmen in two hemispheres, and had observed the condition of the military art at several European capitals. In his retentive memory Miranda had stored many anecdotes of courts and camps with which he later regaled the politicians, merchants, philanthropists, and vagabonds whom he sought to interest in his conspiracies against Spanish rule in America. Even though he may not have pleaded for American independence at every court which he visited, still he must have interested many people in Spanish America.

From 1790 to 1808 the plans which Miranda had been gradually maturing for the separation of the Spanish colonies from the mother country were laid before various cabinets. He generally took advantage of events which threatened to involve Spain in a war. In 1790, when the Nootka Sound controversy arose out of the conflicting claims of Spain and England to territory on the northwest coast of North America, Miranda first formally presented his designs to the English government. At that juncture he proposed to the prime minister, William Pitt, that England should liberate the Indies from the rule of Spain.

In the first plans which Miranda laid before Pitt, he proposed that one independent government should be established in the vast region stretching from the sources of the Mississippi River to Cape Horn, from Brazil to the Bay of San Francisco. The system of government which he thought should be introduced into South America was analogous to the government of Great Britain. The executive power was to be "represented by an Inca with the title of emperor." That office was to be hereditary. The power to make laws was to be vested in a bicameral legislature. The upper house, or senate, was to be composed of a fixed number of senators, or *caciques*, selected by the Inca from citizens who had held important offices. The senators were to hold office for life. The members of the lower house, or "chamber of communes," were also to be selected by the Inca. They were to hold office for five years: they might, however, be reappointed. The members of the federal judiciary were likewise to be chosen by the Inca. Ordinarily they were to hold office for life. Provision was also made for the choice of censors, ediles, and questors for five-year terms. The questors and the ediles were to be eligible for reëlection. The two censors, nominated by the citizens and confirmed by the Inca, were to watch over the morals of the youth, of senators, and of educators. They might expel a senator from the legislature, if they thought such a step necessary for the public welfare. The ediles were to be nominated by the senators and confirmed by the Inca. They were to take care of ports, canals, public monuments, national vessels, and national feasts. The questors, selected by the chamber of communes and confirmed by the Inca, were to take charge of the finances of the empire.

Various provisions were made regarding the amendment of this constitution. No law contrary to the spirit of the constitution was to be valid. The fundamental law of the projected state might be modified in two days: either an amendment to the constitution might be proposed by two-thirds of both houses of the legislature and should become operative if approved by three-fourths of a council composed of the Inca and the judges presiding over the high tribunals of justice; or an amendment to the constitution might be made by two-thirds of this council, if approved by three-fourths of both houses of the legislature. Obviously, the framer of this constitution, who could have been no other person than Miranda himself, had borrowed suggestions from various sources. The clauses concerning the amendment of the constitution were patterned after the Constitution of the United States. The provisions for an hereditary executive and for the upper house of the legislature were modeled upon English institutions. The provisions regarding questors, censors, and ediles were derived from the constitution of Rome. The project of a vast Spanish-American monarchy ruled by an Inca was evidently suggested to Miranda by the papers which he possessed concerning the revolution of Tupac Amaru.

In some particulars Miranda's plan for a monarchy in

America was supplemented by a proclamation found among Pitt's papers, which provided for the establishment of a provisional local government that was to replace the institutions of the Spanish régime. A "Native and Noble Citizen of South America" was temporarily to assume the powers of the Spanish viceroy or captain general. That provisional governor was to hold his office for five years; he was to govern with the advice of a council of thirty-five members who were to be chosen for five years by indirect election. Twenty members of the council were to constitute a quorum; and a majority of the members present was required for the sanction of any measure. In the case of a tie, the governor was to cast the deciding vote. The governor and the council were to have the power to appoint judges, to make laws, and even to negotiate alliances with foreign powers. The laws of the Indies were to remain in force, unless altered by the action of the governor and council. The tithes and properties of the church were to be preserved. The Spanish taxes were still to be levied, but the revenue accruing was to be "the property of the nation." If possible, the governor and council were to diminish the duties, taxes, and contributions. Monopolies were to be swept away. The capitation tax levied upon the Indians was to be "immediately abolished." The inquisition, having become unnecessary, was to be "abolished forever."

To enable Pitt to judge the attitude of the inhabitants of the Indies toward Spanish rule, Miranda sent to that minister his papers relating to the insurrection of Tupac Amaru. The agitator apparently believed that these papers would convince Pitt that the majority of the South Americans were ready for emancipation, if care were taken to adjust properly the delicate problems concerning their religion and independence. He submitted to that minister his plan of attack and operations, elucidating his ideas with the aid of maps and plans. In addition to the information derived from Miranda, the English government gathered data regarding strategic positions in Central America, Mexico, and the Philippine Islands. On his part, the revolutionary promoter tried to enlist the sympathy of General Knox, who had become secretary of war for the United States.

Nothing came of Miranda's elaborate designs in 1790; for the Nootka Sound dispute was adjusted peacefully, and the far-reaching schemes which England's great prime minister had been contemplating were laid aside. Soon afterwards Miranda went to France. There is reason to believe that he hoped to interest French leaders in his designs; as his papers concerning the Nootka Sound controversy followed him to Paris.

Through letters of introduction, and by other means, Miranda soon became acquainted with some of the French leaders, notably Brissot de Warville, leader of the Girondists, and Joseph Servan, minister of war. His arrival in Paris was opportune; for certain Frenchmen were contemplating an attack upon the Spanish colonies in America. Brissot soon selected Miranda as the best leader for such an attack with Santo Domingo as a base. On December 13, 1792, Brissot wrote to Miranda to suggest that the French forces at that island would be aided in the project by a large number of valiant soldiers from the United States, who were "sighing for this revolution." Brissot declared that he had presented his views "to all the ministers," who had appreciated the advantages proposed. His plan was that Miranda should be appointed governor of Santo Domingo from which he might direct the revolution. Miranda was so far interested in the scheme that he held a conference regarding it with Lebrun, the minister of foreign affairs. The French plan to employ Miranda in revolutionizing of Spanish America was most fully presented in a letter of Brissot to General Dumouriez dated November 28, 1792. So we will quote that letter here:

It is necessary to promote this revolution in the Spanish peninsula and in the Indies at the same time. The fate of the revolution in Spanish America depends upon one man; you know him, you esteem him, you love him: that is, Miranda. . . . He will soon check the miserable quarrels of the colonies; he will soon pacify the whites who are so troublesome; and he will become the idol of the people of color. And then with what ease will he not be able to revolutionize either the islands of the Spaniards or the American continent which they possess. At the head of twelve thousand brave troops of the line which are now at Santo Domingo, and of from ten to fifteen thousand brave mulattoes that our colonies will furnish him, having besides a squadron under his orders, with what facility will he not be able to invade the Spanish possessions, while the Spaniards have no forces with which to oppose him. The name of Miranda will be worth an army: his courage, his genius,—all promise success. But in order to ensure success, there is not a moment to lose. It is necessary that he should leave upon the *Capricieuse* which sails for Santo Domingo; it is necessary that he should depart before Spain discovers our plans. I know well that his nomination will strike Spain with terror and confound Pitt with his poor dilatory politics; but Spain is impotent, and England will not move.

Further, Brissot assured Dumouriez that all of the ministers had agreed to the choice and that Monge, the minister of marine, had promised to make Miranda the governor of Santo Domingo, if Dumouriez would consent. Apparently Dumouriez was interested in the execution of Miranda's "superb project." In the meantime Miranda again turned toward the United States; for he hoped to engage General Knox and Henry Lee in the scheme. In all likelihood Lebrun, as well as Miranda, hoped to enlist some American leaders in the campaign against Spanish America. But perhaps because of the belief of certain French leaders that Spain was trying to maintain an attitude of neutrality towards the war between France and other powers, in January, 1793, France laid the project aside. From this ambitious project, however, the revolutionary mission of Citizen Genet to the United States took its origin.

While his favorite project was being considered at Paris, Miranda had become a soldier of France. His thrilling experiences during the French revolution may only be suggested. On April 20, 1792, France had declared war on Austria. In September, 1792, Miranda was placed in command of a division of the French army that was operating in the Austrian Netherlands under General Dumouriez. Early in the following month, he was made brigadier general. General Miranda soon distinguished himself by capturing Antwerp; and a dazzling future seemed to open before him. But he refused to enter into the treasonable designs of General Dumouriez. After the inglorious defeat of the French soldiers at Neerwinden, where the South American commanded a wing of the army, he was recalled to Paris, partly because of the accusations of his former friend, Dumouriez. There he had to stand trial before the revolutionary tribunal. After being triumphantly acquitted, Miranda retired to the suburbs of Paris, where he lived in the midst of books, pictures, and other mementoes of his travels. Suspicion soon gathered around him, however, and in July, 1793, he was cast into the prison *La Force*. *Despite* his vehement protests, it was the beginning of 1795 before he was set at liberty. Miranda soon essayed to formulate a policy and to suggest a frame of government for France: he published his views in a pamphlet entitled *Opinion du Général Miranda sur la Situation Actuelle de la France et sur les Remèdes convenables à ses Maux*. A short time afterwards Miranda was denounced to the convention; hence, on November 27, 1795, he was again imprisoned. But nothing could be proven against him, and he was soon set free. It appears that General Miranda was again accused of engaging in intrigues, or was distasteful to the government, for he was soon ordered to leave the soil of France. While being conveyed to the frontier, he audaciously left his escort, and returned to Paris, where he publicly petitioned the government to pay him for his military services. Although Miranda's name was inscribed on the list of *émigrés*, yet he continued to live in seclusion near Paris until the beginning of 1798, when he crossed the Straits of Dover disguised as a merchant.

On January 16, 1798, Miranda signed a letter to William Pitt which was couched in these words:

The undersigned, principal agent of the Spanish-American colonies, has been chosen by the junta of deputies of Mexico, Lima, Chile, Buenos Aires, Caracas, Santa Fé, etc., to present himself to the ministers of his Britannic Majesty; in order to renew in favor of the absolute independence of these colonies the negotiations which were begun in 1790 and to conduct them, as quickly as possible, to that stage of maturity which the existing circumstances appear to favor, completing them by a treaty of amity and alliance which should resemble (so far as circumstances permit) the treaty concluded by France with the English colonies of North America in 1778. That example can serve as an apology in the absence of strict legality in the present case. . . . The spirit of frankness and loyalty which animates his compatriots and which attaches them to the interests of Great Britain is best expressed in the instrument that serves the undersigned as powers and instructions for this important commission.

Miranda declared that he was happy at being able to claim "by a lucky chance" the "protection of the English nation in

promoting the independence of his country and in negotiating
a treaty of amity and alliance which would be useful and advantageous to both parties." He expressed his confidence in
"the importance and the reciprocal utility of his mission." He
affirmed that circumstances favored his project, because Pitt
had declared to him that a war between Spain and England
would furnish the occasion for the revolutionizing of Spanish
America.

With this letter Miranda submitted a copy of the document
which he declared served him as his instructions. That document was composed of articles purporting to be drawn up
by a South-American revolutionary junta at Paris on December 22, 1797. The junta professed to be composed of deputies
from the principal provinces of Spanish America, who had
been sent to Europe to concert with Miranda a plan for the
liberation of their native land from the rule of Spain. The
instructions affirmed that the Spanish-American colonists,
having unanimously resolved to proclaim their independence
and to place their liberty upon a firm basis, addressed themselves to the British government, which they invited to join
them in the enterprise. Spanish America, it was declared,
agreed to pay England for her assistance. The aid demanded
of England was not to exceed twenty-seven vessels, eight
thousand infantry, and two thousand cavalry. It was declared
that a defensive alliance of England, the United States, and
Spanish America was "the only hope which remained to
liberty, that had been so boldly outraged by the detestable
maxims" avowed by France. It was suggested that a treaty
of alliance be entered into by England and Spanish America,
which, although not granting monopoly privileges, should be
conceived in terms most advantageous for Great Britain. A
proposal was made for the construction of a canal between
the Atlantic and the Pacific oceans by way of Lake Nicaragua,
as well as by the Isthmus of Panama. The freedom of such
transit was to be guaranteed, although not exclusively, to England and the United States. It was provided that, after the
independence of Spanish America had been established, deputies from various sections of America were to meet in a general
representative body in order to make arrangements for commercial intercourse within the liberated territory. It was
pointed out that the relations which the bank of London would
be able to form with the banks of Lima and Mexico would

not be the least advantage which the alliance with Spanish America would secure to England. The thirteenth article of the instructions intrusted the military operations on the American continent, as well as the negotiations with England, to Francisco de Miranda. Certain blank passages in the instructions concerning the amount to be paid England for her assistance and the disposition of the insular possessions of Spain in America, were to be filled out when an agreement had been reached by negotiations.

These instructions constitute the most explicit authorization which has been found for Miranda's activities as a promoter of Spanish-American independence. They bear the signatures of José del Pozo y Sucre, Manuel de Salas, and Francisco de Miranda. It appears that Sucre and Salas were expatriated Jesuits; but no evidence has been discovered to support the statement that they were the authorized agents of certain inhabitants of Spanish America. Still it is possible that the signatories may have been authorized by a group of revolutionary agitators from Spanish America composed of such men as Antonio Nariño. Those agitators may have had some authorization from their revolutionary sympathizers in Spanish America. Such authorization, however, could hardly have been more than an expression of the desire of a minority of the inhabitants of certain sections of America to free themselves from the odious rule of Spain. Viewed in this light, the instrument of December 22, 1797, was a farcical document. Furthermore, it seems likely that the document was, in the main, an expression of Miranda's ideas. To a large extent, Francisco de Miranda was a self-constituted agent.

Following the plan which he had outlined, Miranda soon attempted to engage the aid of the United States. He first approached his friend, Rufus King, the American minister in London, to whom on January 30, 1798, he partly disclosed his scheme. The South American declared that, if England and the United States should be driven to oppose France, nothing would be easier than for these powers by joint operations to separate the Indies from Spain. In the Spanish settlements on the American continents there were ten million people who were civilized and "capable of being happy as members of a polished Society." Everything was ripe for the completion of the plan: Spain had given to the United States good reasons for going to war with her. When King visited Miranda, on February 8, the creole further explained his plan. The attack which he projected was to be made on the east side of the Isthmus of Darien. He wished to secure from England eight thousand infantry and two thousand cavalry—seasoned West Indian troops—besides a naval squadron which should be sent to the Peruvian coast. From the United States Miranda desired five thousand woodmen, or soldiers who understood new countries. He entertained sanguine hopes of coöperation from the Spanish soldiers stationed near the isthmus; for many of the officers, he declared, were in sympathy with his plan. Miranda declared that England was to be paid thirty million pounds for her aid, while England and the United States were to enjoy the trade of liberated Spanish America. Goods from England and the United States which passed across the Isthmus of Panama were to pay lower tolls than the goods of other nations. There is a likelihood that Miranda had in his possession at this time a copy of a Spanish map of that isthmus and the adjacent section of South America, which delineated the strategic positions where fortifications should be constructed.

For a time, Miranda considered the attitude of England toward his plan as favorable. But Lord Grenville, the English secretary for foreign affairs, expressed himself to King unfavorably in regard to Miranda's designs. He stated that he did not favor the plan presented by Miranda, fearing that it might lead to "scenes of wretchedness" on the American continent like those which had characterized the French revolution. By the middle of February, the English ministers had apparently reached a tentative conclusion in regard to the revolutionizing of Spanish America. For Grenville informed King that "if it was really to be apprehended that Spain should fall beneath the control of France, then it was their intention to prevent France from gaining to her cause the resources of South America." At that juncture, they would "immediately open their views and commence a negotiation upon the subject with the United States."

Meanwhile, Miranda and King were attempting to interest the United States in the ambitious design. On March 24 Miranda addressed a letter to President Adams, inclosing a copy of his instructions. He expressed the opinion that Eng-

land's exasperating delay was due to her expectation that the
United States would break definitely with France and to her
desire to coöperate with the United States in achieving "the
absolute independence" of Spanish America. He hoped that
six or eight vessels and four or five thousand men, which
were needed to begin the attack on Spanish America, could
easily be secured in England and the United States. Miranda
also wrote several letters to Alexander Hamilton, asking for
his coöperation in the attack on Spanish America. Rufus King
also wrote to Hamilton suggesting that the spread of French
revolutionary doctrines upon the European continent made it
necessary for the United States to take offensive measures:
"The Destiny of the new world, and I have a full and firm
persuasion that it will be both happy and glorious, is in our
hands." In August, Hamilton wrote to King declaring himself
in favor of the enterprise, and wishing that the United States
would furnish the land forces which should be commanded by
himself. At the same time, Hamilton wrote to Miranda declaring that he could not participate in the scheme unless it was
patronized by the government of the United States, and that
such aid could hardly be hoped for then. Still, he declared
that in a short time the project might mature, and "an effectual coöperation" by the United States might take place. Hamilton's letters evidently encouraged Miranda to entertain sanguine hopes in regard to the outcome of his plans. He wrote
a letter to Hamilton declaring that it was agreed in England
that the auxiliary land forces were to be exclusively American, while the naval forces were to be entirely English. "All is
approved, and we await only the *fiat* of your illustrious
President to depart like lightning."

The revolutionary ardor of Miranda had lead him to disregard the facts; as the contingency of the absorption of
Spain by France was still the pivot on which English policy
toward Spanish America depended. It is possible, of course,
that, if President Adams had decided to favor Miranda's designs, England might have equipped a squadron for an attack
upon South America. However, the government of the United
States—largely because of the reluctance of President Adams
and of his secretary of state, Timothy Pickering—did not even
reply to Miranda's impassioned pleas. The agitator was consequently compelled to dismiss the hope of linking together
the two Anglo-Saxon nations in his pretentious designs.

The regret which Miranda entertained at this outcome was profound. On March 19, 1799, he addressed a memorial to William Pitt reviewing his relations with that minister. An extract from a copy of that document which is preserved in the papers of Timothy Pickering will suggest his mood:

What will be the result when, in place of the long-expected succor which has been so often promised the Spanish-Americans, they learn that England, after having made them wait in expectancy for several years, and after having promised more than fourteen months ago to the agents of Spanish America who were in London an immediate and frank response, has not furnished the slightest succor? It is difficult to judge the effect which despair will produce in such circumstances; but it is certain that the wise and intelligent persons, who hoped to see established throughout the American continent a system of order and morality which might counterbalance the destructive maxims propagated by France, will be deprived of their hopes and will be lowered in the estimation of the Spanish-American people. It is certain that the interests and the future security of the United States of America will be gravely compromised. And that the advantages which would accrue to Great Britain through commerce and by virtue of an alliance with the immense American continent will be a real loss to her. If, on the other side, one supposes that the varied genius of the French directory is capable of successfully executing its plans for a general invasion and of extending its perfidious vengeance to the United States as well as to Great Britain, in view of the colossal and revolutionary power which it possesses at the present moment, one naturally trembles in contemplating the fate of the human race.

From 1799 to 1805 "the agent of the Spanish-American colonies," as Miranda sometimes styled himself, resided for the most part in London. He urged his revolutionary plans upon English ministers whenever circumstances seemed propitious. On certain occasions the cabinets of Pitt and Addington listened to him. Among the persons who became interested in his project was Sir Home Popham. In October, 1800, Miranda crossed the English Channel and succeeded in reaching Paris, where he probably hoped to interest General Bonaparte in his designs. But the former general of the French republic, who was now an indigent soldier of fortune, was viewed with suspicion. He was soon thrust into prison; and, in April, 1801, he left French soil without having been able to present his views concerning Spanish America to Bonaparte. Miranda finally became much dissatified with the attitude of England toward his plans; in June, 1805, he wrote a letter to Pitt, which shows that he was discredited. Speaking of Miranda, a fellow-conspirator, Joseph Pavia, later declared that "Mr. Pitt, who knew him well, kept a strict eye upon him, but granted him protection from no other motive than that of giving uneasiness" to the Spanish government which was always "afraid of his freaks and plans to revolutionize America." This narrow interpretation of Miranda's relations with the English government is probably most correct in regard to the period from 1799 to 1805. It seems impossible to determine the exact amount of aid to encouragement which that government gave to Miranda when, in the end of 1805, he sailed from England for North America.

At that time, Miranda entertained great expectations of aid from the United States, because of the differences existing between that nation and Spain. After landing in New York City, he tried to interest certain Americans in his plans. He made a hasty trip from New York to Washington to solicit the aid or sanction of the government of the United States for his revolutionary undertaking. In the capital city he met President Jefferson and James Madison, the secretary of state. To use Madison's own words, Miranda "disclosed in very general terms his purpose of instituting a revolution in a portion of Spanish America." But the government of the United States would not coöperate. Meanwhile the misleading representations of Miranda's agents in New York City induced a number of adventurous individuals to join an expedition which was destined to attack the Spanish colonies. In February, 1806, the armed vessel *Leander* sailed from New York City, bearing two hundred men, munitions of war, and Miranda. Years of agitation by Miranda had culminated in a filibustering expedition which was directed against his native land.

After the *Leander* reached the high seas, the commander in chief appeared on deck. According to one of his followers, he was attired in a red gown and slippers. The commander soon interested the ship's company by telling marvelous tales of his own adventures. The real object of the voyage became known to all; the recruits were drilled in the manual of arms;

and many speculations were made regarding the attitude of England and the United States toward the enterprise. The expedition first proceeded to the West Indies. There Miranda gathered a few more recruits, and secured the coöperation of some English naval officers, notably Admiral Cochrane. In the meantime the Spanish officials in northern South America had been warned of Miranda's approach by the Marquis of Casa Yrujo, the vigilant Spanish ambassador in the United States. Partly because of those warnings, the first attempt of Miranda to land in the captaincy general of Venezuela failed; and some of the filibusters fell into the hands of the Spaniards. The unfortunate captives were summarily tried and sentenced to imprisonment or death. Miranda's second attack was more successful; for the invaders captured the town of Coro, and marched a short distance into the interior. The tribunal of the inquisition at Carthagena proclamed that Miranda was a traitor to God and his king, while the captain general gathered a small, motley army to repel the invaders. The colonists did not join the filibusters; so that Miranda soon decided to withdraw. When the English naval commanders who were stationed near northern South America declined to aid him, the expedition was disbanded, and the discredited leader took refuge in the British West Indies. The first attempt which Miranda made to revolutionize South America had completely failed, mainly because the inhabitants did not rally to his standard of red, yellow, and blue.

As soon as circumstances seemed auspicious, Miranda sent agents to London to present his views to the English government again. On June 10, 1807, Miranda addressed from Trinidad to Lord Castlereagh, who had become secretary of war and the colonies in the Portland ministry, a letter concerning Spanish America:

The present situation and disposition of the People in the whole Province of Caracas is very favorable to this undertaking yet, notwithstanding the terror that the Government tries to inspire by a few executions, and the tremendous pursuits of the Inquisition, made an absolute political tool on this occasion. The general Orders given to the Commanders of the principal Towns in this Province, with the exception of La Guayra and Puerto Cabello, is to evacuate them in case of my landing with any substantial force, and the inhabitants to retire into the Country;

but these have sent me information, that they will do no such thing, when the opportunity arrives. . . . I really perceive an incalculable mischief in the delay of the proposed operation, for if we do not subtract and protect the Continent of South America now, from the influence and domineering ambition of France, the whole will very soon and ultimately be absorbed in the same fatal and universal dominion. . . . I beseech You, My Lord, on these considerations, to take some prompt and definitive measure that may put a stop to this incalculable evil; or release the American People from the dangerous exertions in which they are embarked, by opposing the French and Spanish Governments' views, which ultimately must be fatal to themselves, if not efficaciously supported by the Government of Great Britain. . . . My own exertions in this Island are almost at an End, if I do not receive the promised support from G. B.

Miranda's hope for aid from England, which was at war with Spain, the ally of France, soon induced him to return to London. On January 10, 1808, he addressed to Castlereagh a long letter which was accompanied by illustrative documents. Miranda averred that the inhabitants of New Granada and Venezuela still favored independence, but that their anxiety had been aroused by rumors that Spain had secretly ceded Cuba and Porto Rico to France. He expressed serious apprehensions in regard to the prospective cession of the captaincy general of Venezuela by Spain to France in return for Porugal, and besought from the English government the assistance which, he declared, it had so often promised, to promote Spanish-American independence. He declared that among the Spanish-American people there was no difference of opinion in regard to emancipation from Spanish rule, if independence was fairly and openly offered to them, and if "the delicate point of their religion" was respectfully attended to.

With regard to the political organization of independent Spanish America, Miranda now proposed that four states should be established upon the "Colombian Continent": the first state should include Mexico and Guatemala; the second, New Granada, Venezuela, and Quito; the third, Peru and Chile; and the fourth, la Plata. He declared that the people of Spanish America had not shown a leaning towards "any particular form of government," but expressed a belief that the identity of language, religion, and civil administration would greatly decrease the difficulty of changing the form of government "without convulsions." Among Miranda's voluminous papers there probably reposed an elaborate project of government for his compatriots.

Miranda wished that an attack on the Spanish dominions should begin in northern South America. If the military operations in Venezuela and New Granada were successful, and, if the governmental arrangements were "wise and acceptable to the people," he thought that the movement would soon spread, on the one hand, through the Isthmus of Panama and Guatemala to Mexico, and, on the other hand, through Quito to Peru and Chile, and even to la Plata. He believed that an army of ten thousand men with a coöperating naval force would be sufficient to execute this plan of operations. Sir Arthur Wellesley, a military officer who had served with distinction in India, became deeply interested in Miranda's projects. He drew up several memoranda concerning a revolution which was "to establish an independent government in a part or the whole" of Spanish America. After carefully weighing the advantages and the disadvantages of an attack upon Mexico or upon Venezuela, Wellesley decided in favor of an expedition of ten thousand soldiers to execute Miranda's designs. Early in June, 1808, thousands of redcoats bivouacked on the Irish coast; a fleet was gathered at Cork; and Wellesley was selected as the commander of an expedition which was to start a revolution in northern South America.

But at this critical juncture, when it seemed that Miranda's hope of English aid to revolutionize Spanish America was at last to be realized, Napoleon's attempt to crush England by extending the continental system to the Iberian peninsula, changed the face of politics. In November, 1807, the invasion of Portugal by French soldiers forced the royal family of Braganza, including the heir to the Portuguese throne, Prince John, and his wife, Carlota Joaquina, the daughter of Charles IV. of Spain, to flee precipitately from Lisbon to Rio de Janeiro, escorted by an English squadron. In the following year French soldiers seized fortresses in northern Spain; a popular tumult at Aranjuez forced the Prince of Peace from power; and Charles IV. temporarily relinquished his right to the Spanish throne in favor of his eldest son, Prince Ferdinand. In May, 1808, by a treaty signed at Bayonne Charles IV. renounced his right to the crown of Spain and the Indies in favor of Napoleon, while Ferdinand VII. was forced to abdicate his right to that crown. Those Napoleonic usurpations provoked a national uprising among the Spaniards, which was stimulated by the news that on June 6, 1808, Napoleon had arrogantly proclaimed his brother Joseph, King of Spain. Juntas, or local assemblies, sprang up, as if by magic, from Oviedo to Granada. On May 25, 1808, the patriotic junta of the principality of Asturias sent two envoys to beseech aid from England against Napoleon. Early in the following month—when Wellesley's soldiers were bivouacking on the coast of Ireland—these envoys were promised munitions and soldiers by England's foreign secretary, George Canning. On July 4, 1808, England published a formal proclamation of peace with Spain. In the speech of King George III. to parliament on that day, it was declared that, because of the resistance of Spain to the usurpations of France, the Spanish nation could "no longer be considered as the enemy of Great Britan" but was recognized by his Majesty as "a natural friend and ally." It was expressly declared that the king had "no other object than that of preserving unimpaired the integrity and independence of the Spanish monarchy."

When England thus decided to aid the Spanish patriots against Napoleon, Miranda's project to revolutionize Spanish America was discarded. Sir Arthur Wellesley was deputed to tell the Venezuelan agitator of the change in England's military plans. Twenty-seven years afterwards, the Duke of Wellington thus described the dramatic scene which ensued:

I think I never had a more difficult business than when the Government bade me tell Miranda that we would have nothing to do with his plan. I thought it best to walk out in the streets with him and tell him there, to prevent his bursting out. But even there he was so loud and angry, that I told him I would walk on first a little that we might not attract the notice of everybody passing. When I joined him again he was cooler. He said: "You are going over into Spain. . . . You will be lost—nothing can save you that; that, however, is your affair; but what grieves me is that there never was such an opportunity thrown away."

To attempt to suggest the outcome of Miranda's plans, if they had been executed by England, is to discuss what might have been. The result might have been to found independent states in Spanish America. On the other hand, viceroyalties of Spain might have been transfromed into dependencies of England. Some South American patriots might have reviled Miranda, the apostle of Spanish-American independence.

But in July, 1808, Sir Arthur Wellesley embarked for the Iberian peninsula to engage in those campaigns which were to play so great a part in thwarting the ambitions of Napoleon. The *rapprochement* between England and the Spanish patriots was an insuperable obstacle to the execution of Miranda's favorite design. His highest hopes of English coöperation sailed away with the soldiers of Wellesley. On January 14, 1809, in the name of Ferdinand VII., the central junta located at Seville and the English government cemented their relations by a formal treaty of peace, friendship, and alliance. For several years England devoted her energies to a life-or-death struggle with Napoleon upon the European continent.

This is a convenient place to notice some common features of the schemes which Miranda urged upon various governments from 1790 to 1808. Against Spanish rule in America he brought the charge that the colonists were "excessively oppressed." As proof of the accusation, Miranda was accustomed to cite the insurrections which had ocurred in Spanish America, for example, the revolt of Tupac Amaru. Ordinarily, he assumed that many Spanish-Americans were dissatisfied with the colonial régime. He was accustomed to argue that the inhabitants of South America would rise against Spain, if he appeared on its coast with a liberating expedition —an argument which was not substantiated by the attitude of the Venezuelans towards the expedition of 1806. In general, he maintained that the Spanish-Americans were not able to cast off the heavy yoke of Spain without assistance. Accordingly Miranda tried to interest one or more important nations in his venture. Burdened with letters, maps, and plans, the enthusiastic creole would appear in the capital of a nation at a crucial juncture in its relations with Spain. Tenacious of purpose, if he failed to interest ministers, he turned to private individuals, merchants, philanthropists, and adventurers. Thus he traveled from court to court, offering, though he knew it not, a New World to European nations for conquest. Miranda argued that, if her colonies were liberated, Spain would be grievously injured. Sometimes he offered her enemies special advantages; such as lower import duties on articles sent to the liberated colonies. After 1797, the upshot of his argument to England was that only the revolutionizing of the Indies would thwart the designs of France upon those dominions. To the imagination of patriot and filibuster, Miranda suggested the alluring vision of a continent of freedmen.

The first objective point of the proposed attack on Spanish America was Miranda's native land. A map found among some papers in the French archives proves that on one occasion, at least, he aimed to get a foothold in northern South America, to secure control of the Isthmus of Panama, to fortify himself there, and gradually to extend the area of freedom. His design was far-reaching, for he glibly talked of ultimately emancipating all the subjects of Spain in America from Tierra del Fuego to the northern limits of the Mississippi Valley. The ambitious scope of these designs tempts one to compare Francisco de Miranda with the anti-slavery fanatic, John Brown.

It is easy to exaggerate or to underestimate the influence of Miranda upon certain leaders of the revolution in Spanish America. His apostolic rôle favors the interpretation that he promoted the revolts which broke out in 1810 from Mexico to Buenos Aires, but contemporary evidence concerning the influence which he exerted upon his compatriots from 1783 to 1810 is fugitive. The evidence shows that Miranda persistently tried to correspond with certain agitators who played a more or less mysterious part in the revolutionary movements in different parts of Spanish-America: as illustrations may be cited Manuel Gual of Venezuela, and Saturino Peña of the viceroyalty of la Plata. While in London Miranda met Bernardo O'Higgins, a young Chilean, Pedro F. Vargas, a revolutionist who had fled from Caracas, Pedro J. Caro, a conspirator from Cuba, and Simón de Bolívar. On these men, and on other Spanish-Americans, Miranda doubtless exerted a stimulating influence which cannot be measured. There is no doubt that Miranda's abiding-place, whether in London or Paris, served as a rendezvous for discontented Spanish-Americans. Some students of Hispanic history have asserted that Miranda founded in Europe a secret revolutionary association, or lodge, which was transplanted to various sections of South America. But this story, which, in its most ample form, would make Miranda the revolutionary godfather of Mariano Moreno, Bernardo O'Higgins, José de San Martín, and Simón de Bolívar, is at present hardly more than a legend.

Amid all the fluctuations of fortune Miranda preserved an interest in learning. His leisure was often employed in the study of government and politics and war. A quondam associate declared that the South American learned Greek when forty years of age. There is also a tradition that he wrote a history of France. Nevertheless he was a dilettante scholar; Joseph Pavia not inaptly said of Miranda that he "deemed himself adept in every science and art; indeed he was a specious smatterer." While living in London Miranda possessed a choice library. A part of that library which was sold at public auction several years after his death contained histories of European countries, voyages and travels in various parts of the world, books on art and art galleries, and a number of Spanish books concerning North and South America. At his elbow Miranda often had a secretary who took charge of his extensive correspondence. At least during a part of his career, he kept copies of his own letters which were filed with the epistles received from his widely-scattered correspondents, who often occupied prominent positions in public and private life. Vanity, or literary ambition, incited Miranda at times to keep a journal, and to collect papers which concerned himself, his family, and his projects.

The following description of Miranda was written by James Biggs, who took part in the expedition of 1806:

He is about five feet ten inches high. His limbs are well proportioned; his whole frame is stout and active. His complexion is dark, florid and healthy. His eyes are hazel colored, but not of the darkest hue. They are piercing, quick and intelligent, expressing more of the severe than the mild feelings. He has good teeth, which he takes much care to keep clean. His nose is large and handsome, rather of the English than Roman cast. His chest is square and prominent. His hair is gray and he wears it tied long behind with powder. He has strong gray whiskers growing on the outer edges of his ears, as large as most Spaniards have on their cheeks. In the contour of his visage you plainly perceive an expression of pertinaciousness and suspicion. Upon the whole without saying he is an elegant, we may pronounce him a handsome man. He has a constant habit of picking his teeth. When sitting he is never perfectly still; his foot or hand must be kept moving to keep in time with his mind which is always in exercise. He always sleeps a few minutes after dinner, and then walks till bed time, which with him is about midnight. He is an eminent example of temperance. A scanty or bad meal is never regarded by him as a subject of complaint. He uses no ardent spirits; seldom any wine. . . . He is a courtier and gentle-man in his manners. Dignity and grace preside in his movements. Unless when angry, he has a great command of his feelings; and can assume what looks and tones he pleases. In general his demeanor is marked by hauteur and distance. . . . In discourse he is logical in the management of his thoughts. He appears conversant on all subjects. His iron memory prevents his ever being at a loss for names, dates, and authorities.

For two years after Wellesley's departure for the Iberian peninsula, Miranda lived in London and attempted the rôle of a propagandist. Although the English ministers—mindful of their pledges to Spain—warned the South American to desist from his revolutionary correspondence with the Indies, yet he busied himself dispatching incendiary letters and pamphlets to certain Spanish-Americans and to the *cabildos* of Buenos Aires, Havana, Mexico, and Caracas. Perhaps his most important letter was addressed to the Marquis of Toro of Caracas and the *cabildo* of that city on October 6, 1808. In that epistle Miranda expressed his fear that a fatal conflict would soon be precipitated between the Spanish officials and the people of Spanish America. He affirmed that, because of the lack of a representative organization, the Spanish patriots were compelled to establish an imperfect system of government; and that afterwards they hardly had time to concert a plan for the general defense before the kingdom was overrun by French soldiers. He declared that although he did not consider the Spanish people capable of enjoying a rational liberty, yet he believed the Venezuelan people capable of enjoying it, for they had not been corrupted. That his fellow-country-men might be prepared for an emergency, he transmitted a "sketch of a representative organization and government" for Spanish America.

The plan of government which Miranda transmitted to the

cabildo of Caracas is worthy of careful consideration. Doubtless it embodied his ripest ideas concerning the government of independent Spanish America. It was probably based upon the plan which he had ready to take him to South America in June, 1808. In October of that year Miranda recommended to the Spanish-Americans a provisional scheme for a federal government. In the provisional scheme he proposed to use the *cabildos* as local organs of government. Extraordinary *cabildos* were to select the members of provincial assemblies, which were to legislate for the province and to supervise the provincial administration. Each provincial assembly was to choose two citizens called *curacas,* who were to exercise the executive authority in their respective provinces. During the war, the armed forces of the patriots were to be commanded by a citizen called the *hatunapa,* who was to be nominated by the general assembly and confirmed by the local assemblies of the provinces. All the existing laws were to remain in force, except those imposing a personal tax. Customs duties were to be levied at the uniform rate of fifteen per cent on importations, and twenty per cent on exportations. All laws relating to the "odious tribunal" of the inquisition were to be swept away. Roman Catholicism was to be the national religion of the Colombian people, but religious toleration was to be observed as "a principle of natural right."

The most significant part of Miranda's plan was the scheme for a general government, which was to be of a federal type. The provincial assemblies were to choose the members of the unicameral legislature, or "Colombian council," which was to make laws for "the entire American federation." In regard to the executive power, it was provided that the council was to select from the citizens two persons at least forty years of age, the owners of two hundred acres of land, who had held one of the great offices of the empire. Those two citizens were to serve as chief executivs for ten years: "They shall be called Incas, a name venerated in the country. One of the Incas shall remain constantly where the legislature is in session at the federal capital, while the other shall traverse the provinces of the empire." As in the plan of 1790, special provision was made for the choice of an executive in perilous times:

In extraordinary circumstances, the council will decree the choice of a dictator, with the same power which he had at Rome: this officer will hold his position for one year; but he may be dismissed before the expiration of that period. The Incas will name the personage who is to fill this sacred office: he must be at least forty-five years of age, and must have occupied at least one of the great offices of the empire.

Careful provisions were made for a provincial and for a national judiciary. Jury trial was to be introduced. It was provided that the federal supreme court was to have jurisdiction over cases relating to the law of nations, those arising from treaties with foreign powers, or from the misdeeds of federal magistrates. Both the provisional and the federal schemes contained age and property qualifications for office-holders, which varied according to the importance of the position.

In 1808 Miranda evidently aimed to include more territory in the projected state than the captaincy general of Venezuela, for this constitution provided that the capital, which was to be named Colombo, should be built at the most central point in the territory of the state, "perhaps on the Isthmus of Panama." Although the plan for a federal government did not designate the boundaries of the projected state, yet Miranda probably desired to include within its limits New Granada as well as Venezuela. The plan of 1808 constituted an attempt, in part, to evolve from the colonial institutions of Spanish America a representative government of a monarchical type. This plan proposed to found in Spanish America not a democracy, or a federal republic, but an empire, or an imperial republic. In 1808 Miranda wished to sponsor an autocratic régime.

Miranda was probably the chief author of the governmental plan. In the letter which he sent to Caracas, enclosing a copy of the plan, he declared that it had been approved by Americans and Englishmen who were well versed in such matters. Perhaps Pitt was partly responsible for some of its provisions. Certain parts of the plan had probably been modified as the result of the suggestions of Sir Arthur Wellesley. Some provisions of the imperial constitution, like the earlier products of Miranda's pen, show that he had borrowed suggestions from various governmental systems. As in the project presented to Pitt, careful provisions, resembling those in the constitution of the United States, were made for the amendment of the fundamental law. Unlike the project of 1790, however, the plan of 1808 provided that the national legislature should be composed of only one house.

In letters which Miranda sent to certain *cabildos* of Spanish America after England had discarded his revolutionary designs, he urged those bodies to seize the reins of government. Likewise he strove to incite the people to rise against the rule of Spain. But the Spanish-Americans could not always appreciate his advice; when the Marquis of Toro received such a letter, he transmitted it to the captain general of Venezuela, and denounced Miranda as a traitor. Meanwhile, that inveterate revolutionist turned some of his energy into journalistic channels. He inspired an article which appeared in the *Edinburgh Review* in January, 1890, entitled *South American Emancipation*. That article was a review of Viscardo y Guzmán's *Lettre aux Espagnols-Américains*. The author of that review, who evidently drew a part of his information from Miranda, took occasion to consider at length the struggle between France and England, the advantages which would result to England if she revolutionized Spanish America, and the persistent efforts of Miranda for the emancipation of his native land. The English people were taken into confidence regarding a subject which for a long time had been "almost exclusively the nursling of Ministers."

Then, too, in March, 1810, a Spanish journal, *El Colombiano*, was founded at London under Miranda's auspices. The second number of that journal, dated April 1, 1810, discussed the extension "of the monstrous power of Napoleon" over the European continent. The hope was expressed that Providence might preserve America from that "most oppressive system." The third number of the journal, dated April 15, 1810, published a decree of the Spanish council of regency to which the central junta had transferred its authority. In the editorial columns the mode in which the central junta had directed the war against France was criticised. The junta was described as an illegal body, which did not possess sovereign authority. A quotation from the article will suggest Miranda's reasoning.

Even if the assumption is made that the junta was legitimate, can one rightly infer that this body could transmit sovereignty? Sovereignty resides solely in the people, and when they deposit that power in an individual, that individual does not acquire the right to dispossess himself of it, or to transfer it without the consent of the people. . . . How can the council of regency say that the supreme junta, without the participation of the nation, is able to create a sovereign authority and to transfer the sovereignty to five individuals, who have no right whatever to it? To admit that sovereignty may be transferred without the consent of the people would not only be absurd, but would also be in contradiction to the actual conduct of the Spaniards themselves.

This number of Miranda's journal, at least, reached Spanish America; for, on October 4, 1810, Mariano Moreno published the above excerpt in the *Gaceta de Buenos Aires*. These two numbers of *El Colombiano*—numbers which have been found in English archives—indicate that the purpose of Miranda was to make the people of Spanish America dissatisfied with the French régime in Spain by spreading broadcast a hatred of Napoleon. Clearly he also strove to disseminate surreptitiously among the Spanish-Americans a spirit of dissatisfaction with the government of the Spanish patriots. Thus in one way or another he hoped to foment a revolutionary spirit.

In 1810 there was also published in London under the nominal editorship of J. M. Antepara, a native of Guayaquil, a book entitled "South American Emancipation, Documents, historical and explanatory, showing the designs which have been in progress, and the exertions made by General Miranda, for the attainment of that object during the last twenty-five years." In the introduction to the volume Antepara stated that the documents had been selected from a large collection of manuscripts in Miranda's archives. These papers were evidently chosen with a view to rehabilitate Miranda, as well as to inform the public of the real scope of his designs. Antepara reprinted in "South American Emancipation" the article from the *Edinburgh Review* concerning Viscardo y Guzmán's *Lettre aux Espagnols-Américains*. The conclusion is irresistible that Antepara must have prepared the book under the supervision of Miranda himself.

At that time Miranda became the leader of a coterie which was seriously interested in the fortunes of Spanish America.

Among its members were Lady Hester Stanhope, the erratic niece of William Pitt, Jeremy Bentham, the philosopher, William Wilberforce, the reformer, and Joseph Lancaster, the educator. In 1810 there were added to the group three fellow-countrymen of Miranda: Andrés Bello, Luis López Méndez, and Simón de Bolívar.

These men appeared in London because of a movement in Miranda's native land which was provoked by Napoleon's usurpations in Spain. After Napoleon had deposed Ferdinand VII., he sent vessels to the Indies bearing the news of the accession of Joseph Napoleon to the Spanish throne. Napoleon's agents who brought the news of the dynastic changes to Venezuela were spurned by the people of Caracas. Soon afterwards leading citizens of Caracas vainly expressed their desire to form a provisional junta in imitation of the Spaniards. Some of the leaders in this movement were evidently loyal to Ferdinand VII., while others probably cherished thoughts of a separation from Spain. The ferment was promoted by the policy of the Spanish patriots. On January 22, 1809, the central junta announced that the American possessions of Spain were not colonies, but that they constituted an integral part of the Spanish nation with the right to representation in the junta. On February 14, 1810, the council of regency addressed a proclamation to the inhabitants of Spanish America which invited them to select delegates to a national cortes. The regency declared that the colonists were now elevated to the dignity of freemen, that they would no longer be viewed with indifference, or vexed by stupid officials, or destroyed by ignorance, and that their destinies did not depend upon ministers, viceroys, and governors but upon themselves. On April 19, 1810, after agents arrived in Caracas with orders that the Spanish regency should be recognized, a *cabildo abierto* deposed the weak captain general and established a provisional junta, which loudly professed to act on behalf of Ferdinand VII. The junta of Caracas soon deposed other colonial officials, organized certain administrative departments, and initiated various political and social reforms. On April 27, 1810, the junta sent a manifesto to the *cabildos* of the important cities of Spanish America inciting them to rise against King Joseph, to declare in favor of Ferdinand VII., and to promote the formation of a Spanish-American confederation. In reality, the proceedings of April, 1810, in

Caracas constituted a revolution in disguise. A short time afterwards the provisional junta addressed a manifesto to the Spanish regency boldly disavowing its authority. Rightly did the junta of Caracas style a "new government."

This junta had commissioned Bello, Mendéz, and Bolívar to proceed to the court of London. They were instructed to solicit the English cabinet to recognize that junta; at least they were to secure from England a promise of aid for the new government of Venezuela. But the alliance between England and the Spanish patriots prevented Marquis Wellesley, who had become the English secretary for foreign affairs, from recognizing the provisional government of Venezuela, or from promising aid to the Venezuelans except to protect them against France. Nevertheless the mission of Bolívar and Méndez to London was important, for it brought Miranda into direct touch with the secessionist movement in his native land, and enabled him to meet Simón de Bolívar. A short time after meeting the Venezuelan commissioners, in October, 1810, Miranda started for South America by way of Curaçao. When he disembarked in Venezuela in December, 1810, he found that his fellow-countrymen, in accordance with the provisions of the junta, were selecting the delegates to a congress.

Since Miranda had left his father's house the conditions in Caracas had changed, for his compatriots had taken a great step along the road toward independence from Spain. The rôle which Miranda attempted in Venezuela was difficult; for he was imperfectly acquainted with conditions there; and the list of his friends or acquaintances was not long. Some of the Venezuelans, who were just awakening to political self-consciousness, hailed Miranda as a gift of favoring Providence, while others considered him an adventurous soldier of fortune. Although he was fifty-four years of age, yet he had not lost his youthful enthusiasm for liberty. There was no Spanish-American leader of this era who was better fitted than Miranda to transmit to South America, the spirit, the doctrines, and the methods of the French revolution.

For some time after the arrival of Miranda in Venezuela, he partly eclipsed Simón de Bolívar, who had landed there several days before him. The ability and prestige of General Miranda enabled him to become the most influential leader

of the independent party in his native land. He was a prominent member of the patriotic society of Caracas,—a society
which resembled the Jacobin club. Further, he was selected
as the delegate for the district of Pao in the Venezuelan
congress. There he became the eloquent champion of an immediate declaration of independence from Spain. On July 3,
1811, he made two harangues in congress in favor of independence. In his first speech Miranda argued that the formation of a republican government was inconsistent with an
acknowledgment of the sovereignty of Spain. In his second
speech he discussed the advantages that a declaration of
independence would afford to Venezuela in her diplomatic
relations with foreign powers: "We ought to declare our
independence; so that we may enjoy the advantages of it: in
order that European nations may make alliances with us,
which will aid us by engaging directly the forces of our
enemies."

July 5, 1811, was a glorious day for Miranda. On that day
the congress composed of delegates from seven provinces
of the captaincy general of Venezuela voted in favor of a
declaration of independence from Spain. Two days later, the
formal declaration of independence was sanctioned by congress. In the declaration the delegates only suggested some
of the evils of the Spanish colonial régime; for, in a chari-
table spirit, they drew a veil "over the three hundred years of
Spanish domination in America." They affirmed that the
usurpation of the throne of Spain by Napoleon had restored
their rights and had summoned Spanish America to a new
existence. The delegates denounced the policy which the
government of the Spanish patriots had adopted toward
America. They affirmed that war had been declared against
them as revolutionists; that their coasts had been blockaded,
and their representation in the *cortes* reduced to a mockery.
They said that the hostile and unnatural conduct of Spain had
forced them out of a position of "political ambiguity." They
spoke of the imprescriptible rights of a people to destroy
"every pact, convention, or association" that did not fufill
the purpose for which governments were established. Accordingly, the representatives of the United Provinces of
Venezuela, as they styled themselves, solemnly declared that
those provinces were and ought to be "by act and right, free,

sovereign, and independent states." In this manner the inhabitants of the captaincy general of Venezuela formally proclaimed their independence of the mother country. Venezuela was thus the first of the revolted Spanish colonies formally to declare herself independent of Spain. While some phrases of the Venezuelans suggest the phraseology of the Declaration of Independence of July 4, 1776, yet the Venezuelan declaration contained neither a philosophy which justified the revolution nor a terrible indictment of the Motherland. Nevertheless, the declaration of independence dated July 5, 1811, voiced the sentiments of Venezuelan radicals.

Miranda became a member of the committee of congress which was chosen to select the design for the flag of the new nation. He succeeded in having the colors red, yellow, and blue which had fluttered from the masthead of the *Leander,* selected for the Venezuelan ensign. When a counter-revolution broke out in Valencia, General Miranda was ultimately entrusted with the army which was sent to subjugate the royalists. He also acted a a member of the committee which was charged with the task of framing a constitution for Venezuela. There is reason to believe that Miranda urged the committee to adopt the plan which he had brought with him from London vesting the executive authority in two Incas. With his intimate friends Miranda pleaded earnestly for the adoption of his imperial constitution. But his arguments were in vain. On September 2, 1811, Francisco Javier de Ustáriz laid a federal plan of government before the constituent congress. Only fleeting references to the congressional debates concerning that plan are available. It is evident that a majority of the delegates, influenced by the example of the United States, favored the adoption of a federal constitution. For, in spite of the opposition of Miranda in congress and of Bolívar outside of congress, on December 21, 1811, that assembly adopted a constitution which provided a frame of government for a federal republic.

In this constitution the provinces of Venezuela were treated as states composing a confederation. In some respects the *pacto federal* was modeled after the Constitution of the North-American Republic, while many clauses showed the influence of the French Declaration of the Rights of Man. Nevertheless, Roman Catholicism was declared to be the religion of the state. The executive authority was vested in the hands of three persons, who were styled the supreme power. The legislative authority was entrusted to a senate and a house of representatives. The judicial power was given to one supreme court and other inferior courts. The constitution contained a provision for the admission into the union of any other province of Spanish America.

Meantime, emmissaries had been sent from Caracas to the United States to plead for aid and recognition. In July, 1811, Venezuela was represented at Washington by Telésforo de Orea and José R. Revenga. Those envoys became the first diplomatic representatives to the government of the United States from an Hispanic-American state which had proclaimed its independence of the motherland. Orea promptly sent a copy of the Venezuelan declaration of independence to James Monroe, the secretary of state of the United States, and tried to secure the recognition of Venezuela's independence by that government. The utmost that Orea could obtain, however, was an assurance in December, 1811, that the ministers of the United States in Europe had been instructed that their government viewed with interest the rise of new states in Spanish America. This friendly attitude was perhaps partly due to the interest of France in the independence of Venezuela. Unofficially, Sérurier, the French ambassador in Washington, assured Orea that a Venezuelan envoy would be favorably received by Napoleon. But the French interest in Venezuela declined when the progress of the revolution was checked.

Events soon demonstrated that the constitution of 1811 was not adapted to Venezuelan conditions. The formation of an independent government inevitably provoked the animosity of a loyalist party. The ambitious designs and intriguing disposition of Miranda, who apparently aimed to form a party devoted to himself, stimulated jealousy and factional strife. The ship of state might have been wrecked even though nature had not conspired against her. On March 26, 1812, an earthquake visited Venezuela, which destroyed towns, crushed patriot soldiers, and inspirited the loyalists. The priests, many of whom were fanatically opposed to independence, harangued the panic-stricken people, and told them that the disastrous earthquake was a punishment from God because they had forsaken their king. After that visitation, the royalist soldiers made rapid progress under the Spanish general,

Domingo Monteverde. Treason thinned the ranks and thwarted the plans of the patriots, while it increased the strength and assurance of their enemies. On April 23 the congress of Venezuela appointed Miranda commander-in-chief of the army; and soon afterwards it entrusted him with the nation's funds. A strange chance thus clothed Miranda with powers similar to those of the dictator in his own governmental projects.

The first dictator of Venezuela pursued a Fabian policy. Instead of immediately making an attack on the enemy, which might have resulted in the discomfiture of the royalists, Miranda paused to gather soldiers and munitions. He sent agents into neighboring provinces to recruit soldiers and to plead for aid. His secretary, Thomas Molini, was sent on a special mission to London, while Pedro Gual, one of Miranda's comrades, was selected as envoy to Washington. But the followers of Miranda were soon disheartened by the news that the fortified city of Puerto Cabello, which had been entrusted to Colonel Simón de Bolívar, had been captured by the royalists. In a letter to Miranda, Bolívar profoundly regretted the loss of the city, expressing his despair that he had not been left lifeless "under the ruins of a city which ought to have been the last refuge of the liberty and the glory of Venezuela." The dismal news of the fall of that port might well have evoked from Miranda the remark which, many years later, Gual attributed to him, "Venezuela is wounded to the heart." The loss of Puerto Cabello, the increasing desertions in the patriot army, and a dislike for bloodshed, evidently influenced Miranda to enter into negotiations with Monteverde for peace.

The outcome was the treaty of San Mateo, July 25, 1812, which was signed by Monteverde and Miranda's agents. That treaty provided that Venezuela was to be relinquished to the Spaniards; but it explicitly stipulated that the persons and property of the Venezuelans were to be respected. Contemporaries and historians alike have questioned the wisdom of the treaty: General Miranda has even been accused of treason to Venezuela because he authorized a capitulation which was not absolutely necessary. A story has been told that he capitulated because he was given a thousand ounces of gold by a royalist, the Marquis of Casa León, but there is scant evidence to support this legend. There is no doubt that Miranda planned to take the national funds with him on departing from Venezuela; but he probably intended to use the treasure to renew the struggle for South American independence, using New Granada as a base of operations. Possibly he may have wished to profit financially by the treaty of San Mateo. It appears, however, that, under the circumstances, this capitulation was a wise step, if the Spaniards had kept their faith.

But Monteverde, who arrogantly assumed the authority of a captain general, treated Venezuela as a conquered province. He ruthlessly thrust some revolutionary leaders into prison, and deported others to the Spanish peninsula. The property of Miranda's followers was confiscated. Such a flagrant violation of the faith of treaties cast a stigma upon the capitulation of San Mateo.

A number of Miranda's companions were so dissatisfied with his actions that they conspired against him. When he was about to embark at La Guaira for the West Indies in an English vessel, the *Sapphire,* which bore his books, papers, and money, he was forcibly detained by Manuel María de las Casas, Miguel Peña, and Simón de Bolívar. The discredited general was thrown into a filthy dungeon. There Monteverde found him, after Las Casas opened the gates of La Guaira to the jubilant royalists. The betrayal of Miranda to the Spaniards is a peculiar incident, which some writers have considered a foul stain upon Bolívar's fame. The writer thinks it likely that Colonel Bolívar took this action in a fit of resentment. One of that officer's intimate friends said that "to the last hour of his life" Bolívar rejoiced because of Miranda's betrayal, which he always asserted was designed "to punish the *treachery* and *treason* of Miranda," who had capitulated to an inferior force, while he intended to embark, knowing that "the capitulation would not be observed." It is only just to compare with this version of the tragical climax of Miranda's career another account given by Louis Delpech, a follower of the Dictator, who rightly declared that much time would be required to respond to the caluminious charges which had been brought against Miranda. Delpech also said that people often judged events "by their results; they have said that Miranda was a traitor because the villain Monteverde infringed the Capitulation, and all the people of property have been delivered up to the assassinous dagger of the infamous Spaniards, but without discussing those unfounded assertions, I venture to believe that, if Miranda had been a traitor, he would certainly not have deceived himself by partaking of the fate of those whom they say he sold to Monteverde; and if I did not have the conviction that he was incapable of such a base action, I would say that it is impossible, that a man who labored all his life for the independence of America was able at the end of his career to forget this glorious enterprise, to stain his white hair, and to dishonor forever his memory in descending to the Tomb, and in return for so much ignominy and crime to receive no other recompense than chains and death."

At last the government of Spain had the arch-conspirator within its grasp. For a short time he was confined in a loathsome prison at La Guaira. Then he was transferred to a dungeon at Puerto Cabello. From that place, on March 8, 1813, he addressed a lengthy memorial to the *audiencia* of Caracas protesting vigorously against the scandalous violation of the capituation of San Mateo. About the middle of 1813, Miranda saw the mountain peaks of his native land fade from view, for he was suddenly transferred from Puerto Cabello to Morro Castle in the island of Porto Rico. In vain did Miranda protest against the infraction of the treaty of San Mateo. In vain did Méndez ask the English cabinet to intercede with the Spanish government: England, the faithful ally of Spain, could not aid the imprisoned agitator. After languishing in a dungeon in Porto Rico for more than a year, he was transported to Spain, where he was incarcerated in the arsenal of la Caracca on the island of Léon.

After reaching Spain, Miranda carried on a correspondence with friends in England who were anxious to help him. The old revolutionist wrote many letters pleading for gold and plotted ceaselessly to regain his liberty. But the restless man did not succeed in escaping from his island prison: his robust frame broke down; and he died early on the morning of July 14, 1816. Long after Miranda had been hastily interred in the cemetery of la Caracca near Cadiz, strange rumors were circulated concerning the mode of his death. In distant Venezuela it was suggested that Spain had used foul means to get rid of an arch-enemy. Thus Francisco de Miranda became a martyr.

This martyr of Venezuelan independence had an interesting personality. His friends were generally faithful and devoted, while his enemies were often bitter and relentless. Miranda could make himself at home whether in the parlor or on the field of battle, at the council-table or in the prison cell. He was a good conversationalist and a persuasive, if not an eloquent, speaker. In the attempt to carry out his master-purpose he displayed a remarkable perseverance. So much of an idealist was Miranda that he has been likened to Don Quixote. Somewhat unscrupulous in regard to methods, he was inclined to exaggerate or to prevaricate in order to promote the success of his designs. There is reason to suspect that Miranda occasionally had amours with women; but the material has not been found to tell the entire story of his private life. South American writers are not always in agreement concerning the mother of Miranda's children. Ricardo Becerra, the Venezuelan biographer of Miranda, asserted that his children were the offspring of a lawful union with a Miss Sarah Andrews. But a letter written by Francisco's son, Leandro Miranda, in 1850—which alluded to a fortune bequeathed to Miranda's children by Lady Hester Stanhope— has been interpreted by C. A. Villanueva to mean that Lady Hester was Leandro's mother.

The life of Miranda indeed furnishes many riddles. A significant query is: what were Miranda's means of support during his long career as a revolutionary promoter? His father's silver undoubtedly purchased for him the captaincy in the company of the Princess. So meager were Miranda's resources after leaving the Spanish military service that he had to borrow money to make his tour of America and Europe. When the South American visited Empress Catherine, she evidently gave him a purse of gold. It does not appear that General Miranda was ever paid for his military services to the French republic. On the one hand, occasionally Miranda was almost a beggar: on the other hand, he sometimes lived in luxury.

During many years Miranda undoubtedly lived upon English gold. For the government of England paid Miranda money in order that it might take advantage of his services, if it decided to attack the Spanish dominions in America. There is no doubt that Miranda was granted money by Pitt in 1790; that he was paid a pension by England from 1801 to 1805; and that in June, 1808, he was again placed upon England's pension roll. In September, 1810, Miranda was enjoying a pension of seven hundred pounds per annum. Incidents in the career of this chronic revolutionist indeed raise the query whether or not he was engaged in the attempt to liberate Spanish America for selfish gain.

Two sharply contrasted views of Miranda's character may be entertained: that he was a mercenary soldier; or that he was a pure-minded patriot. On one side, the view may be taken that Miranda merely sold his services to the best bidder. His career may be interpreted to mean that he was a shifty adventurer, who betrayed the liberty of his fatherland for gold. That conception of Miranda would place him on a level with a soldier of fortune. On the other side, the view may be taken that Miranda was an exalted patriot. Under the influence of this conception, some writers have overemphasized Miranda's services to the cause of South-American independence. One Spanish-American writer characterized Miranda as "the Nazarene of Spanish-American independence," while another writer called South America "the world of Miranda." Such hero-worshipers would place him on a level with Washington. The writer takes an intermediate view: there were many occasions when Miranda must have been impelled by mixed motives: resentment towards Spain mingled with love for Venezuela. With Miranda the revolutionizing of Spanish America became a profession,—he was a patriot-filibuster.

The biography of Miranda demonstrates that certain European powers were interested in the fate of Spanish America long before the outbreak of the great revolution. Frequently he stimulated this interest by appealing to commercial motives. He often directed the thoughts of European and American publicists to the Spanish Indies. On the one hand, the epic of Miranda's life indicates that, at a stormy period in the history of Europe, Spanish America was sometimes viewed as a makeweight in the political balance. On the other hand, the epic of Miranda's life is a part of the history of South America. The prince of filibusters, the chief of the apostles of Spanish-American independence, and one of the founders of the republic of Venezuela, Francisco de Miranda will long live in song and story. In accordance with a decree of the Venezuelan government, the inscription on one side of a cenotaph which was unveiled in the national pantheon of Venezuela at Caracas on July, 5, 1896, at the right of the stately monument to Simón de Bolívar, thus epitomizes Miranda's career: "He took part in three great political movements of his age: the independence of the United States of North America; the French revolution; and the independence of South America."

The patriot-filibuster who figured in the history of both America and Europe, is a type. He had forerunners, companions, and followers. The great precursor of independence, he was the foremost representative of those Spanish-Americans who suffered imprisonment because of their liberal principles, or who wandered through Europe to solicit succor in the task of liberating their native land from Spanish domination. The career of this knight-errant of Venezuela has fired the imagination of many filibusters and revolutionists. The mantle of the unfortunate Miranda fell upon the shoulders of Simón de Bolívar.

Chapter 3

Miguel Hidalgo y Costilla

In 1808 the viceroyalty of Mexico stretched from the Isthmus of Tehauntepec northward to the British possessions. That viceroyalty was composed of twelve provinces, or intendancies. The capital of the viceroyalty, Mexico City, was situated in a beautiful valley on the central plateau. This metropolis was the viceroy's residence, the capital of the province of Mexico, the residence of the chief intendant and of the Mexican archbishop. On the eve of the revolution the viceroy of Mexico was a venal military officer named José de Iturrigaray.

The news of the abdication of Ferdinand VII. profoundly stirred the inhabitants of Mexico City. At the instance of Viceroy Iturrigaray, on August 9, 1808, a junta composed of leading citizens assembled in the viceregal palace. This junta framed and published a manifesto which proclaimed that, until Ferdinand VII. was restored, it would not obey any orders of the French emperor, or of any other personage who was not authorized by its legitimate sovereign. Suspicions that Iturrigarary was scheming to separate New Spain from Old Spain soon caused his disposition. On September 15, 1808, conspirators led by Gabriel de Yermo, an influential Spanish landowner, dragged the viceroy from his palace and thrust him into a dungeon. Shortly afterwards the deposed viceroy was deported to the Spanish peninsula. On September 16 the *audencia* proclaimed that the viceregal power was vested in Pedro Garibay, an old military officer of Spain.

When Viceroy Iturrigaray was deposed, Francisco Primo Verdad, Melchor Talamantes, and several other persons were imprisoned. They were suspected of conspiring to promote the independence of New Spain. It was found that Talamantes, a learned monk, had entertained revolutionary ideas. Among his papers there was found a project entitled "The National Representation of the Colonies," which discussed the circumstances that would justify Spain's colonists in separating from the motherland. But in May, 1809, this monk died in the

82

dungeons of San Juan de Ullúa. It was reserved for another member of the Mexican clergy, Miguel Hidalgo y Costilla, to start the great revolution against Spanish rule in Mexico.

On August 5, 1750, in the Mexican province of Guanajuato, Cristóbal Hidalgo y Costilla married Ana María Gallaga y Villaseñor. From this marriage there sprang several children. The second son was born on May 8, 1753, on the hacienda of San Diego Corralejo, which was situated in the parish of Pénjamo. On May 16, 1753, this child was baptized Miguel Gregorio Antonio Ignacio. The ancestors of Miguel for several generations had been born in the viceroyalty of New Spain: on his mother's side he came of Vizcayan stock; and the patronym Hidalgo—meaning the son of somebody—indicated that his father's family was of noble descent.

In 1753 Cristóbal Hidalgo was managing the haciendo of San Diego Corralejo which belonged to a widow named Josefa Carracholi y Carranza. It appears that Cristóbal had studied for the priesthood, but that a disease of the eyes had compelled him to relinquish his plan of entering the service of the Church. Instead of becoming a priest he engaged in agriculture. Only a few years ago, there could still be seen in the district of Pénjamo the crumbling ruins of Hidalgo's home. At that time there could also be seen a chapel which was erected on the Carracholi estate while Cristóbal Hidalgo was its manager. Cristóbal Hidalgo was fairly prosperous; for he encouraged his sons to prepare for the learned professions: José María prepared to practice medicine; Manuel Hidalgo became a lawyer; while José Joaquín became a priest. Obviously Miguel Hidalgo y Costilla, as he is commonly called by Mexican writers, passed his boyhood days in the shadow of the Roman Catholic Church.

The education of Miguel Hidalgo began on the hacienda of San Diego Corralejo. The years which Hidalgo spent on that estate gave him a great fondness for agricultural pursuits. During this period he acquired a sympathy for industrial laborers and learned to appreciate the viewpoint of Mexicans belonging to the lower classes. When Miguel was about fourteen years of age his father decided to send him to the College of San Nicolás Obispo at Valladolid—the city which was later rechristened Morelia. This college, founded in the sixteenth century, had become a seminary for the sons of Mexicans belonging to the middle class. Hidalgo's sojourn in Valladolid must have influenced him greatly, for this city was the capital of the important province of Michoacán and the intellectual center of an extensive region. Of Hidalgo's life as a student in Valladolid hardly anything is known with certainty, except what has been gleaned from the archives of the metropolitan university.

In March, 1770, Hidalgo took the examination for the degree of bachelor of arts in "the Royal and Pontifical University of Mexico." It appears that Hidalgo had prepared himself for this examination at the College of San Nicolás in accordance with a clause in the constitution of the University of Mexico which provided that, if the students of certain provincial colleges had attended the arts' courses of those colleges for three years, they might become candidates for the bachelor's degree at that university. Hidalgo evidently passed a satisfactory examination before the committee of teachers selected by the rector of the metropolitan university, and he must have defended his thesis in the right fashion; for, under date of March 30, 1770, the archives of the University of Mexico record that Miguel Hidalgo was granted the degree of bachelor of arts. It appears that Hidalgo remained in Mexico City after receiving this degree in order to study theology. On May 24, 1773, he was granted the degree of bachelor of sacred theology by the University of Mexico. According to the mediæval formula customarily used in conferring that degree, Hidalgo was given the right to teach sacred theology, as well as the right to hold, use, and enjoy all the privileges and exemptions that were granted to bachelors of theology by the University of Salamanca. To judge by the stipulations regarding that degree in the constitution of the University of Mexico, Hidalgo had taken courses of study in theology, in the Holy Scriptures, and in the writings of Thomas Aquinas.

Several years after he left the University of Mexico, there seemed to be opening before Hidalgo a promising career. He became a teacher in the College of San Nicolás: at first, of Latin and the arts, and later, of theology. He continued to be a student of theology; for in 1784 he won twelve silver medals which the dean of that college, Dr. José Pérez Calama, had offered as a prize to the student who would submit the two best dissertations—one in Latin and the other in Castilian —on the proper method of studying scholastic theology. In a letter written to Hidalgo on October 8, 1784, to inform him that he had carried off the prize in the contest, Dr. Calama enthusiastically declared:

Both dissertations prove that you are a young man in whom genius and industry are honorable rivals. Henceforward, I shall always call you "the diligent ant" of Minerva, without forgetting that other epithet of "the industrious bee," which knows how to suck from flowers the most delicious honey. With the greatest joy in my heart, I foresee that you will become a light placed in a candlestick, or a city upon a hill.

Perhaps partly because of his success in the prize contest, about 1791 Hidalgo was made rector of the College of San Nicolás. Of his activities as rector we know little beyond an allegation made by a commissioner of the inquisition that Hidalgo introduced certain textbooks of philosophy and theology into the college which merited the censure of the holy office. There is, however, no evidence to show that the holy office noticed those innovations during the brief period when Hidalgo served as rector.

For some unknown reason, Hidalgo relinquished the rectorate of San Nicolás and became a priest in a remote parish. On March 24, 1792, he became the curate of a church at Colima, near the Pacific coast. There he remained only about eight months. In January, 1793, he became the curate of the village of San Felipe in the bishopric of Michoacán where he served until 1803. Some of the actions and words of the curate of San Felipe aroused suspicion, for he was placed under the surveillance of the inquisition. The first evidence lodged with the inquisition against Miguel Hidalgo was a denunciation made on July 16, 1800, to the commissioner of the holy office at Valladolid by a friar called Joaquín Huesca. Subsequently Hidalgo was denounced by other persons. In some particulars the various denunciations lodged with the inquisition against Hidalgo were not consistent. Let it suffice to mention here some of the worst charges. Among the objectionable statements which were ascribed to Hidalgo was the declaration that God did not chastise with temporal punishments. Furthermore, it was alleged that he studied the Holy Scriptures critically; that he spoke disdainfully of the Popes; that he showed little respect for the apostles and for Saint Teresa; that he doubted the virginity of the Mother of Christ;

that he declared fornication to be no sin; and that he lived an immoral life, forgetting the obligations of priesthood and indulging in music, dances, and games. Several persons averred that the home of the curate of San Felipe was known as "little France."

A glimpse of Hidalgo's political ideas at this time may perhaps be obtained from some of the other accusations which were filed in the archives of the inquisition. It was alleged that Hidalgo desired to see French liberty established in Spanish America; that he had provoked an argument as to whether a republic was a better form of government than a monarchy; and that he had declared monarchs to be despotic tyrants. The exact amount of truth in those accusations, it is impossible to determine. Yet it seems reasonable to suppose that the decadence of the holy office made possible Hidalgo's escape from condign punishment. Then, too, it seems likely that the alert curate of San Felipe may have heard of the accusations which were being made against him, and that in consequence he temporarily reformed his manner of life.

In 1803 Miguel Hidalgo succeeded his elder brother, José Joaquín, as curate of the congregation of Our Lady of the Sorrows in the village of Dolores, which was located in the northern part of the province of Guanajuato. Hidalgo served as the curate of that substantial church until September, 1810. There the versatile curate found his mission. At Dolores—now known as Dolores Hidalgo—the curate displayed a keen interest in industrial pursuits: he promoted viniculture and apiculture and sericulture. Lucas Alamán declared that, in the middle of the nineteenth century, there were still flourishing at Dolores eighty-four mulberry trees which Hidalgo had planted for the culture of the silkworm. The curate of Dolores also established a factory where pottery and bricks were made and where leather was tanned. In a history of Dolores a Mexican writer has published a plan of the factory which indicates that it included a carpenter shop, a blacksmith shop, a room devoted to the silk industry, and several rooms used in the manufacture of pottery. On that plan the very spot is marked where, according to the recollections of a contemporary, Hidalgo was accustomed to sit while watching the laborers of the factory. Another contemporary, Carlos María Bustamante, who was a prolific writer on the Mexican revolution, made the assertion that Hidalgo intended to establish at

Dolores a settlement similar to the colony attempted on the pearl coast of South America by Bartolomé de las Casas, the Protector of the Indians.

The home of Miguel Hidalgo at Dolores was a one-story house containing more than a dozen rooms. Certain of these rooms were reserved for ecclesiastical purposes, while others were used by Hidalgo and his family. For there lived with Hidalgo at Dolores his younger brother Mariano, another relative named Santos Villa, and the curate's two illegitimate daughters, Josefa and Micaela. Hidalgo's factory was the industrial center of the parish; his home was the social center of the community. We are told that to the entertainments and dances in the curate's house there came rich and poor, Indians and white men. In that place some foreign and domestic literature was read; and problems of the day were discussed. The curate of Dolores also associated with certain prominent men of the adjacent region: he was on confidential terms with Manuel Abad y Quiepo, bishop elect of Michoacán; he was on friendly terms with the intendant of Guanajuato, Juan Antonio Riaño, and with Antonio de Labarrieta, the curate of Guanajuato.

Hidalgo's industrial activities apparently crowded his religious functions into the background. Aláman averred that the curate of Dolores shared his salary, which amounted to eight or nine thousand pesos a year, with a priest named Francisco Iglesias, who performed many of the duties elsewhere performed by the curate. Certain contemporaries of Hidalgo even alleged that he became so indifferent with regard to his priestly functions that neither did he preach, nor read mass, nor pray. This is probably an exaggeration: José M. de la Fuente, the recent Mexican biographer of Hidalgo, has somewhat repaired his hero's reputation by the statement that three manuscript sermons are still extant which were written by the famous curate of Dolores.

Unfortunately very little evidence has come down to us from Hidalgo himself concerning his literary interests at this time. Evidently he read the *Gaceta de México*. There is no doubt that he read such books of interest as were available. Here, again, a glimpse of the truth may be gained from the records of the holy office. The officials of the inquisition were informed that Hidalgo was accustomed to read the following books: Fleury's "Ecclesiastical History," Buffon's "Natural

History," Andre's "History of Literature," Clavijero's "History of America," Rollin's "Ancient History," Bossuet's "Defence of the Clergy," the works of Muratori, and the orations of Demosthenes and Cicero. At least one of the persons who denounced Hidalgo alleged that he had translated into Spanish some of Molière's comedies, which had been presented upon a stage at Dolores in a rustic fashion. The iteration and reiteration of certain charges against the curate of Dolores in the inquisitorial records furnish ground for the view that in his critical mind doubts had arisen as to the historicity of cardinal doctrines of the Roman Catholic Church, if indeed he did not entertain beliefs which were heretical.

The curate of Dolores was endowed with a strong personality. Alamán described him in the following words:

He was of medium height, with stooping shoulders; his complexion was swarthy; his eyes were of a lively green color; his head inclined somewhat toward his breast; and he was as white-headed and bald as though he had already passed sixty years of age. Although he was neither active nor prompt, yet he was vigorous in his movements: a man of few words in ordinary conversation, when he entered into the heat of a dispute—after the fashion of a collegian, he became animated in his argumentation. He was not elegant in his dress, for he wore no other clothes than those which were ordinarily worn by the curates of small towns.

The costume of a village curate in Hidalgo's day ordinarily consisted of a cloak or long coat of black cloth, a round sombrero, short trousers, and a jacket of Chinese wool, with a clerical collar and neckcloth. The portraits of Miguel Hidalgo which are extant do not necessarily help us to imagine his outward appearance, for some of them may be spurious. His portrait which once hung in the curate's house at Dolores might well have depicted a philosopher. The most authentic picture of Hidalgo, which was first published by Bustamante, suggests that he was a dreamer, a doctrinaire, who possessed, however, some practical talent. His countenance bore the impress of mingled benignity and craftiness. An anecdote has indeed survived the Mexican revolution to the effect that Hidalgo's associates at the College of San Nicolás nicknamed him "the fox." This tradition suggests that possibly Hidalgo's manifold activities at Dolores were intended to conceal certain ulterior designs.

From the smoke of the conflict which has been waged among historical writers of Mexico regarding the respective parts played by certain men in the early Mexican revolution, the curate of Dolores has emerged as the chief conspirator. But the exact time when Hidalgo first entertained revolutionary designs is still somewhat uncertain. La Fuente intimates that Hidalgo probably cherished the idea of revolutionizing Mexico in his youth. Alamán holds that Hidalgo contemplated a rebellion against Spain in January, 1810; for, at that time, he was devouring books on war and conspiracies. There is some contemporary evidence which indicates that Hidalgo may have dreamed of a revolt against Spanish rule as early as 1808.

While Hidalgo was meditating over the distracted condition of his native land, Viceroy Pedro Garibay had been succeeded in July, 1809, by Francisco Javier de Lizanza y Beaumont, archbishop of Mexico, who had been appointed viceroy of New Spain by the central junta. During the rule of Lizanza y Beaumont there were signs of discontent with Spanish rule. Rumors were rife of projected insurrections. One abortive insurrection will serve as an illustration. In December, 1809, a conspiracy was discovered in Valladolid which apparently aimed to establish a junta that was to rule on behalf of Ferdinand VII. On September 13, 1810, Francisco Javier Venegas, lieutenant general in the Spanish army, assumed the heavy responsibilities of viceroy of New Spain. Three days later a revolutionary conflagration was kindled by the curate of Dolores.

In the revolution of 1810 there were associated with Hidalgo a number of discontented Mexicans. Most prominent among those was Ignacio Allende, who, according to Alamán, had descended from a native of Vizcaya. Allende was a strong man with a bold spirit. Early in September, 1810, he was captain of a provincial regiment of dragoons which was stationed at San Miguel el Grande—a town later named San Miguel Allende. A fellow-conspirator of Allende was Juan Aldama, a lawyer and a captain in the same regiment. Another officer of that regiment who entered the plot was Mariano Abasolo, the prosperous son of a Vizcayan. Miguel

Domínguez, the corregidor of Querétaro, was involved in the conspiracy, and also his resourceful wife, Josefa Ortiz de Domínguez. Another conspirator was José Mariano Galvan, an official in the postoffice at Querétaro. In that city some of the conspirators had occasional meetings. There is no doubt that Hidalgo corresponded with the leading conspirators and visited them secretly. It is clear that the conspirators planned to spread the discontent with Spanish rule throughout other sections of Mexico, and that they employed laborers to make lances clandestinely. A day was set for the revolution to begin. Placards were printed bearing the motto: "Americans be alert and do not be deceived. Today all the *Gachupines* are to be killed, September 29, 1810"—a date which appears to have been changed to October 1. So carefully did Hidalgo and his fellow-conspirators conceal their plot, that investigators have not yet discovered how far its ramifications extended.

A short time before the conspirators had perfected their plans, rumors of their activity reached the government. Early in August, 1810, a report in regard to the stealthy meetings of conspirators in Querétaro had been addressed to the viceroy. On September 11 a long report concerning the plot was sent to the viceroy by Juan Ochoa, an *alcade* of Querétaro. That report contained the names of the leaders, mentioned certain preparations which they had made, and declared that Hidalgo was the chief conspirator. A few days after Ochoa's report was written, rumors of the projected insurrection reached José Gabriel Armijo, a commander of the soldiers of the viceroyalty. Meanwhile a rumor that the conspirators had been denounced to the government reached Miguel Domínguez, hence it became his official duty to gather evidence concerning the conspiracy and to incarcerate the leaders.

At this juncture the wife of Domínguez stealthily sent a message to the conspirators that their plot had been discovered. The news reached Captain Aldama late at night on September 15. Startled by the warning, he galloped from San Miguel el Grande to Dolores; early on the morning of Sunday, September 16, he reached the curate's home, where Allende was sojourning. According to the story told by Aldama, when the curate of Dolores was aroused from his slumbers and informed of the discovery of the conspiracy, he exclaimed, "Gentlemen, we are lost: there is now no other recourse than

to seize the *Gachupines!*" Other members of Hidalgo's house-
hold joined the excited group; and armed men appeared upon
the scene. It has been alleged that Hidalgo himself led his
partisans to the village gaol, put a pistol to the head of the
gaoler, and set the prisoners free. Near the curate's house
there soon gathered priests, musicians, laborers, watchmen,
and soldiers, who were armed with pistols, swords, lances,
clubs, and stones. Some of Hidalgo's followers were on foot,
while others were on horseback. With that small, undisciplined, and motley band Hidalgo audaciously dared to initiate
a revolt against Spanish rule.

It appears that the church bell which ordinarily called the
parishioners to mass now invited them to take up arms against
Spain. There is a tradition that, in response to a harangue
from Hidalgo, a cry arose from the people for America and
against the bad government. In a short time that battle-cry,
or a similar one, became known throughout Mexico as the
Grito de Dolores. This uprising at the obscure village of
Dolores signalized the beginning of a war which did not entirely cease for eleven years—a war which crimsoned the soil
of Mexico with blood. Many years afterwards, the bell was
taken from the tower of the church of Our Lady of the
Sorrows at Dolores and hung in the façade of the national
palace at Mexico City. The bell of Hidalgo's church became
known as the independence bell of Mexico.

Why did Hidalgo and his comrades thus throw down the
gage of battle to Venegas? Various motives have been ascribed
to those men by different writers. Carlos M. Bustamante alleged that Hidalgo was enraged because the Spanish government had prohibited the manufacture of wine from the grapes
of Dolores. Alamán scouted this explanation: he jauntily
dismissed the inquiry with the vague statement that the curate
of Dolores was animated by "reasons of general convenience."
The historical student who reads the statements made by
Hidalgo and Allende after their capture by the royalists will
find that both these men asserted that they were provoked
because of the reports of the invasion of Spain by Napoleon's
soldiers. They argued that there was imminent danger of
New Spain falling into the hands of the French and affirmed
that they wished to preserve their native land from Napoleon.
When on trial for their lives, both Allende and Aldama said
that they had contemplated the formation of a provisional

junta in New Spain, while both Allende and Hidalgo admitted that they had thought of making Mexico independent of Spain. Allende boldly avowed that the conspirators had decided to take up arms, should their schemes be discovered, for they anticipated that, if they were cast into prison, they would be at the mercy of the enraged Spaniards. When cross-examined Hidalgo declared that he had not decided upon any plan of government for emancipated Mexico. Perhaps the best contemporary statement in regard to the designs which the conspirators entertained is found in the report made to the viceroy by Juan Ochoa: "Captain Allende is the person to whom they give the title of general. Dr. Hildago, the curate of Dolores, is the chief conspirator; and the person who furnishes the ideas: his plan, in brief, is independence."

As in Venezuela, so in Mexico, the pretext used to justify the insurrection was the necessity of defending the rights of Ferdinand VII. The Mexican insurgents, however, soon appealed to another sentiment besides loyalty to the king. While the motley band was marching from Dolores to San Miguel el Grande, an insurgent—according to some writers the curate himself—took from the sacristy of a chapel at Atotonilco a picture of the Virgin of Guadeloupe, the patron saint of the Mexican Indians, and bore it off in triumph. This revered picture was made the standard of Hidalgo's army: the Virgin of Guadeloupe thus became the patron saint of the Mexican revolution. The rallying-cry of the revolutionists soon became: "Long live religion! Long live our most Holy Mother of Guadeloupe! Long live America! Down with the bad government!" The story of the spread of the insurrection will indicate that Alamán was not animated solely by a malicious spirit when he described that revolutionary battle-cry as "a monstrous union of religion with assassination and plunder."

As Hidalgo marched, his nondescript army increased steadily. Many Indian laborers, or peons, flocked to the sacred banner. The intendant of Guanajuato soon wrote to the viceroy and declared that the inhabitants of Dolores, San Miguel el Grande, Celaya, Salamanca, and Irapuato were joining the insurgents, while disaffection was spreading rapidly in the city of Guanajuato. After the insurgents entered San Miguel el Grande, Allende publicly recognized Hidalgo as the chief of the revolution. Soon afterwards the revolutionists marched towards Celaya; and on September 19 Hidalgo and Allende summoned the *cabildo* of that town to surrender. In a post-script to the summons, the *cabildo* was warned that, if the revolutionists were fired upon, seventy-eight Spanish prisoners would be at once put to death. The *cabildo* yielded; and the curate of Dolores entered Celaya. Soon afterwards the warrior-curate was acclaimed captain general of the army; Ignacio Allende was given the title of lieutenant general, while inferior titles were conferred upon other leaders.

What was the attitude of the Mexican people toward this insurrection? Clearly, it was supported by many persons belonging to the lower classes. But it was vigorously opposed by numerous officials of the viceregal government; by some members of the clergy, especially the higher clergy; and by many landed proprietors. Protests against Hidalgo's revolt and declarations of loyalty to Ferdinand VII. were frequently printed in the *Gaceta de México*. The *ayuntamientos* of several towns and cities denounced the rebels and proclaimed their fidelity to the viceregal government. The rector of the University of Mexico assured the viceroy that the rebel, Miguel Hidalgo, had not received the doctor's degree from that institution. A corporation of Mexican lawyers erased from its roll the name of Ignacio Allende, the rebel.

Viceroy Venegas soon took various measures to quell the revolt. On September 23 he issued a manifesto against the followers of Hidalgo, whom he described as "men deluded by false ideas." Venegas stated his belief that peace would be restored to the viceroyalty when royalist soldiers appeared in the revolutionary districts; and he expressed regret that the first measure of his administration should be the suppression of a rebellion. A few days later the viceroy published a manifesto instructing the loyal inhabitants of the viceroyalty to defend themselves against attacks by the rebels and offering a reward of ten thousand pesos to those individuals who might secure the persons of Hidalgo, Allende, and Aldama, dead or alive. On September 26 the garrison of Mexico City marched toward Querétaro under the command of the Count of Cadena, while other forces were brought to the capital city. Colonel Diego García Conde, military commander of the province of Michoacán, and the Count of Casa Rul, commander of the provincial regiment of infantry of that province, were ordered to leave the capital city and to proceed to their respective commands. Further, on October 5, Venegas published a decree of the Spanish regency which declared that the Indians were no longer to pay tribute. As an anti-revolutionary measure, the viceroy extended the decree so as to include mulattoes and negroes who remained loyal to the government and who helped to subjugate the insurrection. Venegas tried to cast odium upon the curate of Dolores by declaring that he was a tool of Napoleon.

The reports of Hidalgo's insurrection startled the Mexican Church. On September 24, 1810, Bishop Abad y Quiepo issued a proclamation which declared that Hidalgo, "a pastor of souls, a priest of Jesus Christ, a minister of the God of peace," had raised the standard of rebellion and seduced a number of innocent people. Hidalgo and his followers were denounced as disturbers of the peace who had broken their faith to King Ferdinand VII. The indignant bishop proclaimed that as Hidalgo, Aldama, Abasolo, and Allende had imprisoned several priests, they had incurred the pain of excommunication. All persons were prohibited from giving them aid or comfort. Similar proclamations were issued by the bishops of Puebla, Guadalajaro, and Oaxaca, as well as by the archbishop of Mexico. The officers of the inquisitorial tribunal at Mexico City ransacked the archives of the holy office for evidence which would besmirch the character of the curate of Dolores.

After some recruits had joined the army at Celaya, on September 23, Hidalgo led his untrained soldiers toward the city of Guanajuato, which was set in a beautiful valley amid mountains that contained rich silver mines. Here the royalists had stored their treasure in the *Alhóndiga de granaditas,* or public granary,—a fortress-like structure which commanded the main entrance to the city. Urgent appeals for aid were sent by Riaño to Félix María Calleja, the experienced military commander who was stationed at San Luís Potosí. On September 28, Hidalgo summoned Riaño to surrender in the following words:

On the plains near Celaya, the large army which I command elected me to be captain general and protector of the Mexican nation. The city of Celaya, in the presence of fifty thousand men, ratified this election,—an example which has been followed by all the towns through which I have passed. These events will show you that I am legitimately authorized by my nation to undertake a beneficent project which is as advantageous to the Americans as it is to the Europeans who have decided to reside in this kingdom. In brief this project is: the proclamation of the liberty and independence of the Mexican nation. Accordingly I do not view the Spaniards as enemies; but only as obstacles to the success of our enterprise. Be so good as to make known this project to the Spaniards who have gathered in the *Alhóndiga;* in order that they may decide whether they will declare themselves as our enemies, or will agree to become prisoners who will receive humane treatment—like those already in our company—until Mexican liberty and independence are achieved. At that time, such persons will become Mexican citizens entitled to the restitution of their properties, which we use at present because of the exigencies of war. If, however, those Spaniards do not decide to become our prisoners, I shall use every force and stratagem to destroy them without any thought of quarter.

The project embodied in the summons to Guanajuato shows how Hidalgo tried to induce Spaniards to join his cause. This summons is of further significance because it indicates the rudimentary character of Hidalgo's plans with regard to the independence of Mexico from Spain. It furnishes no evidence that he was formulating a plan for the government of independent Mexico.

Riano replied to the summons in a manly fashion. He declared that he recognized no other captain general than the viceroy, and that he would fight Hidalgo as became a soldier. At eleven o'clock on the forenoon of September 28 the intendant sent his last appeal to Calleja, declaring that he was attacked at that very moment. The besiegers were aided by many inhabitants of Guanajuato, who had openly forsaken the intendant. Hidalgo's followers soon swarmed upon the heights which overlooked the *Alhóndiga.* Shortly after the assault began, Riaño was killed; the plans which he had formed for the city's defense were abandoned; and dissensions appeared in the ranks of the defenders. They were soon forced to take refuge in the *Alhóndiga.* There is a story that, during the fierce assault upon the building, a brave insurgent distinguished himself by climbing to the door of the citadel and setting fire to it amid a storm of missiles. That dramatic episode has been immortalized by a Mexican artist in a statue of the hero bearing in his right hand a fiery torch.

The *Alhóndiga* has been compared with the Bastile. The

fall of the *Alhóndiga* was certainly followed by the merciless massacre of the royalists. The treasure stored in that building was seized, while the mines and the haciendas around the city were looted. Hidalgo's undisciplined soldiers became an Indian mob. In the words of Alamán, who as a boy must have witnessed the sack of the city:

Guanajuato presented a most lamentable picture of disorder, ruin, and desolation. The plaza and the streets were full of fragments of furniture, of the remains of merchandise which had been taken from the shops, and of liquors that had been emptied after the conquerors had drunk their fill. The insurgent soldiers abandoned themselves to all kinds of excesses: the Indians of Hidalgo presented the strangest figures; for they had drawn over their own scanty apparel the clothes which they had stolen from the homes of Spaniards. Among these clothes were the uniforms of the regidores of the city; and when the barefooted Indians had bedecked themselves with the embroidered coats and the ornate sombreros of these regidores, they were in a complete state of ecstasy.

Even Hidalgo and the sacred banner of Guadeloupe could not check the frenzied Indians. The capture of Guanajuato —the capital of one of the richest intendancies of New Spain —was followed by an orgy of robbery, murder, and lust, the horrors of which no pen could depict.

After making arrangements for a rudimentary city government in Guanajuato, Hidalgo marched towards Valladolid. Thus he withdrew his followers from their dangerous position between the royalist soldiers under Calleja at San Luís Potosí and the forces under the Count of Cadena which had just arrived at Querétaro. As Hidalgo approached the city of Valladolid, the royalist leaders departed, and the inhabitants relinquished all thoughts of resistance. On October 17 Hidalgo entered that city. Bustamante declared that while the curate was conversing with Manuel Gallegos, a militia officer who had joined the insurgents, this officer frankly advised Hidalgo that, if he wished to defeat the Spaniards, he should retire with fourteen thousand of his followers to the sierra of Pátzcuaro: "In two months," said Gallegos, "I will return these men to you disciplined and serviceable; if such a step is not taken, you will be left alone in the first reverse which you suffer, for all your followers will fly away like doves." If that sound advice was actually given to Hidalgo, unfortunately for the revolutionary cause, he disregarded it.

In the meantime, the holy office was studying Hidalgo's past. On October 10 the officials of the inquisition at Mexico City made a report to the tribunal respecting the curate of Dolores. They declared that Hidalgo was a partisan of French liberty, a libertine, a formal heretic, a Judaiser, a Lutheran, a Calvinist, a rebel, a schismatic, and a suspected atheist. Three days later the inquisition issued an edict concerning Hidalgo. In that proclamation certain denunciations which had been quietly reposing in the inquisitorial archives were published as damning evidence. Hidalgo was accused of denying that God chastised with temporal punishments. He was accused of speaking disdainfully of the Popes and of intimating that a certain Pope who had been canonized ought to be in hell. He was accused of accepting the doctrines of Luther in regard to the eucharist and auricular confession. With apparent inconsistency, he was accused of denying the authenticity of certain portions of the Bible. Further, it was alleged that Hidalgo had described fornication as a natural and innocent act, and that he had made a compact with a woman to foster that crime. It was stated that Hidalgo had declared war on God, his holy religion, and the fatherland. Under pain of excommunication, the accused priest was summoned to appear before the inquisitorial tribunal in Mexico City within thirty days. It was proclaimed that, if he failed to appear, his trial would proceed *in absentia*. The edict concluded by announcing that all persons who supported the revolution, who received revolutionary proclamations, who maintained relations with Hidalgo, who failed to denounce him, or who promulgated revolutionary ideas, would be punished by a heavy fine, by excommunication, and by the other punishments provided by canon law and papal bulls.

In reply to that edict Hidalgo issued a manifesto from Valladolid on December 15, 1810. With a glint of humor he averred that he had never renounced any doctrines held by the Roman Catholic Church:

I have always been thoroughly convinced of the infallibility of her doctrines. . . . I am accused of denying the existence of hell; and, in the same edict, I am accused of affirming that one of the canonized Popes is in that place. How can these two statements be reconciled: to say that there is a Pope in hell, and at the same time to deny the existence of such a place? In a similar fashion, I am accused of having denied the authenticity of the Bible; and I am accused of having accepted the perverse doctrines of Luther: if Luther deduced his errors from the Bible which he believed to be inspired by God, how can one who denies the authenticity of the Scriptures be a Lutheran? . . . My beloved fellow citizens! You may be certain that, if I had not undertaken to liberate our kingdom from the evils which oppress it and from the greater evils which threaten it, . . . never would I have been accused of heresy.

Thus did Hidalgo rightly intimate that the fulminations from the inquisition had been caused by political motives. In this manifesto he also said:

Mexicans, let us break the bonds of ignominy with which we have been so long bound! To break these bonds we need only to unite. If we do not fight among ourselves, the war will be terminated, and our rights will be saved. Let us then unite all those persons who have been born on this happy soil; let us consider as strangers and as enemies of our prerogatives all persons who are not Mexicans. Let us establish a congress composed of representatives of all the cities, towns, and villages of this country. The principal object of that congress will be to maintain our holy religion and to frame wise and beneficent laws adapted to the circumstances of each community. Our lawmakers will rule us with the tenderness of parents. They will treat us like brothers; they will banish poverty; they will check the devastation of the kingdom and the exportation of its money; they will encourage the arts; and they will cause industry to revive. We shall make free use of the richest productions of our fertile soil; and, in the course of a few years, the Mexicans will enjoy all the delights which the sovereign author of nature has bestowed upon this vast continent.

The manifesto responding to the inquisition is of importance because it contains Hidalgo's clever reply to some of the accusations which had been brought against him. It is significant because it contains the most definite statements which the curate of Dolores ever made in regard to a plan of government for emancipated Mexico. Obviously, he intended to summon a congress of delegates which should frame laws for the Mexican people.

During the sojourn of Hidalgo at Valladolid his army

swelled greatly. His followers were evidently rewarded for their services by the rich booty which had been secured and by the contributions which had been levied during the campaign. With his large, undisciplined host, Hidalgo decided to march upon the capital of the viceroyalty. From Valladolid he proceeded towards Mexico City by way of Acámbaro, Maravatio, and Toluca. The royalist general, García Conde, who was a captive in the rebel camp, estimated that, at a review of the army which was held at Acámbaro, there were present about eighty thousand men. Near that town the officers for the army were selected: the curate Dolores was made generalissimo, Allende was made captain general, while Aldama and other leaders were made lieutenant generals. In the meanwhile Colonel Torcuato Trujillo, a cruel and crafty officer who had accompanied Venegas from Spain, had been sent with about eight hundred soldiers to watch Hidalgo. Near the crest of the ridge which bounded the valley of Mexico on the west, the royalists, who had received reënforcements, stationed themselves on the Monte de las Cruces, which commanded the road from Toluca to Mexico City. The stately domes and towers of the capital city were only about six leagues away. On October 30, a fierce and bloody conflict took place at the Mount of the Crosses, after which a small band of royalists cut their way out of the revolutionary soldiers and retired upon the capital. Although the royalists were forced to retreat, yet the encounter had upon them some of the effects of a drawn battle, for the royal artillery had wrought great havoc among the Indian hordes.

The reports of the battle caused much excitement in Mexico City. Attempts were actually made to convey the impression that it was a royalist victory. The merchants of Vera Cruz struck off a medal to commemorate the glorious action. At this time Viceroy Venegas directed that an image of the Virgin in the sanctuary of Los Remedios should be transferred to Mexico City. On October 31 the revered image was accordingly taken to the metropolitan cathedral, where Venegas formally declared it to be the patron saint of the royalist troops. The Virgin of Guadeloupe was thus apparently balanced by the Virgin of Los Remedios: a Mexican writer has said that the Mother of the God of the Christians, like the gods of *The Iliad,* alternately protected two contending parties.

The so-called battle of Las Cruces opened the road to the

capital city. But instead of marching forward immediately, Hidalgo halted for two days. Then he decided not to march against the castle of Chapultepec which guarded the capital. Upon the only occasion when Hidalgo mentioned that momentous decision, he declared that his determination not to march forward was due to a scarcity of munitions. Because of that decision some Mexican writers have stigmatized Hidalgo as timorous, declaring that he thus lost the fruits of his campaign. However, if Hidalgo had led his undisciplined and demoralized soldiers upon Mexico City it is by no means certain that the capital would have fallen.

For, while Hidalgo had been marching toward the capital, Calleja had been ravaging the revolutionary districts with fire and sword. At Querétaro he received despatches from the viceroy informing him of the battle of Las Cruces and urging him tomarch toward Mexico. The royalist commander accordingly marched from Querétaro toward the capital by the very road along which Hidalgo was retiring from the Monte de las Cruces. The two armies met at Aculco on November 6; the conflict which ensued on the following day was a victory for the royalists: the artillery, munitions, and provisions of the rebels were captured by Calleja. In his hour of triumph, the jubilant royalist commander exaggerated the victory, for he informed the viceroy that the insurgent had lost ten thousand men. On their part, the insurgents tried to belittle the royalist victory, for they said that the engagement was merely a skirmish. The truth is that the followers of Hidalgo were dispersed. In the disorderly retreat Hidalgo and Allende were separated: the curate finally turned up at Valladolid, while Allende made his way to Guanajuato. At this crisis in the revolution, a breach between these two chieftains became apparent. But in spite of that breach and the defeat at Aculco, the revolution was still formidable, for it was spreading like wildfire in the region west and south of Mexico City. On the other hand, on November 25, Calleja reconquered the city of Guanajuato, whence Allende fled towards Guadalajara.

In the end of November, 1810, Hidalgo entered the city of Guadalajara amid the plaudits of the inhabitants. While in this city, he published some decrees which indicated that he was forming an administrative policy. On November 29 he issued a decree providing that the owners of slaves should liberate them within ten days upon pain of death. The decree also provided that the tribute which had been laid upon the castes and upon the Indians should be abolished. The Spanish laws and regulations in regard to the use of stamped paper were also abrogated. The restrictions upon the production of tobacco and wine, as well as the powder monopoly, were swept away. To secure revenues for the government, it was provided that an *alcabala* should be levied upon the agricultural products of Mexico and of Europe. On December 1 Hidalgo issued a decree which aimed to prevent his soldiers from arbitrarily impressing supplies. Four days later another decree provided that lands belonging to Indian communities should be cultivated only by Indians. These decrees embody some of Hidalgo's ideas concerning the reforms which were imperatively needed in New Spain. Among the revolutionary leaders of Spanish America, he was the first to strike at negro slavery.

At this stage in the revolution, Hidalgo began to scatter revolutionary doctrines broadcast. On capturing Guadalajara, he had gained possession of a small printing press. Thus he was enabled to found a periodical the *Despertador Americano*, which became the organ of the revolution. As the editor of the periodical, Hidalgo selected Francisco S. Maldonado, who had been the curate of Mascota. The first number of the journal, issued from the press on December 20, 1810, contained a proclamation appealing to the inhabitants of New Spain. Both creoles and Spaniards were urged to march to the field of battle under "the new Washington," Hidalgo, "that grand soul, full of wisdom and goodness, who has enchanted our hearts with his admirable combination of popular and republican virtues." The excesses which had been committed by the insurgents were ascribed to soldiers of the lower class: it was affirmed that Hidalgo's government had not only disapproved of such actions, but had taken steps to check them. Further, it was declared that the insurgents desired to make Mexico an asylum for the Christian religion and that they desired to preserve the rights of Ferdinand VII. The suggestion was also made that they expected to negotiate an alliance with a foreign power.

In fact, just a week before the first number of the *Despertador Americano* was published, Hidalgo had selected Pascasio Ortiz de Letona—a Central American who had joined the revolutionary cause—as agent to the government of the United States. His credentials, dated December 13, 1810, declared that he was made ambassador and plenipotentiary to the congress of the United States. The envoy was authorized to negotiate with the United States a treaty of alliance, offensive and defensive, and a commercial treaty which would be useful and advantageous to both nations. But Letona's credentials —which displayed the ignorance of the Mexican revolutionary leaders in regard to diplomatic procedure—were never filed in the archives at Washington; for before Letona reached Vera Cruz, he was detained by a royalist officer and thrust into prison, where he seems to have committed suicide. The mission of Letona demonstrates that the first Mexican revolutionists hoped to secure succor from the North. Evidently some Mexicans considered the United States as their natural ally. Although in 1810 the government of the United States did contemplate sending an agent to Mexico, yet many years elapsed before a commercial agent was actually sent there.

The credentials of the unfortunate Letona were dated at "the national palace of Guadalajara." Among the officials who signed his papers were Hidalgo, generalissimo of America, Ignacio Allende, captain general of America, José M. Chico, minister of justice, and Ignacio Rayón, general secretary. Those titles show that Hidalgo had established two rudimentary executive departments: in charge of the department of justice he had placed Chico, a young lawyer of Guanajuato; at the head of the department of state he had placed Rayón, who had acted as his secretary. No documents have been found to indicate that the organs of Hidalgo's revolutionary government developed beyond the stage reached at Guadalajara. It seems unlikely that any further growth took place, for the insurgents and the royalists soon met in a decisive struggle.

While Calleja led his soldiers toward Guadalajara where he planned to join forces with General José de la Cruz, Hidalgo was preparing for the battle to which, despite the arguments of Allende, who favored a guerilla warfare, he had decided to entrust the fortunes of his cause. As the march of La Cruz was delayed by an encounter with the soldiers of the insurgent leader, Colonel Mier, Calleja had to fight the insurgents under Hidalgo without the aid of that general. When the news of Calleja's approach reached Guadalajara the insurgent forces, amounting to about ninety thousand men, marched several leagues east of the city and camped on a range of hills near a bridge over the river Calderón: this strategic position controlled the road to Guadalajara. On the eve of battle, we are told, the warrior-priest made this boast: "I go to breakfast at the bridge of Calderón, to dine in Querétaro, and to sup in Mexico City." This was not altogether an idle boast; for Hidalgo's army vastly outnumbered the royalists, who perhaps had no more than ten thousand men. However, those were disciplined and well-armed soldiers directed by a valiant and skillful commander. More than once did the scale of battle incline toward the insurgents, but a disastrous fire finally broke out in the revolutionary camp; so that, after a conflict lasting about six hours, the insurgents were compelled to retire precipitately. The retreat of the insurgents was soon turned into a rout, and the revolutionary leaders fled in a northerly direction. The battle of Calderón, January 17, 1811, was thus the turning-point of Hidalgo's revolution.

The defeat at the bridge of Calderón shattered the prestige of Hidalgo. While the revolutionists were trying to escape from Calleja's soldiers, Allende evidently determined to take the leadership of the enterprise from the discredited curate. According to a statement made by Hidalgo, it was at a hacienda located between Aguascalientes and Zacatecas that he was forced to transfer his authority to Allende. Thenceforward the deposed commander was watched by the adherents of Allende, who threatened him with death, if he, or any of his friends, should dare to leave the insurgent army. With the dejected generalissimo in his train, Allende led the disheartened revolutionists into Zacatecas.

The new generalissimo soon decided to march into the provinces further north, where many inhabitants had declared in favor of the revolution. In consequence, early in February a small force under Allende left Zacatecas for Saltillo. At that point Hidalgo received a proposal of pardon which was made by General la Cruz in accordance with a degree of amnesty issued by the Spanish *cortes*. In response to the proposal Hidalgo declared that he considered himself pledged to the Mexican patriots not to lay down his arms "until the priceless jewel of liberty had been torn from the hands of the oppressors." He firmly declared that he would enter into no negotiations with Spain which did not have as their basis the recognition of the liberty of the Mexican nation. He expressed a belief that Calleja would yet be humbled by the revolutionists, for Mexico was in a condition of ferment. "Pardon," said Hidalgo, "is intended for criminals and not for defenders of their native land, especially if they possess forces which are superior to their enemies." Despite the sanguine tone of the response, Allende and his companions evidently realized that they were in a desperate plight. In their hour of extremity, they turned again to the North. Evidently they contemplated marching into the province of Texas, or even into the United States. Ignacio Aldama was selected to proceed as their agent to that country. According to statements made by Juan Salazar, a Franciscan friar who accompanied Aldama, the latter was instructed to solicit aid from the government of the United States. Whatever was the exact nature of the mission, it was frustrated; for on March 1, Aldama, who carried with him a quantity of silver, was imprisoned at Béjar, Texas, by José M. Zambrano, the leader of an anti-revolutionary movement. Many Mexicans now turned their eyes from the Virgin of Guadeloupe to the Virgin of Los Remedios.

Among the soldiers of the revolution who secretly passed over to the camp of the royalists about this time was Colonel Ignacio Elizondo, who had become disgruntled with Allende. Elizondo soon placed himself at the head of a band of royalists and laid plans to intercept Hidalgo and Allende, who were journeying northward with a small escort. On the morning of March 21, as the revolutionary caravan was crossing the arid plains near Monclova, it fell into an ambuscade which had been laid by Elizondo. The military leaders were dragged from their coaches, while Hildago, who was at the rear of the caravan, surrendered. By that exploit Elizondo captured about nine hundred men, twenty-four cannon, a small sum of silver money, and a considerable quantity of bar silver. Besides the curate of Dolores, Elizondo captured Mariano Hidalgo, Ignacio Allende, Juan Aldama, Mariano Jiménez, and Mariano Abasolo. Generals, lieutenants, and friars were alike conveyed to Monclova, where the leaders were fettered and cast into prison.

On March 26, under the escort of Colonel Manuel Salcedo, the principal prisoners began the long journey to Chihuahua which was the residence of Nemesio Salcedo, the commandant of the interior provinces. After a tiresome journey, on April

23, the caravan reached Chihuahua. There the prisoners of state were incarcerated in a building which had once served the Jesuits as a college. On May 6 Nemesio Salcedo appointed a military junta of seven men to try the conspirators; about the same time he commissioned Juan de Bustamante and Angel Abella to examine them. We know that before the trial began, Viceroy Venegas had sent to Calleja the mandate that the insurgent leaders should be punished as traitors. Technically, the case for the government was based upon the statements of the accused men.

After the minor conspirators had been examined, the legal counselor of the military junta, Rafael Bracho, wrote his opinion, and the junta passed judgment. It declared that eighteen men were traitors, and decreed that they should be shot in the back. In this ignominious manner, on June 26, Ignacio Allende, generalissimo, Mariano Jiménez, captain general, and Juan Aldama, lieutenant general, were executed. About the same time that the judgment was announced, Ignacio Aldama and Juan Salazar were brought from Texas to Monclova, where they were executed. Mariano Abasolo, who tried to absolve himself from the charge of treason, was condemned to life imprisonment in Spain: about five years later he died in a prison at Cadiz. Many of the priests who had joined the curate of Dolores were taken to Durango, where they were degraded from the priesthood and executed as traitors.

The trial of the chief conspirator was the last to terminate. On May 7, 8, and 9 Hidalgo was skillfully cross-examined by Abella. Although the curate of Dolores was unfrocked, disgraced, and manacled, yet he bore himself with fortitude. He displayed much ingenuity and acumen in his responses to Abella's forty-three questions. The patriot, the dialectician, and the priest were reflected in the answers which his mortal foes preserved. Those answers indicate that Hidalgo did not try to shift the responsibility for the leadership of the insurrection from his own shoulders,—quite otherwise. Although he apparently admitted that the thought of inciting a revolution against Spain had originated with Allende, yet he boldly declared: "I placed myself at the head of the revolution, raised armies, manufactured small arms and cannon, appointed chiefs and officers, directed a manifesto to the nation, and sent to the United States a diplomatic agent, Ortiz de

Letona, who, as I know, died before he reached his destination." Evidently, Hidalgo averred that the object of the revolution was to preserve the viceroyalty of New Spain from conquest by the French. In vain did Abella try to make Hidalgo admit that he had been incited to revolt by Napoleon's emissaries. More than once did the prisoner avow that it had been his purpose to establish the independence of his native land. He declared that he had not adopted any plan of government for emancipated Mexico. He acknowledged that he was partly to blame for the executions and murders which his followers had committed. Relentlessly, Abella drove Hidalgo from one response to another. The priest's answers to the last interrogatories, which concerned the doctrines of the Church, showed signs of regret for the evils which his revolt had brought upon New Spain:—at last Hidalgo besought pardon from the bishop, the viceroy, and the inquisition. Apparently, the pardon which Hidalgo thus solicited was rather for the evils which his rebellion had brought upon the people of Mexico than for his attempt to establish in New Spain a government independent of Old Spain.

It is in the light of this apparent repentance that the writer would view the manifesto of Hidalgo dated May 18, 1811, addressed "To All the World"—the authenticity of which has sometimes been questioned. Extracts from that curious confession will suggest the mood into which the repentant priest had apparently fallen:

Who will furnish water for my head and fountains of tears for my eyes? Who will cause to exude from the pores of my body the blood which flows through my veins in order that I may mourn day and night for those Mexicans who have died, and that I may bless the never-ending mercy of the Lord? . . . The night of darkness which blinded me has been changed into luminous day; and, in the midst of the prison which I have deserved, the evils which I have brought upon Mexico are presented to me so clearly that sleep deserts my eys and repentance prostrates me upon my bed. Not far distant I behold the scene of my sacrifice. I exhale each moment a portion of my soul. I feel as though I might die a thousand times because of regret for my wickedness before I die once. . . . I see that the supreme judge has written down charges against me which fill me with bitterness. He wishes to destroy me because of the sins of my youth. What then will be my astonishment when I see enumerated

the many sins which I committed as the leader of the insurrection? Oh, Mexico, my beloved fatherland! Oh, Mexicans! my
compatriots; Europeans! my progenitors, pity me! I see the devastation of this country which I have caused, the ruins of the
properties which I have destroyed, the infinite number of orphans
whom I have made desolate, and the blood which I have shed
with so much profusion and temerity. I behold . . . the multitude
of souls that will sink into the bottomless pit because they
followed me. . . . Now I see that, if you, deluded insurgents of
Mexico, wish to practice the perverse doctrines of revolution,
my sins will increase and the resulting evils for America, and
more particularly for the Mexicans, will have no end. . . . Know
ye that the person who resists the lawful authorities, resists the
will of God; lay down your arms; throw yourselves at the foot
of the throne; fear not prison or death: fear rather him who
has power to consign the soul to hell after it has departed from
the body!

Lastly, Hidalgo declared himself to be a Roman Catholic.
He abjured whatever he had said against the Church; and he
asked the faithful to pray that God might have mercy upon
his soul. If indeed Hidalgo wrote the manifesto willingly, and
signed it in sincerity, perhaps he did so with the secret hope
that his judges might be merciful unto him.

Early in June the examination of Hidalgo by the military
junta terminated. Then the bishop of Durango, at the instance of Commandant Salcedo, named Fernández Valentín, a
canon of Durango, to judge the accused priest on behalf of the
Church. On June 14 Valentín expressed his approval of the
trial and directed that Hidalgo's case be turned over to Rafael
Bracho. On July 3, Bracho wrote his opinion of the case,
pronouncing Hidalgo a traitor whose punishment was prescribed by the laws of Spain: "Hidalgo is a conspirator guilty
of high treason and an instigator of treacherous murders.
Therefore he should be put to death. According to the laws
of Spain, his property should be confiscated. His proclamations and seductive papers should be cast into the fire publicly
and ignominiously." Bracho declared that the most shameful
mode of execution would scarcely satisfy the vengeance of the
government. The traitor, however, being a minister of the
Almighty, was entitled to merciful treatment. The judgment
of Bracho was that, after having been degraded from the
priesthood by the ecclesiastical authorities, Hidalgo should be

shot as a traitor. Accordingly, on June 19, Hidalgo was clad in the garb of a priest. Then the curate of Dolores was publicly stripped of his sacred vestments by an agent of the bishop of Durango. Whereupon the condemned priest was turned over to Manuel Salcedo, president of the military junta, and he was informed of the death sentence, which, in accordance with Bracho's judgment, had been pronounced against him on July 26. A confessor was brought to Hidalgo, in order that he might prepare "to die like a Christian."

The ominous news of his death sentence did not humiliate the condemned man, who evidently had recovered his remarkable poise. Francisco de Jáuregui, an eyewitness of the solemn ceremony of degradation, declared that, when Hidalgo was being ignominiously stripped of the priestly vestments, he bore himself with such serenity that the priests engaged in the ceremony were horrified. Further, this observer declared that, when the sentence of death was read, Hidalgo received it with surprising indifference, and, that when he was asked if he had anything to say, he blandly requested that an attendant should bring him some sweetmeats. "During the entire day," said Jáuregui, "he spoke of unimportant matters; he slept well at night, breakfasted with pleasure, and showed few signs of repentance." Hidalgo's keepers evidently treated him humanely, for, on the eve of his execution, he expressed his gratitude to the gaolers in two stanzas of poetry which he scrawled upon the walls of his dungeon. Early on the morning of July 30, after being quietly escorted out of his cell into the courtyard of the prison, Hidalgo was shot by a squad of soldiers. Many years later, Lieutenant Armendariz, who commanded these soldiers, declared that Hidalgo died while holding aloft a crucifix.

The bodies of Miguel Hidalgo, Ignacio Allende, Juan Aldama, and Mariano Jiménez were interred at Chihuahua. Their heads were sent to Guanajuato. And, enclosed in iron cages, they were displayed at the four corners of the *Alhóndiga* for ten years. At the principal entrance to that building was placed the following inscription: "Here are the heads of Miguel Hidalgo, Ignacio Allende, Juan Aldama and Mariano Jiménez, who were notorious imposters and the chief leaders of the revolution. They sacked and robbed the Church of God and the royal treasury; they brutally shed the blood of faithful priests and just magistrates; they were the cause of the disasters, the disgraces, and the calamities which we suffered,—occurrences which all the inhabitants of this integral part of the Spanish monarchy lament and deplore. Their heads were placed here by order of Señor Brigadier Don Félix María Calleja del Rey, the illustrious victor of Aculco, Guanajuata, and Calderón—the restorer of peace to Mexico."

Even after Hidalgo had been shot, the holy office did not cease to persecute him. More than a week after Hidalgo's body had been interred at Chihuahua, a report was made to the inquisitorial tribunal in which opprobrious epithets were applied to the dead priest. It was not until March 15, 1813, that the tribunal closed the famous case by ordering that the documents concerning Hidalgo should be deposited in the archives of the holy office.

The rôle of Miguel Hidalgo in the drama of the Mexican war for independence is thus suggested in a history of Mexico: "By his admirers, Hidalgo has been termed an angel of light; by his enemies, a bloodthirsty rebel whose sole delight was in revenge and cruelty." There is some truth in both of these characterizations. The excesses committed by Hidalgo's followers, however, were due rather to his defects as a leader than to a preconceived design. These defects naturally resulted from his lack of ability as a military organizer and from his ignorance of the art of war. Among the glaring mistakes of that shepherd of souls was his failure to formulate a program of action for the people of Mexico. Unlike Miranda, the curate of Dolores was not a framer of constitutions. In light of the subsequent history of Mexico, it would be vain to suppose that, of Hidalgo had promulgated a project of a constitution, he would have solved a grave political problem; but he probably would have secured the support of some Mexicans of the upper classes, who held studiously aloof from his movement for independence. Then, too, at times he utterly failed to manage his own turbulent followers. His lack of the power to command masses of undisciplined soldiers, coupled with his ignorance of military tactics, undermined his prestige; for his voice lacked authority at the council-table, and he could not, like Morelos, inspirit his soldiers upon the field of battle. An experienced military commander would scarcely have risked the fate of a revolution, as Hidalgo did at the bridge of Calderón, upon a pitched battle between undisciplined peons and the experienced soldiers of Spain.

It is only fair to Hidalgo to say, however, that the royalists in Mexico were so strongly entrenched that even a brave and experienced military commander might have failed to plant the revolutionary banner upon the summit of Chapultepec. Then, too, it must be said that the schemes which the curate of Dolores formed were sometimes blighted by untoward circumstances. But in spite of Hidalgo's defects and mistakes and misfortunes, the truth is that he still has an enduring claim to the title given him by the Mexican people,—"the Father of Mexican independence." For, although that priestly iconoclast did not indeed originate the idea that Mexico should be separated from the Spanish monarchy, yet at the psychological moment he awoke the slumbering spirit of discontent with Spanish rule. The spirit of Mexican nationality may be said to date from the rebellion of Hidalgo; for, at his behest, thousands of Mexicans flocked to the revolutionary standard. In 1810 the creoles and the Indians of Mexico measured their strength against the soldiers of Spain upon the field of battle. But the victories which were won by the insurgents at the opening of the Mexican revolution were won at an extravagant price, the price of anarchy. In the lurid background of Mexican national history, there may be discerned standing beside the sacred banner of Guadeloupe the figure of the curate of Dolores,—the daring but unfortunate leader of a bloody revolt of the lower classes in Mexico against the dominant aristocracy. At his death, the curtain falls upon the first act of the Mexican revolutionary drama.

Chapter 4

Agustín de Iturbide

In March, 1812, a *cortes* which the council of regency had summoned at Cadiz promulgated a constitution for distracted Spain. According to the constitution, the executive authority was vested in a monarch; and the legislative power was to reside in the king and a *cortes*. The unicameral legislature was composed of deputies chosen from the provinces in Spain and the Indies. Provision was made for several secretaries of state, including a secretary for the colonies. The government of each province, peninsular or transatlantic, was vested in a superior political chief selected by the king,—the office of viceroy was not mentioned. Among the reforms embodied in the fundamental law was an article providing that all Spaniards were to have the liberty to write and to publish their political ideas. In May, 1812, the *cortes* decreed that an oath of allegiance to this constitution should be taken throughout the Spanish dominions in both hemispheres.

On September 30, 1812, at Mexico City, the viceroy, members of the *audiencia* and of certain corporations solemnly swore to observe the new constitution. A similar ceremony took place in other cities of Spanish America which remained loyal to Spain. Periodicals which ridiculed the viceregal government soon burst forth from the emancipated press of Mexico. In consequence the superior political chief of New Spain, Venegas—who still used the title of viceroy—soon suspended the constitutional guarantee of a free press. In certain parts of New Spain the promulgation and partial revocation of the liberal constitution of 1812 stimulated the spirit of dissatisfaction with the existing régime.

In that viceroyalty some of Hidalgo's surviving followers kept the revolutionary fire burning. At the very time when the *cortes* was framing a constitution for the Spanish monarchy, certain revolutionists were planning a congress for New Spain. The movement for a new government in Mexico was initiated by Ignacio Rayón, who, after the execution of Hidalgo, became a revolutionary chief in the rugged region

111

south and west of Mexico City. In August, 1811, in the picturesque hamlet of Zitácuaro, a group of revolutionists created a council composed of three men, which styled itself "the supreme governmental junta of America." The president of the first Mexican junta was Ignacio Rayón. The three members of the junta took a solemn oath to support the Church of Rome as well as the king of Spain. Not all of the Mexican revolutionists, however, were satisfied with the actions of this junta. The resourceful leader of the revolutionary soldiers, José María Morelos, strongly disapproved of its professions of loyalty to Ferdinand VII.

José María Morelos was born at Valladolid on September 30, 1765. As his parents were poor, it was not until Morelos had reached manhood that he entered the College of San Nicolás at Valladolid, where in 1795 he received the degree of bachelor of arts. A few years later he became a village priest; in 1810 he was curate of Cáracuaro in Michoacán. No sooner did Morelos hear of the *Girto de Dolores* than he sought Miguel Hidalgo. The latter soon commissioned the curate of Carácuaro to recruit soldiers and to lead the revolution in the coastal region south of Mexico City. In a brilliant campaign Morelos eventually drove the royalist soldiers from the district between Acapulco and the valley of Mexico. In his military exploits Morelos was aided by the valiant members of the Galeano and Bravo families, notably the youthful Nicolás Bravo; by Mariano Matamoras, the little curate of Jantetelco; and by the unyielding revolutionist who became famous under the sobriquet of Guadeloupe Victoria. Morelos elucidated his political ideals to a congress which assembled in September, 1813, in the village of Chilpancingo.

The congress of Chilpancingo was originally composed of only eight delegates. In the regions dominated by the insurgents the delegates had been chosen by revolutionary sympathizers: elsewhere they had been selected by Morelos. To those delegates that leader expressed a wish that Mexico should be independent of all nations; he declared in favor of the Roman Catholic religion without the toleration of any other faith; he argued that sovereignty was vested in the people; and he proposed that a new Mexican government should be formed. He suggested that there should be three departments in the revolutionary government. He maintained that only Mexicans should hold office, and that slavery, torture, monopolies, and *alcabalas* should be abolished. The measures which were vigorously championed by Morelos naturally gained favor in congress. In October it issued a manifesto written by the Yucatanese scholar, Andrés Quintana Roo, denouncing Spain's colonial policy and avowing that the Mexicans desired independence.

On November 6, 1813, despite the opposition of Ignacio Rayón, seven members of the congress of Chilpancingo signed an act which declared that Mexico was independent of Spain. This act, which was the first Mexican declaration of independene, asserted that the decision to take such an important step was due to conditions in Spain which had restored to Mexico the exercise of her usurped sovereignty and had forever ended her dependence upon the Spanish king. The declaration provided that no religion except the Roman Catholic was to be tolerated publicly or secretly: the government was to protect that religion and to guard the purity of its faith. Further, congress appointed Morelos the commander-in-chief of the revolutionary army and the chief executive of the Mexican state. After accepting these appointments which conferred upon him the title of highness, Morelos used with that title the modest phrase, "servant of the nation." Thus, under the inspiration of Morelos, the Mexican revolutionists in the congress of Chilpancingo took measures which clearly indicated that a new nation was being created. But the political and military prestige of the warrior-priest soon began to wane. About two months after the declaration of independence was signed the soldiers of the viceroy forced the revolutionary congress to flee from Chilpancingo.

While the Mexican congress was seeking a refuge from the royalists, "the sword of Wellington" restored Ferdinand VII. to the throne of Spain. At Valencia the faithless Ferdinand issued a decree dated May 4, 1814, proclaiming his intention to disregard the constitution of 1812 and the decrees of the liberal *cortes*. Thus Spain again fell under the sway of an absolute king. On August 16 the decree of Valencia was published in Mexico City. Four months later, Félix María Calleja, who had succeeded to the viceregal authority, issued a decree which provided that the *ayuntamientos* established according to the constitution of 1812 were to be abolished. Calleja also ordered that no person should criticise the royal prerogative, and that the language of the constitution should be suppressed in all documents, public and private. Copies of the decree of Valencia were sent to various officers and dignitaries throughout the viceroyalty. By such measures Calleja strove to restore the administrative system of the viceroyalty as it had existed before the deposition of Charles IV.

In the meantime the revolutionary congress was framing a fundamental statute for independent Mexico. On October 22, 1814, in the remote hamlet of Apatzingan, the congress adopted a provisional constitution enunciating certain political principles and providing a government for the revolutionists. The constitution declared that the sovereignty of the people was vested in congress and that the religion of the state should be Roman Catholicism. The governmental authority was vested in an executive composed of three persons, each of whom was to serve as the president for four months; in a congress composed of deputies from the provinces; and in a national judiciary chosen, like the executive, by congress. Under this constitution a government was soon established: Jose M. de Liceaga, Morelos, and Doctor Cos being chosen to act as the executive power. There was a provision in the constitution to the effect that, after peace with Spain was established, a constituent congress was to assume the sovereign authority. To most Mexicans, however, the constitution of Apatzingan remained a paper constitution, for Spanish soldiers still patrolled the larger part of the viceroyalty.

About a year after this constitution was promulgated, while he was convoying the migratory congress from Ario to Tehuacán, Morelos was captured by the royalists. In November, 1815, the jubilant Spaniards thrust him into a cell of the inquisition in Mexico City. The trial of Morelos has been described by Henry C. Lea as "the most expeditious in the annals of the Holy Office": on November 24, the inquisitorial tribunal accused Morelos of being a heretic and an insurgent; two days later, it announced the judgment which condemned the curate of Carácuaro to degradation and execution. On December 22, 1815, after being stripped of his priestly vestments, the "invincible" Morelos was shot in the back by the soldiers of the viceroy. The execution of Morelos, the ablest military commander that the Mexican revolution had produced, was a heavy blow to the cause of independence.

Another phase of the early Mexican revolution may be suggested by the career of Francisco Xavier Mina, a brave native of Navarre. Utterly disgusted at the absolute rule of Ferdinand VII., Mina fled from Spain to England, where he dreamed of promoting the cause of liberty and independence in New Spain. In April, 1817, with a small band of daring filibusters, recruited mainly in the United States, Mina landed at Soto la Marina on the Mexican Gulf. With a part of "the auxiliary division of the Mexican republic," as he styled his soldiers, Mina marched into the exterior of Mexico. Although he gained some signal successes against the royalists, yet he failed to secure the sincere coöperation of the Mexican insurgents led by a local chieftain, Padre Tórres; he was captured by the royalists and executed on November 11, 1817. The prestige of the revolutionists sank still lower after Mina's execution: the publication of insurgent periodicals was suspended; and a number of prominent revolutionary leaders, among them Quintana Roo, accepted the pardon which was offered by Ferdinand VII.

Although Hidalgo, Morelos, and Mina had failed to establish the independence of Mexico, yet they had not died in vain. Hidalgo's memory was revered by many Mexicans. The career of Mina indicated what a capable military commander might accomplish. The political achievements of Morelos presaged the founding of an independent nation. The sequel will show that many Mexicans were ready to take up arms against the motherland, if, at an auspicious moment, a resolute leader appeared with an attractive political program. Such a man was Agustín de Iturbide, who, during the early Mexican revolution, had served under the Spanish standard.

Agustín de Iturbide, the son of José Joaquin de Iturbide and María Josefa Arámburu, was born in the city of Valladolid, Mexico, on September 27, 1783. His mother's family was evidently of Vizcayan origin. Augustín's father, a prosperous landowner, was a native of Pamplona, the ancient capital of Navarre. On October 1, 1783, in the cathedral of Valladolid, the son of José de Iturbide was baptized Agustín Cosme Damian. There is a tradition that the name Agustín was bestowed because a pious Augustinian friar had prayed for the safe delivery of the child. At present the early life of Agustín de Iturbide cannot be reconstructed with fullness, for only a few prejudiced documents and some traditions of varying degrees of authenticity have come down to us in regard to that period of his career. Various documents show that his mother, who had been educated in a convent, was throughout life a devout Roman Catholic. Accordingly we may safely assume that Agustín grew up in a home where the Catholic Church was regarded with veneration. Although the boy passed his early years in a city which was one of the intellectual centers of Mexico, yet he did not profit greatly by its educational advantages. Alamán alleged that Agustín was not a studious youth, and that he never acquired more than the rudiments of an education. Vicente Rocafuerte, a bitter political enemy of Iturbide, asserted that, although the youth was sent to college in his native city, he did not complete his course of study because of idle and vicious habits. Those assertions evidently embody a belief which was current in Mexico during the revolutionary epoch to the effect that the education of Iturbide had been somewhat neglected,—a view which is borne out by the marks of illiteracy found among his papers.

At an early age Iturbide displayed an interest in military affairs. The earliest report of his military services preserved in the archives of Simancas shows that, on October 16, 1797, Iturbide was given a provisional appointment as ensign in the provincial regiment of infantry of Valladolid. On July 6, 1798, that appointment was confirmed by a royal order. In a report of Iturbide's military services which was written in December, 1800, the following statements were made: that he was of noble descent; that his health was good; that he posessed application and ability; and that he was unmarried. It was in 1805 that Agustín de Iturbide married María Huarte, who belonged to a well-known family of his native city. By the end of December, 1806, Iturbide had been promoted to a lieutenancy in his regiment. Service in a militia company did not engross Iturbide's time; for Mexican militiamen were ordinarily required to do little more than to attend occasional reviews. During his early manhood Iturbide evidently spent considerable time helping his father to manage the haciendas of the family. As early as 1809 the dissastisfaction with Spanish rule attracted Iturbide's attention. José Michelena, the leader of a conspiracy which was formed against the viceregal government at Valladolid, obviously referred to Iturbide when he later declared that a young creole, who became aware of the plot, had denounced the conspirators. In an autobiographical sketch written thirteen years later, Iturbide thus described his situation in life when the *Grito de Dolores* was heard:

In the year 1810, I was simply a subaltern officer, a lieutenant in the provincial regiment of Valladolid, my native city. . . . When the revolution set on foot by Don Miguel Hidalgo, curate of Dolores, broke out, he offered me the rank of lieutenant-general. The offer was one which might have tempted any young man without experience, and at an age when his ambition might be excited. I declined it, however, because I was satisfied that the plans of the curate were ill contrived, and that they would produce only disorder, massacre, and devastation, without accomplishing the object which he had in view. . . . The word insurrection in that instance did not mean independence and equal liberty;—its object was, not to reclaim the rights of the nation, but to exterminate all the Europeans, to destroy their possessions, and to trample on the laws of war, humanity, and religion.

This statement embodies the opinion of conservative Mexicans respecting the insurrection of Hidalgo. Not only did Lieutenant Iturbide decline to follow the sacred banner of Guadeloupe, but he took up arms against the insurgents as "against a lawless band" which "harassed the country." He gained distinction under Colonel Trujillo at the battle of Las Cruces. In June, 1812, he captured the insurgent leader Albino García in the town called the Valley of Santiago. Four months later he carried a rebel stronghold, Fort Liceaga, by storm. In April, 1813, he drove the insurgents under Ramón Rayón from Salvatierra. In December of that year he participated in a battle at Valladolid which resulted in the defeat of Morelos. In September, 1815, Viceroy Calleja rewarded Colonel Iturbide for these achievements by appointing him commander of a military district composed of Guanajuato and Michoacán. In a short time the actions of Iturbide as military commander of that district caused great dissatisfaction among its inhabitants. Because of this discontent, early in April, 1816, Calleja ordered Iturbide to leave his command and to proceed to Mexico City. In an official report of Iturbide's case which was printed in the *Gaceta de México* on September 1, 1816, it was stated that although there was not enough evidence to convict the accused officer, yet the appearance of new and adverse witnesses made it seem advisable

not to restore him to his command. Apparently Colonel
Iturbide was neither dismissed nor reinstated. In April, 1816,
the hero of many bloody engagements ceased to fight under
the Spanish standard.

While the royalist commander who had won an unsurpassed reputation for cruelty and bravery was nursing his
real or fancied wrongs, events occurred in Spain which influenced Spanish America profoundly. In 1819 Ferdinand
VII. prepared to quell the insurrection in America. A fleet
was brought to Cadiz. Thousands of soldiers bivouacked in
that city. But discontent with Ferdinand's absolute rule and
a conviction that the soldiers destined for America constituted
a forlorn hope, provoked an uprising. On January 1, 1820,
Rafael Riego, the colonel of an Asturian regiment, boldly
proclaimed his adherence to the constitution of 1812. A wave
of revolution swept over Spain; Ferdinand VII. was compelled
to relinquish his absolute authority: on March 7 he proclaimed his intention to support the liberal constitution. A
short time afterwards he solemnly swore to observe this constitution and accepted liberal statesmen as his ministers.

News of the Spanish revolution startled the citizens of
Vera Cruz in April, 1820. In the end of the following month,
Juan Ruíz de Apodaca, who had become viceroy of New
Spain shortly after Iturbide was recalled from his command,
directed that the officials and corporations of Mexico City
should take an oath to support the new régime. About the
middle of June the freedom of the press was again proclaimed
in Mexico City. On June 24 Apodaca addressed a circular to
the inhabitants of New Spain informing them that they were
to take an oath to support the constitution of 1812. In September, 1820, deputies were chosen to represent Mexico in
the Spanish *cortes*. In September and October, before these
deputies sailed from Vera Cruz, the *cortes* passed some decrees which disturbed many Mexicans. On the one side, it
passed a decree providing that when the American rebels who
lived in regions that had been pacified took an oath to support
the constitution, they were to be pardoned. On the other side,
it passed decrees suppressing certain religious orders and re-
stricting other religious orders. Consequently many members
of the higher clergy became apprehensive of the results which
constitutional government might have upon the Mexican
Church. Further, the promulgation anew of the constitution

of 1812 encouraged liberal ideas and stimulated discussion in regard to the best form of government for Mexico. There is perhaps no better contemporary statement of the conditions than that which was made by Iturbide.

The new order of things, the ferment in which the Peninsula was placed, the machinations of the discontented, the want of moderation amongst the supporters of the new system, the vacillation of the authorities, and the conduct of the government and Cortes at Madrid, (who, from the decrees which they issued, and the speeches which some of the deputies pronounced, appeared to have determined on alienating the colonies), filled the heart of every good patriot with the desire of independence, and excited amongst the Spaniards established in the country, the apprehension that all the horrors of the former insurrection were about to be repeated. . . . In such a state of things the richest and most beautiful part of America was about to become again the prey of contending factions. In every quarter clandestine meetings took place, for the purpose of discussing the form of government which ought to be adopted. Among the Europeans and their adherents, some wished for the establishment of the Spanish constitution. . . . There were some who conceived that it ought to undergo modifications, inasmuch as the constitution framed by the Cortes at Cadiz was inapplicable to "New Spain." Others there were who sighed after the old absolute government as the best support of their lucrative employments, which they exercised in a despotic manner, and by which they had gained a monopoly. The privileged and powerful classes fomented these different parties, attaching themselves to the one or the other, according to the extent of their political information, or the projects of aggrandizement which their imaginations presented. The Americans wished for independence, but they were not agreed as to the mode of effecting it, still less as to the form of government which they should prefer. With respect to the former object, many were of opinion that in the first place, all the Europeans should be exterminated, and their property given up to confiscation. The less sanguinary would have been contented with banishing them from the country, thus reducing thousands of families to a state of orphanage. The moderate party suggested only that they should be excluded from all public offices, and degraded to the condition in which they had kept the natives of the country for three centuries. As to the form of government, one party proposed a monarchy, tempered by the Spanish, or some other constitution; a second party wished for a federative republic; a third for a central republic; and the partisans of each system, full of enthusiasm, were impatient for the accomplishment of their different objects.

In 1820 only a few bands of Mexicans still followed the standard of independence. Most of the insurgents were waging a guerrilla warfare against the royalists in the region south of the capital city. The operations of the royalists in that quarter had been entrusted to General José Gabriel Armijo. To the chagrin of Apodaca, that general had not made much progress in subjugating the enemy. When in the end of 1820, Arijo relinquished his command, Apodaca looked for a man who might complete the pacification of Mexico. His eyes finally fell upon the renowned and discredited commander, Agustín de Iturbide, to whom he offered an appointment as commander of the royalist forces in the field. On November 9, Colonel Iturbide accepted the appointment. About a week later he left Mexico City obviously charged with the task of terminating the revolution. Viceroy Apodaca has been severely criticised because he selected Iturbide for this command: it has been alleged that the latter owed his appointment to the influence of certain members of the clergy who secretly hoped to use him in the execution of their disloyal designs. But the writer has found no evidence to indicate that Apodaca was animated by any other motive than a desire to re-establish the authority of Spain throughout the length and breadth of his viceroyalty.

The insurgent leader against whom Iturbide marched in November, 1820, was Vicente Guerrero. Little is known of Guerrero's early career. It appears that this leader was born in 1782 of humble parents at Tixtla in the province of Mexico. His parents were of Indian race, or, at least, had some Indian blood in their veins. Vicente Guerrero spent his early life as a laborer: Julio Zárate, the historian of the Mexican revolution, declares that he was employed for a time as a muledriver. Guerrero seems to have entered the revolutionary ranks in 1810 under a subordinate of Morelos. After the execution of that warrior-priest, Guerrero became the soul of the Mexican revolution. If it had not been for Guerrero's reputation as a sincere, daring, and valiant man, in 1820 the revolt against the rule of Spain in Mexico might have been little more than a memory.

Instead of making war on Guerrero, as he had warred upon

other patriot leaders, Iturbide, without informing the viceroy, soon entered into negotiations with that leader for the pacification of Mexico. The upshot of the negotiations was an agreement between Iturbide and Guerrero to join forces and pacify Mexico. Their agreement was embodied in a plan which Iturbide first published in the obscure hamlet of Iguala on February 24, 1821.

The Plan of Iguala—an original copy of which the writer has seen in the Mexican archives—was a unique document. That plan was a crude *pronunciamiento* which contained not only a declaration of independence from Spain but also a sketch of a provisional government for New Spain. The preamble of the plan, addressed to Mexicans of all races—Europeans, Africans, and Asiatics—suggested that the independence of Mexico from Spain was destined to be established in the natural course of events. It declared that the viceroyalty of Mexico had been for three hundred years under the tutelage of the most pious, heroic, and magnanimous of nations, but that the evils which naturally arose because of the distance of that viceroyalty from the government at Madrid could only be remedied by the absolute independence of Mexico from Spain. The branch of the tree was now as large as the trunk. Only a general union of Europeans, Indians, and creoles would furnish a solid basis for the happiness of the Mexican people. An appeal was made to their spirit of nationality in these words: "The moment has arrived when you should manifest a common sentiment. You should show that our union is the powerful hand which emancipates America without any foreign aid. At the head of a determined and valiant army, I have proclaimed the independence of Mexico."

In twenty-three articles, which were not always perfectly consistent with each other, suggestions were made in regard to the system of government that Iturbide proposed to establish. One article provided that only the Roman Catholic religion should be tolerated in Mexico. The members of the regular and secular clergy throughout the country were to be protected in all their rights and properties. In form the new government was to be a monarchy, but it should be regulated by a constitution suitable to the condition of the country. The monarch of Mexico was to be Ferdinand VII., a member of his family, or a member of some other ruling dynasty of

Europe. Until the emperor was selected, the governmental authority was to be vested in a junta, which was to frame regulations for the election of delegates to a Mexican congress. Until the arrival of the Mexican monarch, this congress, or *cortes,* was to decide whether the junta should govern or be replaced by a regency. As soon as the *cortes* assembled, it was to frame a constitution and to make laws for the state. All the inhabitants of the empire, without any distinction of race or class, were declared to be citizens of Mexico who were entitled to protection in their persons and properties. According to their merits, they were to be eligible to all the offices of the new empire. The existing governmental bureaus were to remain intact, but those officials who opposed the Plan of Iguala were to be replaced by men who were distinguished by loyalty, virtue, and merit. The new government was to be sustained by the army of independence. That army should be called the army of the three guarantees:—it was to sacrifice itself, if need be, for the preservation of the Roman Catholic religion, the establishment of independence, and the maintenance of the union of Mexicans and Spaniards.

These three principles, or guarantees, as they were designated by Mexican contemporaries,—religion, independence, and union, were the distinctive features of the project, as viewed by Mexicans of the revolutionary era. In reality the Plan of Iguala was a bid for the support of the various classes or castes of New Spain: royalists, insurgents, creoles, Indians, peninsular Spaniards, and clergy. To the rulers of Old Spain the Plan of Iguala apparently offered a mode of adjustment with New Spain which provided that the titular sovereignty over Mexico might be vested in a Spanish prince. According to that scheme for a constitutional government in Mexico, a person born there could not become its monarch. With what seems like a lack of wisdom, when the liberal *cortes* of Spain heard of Iturbide's revolution, that body scarcely entertained the thought of accepting the Plan of Iguala as a solution for the vexatious colonial problem. To many Mexican insurgents this plan was attractive because it embodied some of the political ideals of Morelos.

The Plan of Iguala differed from the Declaration of Independence of July 4, 1776, because it did not present an indictment of the mother-country. Neither did it contain a philosophy of the revolution. It did, however, formulate a definite scheme of government for the revolutionists. According to Iturbide's own statement, the Plan of Iguala was formed after he had made a careful study of conditions in Mexico. He explained the origin and the purpose of the plan in these words:

A pamphlet, which I have seen, has asserted that the project was the work of a club of serviles, who held their meeting at the *Profesa,* a building belonging to the congregation of St. Philip, in Mexico. Any person who reads the document must be convinced, from its contents alone, that it could not have been dictated by servilism; I put out of the question the opinions of those persons to whom it is attributed, and shall only say that they are matters upon which the multitude is very commonly mistaken. . . . After the plan had been drawn out, I consulted upon it with distinguished individuals of different parties; not one of them disapproved of it; it was not modified in any manner; nothing was added or erased.

In tracing out this project, my aim was to give independence to my country, because such was the general desire of the Americans; a desire founded on natural feelings, and on principles of justice. It was, besides, the only means by which the interests of the two nations could be secured. The Spaniards would not allow themselves to be convinced that their decline began with their acquisition of the colonies, while the colonists were fully persuaded that the time of their emancipation had arrived.

The Plan of Iguala guaranteed the religion which we inherited from our ancestors. To the reigning family of Spain, it held out the only prospect which survived for preserving those extensive and fertile provinces. To the Mexicans, it granted the right of enacting their own laws, and of having their government established within their own territory.

The sagacity which Iturbide had shown in framing the Plan of Iguala was soon demonstrated. This plan received the support of many members of the clergy who had remained studiously aloof from Hidalgo. A large number of royalist soldiers were attracted by the movement because of Iturbide's prestige as a royalist commander, while the acceptance of the Plan of Iguala by Guerrero guaranteed the support of many revolutionists. Thus, because of one motive or another, supporters of that plan soon appeared in various parts of Mexico. On March 29, 1821, the garrison of Vera Cruz, which was commanded by Captain Antonio López de Santa Anna, proclaimed its adherence to Iturbide's program. Nicholás Bravo, who had just been released from prison by Apodaca, soon began to recruit soldiers for the army of the three guarantees. Vicente Filisola, an Italian who had been a comrade-in-arms of Iturbide, joined his adherents. Meanwhile Iturbide had invested his native city: on May 22, after a brief siege, he entered Valladolid amid the rejoicings of his fellow-townsmen. On June 28 Querétaro fell into his hands. In the gazette of Iturbide's army and in his official newspaper, the *Diario Político Militar Mejicano,* reports were regularly published of the progress of his arms and of the viceroy's declining power. The first number of that newspaper, September 1, 1821, spoke of Iturbide's "just, liberal, and beneficient government."

Iturbide had evidently hoped that Viceroy Apodaca would accept his scheme as the basis for an adjustment between Mexico and Spain. For the Plan of Iguala provided that Apodaca should become the president of the provisional junta. But Apodaca refused to join hands with Iturbide. On March 8 he issued a manifesto exhorting the Mexicans to support the constitution and the laws; on March 14 he published a proclamation announcing that Iturbide was an outlaw. Apodaca also took various measures for the defence of the capital city; soldiers were gathered and placed under the command of a royalist officer named Pascual de Liñan. Early in June the viceroy felt compelled to impress soldiers whom he called "the defenders of the integrity of the Two Spains." However, when reports reached the capital of the capture of Valladolid and Querétaro by the soldiers of the three guarantees, the discontent of the royalists became intense; and hence the chief military officers in Mexico City insisted that Apodaca should relinquish his office. The hapless viceroy yielded to the storm:—July 6 he resigned his command in favor of General Francisco Novella.

Like the last titular emperor of Rome, the last titular viceroy of New Spain was deposed by a mutiny of his own soldiers. The viceroy soon journeyed to Vera Cruz where he embarked for the Spanish peninsula on the ship *Asia.* It seems odd that this vessel had just brought to Mexico General Juan O'Donojú, the last representative of the Spanish monarchy to exercise viceregal authority in North America.

In January, 1821, General O'Donojú had been appointed captain general of New Spain. In accordance with the constitution, he was given the title of superior political chief. If any detailed instructions were written by the liberal statesmen of Spain for the guidance of O'Donojú, investigations by the writer in the Spanish archives have not brought them to light. In view of the extraordinary conditions in Spain, it is possible that O'Donojú was not given any instruction regarding the policy which he was to follow as captain general of New Spain. At the critical juncture when rumors of the revolutionary projects of Iturbide reached Madrid, O'Donojú was nearly ready to leave the Spanish peninsula for the New World. The commander of New Spain left Cadiz for America on May 20, 1821, accompanied only by a few military officers. Two months later he reached the fortress of San Juan de Ullúa. When O'Donojú discovered that many of the important towns and cities of Mexico had proclaimed their adherence to the Plan of Iguala, that the army of the three guarantees had besieged the capital city of the viceroyalty, and that Vera Cruz had actually been attacked by the soldiers of Iturbide, his amazement was prodigious. It seemed as though a magician's wand had almost transformed the ancient viceroyalty of New Spain into an independent state.

The Iturbidista revolution indubitably influenced the policy which was adopted by O'Donojú, the liberal. From Vera Cruz on August 3 the captain general issued an address to the inhabitants of Mexico in which he frankly declared that if his government did not suit the Mexicans, at the first sign of disgust with his rule he would relinquish his post and quietly allow them to select their own ruler. He suggested, however, that the Mexicans should suspend their projects until they received fresh tidings from the Spanish peninsula. A few days later, perhaps at the instance of the wily insurgent, Santa Anna, O'Donojú sent to Colonel Iturbide two agents who were empowered to propose the negotiation of a treaty which might ensure the pacification of New Spain.

Those agents soon made arrangements for an interview between O'Donojú and Iturbide. The interview was held in the town of Córdoba. There, on August 24, the commander of the army of the three guarantees and the superior political chief of New Spain agreed to a treaty. The preamble of the treaty of Córdoba alleged that O'Donojú desired to reconcile

Old Spain and New Spain by untying the bonds which had united them. O'Donojú agreed that New Spain was to be recognized as a sovereign and independent nation. The government of the new nation was to be a monarchy limited by a constitution. With regard to the monarch, article three of this convention provided that Ferdinand VII. was first to be offered the throne of Mexico. If the king of Spain declined to accept that throne, it was next to be offered to his brother, Prince Charles; if Charles did not accept the kingship, the throne was then to be offered to Prince Francisco de Paula; if that prince did not wish to accept the Mexican throne, it was then to be offered to Prince Charles Louis, Duke of Lucca. In case no one of those personages accepted the kingdom of Mexico, then the *cortes* of the Mexican empire was to elect a monarch who should erect his court in Mexico City. His Catholic Majesty, Ferdinand VII., was to be solicited to promote the selection of a prince of his dynasty to reign in Mexico.

Meanwhile, "in accordance with the spirit of the Plan of Iguala"—so ran the treaty—a junta was to be formed from the leaders of the Mexican empire, including O'Donojú. This junta was to be styled the provisional governmental junta. It was to select its own president, to inform the people that deputies were to be elected to a Mexican *cortes,* and to choose a regency of three persons who were to constitute the supreme executive authority until a monarch grasped "the sceptor of the empire." Until the *cortes* assembled, the provisional junta was to legislate in accordance with the existing laws that harmonized with the Plan of Iguala. The regency was to convoke a constituent *cortes* for Mexico. The treaty of Córdoba also contained a provision that the Spaniards might freely depart from Mexican soil with their families and property, whereas those officials who were notoriously opposed to Mexican independence might be compelled to leave the empire. The occupation of Mexico City by Spanish soldiers being an obstacle to the fulfillment of the treaty, O'Donojú agreed to use his influence to secure the peaceful evacuation of that city by an honorable capitulation.

This epitome of the treaty of Córdoba shows that it confirmed the Plan of Iguala, with some modifications. Of special significance was the clause which provided that in case none of the personages designated in the treaty deigned to accept the throne of Mexico, the emperor should be chosen by the Mexican *cortes*. The treaty contained no provision to the effect that the monarch must be selected from a reigning dynasty of Europe. Thus the road was cleared for the choice of an emperor who had been born in Mexico. It is not strange that some writers should have considered that the treaty of Córdoba embodied a plan which prepared the way for the selection of the aspiring commander of the army of the three guarantees as emperor of Mexico.

After Iturbide and O'Donojú had affixed their signatures to the convention of Córdoba, there was a tilt between O'Donojú and Novella; for the latter maintained that O'Donojú was not authorized to sign such a convention, while O'Donojú demanded that Novella should place the garrison of Mexico City at his disposal. In the end Novella was reluctantly induced to recognize O'Donojú as the rightful commander of the royalist soldiers. In accordance with O'Donojú's wishes, on September 14, Novella transferred his military authority to Pascual de Liñan and bestowed his civil authority upon Ramón Gutierrez del Mazo. A few days later the grenadiers of Iturbide took possession of the fortress-palace of Chapultepec. His troops displaced the peninsular soldiers who had garrisoned the city. Elaborate preparations were made for the entry of Iturbide and his followers into the capital. On September 27, 1821—his thirty-eighth birthday—Iturbide marched into the city from Chapultepec at the head of the victorious army of the three guarantees. As the triumphal procession wended its way into the city, it deeply impressed the inhabitants. The first number of the *Gaceta Imperial de México,* which replaced the *Gaceta de México,* declared that Iturbide was hailed by the people of Mexico City as "the father of his country, the liberator, and the tutelar genius of New Spain." In the enthusiasm of the moment that gazette exclaimed that "Rome had never witnessed such a triumph." The *ayuntamiento* of Mexico City, says Bustamante, presented Iturbide with a key of gold upon a platter of silver. These demonstrations of joy signalized the termination of the struggle for the independence of Mexico from Spain,—a struggle which Hidalgo had begun on September 16, 1810. By what may rightly be characterized as a bloodless revolution the author of the Plan of Iguala had overthrown Spanish rule in the region that had been conquered by Hernando

Cortés and his followers. In the words of Iturbide himself, "Six months were sufficient to untwist the entangled knot which had bound the two worlds."

While the royalist soldiers were evacuating the capital, Iturbide was selecting the members of the provisional govenrmental junta provided by the Plan of Iguala. Among the leaders selected to serve on the junta were Iturbide, O'Donojú, and Antonio Joaquín Pérez, the bishop of Puebla. On September 28, this junta met in a hall of the former viceregal palace. The members soon elected Iturbide as president. They chose as their secretary Juan J. los Monteros, one of Iturbide's intimate friends. After solemnly swearing to support the Plan of Iguala and the treaty of Córdoba, they signed "the act of independence of the Mexican Empire." The act proclaimed that Mexico had just emerged from three hundred years of oppressive rule: "the heroic efforts of her sons have been crowned with success; this measure consummates an eternally memorable enterprise which a hero who is worthy of admiration, praise, love, and glory began in Iguala and brought to a successful termination in spite of almost insurmountable obstacles." The declaration of independence announced that Mexico was a sovereign nation independent of Spain with which she would maintain friendly relations as prescribed by treaties. In contrast with the first Mexican declaration of independence framed under the inspiration of Morelos, this declaration announced to the world that Mexico was an empire. The governmental junta provided that the inhabitants of the Mexican empire were to swear to support its declaration of independence.

The junta soon appointed a regency to serve as the executive body until an emperor was elected. The members of the executive power were Agustín de Iturbide, Juan O'Donojú, Manuel de la Barcena, José Isidro Yañez, and Manuel Velásquez de León. When he became president of the regency, Iturbide relinquished the presidency of the junta. The regency soon conferred upon Iturbide the command of the army with the grade of generalissimo and the title of highness. That body also established four secretaries: a secretary of state, of justice and ecclesiastical affairs, of war and the navy, and of the treasury.

On February 24, 1822, the congress which had been convoked in accordance with the treaty of Córdoba assembled.

At once it declared that the provisional junta had ceased to exist and that the legislative authority was vested in itself. In a short time it sent a decree to the regency providing that all the cities, towns, villages, and corporations of the Mexican empire should take a solemn oath to recognize the sovereignty of the nation as represented by congress. The regency ordered that this decree should be observed by Mexican civil, military, and ecclesiastical authorities of whatever class or dignity. Nevertheless a struggle soon began between congress and the regency for the supreme authority. Some members of congress desired the establishment of a republic in Mexico. "The Republicans were hostile to me," said Iturbide, "because they well knew that they could never bring me to contribute to the establishment of a government, which, whatever might be its attractions, did not suit the Mexicans." Another group of Iturbide's opponents was composed of persons who wished to see that provision of the Plan of Iguala carried out which arranged for the coronation of a Bourbon prince as emperor of Mexico,—a provision which the action of Spain rendered nugatory.

According to an article of the treaty of Córdoba, O'Donojú selected two commissioners to carry the news of that agreement to the court of Madrid. He entrusted those commissioners with a dispatch addressed to Ferdinand VII. In this dispatch O'Donojú expressed the opinion that the independence of Mexico from Spain was inevitable; he described the unexpected pleasure with which he had witnessed Iturbide sign the treaty of Córdoba, and pointed out that a prince of Spain might still become emperor of Mexico. But the treaty of Córdoba, which became known to the Spanish government in November, 1821, was given a cold reception. On December 7, Ramón Pelegrín, the secretary for the colonies, addressed a circular to various *ayuntamientos, audiencias,* and archbishops in the New World declaring that neither O'Donojú nor anyone else had been authorized to agree to a convention which recognized the independence from Spain of any transatlantic province. In the same month Juan Moscoso, who had been employed in the Spanish service in the West Indies, was quietly appointed captain general of New Spain to replace O'Donojú. Early in 1822 the treaty of Córdoba was laid before the Spanish *cortes*. After an interesting debate, on February 13, 1822, the extraordinary *cortes* passed a decree which solemnly declared that the recognition of the independence of any Spanish colony by a foreign state would be considered as an act of hostility toward Spain. The Spanish ambassadors in Europe were soon instructed to make known to the govenrments to which they were accredited the views of Spain regarding the independence of Spanish America. Thus did the members of the liberal *cortes*—which had rejected the Plan of Iguala—spurn a convention by which Spain might have held Mexico as an appanage.

Pelegrín's circular disavowing the treaty of Córdoba was printed on March 28, 1822, by the *Gaceta Imperial de México,* the official organ of Iturbide's government. In commenting upon that circular the gazette intimated that the Mexicans would never bow their necks to the Spanish yoke again. The truth of the matter is: that to Iturbide's adherents the policy announced by Spain appeared to make effective the article of the treaty of Córdoba which provided that, in a certain contingency, the Mexican nation might elect its own sovereign. The dramatic sequel was not long delayed. On the night of May 18, 1822, Pio Marcha, a sergeant in Iturbide's old regiment, and the rabble in the streets of the capital city, with loud shouts which were accompanied by a rattling fire of musketry, proclaimed Iturbide as Agustín I., Emperor of Mexico. According to Iturbide's own version of the affair, his first impulse was to decline the imperial dignity which the people so unceremoniously thrust upon him:

If I restrained myself from appearing before them for that purpose, it was solely in compliance with the counsel of a friend who happened at the moment to be with me. "They will consider it an insult," he had scarcely time to say to me, "and the people know no restraint when they are irritated. You must make this fresh sacrifice to the public good: the country is in danger; remain a moment longer undecided, and you will hear their acclamations turned into death-shouts." I felt it necessary to resign myself to circumstances; and I spent the whole of that night allaying the general enthusiasm, and persuading the people and the troops to give time for my decision, and in the meanwhile to render obedience to the Congress.

On May 19, Iturbide was invited to attend an extraordinary session of congress. When he was ready to proceed there, some enthusiastic Mexicans unfastened the horses from his coach and drew him triumphantly through the streets to the hall of congress. The building was surrounded by his turbulent soldiers, while excited civilians crowded into the galleries. Nevertheless, the proposal to proclaim Iturbide the supreme ruler of Mexico provoked a spirited opposition. Only after a debate which lasted several hours did a majority of the members of congress who were voting announce themselves in favor of Agustín de Iturbide as emperor of Mexico. On the same day congress passed an act which asserted that, as certain members of the ruling dynasty of Spain had renounced the crown of Mexico or had refused to accept that crown, in accordance with article three of the treaty of Córdoba, it had selected as "the constitutional emperor of Mexico, Agustín de Iturbide, first of that name, according to the bases proclaimed in the Plan of Iguala, which was generally supported by the Mexican nation." On May 20 congress formulated an oath of fidelity to the imperial government of Mexico. On the following day Iturbide took that oath in the halls of congress. After this ceremony Emperor Agustín I. apparently made an address declaring that he was fettered with chains of gold.

Bells were rung in the city of Mexico when the election of Iturbide as emperor was proclaimed. Felicitations were showered upon Agustín I. by various individuals and corporations. He was congratulated by the *ayuntamiento* of the capital city and by the leading military commanders, notably by Guerrero and Santa Anna. At Guadaljara and at Valladolid the accession of Iturbide to the throne of Mexico was celebrated by public rejoicings. Congress soon passed important measures concerning the Iturbidista dynasty. On June 22 it passed a law providing that the Mexican monarchy was to be moderate, constitutional, and hereditary. The successor of Emperor Agustín I. was to be his eldest son, Agustín, who was to be styled Prince Imperial; the other children of the emperor were to be called princes or princesses of Mexico; his father was to be entitled Prince of the Union; and his sister was to be styled Princess Iturbide. In accordance with the provisions of congress elaborate preparations were made for the coronation of the newly elected emperor. On July 21, 1822, in the stately cathedral of Mexico City, in the presence of several bishops and a large concourse of people, Iturbide was ostentatiously crowned emperor of Mexico. After the ceremony of coronation was completed, medals were scattered among the populace which bore on one side the bust of the emperor and on the other side the inscription: "Agustín, First Constitutional Emperor of the Mexicans."

Emperor Agustín I. soon established an imperial court with pages and chamberlains and almoners and ladies-in-waiting. He also instituted a military order, the imperial order of Guadeloupe, ostensibly to reward the soldiers who had fought for Mexico's emancipation. Agustín I. became the grand master of the Order of Guadeloupe. Many other leaders in the Iturbidista revolution, as well as some of the friends or relatives of the emperor, were decorated with the grand cross, the insignia of the order.

In 1821 and 1822 the authority of the Mexican empire was extended southward far beyond the confines of the viceroyalty of New Spain. On September 8, 1821, a junta in the province of Chiapas, which was situated within the captaincy general of Guatemala, swore to support independence from Spain in terms which indicated an intention to adhere to the Plan of Iguala. A week later a junta at Campeche, Yucatan, declared that province to be independent of Spain; and at the same time it expressed a hope that the system of independence embodied in the treaty of Córdoba was not contrary to civil liberty. On September 15 the members of a junta convoked by Gavino Gainza, the captain general of Guatemala, in Guatemala City, declared in favor of independence from Spain. On September 28 in Comayagua, the capital of the province of Honduras, a junta declared that province to be independent alike of Spain and of Guatemala. In the same month similar action was taken in the province of Nicaragua. On December 27, 1821, Agustín I. ordered Vicente Filisola to take command of a military expedition, which, "in accordance with the Plan of Iguala," was to protect the provinces of the captaincy general of Guatemala. After Filisola marched for Guatemala, the provinces of Salvador and Costa Rica also decided in favor of independence from Spain and union with Mexico. On September 5, 1822, orders were sent out from Mexico City to the effect that Agustín I. should be proclaimed emperor in the principal towns of Guatemala, according to the ceremony which had been used in proclaiming the Spanish monarchs. Agustín I. thus became the titular ruler over an immense empire. In 1822 his dominions included the former viceroyalty of New Spain and almost all of the former captaincy general of Guatemala, or Central America. At its greatest extent the first Mexican empire stretched from "Great Colombia"—which had just been founded by Simón de Bolívar—to the forty-second parallel of north latitude, the southwestern boundary of the United States of North America.

Joel R. Poinsett of South Carolina, who was sent to Mexico by President Monroe to investigate conditions in that empire, thus described Emperor Agustín I:

I was presented to His Majesty this morning. On alighting at the gate of the palace, which is an extensive and handsome building, we were received by a numerous guard, and then made our way up a large stone staircase, lined with sentinels, to a spacious apartment, where we found a brigadier general stationed to usher us into the presence. The emperor was in his cabinet and received us with great politeness. Two of his favorites were with him. We were all seated, and he conversed with us for half an hour in an easy unembarrassed manner, taking occasion to compliment the United States, and our institutions, and to lament that they were not suited to the circumstances of his country. He modestly insinuated that he had yielded very reluctantly to the wishes of the people, but had been compelled to suffer them to place the crown upon his head to prevent misrule and anarchy.

He is about five feet ten or eleven inches high, stoutly made and well proportioned. His face is oval, and his features are very good except his eyes, which were constantly bent on the ground or averted. His hair is brown with red whiskers, and his complexion fair and ruddy, more like that of a German than of a Spaniard. . . . I will not repeat the tales I hear daily of the character and conduct of this man. . . . In the interval between the defeat of the patriot cause and the last revolution, he resided in the capital, and in a society not remarkable for strict morals, he was distinguished for his immorality. His usurpation of the chief authority has been the most glaring, and unjustifiable; and his exercise of power arbitrary and tyrannical. With a pleasing address and a prepossessing exterior, and by lavish profusion, he has attached the officers and soldiers to his person, and so long as he possesses the means of paying and rewarding them, so long will he maintain himself on the throne; when these fail he will be precipitated from it. It is a maxim of history, which will probably be again illustrated by this example, that a government not founded on public opinion, but established and supported by corruption and violence, cannot exist without ample means to pay the soldiery, and to maintain pensioners and partisans. Aware of the state of his funds, and of the probable consequence to himself of their failure, he is making great exertions to negotiate loans in England; and such is the infatuation of the monied men in that country, that it is possible he may effect his object. The conditions of a loan have been agreed upon, and an agent has lately gone to London—another is preparing to set out for the same destination with all the pomp of an embassy—and the professors of Botany and Mineralogy told me with great dismay yesterday, that they had received orders from his Majesty to prepare collections to be sent to England. . . .

To judge Iturbide from his public papers, I do not think him a man of talents. He is prompt, bold and decisive, and not scrupulous about the means he employs to obtain his ends.

After Iturbide had been crowned emperor of Mexico, he no longer dreamed of inviting a European prince to occupy the throne of the new state. It is evident, however, that he still hoped to make an amicable arrangement with the motherland. The policy which he wished to follow is suggested in an official memorandum concerning the choice of an envoy to the court of Madrid. The memorandum declared that Mexico was anxious to establish friendly relations with Spain and desired to enter into an offensive and defensive alliance with her. Nevertheless, Mexico considered as an indispensable preliminary to all negotiations, the acknowledgment of her independence from Spain and the recognition of Agustín I. as her legitimate emperor. About the time that this memorandum was written, the liberal government of Spain sent two commissioners to New Spain to enter into negoitiations for the pacification of that country. Spain's commissioners informed the Mexicans that they were empowered to terminate the dissensions between Old Spain and New Spain by frank and amicable negotiations. The Mexican empire selected commissioners to negotiate cautiously with the Spanish agents. Those commissioners were instructed not to agree to a treaty with the Spaniards until the absolute independence of the Mexican empire from Spain was recognized. However, the negotiations for a treaty of peace between imperial Mexico and liberal Spain came to an end when the emperor abdicated.

No attempt will be made here to consider in detail the

events which precipitated the downfall of Agustín I. Let it suffice to say that republicans and Bourbonists alike opposed his policies. Congress became the focus of opposition to his domination. Hence, by an imperial decree dated October 30, 1822, the emperor dissolved congress, having already incarcerated some leaders of the opposition. To replace congress the emperor invited certain congressmen to serve as members of a junta. That body tried to improve the finances by authorizing forced loans and by issuing paper money. These measures increased the discontent with imperial rule. At Vera Cruz on December 2, 1822, Santa Anna issued a *pronunciamiento* against the government. Soon afterwards General Guadeloupe Victoria joined him. While in southern Mexico, Bravo and Guerrero supported the anti-imperialistic movement. Agustín I. sent a detachment of soldiers under General Echávarri against Santa Anna, but the imperial commander failed to crush the insurrection. Instead Echávarri ultimately joined hands with Santa Anna and agreed to support the Plan of Casa Mata. This plan, signed at Casa Mata on February 1, 1823, was a proclamation by a group of military officers against the autocratic rule of Agustín I. and in favor of representative government. In a short time the plan found adherents in many parts of Mexico. Iturbide strove in vain to reach an adjustment with the leaders of the republican movement. In his memoirs he said:

I repeatedly solicited a private interview with the principal dissenting chiefs, without being able to obtain anything more than one answer in a private note from Echávarri. . . . The events which occurred at Casa Mata untied the republican and the Bourbon parties, who never could agree but for the purpose of opposing me. It was as well, therefore, that they should take off the mask as soon as possible, and make themselves known, which could not have happened if I had not given up my power. I re-assembled the Congress, I abdicated the crown, and I requested permission, through the minister of relations, to exile myself from my native country.

I surrendered my power, because I was already free from the obligations which irresistibly compelled me to accept it. The country did not want my services against foreign enemies, because at that time it had none. As to her domestic foes, far from being useful in resisting them, my presence might have proved rather prejudicial than otherwise because it might have been used as a pretext for saying that war was made against my ambition, and it might have furnished the parties with a motive for prolonging the concealment of their political hypocrisy. I did not abdicate from a sense of fear; I know all my enemies, and what they are able to do.

In a letter to congress abdicating the imperial dignity, on March 19, 1823, Iturbide declared that, as he wished to prevent his name from being made a pretext for civil war, he was willing to expatriate himself. After some debate, on April 7, 1823, congress passed a decree announcing that, as the coronation of Iturbide was the work of violence, that action was therefore null and void. The laws which congress had passed regarding the succession to the throne, as well as all acts of the empire from May 19, 1822, to March 29, 1823, were declared null. Further, congress made provision for the transportation of the ex-emperor from Mexico: it voted a pension of twenty-five thousand pesos annually to Iturbide, on the express condition that he should reside in Italy. On April 8 congress passed another decree announcing that the provisions of the Plan of Iguala and the treaty of Córdoba were null and void in so far as they made arrangements for a governmental system, but declaring that the other stipulations of the Plan of Iguala which concerned religion, independence, and union were still valid. On April 16 it decreed that anyone who might call Iturbide emperor of Mexico should be considered a traitor. It also provided that in all governmental offices the word imperial should be replaced by the word national. Lastly, on May 31, congress issued a decree providing that delegates should be chosen to a constituent congress which was to frame a federal republican government for Mexico. In the meantime a provisional government was established composed of three persons, known as the executive power.

On May 11, 1823, the ex-emperor, with his family, accompanied by a few loyal friends and dependents, sailed from Mexico on the English vessel *Rawlins* for Italy. In a country house near Leghorn Iturbide lived a quiet and secluded life for a few months. Meanwhile, an army sent into Spain by France, acting as the informal agent of that mysterious association of European powers known as the Holy Alliance, overturned the liberal government and restored Ferdinand VII. to the plenitude of his power. A short time after the restoration of the absolute king, apparently because of a dread that the Holy Alliance was intriguing against him, Iturbide decided to leave Italy. In December, 1823, he traveled hastily across the continent to Ostend, where he took ship for England. Early in January, 1824, the ex-emperor reached London. In that city a secret agent of the Mexican government spied upon the exile's movements and sent reports to Mexico in regard to his supposed designs. While in England Iturbide evidently received letters from misguided adherents in his native land urging him to return. On February 13, 1824, he sent a memorial to the constituent congress of Mexico offering to place his sword at its disposal: congress replied to his overture on April 28, 1824, by a decree announcing that, if the ex-emperor dared to set his foot on Mexican soil, he was to be considered a traitor and an outlaw. Without any knowledge of the decree of death, on May 11, 1824, Iturbide, accompanied by his wife, his two youngest children, a few servants, a printer, two faithful friends, and two priests, left England on the vessel *Spring* bound for America.

Why did the proscribed man thus return to his native land? An address written while on shipboard suggests his motives. In this paper Iturbide expressed a fear that Spain, with the aid of the Holy Alliance, was conspiring to re-conquer Mexico. He also expressed a hope that he might be able to act as a mediator between dissenting factions. "My sole object," said Iturbide, "is to contribute by my voice and by my pen to the support of the liberty and the independence of Mexico."

On July 12, 1824, the *Spring* cast anchor near Soto la Marina in the province of Tamaulipas. Three days later, with one companion, the ex-emperor landed near that town incognito. He was soon recognized, however, and detained by General Felipe de la Garza, the military commander of the district. That commander submitted Iturbide's case to the judgment of the legislature of Tamauipas which was assembled at Padilla. The legislature ordered that the decree of the national congress dated April 28 should be enforced immediately. At the request of the condemned man, his execution was postponed for a short time in order that he might prepare to die like a Christian. After he had confessed his sins, heard mass, and made his will, Iturbide was shot at Padilla, on July 19, 1824. He seems to have met his fate with the fortitude becoming a soldier who had so often faced death upon the battle-field. According to a comrade who was present at the execution, Iturbide objected to an attempt to bandage his eyes, but when told that this was necessary "the ex-emperor drew forth his handkerchief and bound it on *with his own hands;* this done he knelt down, and having received two balls in his forehead, and two in his breast, fell dead. They instantly removed the corpse and deposited it in a chapel for the pupose of interring it the ensuing day. It was then buried with all the propriety and solemnity which could have been expected in a small inland town; the Legislature and all the public authorities followed his remains to the grave and assisted in consigning the *Liberator of Mexico* to his last abode."

In his last words Iturbide evidently denied that he was a traitor to Mexico and declared that he forgave his enemies. Unfortunately for the student of history, after the execution of Iturbide many of the papers which he had brought with him were burned by the Mexicans. But among Iturbide's posthumous papers there is found a memorial addressed to the Mexican congress which serves as his apology.

I asked if it was a crime to form the Plan of Iguala and to organize the army of the three guarantees which rapidly transformed the country from a state of serfdom to that of independence. I asked if it was a crime to have established the constitutional system in Mexico and to have assembled a congress which gave her laws suitable to her own wishes and convenience. I asked if it was a crime to have twice destroyed the plans which were formed after the year 1821 to elevate me to the position of a king. I asked if having accepted the crown when I was not able to avoid doing so, thus making a great sacrifice to liberate Mexico from the threat of anarchy, constituted a crime. I asked if it was a crime not to have given offices to my nearest relatives or to have augmented their fortunes. . . . I asked if it was a crime that, when the nation had scarcely indicated through two or three provincial deputations and a part of the army the desire for a new government, I voluntarily relinquished the crown which I had been compelled to accept. . . . I asked if it was a crime to leave my honorable, virtuous, and venerable father in need and to depart from Mexico with my wife and eight children for a country two thousand leagues distant where it was very probable that I would have to beg a livelihood. . . . I asked if it was a crime for me to risk the threats of the

Holy Alliance and to prepare to return to my country when that alliance was conspiring against her. . . . I beseech your Highness not to consider me as an enemy, but as the truest lover of his native land.

Although the apprehensions of Iturbide concerning the designs of the Holy Alliance upon Mexico appear to have been almost without foundation, yet similar sentiments were entertained by many American contemporaries.

When on September 30, 1824, the *Gaceta de Madrid* published the news of the execution at Padilla, it not inappropriately said that upon Iturbide the attention of both worlds was focused. Among the prominent leaders of the revolution in Spanish America, just one man, Agustín Iturbide, was granted not only the office of chief magistrate by the nation which he had founded, but also the ephemeral dignity of a crowned monarch. Far from blameless in his private life, extravagant and despotic as emperor, yet the martyr of Padilla had played the most important rôle in the protracted drama of the Mexican revolution. From the standpoint of Mexican independence, Iturbide's part as emperor of Mexico shrinks in contrast with his majestic rôle as liberator. When the revolt against Spain in Mexico had reached a critical stage, Iturbide seemed to essay the part of a pacificator. This rôle culminated in a movement which severed forever the political bonds that had united Mexico to Spain. It is indeed one of the riddles of Mexican history that an illiterate military commander should have proclaimed a plan which so readily won the support of the discordant and belligerent classes—a plan that laid the foundations for a new order in Mexico. Thus did Iturbide bear to triumph the banner which Hidalgo had raised. In singular contrast with the treatment which the Mexican people have graciously accorded to Hidalgo, they have been peculiarly ungrateful to Colonel Iturbide, who rightly deserves the title of liberator of Mexico. It is significant that Iturbide's plan for the independence of Mexico from Spain unwittingly resembled a design for the liberation of Peru which, as will be shown in chapter six, was cherished by José de San Martín.

While Iturbide was pining in exile, the state which had been liberated by his sagacious plan had broken into two parts. On July 1, 1823, a congress of delegates summoned by General Filisola from Guatemalan provinces proclaimed the independence of the United Provinces of Central America. In the following year a constituent assembly adopted a constitution for these provinces which, in some respects, was modeled upon the Constitution of the United States. The confederation of Central America, which stretched from Mexico to the Isthmus of Panama, did not include all the territory which had been under the control of Captain General Gainza, for the province of Chiapas remained a part of Mexico. Consequently, even after the secession of Central America, the state of Mexico extended south beyond the boundary of the former viceroyalty of New Spain, while on the north its boundary remained as under Agustín I. About three months after the death of Iturbide, on October 4, 1824, the constituent congress of Mexico promulgated a constitution for the Mexican republic,—a constitution which, in some particulars, was patterned after the Constitution of the United States. The constitution of the "United Mexican States" provided for a government which was to be republican, democratic, and federal. A short time afterwards, Generals Bravo, Negrete, and Victoria, who had composed the executive power, relinquished their authority, and General Guadeloupe Victoria was inaugurated as the first president of the Mexican republic.

On July 19, 1823, the congress of Mexico decreed that Hidalgo, Allende, Aldama, Jiménez, Morelos, and other revolutionary leaders were *beneméritos de la patria* and provided that their remains were to be transferred to Mexico City. There, on September 17, 1823, their bones were solemnly deposited in a crypt of the great cathedral. In 1838 the remains of Iturbide were likewise transferred to the capital city and interred in a chapel of the same cathedral. The mortal remains of the greatest leaders of the revolutionary period in Mexico thus at last reposed together within the city which had witnessed so many scenes in the strange pageant of Mexican history.

Chapter 5

Mariano Moreno

THE NAME at the head of the chapter is not familiar to English readers. Of the seven worthies who are sketched in this book, Mariano Moreno is probably the least known. But his meteoric career furnishes a good illustration of the course of the early revolutionary movement against Spain in southern South America. On the eve of the revolution the fair viceroyalty of la Plata, which was composed of eight provinces, stretched from the viceroyalty of Peru to Cape Horn. The most important of these districts was the littoral province of Buenos Aires. The capital of that province, as well as of the viceroyalty, was the city of Buenos Aires. That metropolis was the heart of the viceroyalty: it was an economic center of southern South America, for much foreign commerce passed through its custom-house; it was also the political focus of the viceroyalty, for there was the residence of the viceroy and the chief intendant.

In the latter half of the eighteenth century an enterprising Spaniard called Manuel Moreno, a native of Santander, sailed from Cadiz for South America. After arriving in the viceroyalty of la Plata, he secured a position in the royal service in the capital city. There he married María Valle, a native of Buenos Aires. From that union there sprang a number of children: the first-born child is the subject of this study. At present the chief source of our information concerning the early life of Mariano Moreno is a biography written by his brother, Manuel. According to that biography, Mariano was born in the city of Buenos Aires on September 23, 1778. His education was begun at home, and, as his father was in moderate circumstances, it was continued in the best schools of Buenos Aires. Manuel Moreno declared that his eldest brother became so fond of books that his father prohibited him from reading them after the family had retired to rest. It appears that Mariano gained some distinction in the study of Latin, theology, and philosophy in the local College of San Carlos. An estimable friar became so much interested

141

in the studious youth that he allowed him to browse in the library of the Franciscan monastery.

Mariano's worthy parents wished to consecrate their eldest son to the service of the altar. In 1799, encouraged by a priest from Upper Peru who was sojourning in Buenos Aires, Mariano Moreno made a toilsome journey to Chuquisaca where he entered the University of San Francisco Javier, a center of legal and theological study in South America. At that university one of his favorite studies was theology. Manuel Moreno declared that Mariano was granted the degree of doctor of theology by that institution. Whlie attending the University of San Francisco Javier the earnest student won the friendship of Canon Terrazas, a prominent ecclesiastic, who gave him access to his library. As prohibited books sometimes found their way to Chuquisaca, Mariano Moreno extended his knowledge of foreign authors: he read the works of Montesquieu, Raynal, and other celebrated writers of France.

For some reason or other, Mariano Moreno discarded the design of becoming a priest. Instead he undertook the study of law. According to his brother's story, two years after completing a course of study in theology, Mariano was granted the degree of bachelor of law. Certain it is that in 1802, as a candidate for a degree in law, he presented to the Carolinian academy of Chuquisaca—an institution which appears to have been affiliated with the University of San Francisco Javier—a dissertation which explained and interpreted a mediæval Spanish law that contained provisions concerning the disposition of the property of a woman who married more than once. After completing his preparation for the legal profession, Mariano Moreno began to practice law in the city of Chuquisaca. The ambitious young advocate evidently continued to extend his knowledge of men and books; when describing that period of his brother's career, Manual Moreno said:

Never would he have been contented with the humble studies of an ordinary advocate. A presentiment that his native land would some day employ him in important affairs coupled with a noble ambition to gain celebrity, caused him to study with the greatest care oratory, politics, history, and geography. Because of the situation and the relations of its master, the house in which Mariano lived became the resort of society and the center of affairs for the people of Upper Peru. These circumstances served to give him a singular dexterity in the management of affairs and an exact knowledge of the human heart. His observations were indeed so exact and so penetrating, that seldom did he fail rightly to judge men and to divine their interests or their passions. This ability helped to promote his success in the courts of justice and in the position of magistrate with which he was subsequently entrusted.

As this statement was written after Mariano Moreno had achieved fame, it must be considered with a grain of salt. His brother also declared that the zeal of the eloquent advocate in the cause of justice soon provoked such powerful enemies that Mariano decided to leave Chuquisaca. In the latter part of 1805, Mariano Moreno returned to his native province. There his genuine ability was soon recognized, for he was appointed legal counselor of the royal *audiencia* at Buenos Aires. While he was serving in that capacity the viceroyalty of la Plata was attacked by Beresford's soldiers. In a patriotic memoir Moreno declared that he "wept more than anyone else" when English redcoats were quartered in the fortress and throughout his native city. Manuel Moreno assures us that as an adviser of the *cabildo* of that city his brother inspired some of the acts which had their fruition in the defeat of General Whitelocke.

In the second and third chapters the influence of Napoleon's usurpations in Spain upon Venezuela and Mexico was discussed; in this chapter the influence of those usurpations upon the Spanish colonists in southern South America must be considered. To the viceroyalty of la Plata Napoleon sent the Marquis de Sassenay as agent. On his arrival in the city of Buenos Aires the emissary was publicly informed by De Liniers that the colonists desired no other ruler than Ferdinand VII. When news of the startling changes in Spain became known in that city, the populace was agitated, many people loudly professed their loyalty to Ferdinand VII., and substantial contributions were made to the cause of the Spanish patriots. Nevertheless in Buenos Aires, as in Caracas, there were some alert colonists who thought that the accession of a new dynasty to the Spanish throne had radically altered the relations between Spain and her colonies. In the viceroyalty of la Plata discontent with the existing régime was also stimulated by the proceedings of Carlota Joaquina. In the latter part of 1808, there was circulated in South America a proclamation of Carlota Joaquina asserting that she was the presumptive heir to the throne of Spain and the Indies. A group of conspirators was soon formed in the Platean viceroyalty who seemed to support Carlota's pretensions. Among the members of the secret coterie were Manuel Belgrano, a young lawyer of Italian descent who had been educated in Spain, his friend Juan José Castelli, who belonged to the same profession, Nicolás Rodríguez Peña, a merchant of Buenos Aires, and Juan Hipolito Víeytes, a friend of Peña who was a manufacturer of soap. It is significant that several leaders who in 1808 seemed to favor the establishment at Buenos Aires of a monarchy ruled by a scion of the Bourbon dynasty at a later time advocated the separation of the viceroyalty of la Plata from Spain.

At this critical juncture, to replace the valiant De Liniers as viceroy of la Plata the central junta selected Baltasar Hidalgo de Cisneros, lieutenant general of the Spanish navy. The new viceroy reached the banks of la Plata in July, 1809. The economic condition of the viceroyalty was deplorable; for the Spanish colonial system, as it had existed before the English invasion, had been restored. In general commerce and agriculture were languishing, while illegal trade was flourishing, and the royal treasury was being cheated of its revenues. Consequently many colonists clamored that the ports of the viceroyalty should again be opened to English commerce regularly. When he became acquainted with economic conditions, Viceroy Cisneros favored a reform in the tariff regulations. On September 30, 1809, a memorial on behalf of the discontented landowners of la Plata basin was presented to the viceroy by their advocate, José de la Rosa:—after the uprising of 1810 the real author of this *Representación* became known; for its was published in Buenos Aires with the statement that it had been written by Mariano Moreno.

Some excerpts from this memorial will indicate the economic condition of the fertile viceroyalty of la Plata. Moreno declared that when Cisneros became viceroy the treasury was so depleted that proper measures for the defence of the viceroyalty could not be taken.

In this sad plight there is no other remedy than to grant English merchants permission to introduce their goods into the city of Buenos Aires and to export the products of the country. Thus the revenues accruing to the treasury will be immediately increased from the duties upon this double exchange, and an impulse will be given to our declining trade. . . . Since the English expedition appeared on our coasts in 1806, the merchants of that country have not lost sight of the Río de la Plata in their speculations. A continuous series of commercial adventures have been carried on which have provided almost entirely for the consumption of this country. Large importations made in defiance of the law and in spite of repeated prohibitions have met with no other obstacles than those necessary to deprive the treasury of customs duties and to rob the country of the advantages that it might have received from the exportations which would result from a free exchange.

The effect of this system has been to allow the English the exclusive privilege of providing the country with all the merchandise that it requires, while the treasury has lost the revenues which the importation of such a large amount of merchandise and the consequent exportations should have produced, because of a scrupulous regard for laws that were never more flagrantly disregarded than at the very time when their observance was insisted upon by the merchants of the capital. Sir! what can be more ridiculous than to hear a merchant clamoring for the enforcement of the laws which prohibit the introduction of foreign merchandise at the door of a shop that is filled with English goods imported clandestinely?

To the gain which the government will derive from the lawful introduction of foreign goods should be added those advantages which the country will receive from the free exportation of its products. Fortunately the products of this province are all valuable; their yield is constant; and most of them are today necessities. With what rapidity would our agriculture progress, if the ports were opened for the exportation of our products, so that the farmer could count with security upon a lucrative sale.

Moreno denounced the monopoly of colonial commerce which had been enjoyed by the merchants of Cadiz. He declared that events in Spain had "destroyed all the pretexts which supported the prohibitory laws." To meet an argument of Miguel de Agüero, the representative of the consulate of Cadiz, to the effect that to legalize trade with the English would loosen the bonds which united the Platean provinces to

Spain, Moreno praised "the loyalty of the Spanish-Americans, declaring that Spain had never needed "any other guarantee for the security and preservation" of those provinces. He declared that the repulse of the English attacks upon the viceroyalty should make the colonists "the envy of the Spanish people"; for the English still viewed "with respect the victors of July 5," while the Spaniards would not soon forget that the people of la Plata had defended "the land in which they were born, shedding their blood for a régime which they loved and venerated." Moreno also presented an argument drawn from the writings of the Italian publicist, Gaetano Filangieri, to the effect that a dependent rôle became unendurable to colonies only when it meant misery and oppression, the Roman colonies being cited as an example. He quoted Filangieri approvingly as follows: "The same reasoning could be applied to modern colonies. Happy under the rule of their mother, they would not dare to throw on a light and easy yoke in order to see an independence which would deprive them of the protection of their mother without assuring them of the power to defend themselves against the ambition of a conqueror, or the intrigues of a powerful citizen, or the perils of anarchy. It was not an excess of riches and prosperity which made the English colonies revolt: excessive oppression caused them to turn against their mother those very arms which they had so often employed in her defense."

In this argument there may indeed be found a subtle suggestion that in the viceroyalty of la Plata a revolutionary spirit was being stimulated by economic discontent. Still, it requires a lively imagination to liken Mariano Moreno's *Representación* to Thomas Paine's "Common Sense." In fine, the lengthy and important memorial which Moreno prepared for Viceroy Cisneros declared that commerce with English merchants should be allowed by law; that such a reform would destroy the commercial monopoly which had been enjoyed by the merchants of Cadiz; that it would relieve the misery of the inhabitants of the pampas; that it would stimulate agriculture and commerce; that the revenues accruing from the import and export duties would replenish the depleted colonial treasury; and that Spain could then be given substantial aid in her critical struggle with Napoleon. To suppose that Moreno argued for free trade in the ordinary sense is to misinterpret his plea; what he sought was such freedom of trade as would permit the inhabitants to obtain English goods legally, and as would permit them to export the produce of their fertile plains. Whether or not Moreno's memorial had much influence upon the viceregal government, it is clear that, acting upon the advice of a junta, early in November the viceroy issued a decree which provided that vessels of friendly or neutral powers laden with products of their respective countries might be admitted into the port of Buenos Aires according to special regulations. But despite the assurances of colonial loyalty which Moreno voiced in his argument for freer trade, it is evident that when this reform was actually made the loyalty of some prominent citizens of Buenos Aires declined.

As suggested in the second chapter, the increasing disaffection in Spanish America was partly due to the policies adopted by the changeling governments of Spain. The disaffection in Buenos Aires was not diminished by the temporizing policy of Viceroy Cisneros. On May 15, 1810, he published a proclamation which was addressed to "the loyal and generous citizens" of his viceroyalty. In that proclamation Cisneros spread broadcast the recent and startling news from Spain: he declared that French soldiers had swept over Andalusia, and that they were approaching Cadiz where the central junta had taken refuge. Foolishly did the viceroy vaunt that even though the peninsular Spaniards should lose their liberty, still France could not enslave the entire Spanish nation. He boasted that "within the confines of the American continent the liberty and independence of the Spanish monarchy would be preserved." He even announced that if the central junta should be subverted by French Soldiers, he would take no measures which were not approved by a representative assembly of the citizens of Buenos Aires. This indiscreet proclamation furnished tinder for the revolutionary fires which were smouldering within the capital city.

The organ of the discontented citizens of Buenos Aires was the *cabildo*. On May 21 it asked the viceroy for permission to summon a *cabildo abierto* which might voice the popular will. With some reluctance Cisneros granted its request. Prominent citizens, both clergy and laity, were accordingly summoned to meet with the *cabildo* to consider political affairs. On May 22 those citizens met as an open council in the hall of the *cabildo*. There many different views with regard to the proper course of action were expressed. Some citizens proposed that Cisneros should be left in command but that two military officers should be selected to aid him in the government. Colonel Saavedra proposed that the viceroy's powers should be temporarily assumed by the *cabildo*. Among those citizens who supported Saavedra's proposal were Mariano Moreno, Manuel Belgrano, Juan José Castelli, and Bernardino Rivadavia, a talented leader of Italian descent. After an exciting debate, the *cabildo abierto* voted that the *cabildo* itself should decide what action should be taken concerning the government. Whereupon the *cabildo* voted that the viceregal authority should be temporarily vested in itself. Perhaps that council was trying to steer a middle course; for Cisneros was soon made the president of a provisional junta, installed on May 24, which was declared to be the repository of governmental authority.

It was probably the discontent of the people, as well as the machinations of conspirators, which induced the *cabildo* again to promote the insurrection. For that council soon formed a new junta composed of nine members from which the deposed viceroy was excluded. Both Castelli and Belgrano became members of this junta. Saavedra was made its president, while Juan José Paso, a graduate of the University of Córdoba, and Mariano Moreno became its secretaries. On May 25, 1810, on bended knees, the members of the new junta solemnly swore to preserve the integrity of the provinces of la Plata River for their beloved sovereign, Ferdinand VII. Salvos from English vessels celebrated the junta's inauguration. This kaleidoscopic scene was a revolution in disguise. In reality the establishment of the provisional junta of May 25 was a step towards the formation of an independent government. When describing the choice of Mariano Moreno as a secretary of the junta, Manuel Moreno ascribed the following remarks to his brother:

I know the perils which a magistrate will have to overcome in order to manage affairs during such a critical period. The present change should not end with the displacement of viceregal officials and the imitation of their corruption and indolence. The new government must destroy administrative abuses, display an unprecedented activity, remedy the evils which afflict the state, stimulate and direct public spirit, educate the people, destroy their enemies, and give new life to the provinces. If the government evades this task, it will follow in the footsteps of its predecessors, sanctioning confusion and corruption in the execution of the important functions which have been entrusted to it. Accordingly to avoid the obstacles with which despotism, venality, and prejudice have for centuries prevented the happiness of this continent, the government will have to pursue an untrodden path. After the new government shall have escaped the attacks to which it will be exposed simply because it is new, it will have to encounter attacks due to the passions, the interests, and even the inconstancy of those persons who now promote the reform. A just man who is in charge of such a government will become the victim of ignorance or of jealousy. The tranquillity which I have heretofore enjoyed in the midst of my family and my books will be interrupted. But none of these apprehensions will deter me in the least, if the people invite me to take a part in the administration of their affairs. If I am needed, I cannot deny my country the sacrifice of my tranquillity, my profession, my fortune, and even my life.

The junta of Buenos Aires, which was installed on May 25, 1810, generally styled itself "the provisional junta of the provinces of la Plata River." It soon issued a circular letter which announced the creation of the junta and invited the people of the interior provinces of the viceroyalty to select deputies to represent them at Buenos Aires. The members of the *cabildo,* as well as many viceregal officials and military officers, took an oath to obey the junta. Soon afterwards the junta formed certain rules to regulate its own organization. It entrusted the administration of the government to two departments which were placed under the control of the secretaries. Paso was given charge of financial affairs, while Moreno was placed in charge of military and political affairs. Provision was made that in important affairs the junta, or a part of it, was to take action; in minor matters, the president of the junta and a secretary were authorized to act. It also provided that its president should be addressed as his excellency and otherwise accorded the same honors as the former viceroy. The junta soon began to exercise executive and legislative functions: it made ecclesiastical appointments, provided for the reorganization of the military forces, and replaced the royal governors of interior provinces by governors of its own selection. The junta also issued decrees which reduced the duties on imports and exports and aimed to prevent smuggling. Further, the junta prudently arranged that the viceroy and the *audiencia* should be deported on a vessel sailing for the Canary Islands.

Although Mariano Moreno apparently accepted the position of secretary of the junta with considerable reluctance, yet he performed the duties of that office with zeal and energy. Being allowed a vote and a voice in the meetings of the junta, he exercised a potent influence in its deliberations. His facile pen was probably employed to draft some of its most important decrees. On June 2, 1810, a decree was issued, signed only by Moreno, which founded the *Gaceta de Buenos Aires*. That decree expressed the opinion that the provisional government should furnish the people with a knowledge of public affairs. It declared that the junta had decided to issue from the press "a new weekly periodical with the title of the *Gaceta de Buenos Aires,* which would furnish the people with the foreign and domestic news which they ought to consider of interest." It stated that the *Gaceta* would publish information concerning the foreign relations of the junta, the condition of the treasury, and measures for the improvement of the finances. It expressed the hope that this journal might serve as an organ for the expression of the views of private individuals on matters of common welfare.

The first number of the *Gaceta de Buenos Aires* was published on June 7, 1810. Of that journal Mariano Moreno became the editor. The *Gaceta* spread the news of important events throughout the provinces of la Plata, and became the junta's mouthpiece. While under Moreno's direction, the gazette contained such items as the following: communications from citizens of Buenos Aires, lists of persons who made voluntary contributions to the support of its junta, decrees of the junta, orders of the Spanish regency, articles respecting the French invasion of Spain, documents concerning the revolts in Spanish America, and extracts from newspapers of Europe and North America. A phrase of Tacitus, which was adopted as a motto for the gazette, served as a program: *Rara temporum felicitate, ubi sentire quae velis, et quae sentias, dicere licet.* Some of the political articles which appeared in the gazette were doubtless written by the editor himself. He contributed a noteworthy article to the *Gaceta* on June 21, 1810, concerning freedom of thought.

In this article Moreno pointed out that in all ages men had been misled by erroneous conceptions and "shameful prepossessions." He declared that it was a worthy occupation for a writer to attack such prepossessions publicly and pitilessly; for if liberty of speech were not permitted in all matters which did not prejudice the Roman Catholic religion or the policies of the government, the people would continue to chreish errors and would remain in "a shameful state of stupefaction." He asked the people to discard their "antiquated opinions," for otherwise there could be "no advance in the arts or in useful knowledge." He urged them freely to allow the introduction of truth and light and learning. "Truth, as well as virtue, contains within itself the most convincing apology; discussion and examination cause their splendor and luster to become fully apparent. If restrictions are placed upon speech, the spirit of man will vegetate as does matter: error, falsehood, prejudice, fanaticism, and stupefaction will become the devices of the people, and will cause their perpetual decadence, ruin, and misery."

Thus Moreno became the champion of free speech in certain political matters. In the *Gaceta* be bewailed the decadent condition of education at Buenos Aires. He eulogized the famous libraries of antiquity. About the middle of September, when the junta decided to establish a public library at Buenos Aires, the editor of the gazette was selected to be "the protector" of the library, that is to say, the director. Evidently it was at the request of Moreno that popular subscriptions were made for this library and that books were collected from individuals, colleges, and religious establishments. Accordingly Mariano Moreno may be designated as the founder of the national library of Argentina. That alert scholar also promoted the establishment of an academy of mathematics which was placed in charge of his colleague in the junta, Manuel Belgrano. So strong an influence did Moreno exert upon the policy of the junta, that its educational, commercial, fiscal, and military policies have often been indiscriminately ascribed to him. In truth, the matters directly under control of Secretary Moreno were political affairs and war. To him there evidently belonged a large share of the responsibility for the execution of De Liniers, who had placed himself at the head of an unsuccessful counter-revolution in the province of Córdoba. Moreno evidently opposed the recognition of the council of regency by the junta of Buenos Aires. This repudiation of the patriot government of Spain led that junta farther along the thorny path toward independence.

The provisional government of Buenos Aires—which professed to rule on behalf of Ferdinand VII.—not only repudiated the authority of the patriot government of Spain, but also attempted to extend its authority over important provinces of the former viceroyalty of la Plata. To Paraguay and to *la Banda Oriental*—the region lying between the Uruguay River, Brazil, and the Atlantic Ocean—it sent letters inviting the people to join the movement initiated by the capital city. It sent commissioners to Asunción and Montevideo who were instructed to convert those cities to the cause of Buenos Aires. But these measures were in vain; and hence the junta soon felt compelled to take drastic action. Subscriptions were gathered for the equipment of an expedition to the interior provinces. At the head of the list of contributors published in the gazette on June 21, 1810, was the name of Mariano Moreno, who had donated six ounces of gold. Early in August, 1810, the junta issued a decree which severed communications between Buenos Aires and Paraguay, where Governor Velazco had announced his fidelity to the council of regency. In September, 1810, Manuel Belgrano was given charge of a small military force, which was sent to spread in Paraguay the news of the revolution of May at Buenos Aires. Although in March, 1811, Belgrano's soldiers were checked by the Paraguayans, still his expedition fomented a seditious spirit in Paraguay. The junta of Buenos Aires also turned its attention to the Pacific coast; in November, 1810, it appointed Antonio Álvarez Jonte agent to a provisional government which, as will be shown later, had been established in Santiago de Chile. That emissary was instructed to solicit the coöperation of the Chilean junta to promote the "glorious system" which southern South America had adopted. Thus, at the very beginning of the movement which developed into a revolution, the junta of Buenos Aires tried to incite other parts of South America to separate from the motherland.

The efforts of the junta of Buenos Aires to disseminate information concerning the separatist movement were not confined to Spanish America. As early as May 28, 1810, it wrote to Lord Strangford, the influential English ambassador at Rio de Janeiro, to inform him of the creation of a new government at Buenos Aires. In response Lord Strangford declared that, as the junta had expressed its loyalty to Ferdinand VII., he would write to it with the same consideration as though it had been formally recognized by the English government. He advised the junta to shun all relations with the French. He urged it to preserve peace and concord, and assured it of the pacific intentions of the Portuguese court. He also expressed his willingness to aid the junta personally and promised to make a favorable report to the English government regarding its actions. In November, 1810, Strangford confidentially advised Moreno that the junta of Buenos Aires should preserve the fidelity which it had professed to the Spanish king and avoid "a premature declaration of independence"; for this would preclude amicable intervention by England in the dispute between Spain and her colonies. The English ambassador, however, dropped thinly veiled hints that he was not at heart opposed to the movement for the separation of Spanish America from Spain.

The correspondence between Moreno and Strangford suggests that the junta of Buenos Aires was confronted by perplexing diplomatic problems. Some audacious solutions of those problems were soon proposed to it. On July 15, 1810, Manuel Belgrano presented a scheme to the junta which proposed that it should revolutionize *la Banda Oriental* and the southern provinces of Brazil, while negotiating secretly with Spain, Portugal, and England. Further, he recommended that a committee should be selected to form a diplomatic program. After some discussion the junta evidently decided to select Mariano Moreno to formulate a foreign policy because his "vast knowledge and well-known talent" qualified him to execute the unique commission. With such secrecy did Moreno perform his duty that some doubts have been raised concerning the authorship of the plan, ascribed to him, which was completed by the end of August, 1810. Apparently that plan was first printed, in part, by a Spanish historian, who seems to have secured it from the Spanish archives. Subsequent investigators have not rediscovered the original manuscript; but among the papers of the archives of the Indies the writer found a list of inedited documents which at one time evidently reposed there: in this list was mentioned Moreno's "Plan of Operations which the Provisional Government of the United Provinces of the Rio de la Plata should Pursue to Consolidate the Great Work of Our Liberty and Independence." The ultra-republican spirit of this unique and elaborate plan of operations is suggested by the following excerpts:

Let me say here that at times accident is the mother of events; for, if a revolution is not directed aright, if intrigue and ambition destroy public spirit, then the state will relapse into the most horrible anarchy. My fatherland, what changes you may suffer! Where, Oh noble and grand Washington, are the lessons of your politics? Where are the rules which guided you in the construction of your great work? Your principles and your system would be sufficient to guide us:—lend us your genius so that we may accomplish the results which we have contemplated!

The foundations of a new republic have never been cemented unless rigor and punishment were mingled with the blood of all those citizens who might obstruct progress. . . . If a revolution is not directed aright, if intrigue, ambition, and egotism smother the spirit of patriotism; in a word, if the general welfare is subordinated to private interest, then the emancipation of a nation will produce all sorts of excesses, and will cause the upheaval of the social order. . . . Never will there be offered to South America a better opportunity than the present for the establishment of a republic upon the basis of moderation and virtue. The dynasty of the Bourbons has been brought to the ground; none of its cowardly friends came in time to lend it a hand: all that is now necessary is to let it lie and to forget it. . . . Why is liberty pictured to us as being blind and armed with a dagger? Because neither an aged state nor a province can be regenerated or purged of corrupt abuses without rivulets of blood being spilled. . . . Finally, let us give a most solemn character to our new edifice; let us look solely to our native land; and, when the constitution of the state secures to every person the legitimate enjoyment of the rights of true liberty in practice and in quiet possession, without the existence of abuses, then will an American state solve the true and great problem of the social contract.

The plan contained certain suggestions concerning the policy of the junta. Among these were the following proposals. The provisional government should observe a wise secrecy with respect to the management of its internal and external affairs. Adherents of the new order should be punished only for disloyalty to the sacred cause of liberty. Rewards should be provided for successful soldiers. Cruel and sanguinary measures should be used against the avowed enemies of independence. Trusty spies should be stationed throughout the country to watch suspicious characters. Foreigners should be given governmental offices according to their merits. Caste distinctions should be swept away. The importation of slaves should be prohibited. Those slaves who enlisted under the banner of liberty should be rewarded.

With regard to "the mystery of Ferdinand"—the plea of allegiance to Ferdinand VII.—the author intimated that in negotiations with foreign states the junta might advantageously use that plea to veil its real designs. He sketched a project for the revolutionizing of *la Banda Oriental*. His object was to subjugate Montevideo and to attract the inhabitants of the adjacent region with seductive proclamations of liberty, equality, and felicity. By such measures he hoped that *la Banda Oriental* might ultimately be incorporated into the Platean state. Toward Spain he proposed that a policy of dissimulation should be adopted. Memorials to the Spanish government should be drawn up by the *cabildos* of important towns and cities expressing their intention to preserve la Plata for "Ferdinand VII. and his successors." Those *cabildos* were to suggest that the corrupt viceregal government had designed to transfer the colony to France. They were to praise the provisional government for its energy in promoting art, agriculture, and industry. They were to affirm that succor would soon be furnished to Spain in the struggle against Napoleon. With these memorials, *mutatis mutandis,* should be sent similar representations from towns and villages. The object of the memorials was to mislead the peninsular Spaniards, while the people of Buenos Aires screened their real intentions.

Of greater interest were the proposals regarding the diplomatic relations of the junta with Portugal and England. The plan urged that a liberal policy should be followed towards those nations. Their commerce should be protected. Import duties on their goods should be reduced. They should be given preferential treatment. A secret plan should be presented to England which would point out the advantages that her merchants might derive from the Platean provinces. Portuguese intrigues in *la Banda Oriental* should be foiled by negotiations with the court of Rio de Janeiro. England should be induced to preserve a strict impartiality in the internecine struggles of Spanish America. She should be asked to make a public declaration that, under no circumstances, would she interfere in the political dissensions which might arise in the Spanish-American colonies, so long as these colonies demonstrated their hatred of Napoleon and their fidelity to Ferdinand VII. Agents of the junta were to plead that England should aid the cause of Platean independence by selling munitions secretly to Buenos Aires and by conveying the envoys of the junta oversea under the protection of her flag. These emissaries were to negotiate an offensive and defensive alliance between England and la Plata. To induce England to enter into such an alliance, she was to be offered the island of Martín García at the mouth of la Plata River. The upshot of the diplomacy was to be the isolation of Portugal from England and the absorption of Brazil by the Platean state.

Whether or not Mariano Moreno was the author of this plan, it discloses the thoughts of a leader of the Platean provinces at a stormy period. It reveals that by means of spies, intrigues, and subtle negotiations, the author aspired to found in the broad basin of la Plata River a state which would be absolutely independent of Spain. Draconian punishments were to be meted out to persons who obstructed the crusade for liberty and independence. The new state should include *la Banda Oriental;* it should annex Brazil. This ambitious and visionary project displays the ignorance, as well as the knowledge, of the author in regard to international politics. An alliance with England—which was pledged to maintain the integrity of the Spanish dominions in both hemispheres—was the pivot upon which the author made the policy of political independence and territorial expansion depend. The methods which the author of this plan proposed to use were Machiavellian and the state which he wished to create was to be the colossus of Hispanic America.

Moreno's thoughts concerning society and government were affected by various influences. For a Spanish-American of the early revolutionary period he was exceptionally well versed in the literature of foreign lands. Moreno was acquainted with Spanish writers on economic subjects: he praised the treatise of Gaspar Melchor de Jovellanos concerning an agrarian law. When arguing against the commercial policy of Spain in his memorial to Viceroy Cisneros, he quoted approvingly from Filangieri. The Argentine writer, Vicente F. López, declared in his history of Argentina that he had seen Moreno's suggestions for that memorial penciled upon the margins of the writings of Campillo, who was a disciple of Quesnay, the French physiocrat. To a considerable extent Moreno was influenced by the physiocratic school of political economy: he frequently argued that the prosperity of his native land depended upon the prosperity of agriculture.

Most of all was Mariano Moreno, "the soul of the revolution of 1810" at Buenos Aires, influenced by Jean Jacques Rousseau. Some time after the provisional government was established, Secretary Moreno edited a Spanish translation of *Le Contrat Social* which was published in his native city. In the introduction to this work Moreno said that among various books composing a precious collection that he wished to offer to his compatriots, he had given the first place to "The Social Contract." He characterized Rousseau as an "immortal man, the pride of his century,"—a man who had "placed in a clear light the rights of the people," who "taught them the true origin of their obligations, and showed them what were the corresponding obligations which the rulers contracted." He declared that Rousseau had taught the people "to seek in the social compact the root and only origin of obedience. . . . The study of this book should produce good results in all classes of readers. . . . Those persons who desire to improve themselves will find models to kindle their imagination and to rectify their judgment; those who wish to comprehend the basis of our society will find its true principles analyzed with simplicity. The citizen will learn what he owes to the magistrate; similarly, the magistrate will learn what may be required of him: all classes, all ages, all conditions, will share in the benefits which this immortal book brings to the world,—benefits which should secure for its author the just title of the legislator of nations. . . . Happy my country, if her sons know how to profit by such important lessons!"

The political ideas of Moreno were most clearly presented in a series of articles published in the editorial columns of the *Gaceta de Buenos Aires* from November 1 to December 6, 1810. In those articles he proposed that the citizens of the former viceroyalty should convoke a congress to consider certain political problems. In the gazette for November 6 he declared that the laws of the Indies—a collection of precepts which constituted a monument of their degradation—could not serve the Spanish-Americans in place of a constitution. He suggested that the proposed congress should frame a fundamental law. He spoke in favor of a division of powers in the projected government. Yet he praised the English government as a model for modern peoples. He intimated that the former viceroyalty of la Plata constituted a sovereign state. In an editorial on December 6, Moreno presented his views regarding a great Spanish-American state:

If we consider the diverse origin of the group of states which forms the Spanish monarchy, we cannot discover a single reason why they should remain united in the absence of the king, who was the bond of their unity. The laws of the Indies declared that America was a part or an appendage of the kingdom of Castile from which it could never be separated. I do not comprehend the legitimate basis of this opinion; but the submission of Castile to the yoke of a usurper separated our provinces from that kingdom, and our people entered upon the enjoyment of rights which they had been deprived of since the conquest. . . . It is chimerical to claim that all of Spanish America should form one state. How could we reach an understanding with the Philippine Islands of which we have hardly any other information than that which is derived from a geographical chart? How could we reconcile our interests with those of the viceroyalty of Mexico? . . .The colonies should form constitutions; they should do so for themselves; nature herself has ordained this conduct because of the products and the boundaries of their respective territories. Every arrangement which diverts them from this procedure is a trick to misdirect the enthusiasm of the people until the occasion is ripe to furnish them with a new master.

I hear much talk of a federal government as being the most suitable to the present circumstances and to the condition of our provinces; but I fear that its advocates are ignorant of the real character of such a government, and that without discernment they ask for a system which they would consider unsuitable when they became acquainted with it. . . . This system is perhaps the best which has ever existed among men, but it would be difficult to apply such a system to Spanish America. At what point would the general assembly meet so that this body might conveniently receive instructions from distant peoples in regard to the urgent needs of the state? I desire that the provinces would restrict themselves to the limits which they have had up to the present time; that they form separately the constitutions adapted to promote the happiness of each of them; that they always observe the just maxims of mutual aid and succor; and that, postponing all thoughts of a federal system which under present conditions is not suitable and may be injurious, they consider only the formation of close alliances which would encourage the fraternity that should always reign, and which is the only thing that can save us from domestic passions,—a more terrible enemy to a state that is in process of formation than the armies of foreign nations which oppose it.

Thus Moreno evidently wished to promote the formation in Spanish America of several democratic states. In the provisional junta his democratic ideas provoked the opposition of a clique led by President Saavedra,—a clique which cherished some customs of the viceregal régime. Moreno's adherents even suspected that the partisans of Saavedra wished to acclaim him viceroy, or emperor, of la Plata. When the impetuous Moreno decided that the provisional government should be stripped of the vestiges of viceregal days, the radical and the conservative factions clashed. On December 6, 1810, Moreno triumphed, for upon that day the junta adopted a decree abolishing the honors which had been previously accorded to President Saavedra and declaring that the members of the junta were equal. Secretary Moreno probably wrote the decree which contained the following expression of democratic sentiment:

The liberty of the people does not consist in words, nor should it merely appear in documents. Any despot can force his subjects to chant hymns to liberty,—mechanical hymns which accord with the chains and the oppressions of the singers. If we desire that the people should be free, we should scrupulously observe the sacred dogma of equality. If I consider myself equal to my fellow citizens, why should I present myself in a garb which indicates that they are less important than I am? My superiority consists only in the exercise of the functions of magistrate which have been confided to me: in the other activities of society, I am a citizen without the right to any other consideration than that which I deserve because of my virtues.

After the passage of the decree depriving Saavedra of his cherished titles and honors, his discomfited friends evidently schemed to retaliate by diminishing the power and influence of Moreno. An opportunity for revenge was afforded when there appeared in the city of Buenos Aires nine deputies from the interior provinces who were led by Dean Funes of Córdoba, an aggressive ecclesiastic. With a show of legal right, those reactionary deputies, who had been chosen in accordance with the junta's decree of May 27, demanded to be incorporated in the junta. Evidently the demand was favorably received by several members of the provisional government. Moreno, however, opposed such action and advocated that a congress should be convoked to regulate governmental affairs. The enemies of Moreno achieved a triumph when, on December 18, the members of the junta decided to allow the provincial deputies to vote with them on the question as to whether or not those deputies should be incorporated in the provisional government. Only the secretaries of the junta ventured to vote against such action, maintaining that it was contrary to law and opposed to the welfare of the state. After the decision was reached to incorporate the provincial deputies in the provisional government, Moreno, who seemed to consider this action as an attack upon himself, resigned his position as secretary, declaring that "a discredited magistrate" should not remain in office.

This decision checked the democratic movement in the Platean provinces. It initiated a protracted struggle between the citizens of Buenos Aires and the inhabitants of the country provinces,—the *porteños* and the *provincianos*. Moreno's proposed congress did not assemble. Viceregal honors were restored to Saavedra. Several years passed before the provinces of the Río de la Plata discarded the plea of allegiance to Ferdinand VII. and adopted a declaration of independence from Spain.

In December, 1810, the junta of Buenos Aires selected Moreno to act as its diplomatic agent in certain foreign countries. Originally, the junta intended that Moreno should negotiate with the Portuguese court, with Lord Strangford, and with the cabinet of England. On December 25 the junta signed Moreno's credentials as its diplomatic agent to Rio de Janeiro. On January 17, 1811, that junta wrote a letter to Lord Strangford declaring that the addition to it of the deputies from the interior provinces had furnished the best opportunity to promote its relations with foreign powers. The quaint translation of the letter which is preserved in the English archives runs as follows:

Under these Notions it resolved to send its Secretary D. Mariano Moreno to the Courts of London and Brazil, to the End, that making known in each Court, the true sentiments of this Junta, he might conclude arrangements upon solid and lasting Principles. However, as an assurance of his personal safety was wanting on the part of Brazil, it was finally resolved that he should refrain from proceeding there until such an assurance should be obtained for him by the Mediation of Your Excellency; and that he should without delay, prosecute his Voyage to the former Place.

The Junta has furnished him with sufficient Powers for the purpose of treating with the Ministers of His Royal Highness, and of conferring with Your Excellency, but persuaded that this object is not to be obtained, in consequence of Captain Elliot having refused to grant him the protection of the British Flag, the Junta entreat Your Excellency to recommend him and the object of his Mission which is in no manner opposite to the Interests of Great Britain.

The indefinite statements of this letter with regard to the purpose of Moreno's mission are supplemented by a letter which the junta addressed on December 24, 1810, to Marquis Wellesley, the English secretary for foreign affairs. That letter declared that the "close friendship" between Great Britain and the provinces of la Plata which had been promoted by the provisional government had produced "the most sincere satisfaction in the minds of the deputies of the provinces." As those deputies desired to promote that friendship, they had conferred "all their power and authority upon Doctor Don Mariano Moreno"; so that he might proceed to the court of London to inform the English king and his ministers "of the real desires of these provinces." The letter affirmed that, as the wishes of Buenos Aires were "intimately related to the interests of the British nation," the junta expected "a favorable hearing" from the British government. The junta declared that Moreno carried documents to show the actual condition of la Plata provinces and that he was vested "with all the powers" necessary "to establish the political relations between those provinces and Great Britain which the existing circumstances imperiously demanded." The hope was expressed that Wellesley would receive Moreno as "a legitimate representative" of the junta, "a trusty medium of its intentions, a depositary of its confidence and of its most intimate sentiments." The instructions to Moreno said that he should declare the fidelity of the junta to Ferdinand VII., while avowing that, in case of his decease, the junta would consider itself empowered to manage the government on behalf of a people who had reassumed their sovereign rights. Moreno was directed to negotiate a commercial treaty with England and to solicit munitions. On January 2, 1811, the junta voted that besides an allowance for the expenses of the trip to England, Moreno should be granted eight thousand pesos per annum. Mariano's brother, Manuel, and Tomás Guido, who held offices under the provisional government, were made the salaried secretaries of the junta's diplomatic agent.

The attendant circumstances of the mission of Mariano Moreno raise the question as to whether or not the junta intended thus to consign him to political exile. On that question the available documents emanating from the provisional government are almost silent: in his credentials Moreno was indeed styled the secretary of the junta. Manuel Moreno merely declared that his brother was extremely depressed when he started on the voyage to England. But, in a letter to Marquis Wellesley on February 20, 1811, the vigilant Strangford transmitted the rumor that "the Talents and Influence of Moreno had begun to excite the jealousy of his Colleagues," and that the diplomatic mission was "merely a pretext to remove him." Possibly the junta was animated by mixed motives. It would certainly have been difficult for that body to have selected a more capable agent to speak for Buenos Aires at the court of London than the author of the memorial of 1809.

In the end of January, 1811, the first important embassy from southern South America to the Old World left the city of Buenos Aires. Accompanied by his secretaries, Moreno embarked on an English vessel en route for England. It soon appeared that the harassing cares of a revolutionary magistrate had injured Moreno's health; he was unable to endure the stormy voyage, and was soon prostrated by a violent illness. According to his brother's account, Mariano Moreno died in the arms of his secretaries, exclaiming, "Long live my country although I perish!" Early in March, 1811, at a point south of the equator, the corpse of Moreno, which seems to have been shrouded in the English flag, was lowered into the sea. On hearing the news of the sudden death of his protagonist, President Saavedra is said to have ejaculated, "It took so much water to extinguish so much fire!"

Manuel Moreno and Tomás Guido proceeded to London.

Whatever approaches Moreno may have made to the English ministry were fruitless: that ministry had formulated its policy in regard to Spanish America to the Venezuelan commissioners. Guido soon returned to his native land, where he promoted the revolution against Spain. For a time Manuel Moreno eked out a scanty livelihood in the busy English metropolis, and then he also proceeded to Buenos Aires. To Mariano Moreno's widow—a woman whom he had married while living in Upper Peru—the provisional government granted a pension.

Information concerning Moreno's private life is not plentiful. Our knowledge of the personality of Mariano Moreno must be drawn almost solely from the biographical sketch which was written soon after his death by Manuel Moreno. In its pages Mariano is portrayed as a man who did not possess a robust constitution, but who was endowed with a strong will and a fine intellect. Somewhat fanatical in his religious opinions, he was fond of the Church and revered her doctrines. In Chuquisaca and Buenos Aires Moreno's home was the scene of animated political discussions. In his professional duties Moreno was animated by a stern love of justice and by a desire to protect the innocent from oppression. His love for learning was displayed during his career at Chuquisaca. While living in Upper Peru he had become vividly impressed with the evils of Spain's colonial system. Moreno resented Spain's policy of subordinating the creoles to the peninsular Spaniards. A contemporary estimate by an Englishman is afforded by a letter from Strangford to Marquis Wellesley, February 20, 1811, in which the former described Moreno as "a man of extraordinary Merit, and of a virtuous and honorable Character." The following passage written in 1855 by Tomás Guido contains a somewhat extravagant eulogy of Mariano Moreno's services during his brief public career:

As eloquent as Mirabeau, as ardent as Camille Demoulins, as republican as Junius Brutus, he was endowed with a remarkable faculty for the transaction of administrative affairs. His comprehensive intelligence appreciated all the circumstances of a situation which was beset with difficulties. The light of the junta, he dispelled doubts, and calmly promulgated the most audacious reforms. Under the guidance of his surpassing talents and copious knowledge, the press freely scattered ideas upon all subjects concerning which the American people were summoned to act when extricating themselves from the rule of Spain. An indefatigable worker in the organization of the government, familiar with the history of modern times, and enriched by the philosophy of the ancients, he realized his sublime mission. With undaunted front he fought prejudices, attacked abuses, and laid the foundations of the Argentine republic.

There remains to indicate how Paraguay separated from Spain. As already suggested, Belgrano's expedition stimulated a spirit of dissatisfaction with Spanish rule in that province. Further, the apprehensions of Paraguayan leaders were provoked by the suspicious designs of the Portuguese. Consequently, in the middle of May, 1811, certain Paraguayans quietly deprived Governor Velazco of the supreme authority and installed a provisional government at Asunción. On June 20 a junta of five members with a secretary was established. In July, 1811, the Paraguayan junta announced its decision to suspend the recognition of the Spanish *cortes* and the regency; it declared in favor of common action with Buenos Aires in support of Ferdinand VII.; and it expressed its intention to govern Paraguay. The leaders of this junta were Pedro Juan Caballero, José Rodríguez de Francia, and Fulgencio Yegros. Tradition properly ascribes an influential rôle in the revolution which thus altered the political status of Paraguay to José Francia, a doctor of theology of the University of Córdoba, who had gained a reputation in Asunción for being a capable and upright lawyer. A story has been preserved that, soon after the junta was installed, Francia stalked into the midst of some officials who were considering the policy which should be pursued toward Spain, and, laying two loaded pistols upon the table, he declared, "These are the arguments which I bring against the supremacy of Fernando Septimo."

A short time after the inauguration of that junta, Francia retired from its council table. But he forsook his country villa when the junta at Buenos Aires dispatched Nicolás Herrera as emissary to Asunción ostensibly to promote closer relations with Paraguay. At Francia's suggestion a congress was convoked at Asunción to consider Paraguayan affairs. To that motley assembly Francia presented a play of government, which, on October 12, 1813, it adopted by acclamation. This constitution provided that the supreme power of Paraguay should be vested in "two citizens, Don Fulgencio Yegros and Don José Gaspar Francia, with the titles of *Consuls of the Republic of Paraguay.*" The title of brigadier in the Paraguayan army was also conferred upon each of these men. Each consul was to wear the consular insignia, "a sombrero decorated with a blue fringe and bearing the three-colored cockade of the republic." These magistrates were to possess equal authority; they were to sign every act of the government. Their primary duty was to preserve and defend the republic: the soldiers of Paraguay were to be under their joint control. They were to hold the supreme power alternately for a period of four months: the first term of this joint investiture was to be filled by Francia. If one of the consuls died, or was unable to act, the survivor was to convoke a congress within one month. A congress was to be assembled annually to consider the measures which were necessary for "a free and sovereign people." It is apparent that Francia was aping the government of Rome in this constitution which transformed the province of Paraguay into the republic of Paraguay. The Paraguayan historian, Blas Garay, alleges that on October 12 the constituent congress declared that Paraguay was absolutely independent.

Two decrees which were issued by Francia and Yegros during their joint consulate will suggest the policy which they adopted toward the Spaniards. On January 5, 1814, they issued a decree announcing that all peninsular Spaniards residing in Paraguay who were in the capital should appear in the plaza at a fixed hour in order that a register of Spaniards might be formed and declaring that those Spaniards who did not appear should be put to death immediately. A decree of March 1 provided that henceforth no marriages should be solemnized between peninsular Spaniards and Paraguayan women of Spanish descent under penalty of exile and confiscation of property for the priests or curates authorizing such marriages and the imprisonment of the offending Spaniards for ten years with the confiscation of their property. Peninsular Spaniards, however, might marry Indian women, mulattoes, and negroes. Evidently it was the intention of the consuls to diminish the prestige of Spaniards. One year after the fantastic republican constitution was adopted, a subservient congress which assembled at Asunción made the first consul dictator of Paraguay. On June 1, 1816, another congress appointed Francia the ruler of the republic for life. That unique authority was conferred by congress upon Francia in these words: "Because of the complete confidence which Citizen José Rodríguez de Francia has justly merited of the people, he is made perpetual dictator of the republic during his lifetime in the position of a personage without any equal. . . . The republic will have a congress whenever the dictator considers it necessary." The congress proposed that the bishop of Asunción should direct the prelates and priests of Paraguay that in all future masses they should replace the word king by the word dictator.

After congress thus made Francia dictator of the republic, he ruled over the state with an increasingly despotic sway. In 1819 he issued a decree depriving the bishop of Asunción—because of alleged lunacy—of his ecclesiastical authority, appointing in his place a provisor and a general vicar, and providing that no profession of religious faith should be valid without the consent of his government. As the printed records of Francia's administration are incomplete, at present our knowledge of his policy depends largely upon the reminiscences of foreigners who ventured into his dominions. European visitors described Dictator Francia as an extraordinary character: a man of good education and remarkable ability, but inordinately vain, ambitious, cruel, and despotic. As the dictator became obsessed with the idea that his subjects were conspiring against him, he developed an insidious system of espionage: Asunción became a whispering gallery. Those ill-fated persons who were supposed to be disaffected toward the supreme ruler were manacled and thrust into filthy prisons. They were whipped, tortured, and exiled from their homes, or put to death in a revolting manner under the windows of Francia's palace. It has been estimated that thousands of Paraguayans were arbitrarily executed during this prolonged reign of terror, when decrees and judgments were written at Francia's dictation. Although Francia was at times aided by a secretary and other officials, yet, for the most part, his method of administration was personal: he was not only the chief executive and the legislator but also the supreme court of Paraguay and the virtual head of the Church.

But there is another side to the shield besides that harsh

picture drawn by some foreign visitors to Paraguay. To an
extent the rule of Francia was animated by a paternalistic
spirit like that which marked the administration of the Jesuit
missions among the Guaraní Indians. Under Francia's autocratic rule, the Paraguayans were almost completely isolated
from the world, politically and commercially. The most striking exception to his jealous policy of isolation was the negotiation of a convention between Brazil and Paraguay in April,
1823, which stipulated that trade might be carried on between
these two countries through Encarnación, provided that the
traffickers were persons addicted to the sacred cause of liberty.
By one method or another, Francia gave an artificial stimulus
to agriculture, cattle raising, and primitive manufactures.
During his administration the Paraguayans evidently enjoyed
a comparatively large measure of economic prosperity. A
frugal administrator, at his death Francia left a surplus in the
coffers of the Paraguayan state. It is possible that when a
thorough and scientific investigation of Francia's administration shall have been made, the future historian may feel fully
justified in appreciating him as a South American type of the
benevolent despot. In any case, it is only just to Francia to
realize that the rich province of Paraguay owed her independence of the neighboring nations, as well as of Spain,
largely to his influence:—this remarkable character was the
founder of Paraguayan nationality, as well as the historical
antecedent of the López dynasty.

In an account of the rule of the Paraguayan dictator, John
Rengger, a Swiss physician, thus described his first meeting
with Francia:

On July 30, 1819, we disembarked at Asunción, and some days
afterwards were presented to the dictator. He is a man of medium
height, with regular features, and those fine black eyes which
characterize the creoles of South America. He has a most penetrating look, with a strong expression of distrust. On this occasion
he wore his official costume, which consisted of a blue laced coat
—the uniform of a Spanish general—waistcoat, breeches, stock-
ings of white silk, and shoes with gold buckles. . . . Dictator
Francia was then sixty-two years of age, though he did not
appear to be more than fifty. He asked me with a studied haughti-
ness of manner, several questions, by which he sought to em-
barrass me; but he soon changed his tone. Having opened my
portfolio to take out some papers which I had to present to him,

he perceived a portrait of Bonaparte, which I, aware of his admiration for the original, had designedly placed there. He took it up, and examined it with great interest, when I told him whose likeness it was. He then began conversing familiarly upon the political affairs of Europe, with which he seemed to be better acquainted than I could have supposed. He asked me for news from Spain, for which country he expressed the most profound contempt. Louis the Eighteenth's charter was not to his taste; he admired much more the military government and conquests of Napoleon, whose downfall he deplored. . . . But the principal subject on which he talked, was the monks. He reproached them with pride, depravity of manners, and every species of intrigue; and declaimed, particularly, against the tendency which the clergy in general have to reject the authority of government. The better to make known his principles upon this point, he said, "If his holiness the Pope should come to Paraguay, I should make him merely my almoner." . . . In speaking of the emancipation of Spanish America, he warmly declared his devotion to that cause, and his firm resolution to defend it against any attack.

The ideas he expressed relative to the manner of governing these new states, as yet but little advanced in civilization, appared to me sufficiently reasonable; but, unfortunately, he had himself put none of them into practice. He condescended to show us his library; it was small, indeed, but it was almost the only one existing in Paraguay. I saw in it, besides the best Spanish authors, the works of Voltaire, Rousseau, Raynal, Rollin, La Place, etc., all of which he had procured since the revolution. . . . He dismissed us with these words: "Do here whatever you please, profess the religion you wish,—no one shall molest you; but take care not to meddle with the affairs of my government." . . .

I am inclined to think that, at first, his intentions were good; at least his public life, before the revolution, and the use which he, in the beginning, made of his power, would lead to that belief. But soon hurried on by the love of sway, and giving way to his suspicious and violent temper, he strayed from the right path and became a veritable tyrant; at the same time that he justified his conduct to himself by the maxim, that liberty should be in proportion to civilization; and that to a people who felt not the want of it, could only prove injurious.

Rengger's account impresses the writer as a discriminating characterization of the "Supreme, Perpetual Dictator of the Republic of Paraguay." But the eccentric dictator was much provoked by this account of this rule. Francia published a reply to Rengger's book: he described it as an "Essay of Lies";

he denounced its author as an "assassin," a "barbarous atheist," and an "infamous impostor and deceiver." This biting criticism may help to reveal the character of *El Supremo,* who dominated the destinies of Paraguay, the hermit state, for almost a quarter of a century.

This chapter shows that some revolutionists in the viceroyalty of la Plata were inclined to adopt radical measures. Strange though it may seem to some Anglo-Saxons, certain revolutionary leaders of South America did not wish to found true republican governments upon the ruins of Spain's colonial system. Under the guise of a republic, Francia founded an autocratic state in Paraguay. In contrast with the Paraguayan dictator, Mariano Moreno stands forth like a tribune. He was the democrat, who dreading anarchy, and fearing that the people of la Plata provinces were not ready for a federal government, wished to found a republic at Buenos Aires. His ideas on government, however, were too democratic for his associates. Moreno was not only a publicist, he was also a scholar; the national library of the Argentine republic is "the best monument to the memory of its founder."

Chapter 6

José de San Martín

THE GAP between Mariano Moreno and José de San Martín may be partly filled by the picturesque figure of José Artigas, who is the hero of the struggle for independence in *la Banda Oriental*,—the territory later known as Uruguay. His father was a member of a well-known family of Montevideo who owned a hacienda where José spent some years of his boyhood. The youth early became inured to the hardships of frontier life. On the wide pampas he acquired a love for personal liberty. With regard to his career before the English attack upon Buenos Aires, it is particularly difficult to distinguish between Artigas in legend and in history. There is a tradition that José Artigas became the chieftain of a roving band which stole herds of cattle and shared the illicit gains of smugglers. Whether or not he was for a time "the Robin Hood of South America," it is clear that being eventually induced to enter the employment of the Spanish governor at Montevideo, Artigas then upheld the rule of law and order in *la Banda Oriental*. In 1810 he was an officer in a corps of lancers in the Spanish service.

Early in 1811 Artigas openly forsook his post. He became the leader of a nondescript band which acknowledged the governmental authority of the junta of Buenos Aires. On April 11, 1811, Artigas issued a proclamation to his fellow-countrymen: he invited them to join him in defense of "a just cause," declaring that they ought "to die with honor rather than to live ignominiously in frightful captivity." On May 18, 1811, at the head of some insurgents who, according to his own report, were mostly armed "with poles to which knives had been fastened," Artigas defeated at Las Piedras a detachment of royalist soldiers which had been sent from Montevideo by Francisco Xavier Elío, who was the successor of Cisneros as the viceroy of la Plata. Artigas then became the leader of the insurrectionary movement in his native province.

On April 13, 1813, in his camp before Montevideo, Artigas signed the instructions to five delegates from *la Banda Ori-*

ental to a constituent assembly which had been convoked in the city of Buenos Aires. His delegates to the assembly were directed to urge that it should adopt a declaration of absolute independence from Spain. Their instructions proposed that a compact between the provinces of the Platean basin should establish a confederation which would ensure complete civil and religious liberty. Each province, as *la Banda Oriental,* should be allowed to organize its own government. The central government should direct only the general business of the state, while other matters should be managed by the provinces. The suggestion was made that, for the time being, the provinces of la Plata should form a firm league of friendship for their common defense, liberty, and mutual happiness. Article eleven of the instructions provided that *la Banda Oriental* retained "its sovereignty, liberty, and independence, and every power, jurisdiction, and right" which was not expressly delegated by the confederation to the congress of "the United Provinces." Article fourteen provided that "no tax or duty should be imposed upon articles exported from one province to another; nor should any preference be given by any regulation of commerce or revenue to the ports of one province over those of another; nor should vessels sailing from this province to another province be obliged to enter, anchor, or pay duties in another." The instructions contained a provision that each province should have the right to raise and to organize its own militia; this was accompanied by a statement that military despotism should be completely prevented by constitutional checks. It was affirmed as necessary and indispensable that the capital should be located at some other place than the city of Buenos Aires. With regard to the type of government, there was a provision that the provinces should form their own constitutions. Each province should also have the right to sanction the constitution for the United Provinces which should be framed by the assembly. That constitution was to guarantee to the provinces a republican form of government which would save them from domestic violence, as well as from any usurpation of their rights of sovereignty. The "instructions of the year thirteen," as they are known in Platean history, were obviously based in part upon North-American example. Whether or not Artigas was the sole author of these instructions, they embodied his federalist ideals.

But the assembly at Buenos Aires declined to admit the federalist delegates, alleging that their credentials were not acceptable. Still the battle of Las Piedras was one of the victories mentioned in a patriotic hymn which, in May, 1813, was declared by the assembly to be the song of the Platean provinces. A literal translation of the first stanza of the song will suggest the sentiments of some Platean leaders at this time.

> *Hear, Oh Mortals! the sacred shouts,*
> *Of liberty, liberty, liberty,*
> *Hear the sound of broken chains,*
> *Behold equality enthroned;*
> *Behold in the face of day arising,*
> *A new and glorious nation,*
> *Her brows are crown'd with laurel,*
> *A vanquished lion at her feet.*

It was probably a dislike for the government at Buenos Aires which impelled Artigas in January, 1814, to leave the Platean soldiers who, under General José Rondeau, were besieging Montevideo. Consequently, on February 11, 1814, Gervasio Antonio Posadas, who had just become the supreme director of the provinces of la Plata, declared the federalist leader to be a traitor, and set a price upon his head. Despite the attempts which were subsequently made to reconcile the proscribed leader with Buenos Aires, the breach could not be healed. Thus Artigas, the advocate of independence and federation, became the champion of those inhabitants of *la Banda Oriental* who struggled fiercely against the domination of the government at Buenos Aires, the emperor of Brazil, and the king of Spain. His spirit is preserved in the response which he made to an agent of Spain who tried to induce him to join the cause of the royalists: "I cannot be purchased; I wish no other reward for my hardihood than to see my nation free from Spanish rule; and, if the noise of cannon cease during my lifetime, my hands will drop the sword which they have seized to defend my native land." In 1815 this revolutionary chieftain had reached the climax of his power; for the city of Montevideo, and several provinces of the viceroyalty of Buenos Aires, as well as the region of the Guaraní missions, had recognized his ascendancy. His seat of power was at el

Hervidero upon the banks of the Uruguay River; his pretentious title was "the Protector of Free Peoples." A Scotchman
who sailed up the Uruguay River to the headquarters of the
"protector" thus described him:

And there (I pray you do not turn skeptic on my hands),
what do you think I saw? Why, the most excellent Protector
of half of the New World, seated on a bullock's skull, at a fire
kindled on the mud floor of his hut, eating beef off a spit, and
drinking gin out of a cow-horn! He was surrounded by a dozen
officers in weather-beaten attire, in similar positions, and similarly occupied with their chef. All were smoking, all gabbling.
The Protector was dictating to two secretaries, who occupied, at
one deal table, the only two dilapidated rush-bottom chairs in
the hovel. . . . To complete the singular incongruity of the scene,
the floor of the one apartment of the mud hut . . . in which the
general, his staff, and secretaries were assembled, was strewn with
pompous envelopes from all the provinces (some of them distant
1,500 miles from that centre of operations), addressed to "His
Excellency the Protector." At the door stood the reeking horses
of couriers arriving every half-hour, and the fresh ones of those
departing as often. Soldiers, aides-de-camp, scouts, came galloping
in from all quarters.

The prestige of this *caudillo,* rude, wild, and strong—who
cherished some extravagant ideas concerning liberty—declined
from 1817 to 1820. In 1817 Portuguese soldiers under General Lecor took possession of Montevideo. Early in 1820 one
of his own lieutenants, Francisco Ramírez, raised his hand
against the "protector." In September, 1820, the dejected
leader of Gauchos withdrew to Paraguay, where he was given
an asylum by Dictator Francia. While the enigmatical Artigas
was living near Asunción, he was quoted as having described
his career in the following words:

I did no more than to respond to the dark measures of the
directory of Buenos Aires and to the war which it made upon
me because it considered that I was an enemy of centralization.
. . . Taking the United States as a model, I desired the autonomy
of the Platean provinces, granting to each state its own government, its constitution and its flag, with the right to elect its
representatives, its judges, and its governors from its own natural-
born citizens. This is what I attempted to do for my province
and for those other provinces which proclaimed me their Pro-

tector. . . . But the Pueyrredons and their assistants wished to make of Buenos Aires a new imperial Rome which could send its proconsuls to govern the provinces in a military fashion and deprive them of all political representation, just as it rejected the deputies whom the people of la Banda Oriental selected for the constituent assembly, and as it set a price upon my head.

Thus did Artigas apparently interpret his rôle in Platean history.

In 1825 a compatriot of Artigas, Juan Antonio Lavalleja, with an immortal band of about thirty-three followers, initiated another struggle for the liberation of *la Banda Oriental*, with the aid of Buenos Aires. Lavalleja was soon joined by Fructuoso Rivera and other patriots. On August 25 of that year, in the town of Florida, an assembly of delegates from various sections of the province framed a declaration of independence. That declaration announced that all measures of incorporation or oaths of allegiance which had been forcibly imposed upon the people of the province by the intrusive agents of Portugal and Brazil were null and void. "In consequence of the foregoing declaration, *la Banda Oriental*—reassuming those rights, liberties, and prerogatives inherent to the peoples of the earth—declares itself by fact and right, free and independent of the king of Portugal, of the emperor of Brazil, and of any power of the universe, with ample power to assume in the exercise of its sovereignty whatsoever form it may consider convenient." On the same day this assembly decreed that the "Oriental Province" should be united to the other provinces of the Río de la Plata:—thus did it secure the coöperation of the United Provinces against its colossal neighbor, the empire of Brazil. In reality, the struggle for the independence of *la Banda Oriental* was not crowned with success until August 27, 1828, when the United Provinces of the Río de la Plata and Brazil by a solemn treaty mutually recognized its dependence. In the following year a constitution was formed for "the Oriental Republic of Uruguay"; and in 1830, under the presidency of General Rivera, that republic was launched upon an independent career.

While Artigas was struggling to found a vast federation in the Platean basin, or, at least, to establish a new nation in one province of the ancient viceroyalty of la Plata, José de

San Martín was winning the independence of South America from Spain. José Francisco de San Martín was born on February 25, 1778, in the village of Yapeyú, which was located on the right bank of the Uruguay River. Yapeyú was a mission which had been planted by Jesuit padres among the Guaraní Indians. In 1778 Juan de San Martín, the father of José, was the administrator of that mission. Juan de San Martín was a native of Cervatos de la Cueza in the province of León, Spain, who had served as lieutenant, adjutant, and captain of a battalion of Spanish militia in the city of Buenos Aires. Gregorio Matorras de San Martín, the mother of José was the daughter of Domingo Matorras, who had undertaken to conquer the Indians of Chaco. On the paternal side, she traced her descent from Spaniards who had emigrated from the province of Asturias; and, on the maternal side, from natives of old Castile.

The earliest years of José de San Martín were spent in the Indian village of Yapeyú. When his father was again stationed in the city of Buenos Aires, José was taken from the frontier village to the metropolis of the viceroyalty. By an order of Charles III., dated May 21, 1785, Captain San Martín was transferred from his post at Buenos Aires to Málaga. His fourth son, José, profited by the change, for he was soon sent to a school in Madrid, where, at least, he acquired some knowledge of mathematics. The example of his father, and of his three older brothers, who had also become soldiers of Spain, obviously influenced José, for, on July 1, 1789, he asked the Spanish government to be allowed to join the infantry company of Murcia, in order, as he expressed it, that he might "follow the distinguished profession of arms."

This boy volunteer fought for the first time under Spain's banner of blood and gold against the Moors in North Africa. In 1793 he served in the campaign of the Spaniards against the French in Roussillon. In 1797 and 1798 he served on the Frigate *Dorotea* in the Mediterranean Sea. With the regiment of Murcia, San Martín then saw service in Spain's campaign of 1801 against Portugal. In 1804, as captain of the infantry company of *Voluntarios de Campo Mayor,* to which he had been transferred, San Martín served in the garrison at Cadiz, where he read books of history, geography, and military science. Later, as a reward for bravery in the guerilla warfare against the soldiers of Napoleon, the junta of Seville made

San Martín a captain in the cavalry regiment of Bourbon. For his services in the engagements which preceded the surrender of the French army under General Dupont at Bailén in July, 1808, San Martín was granted a medal and appointed lieutenant colonel of cavalry. About a year later, he was made aide-de-camp of the Marquis de Coupigny in the army of Catalonia. According to his own statement, in July, 1811, San Martín was appointed commander of the regiment of dragoons of Saguntum.

From 1789 to 1811 José de San Martín had faithfully served his king. He had passed through many varied experiences as a Spanish officer. His valiant services had frequently been recognized by the government of Spain. Such a distinguished and honorable reputation in the military service of a European power had not been earned by any other Spanish-American of the revolutionary epoch,—not even Francisco de Miranda. Possibly the creole colonel, San Martín, felt that his services had not been sufficiently appreciated. Many years afterwards he explained his departure from Spain in these words: "In 1811, I was serving in the Spanish army. Twenty years of honorable service had gained for me some consideration in spite of the fact that I was an American; I heard of the revolution in South America; and—forsaking my fortunes and my hopes—I desired only to sacrifice everything to promote the liberty of my native land. I arrived at Buenos Aires in the beginning of 1812:—thenceforward I consecrated myself to the cause of Spanish America."

On March 9, 1812, Colonel San Martín disembarked at the city of Buenos Aires, having proceeded from the Iberian peninsula to South America by way of England. A short time after arriving in Buenos Aires, he married María de los Remedios Escalada, the daughter of a well-known inhabitant of that city. The Argentine biographer of San Martín, General Mitre, has asserted that his hero transplanted to South America a secret society, sometimes called the Lautaro lodge, which solemnly pledged its members to consecrate themselves to the task of liberating America from the odious rule of Spain. It is possible that San Martín did establish at Buenos Aires a society, which, in some respects, resembled a masonic lodge. But the writer has not found evidence to prove that such a society was a potent force at Buenos Aires in 1812. At a later stage in the South-American revolution evidence can be found of the activity of a secret association to which certain leaders belonged. For example, San Martín's correspondence contains occult allusions to "O-O", and to *"los Amigos"*—allusions which evidently veiled a mysterious fraternity that influenced the actions of prominent revolutionary leaders.

At once San Martín felt that the South American soldiers were deficient in discipline and ignorant of the military art, while the government of Buenos Aires realized that Colonel San Martín might render valuable services to the revolutionary cause. Accordingly, on March 16, 1812, the junta of Buenos Aires appointed San Martín lieutenant colonel of cavalry and commander of a projected squadron of mounted grenadiers. On April 3 his name was published in the *Gaceta de Buenos Aires* in recognition of his offer of one-third of his salary and a monthly contribution of fifty pesos for the support of the provisional government. San Martín soon took steps to improve the soldiers of Buenos Aires: he established a military training school, and provided for the supervision of the conduct of the soldiers through a monthly assembly of grenadiers. That gathering, which, in some respects, resembled a secret lodge, may have been the hazy nucleus of the Lautaro society. In any case the *esprit de corps* of the citizen soldiery was stimulated, if not indeed created. A token of what a trained soldiery might accomplish under a brave and experienced commander was soon given. On February 3, 1813, Colonel San Martín's grenadiers attacked a small detachment of royalist soldiers at San Lorenzo on the right bank of the Paraná River. The Spanish soldiers were routed and forced to retreat to Montevideo. A Scotchman who witnessed this conflict likened San Martín's grenadiers, who had screened themselves from the royalists in the cloisters of the monastery of San Lorenzo, to the Grecian warriors who were introduced into the city of Troy in a wooden horse.

While San Martín was training his grenadiers, the soldiers of Buenos Aires under General Belgrano had defeated the royalists in an engagement at Tucumán on September 24, 1812, and in an engagement at Salta on February 20, 1813. But in October and in November, 1813, the royalists defeated Belgrano. Hence in the following month, San Martín was given command of an expedition which was sent to reënforce Belgrano's dispirited soldiers near the city of Tucumán. On January 18, 1814, San Martín was made "general in chief" of the army of Buenos Aires near Tucumán. That was indeed a "heavy cross"; for the army was poorly disciplined; some of the officers were incompetent; and San Martín was ignorant of the nature of the country. Upon reaching the defeated army San Martín began to reform it: he established an entrenched camp at Tucumán; he gathered recruits, reorganized the soldiers, and provided for instruction in mathematics and engineering. So successful was San Martín in directing a guerrilla warfare that the victorious royalists were checked.

In April, 1814, San Martín relinquished his position as commander of the army which the government at Buenos Aires had designed for use against the royalists in Upper Peru: on August 10, 1814, the supreme director of la Plata appointed him governor-intendant of the province of Cuyo, which was south of Tucumán. With regard to the cause for this significant transfer, it is evident that San Martín had asked to be relieved of his position at Tucumán and to be given instead a position at Cuyo because of poor health. But that plea probably masked his main motive. For it is certain that coupled with the desire to improve his health in the delicious climate of Mendoza, the capital of the province of Cuyo, was the ambition to become more serviceable in the struggle against the royalists. As early as April, 1814, San Martín had written to Nicolás Rodríguez Peña and declared that in Upper Peru he could only wage a defensive war. In confidence he also imparted to Peña his "secret." This was the project which he had conceived for the prosecution of the war against Spain, as contrasted with the plan of the provisional government of Buenos Aires to attack the Spanish stronghold in Peru through Upper Peru: "A small well-disciplined army in Mendoza to cross the Andes in order to exterminate the royalists in Chile and to aid a government of trusty friends to put an end to the anarchy which reigns there. Then, allying our forces, we shall go by sea to capture Lima. This is the road and not the other: you may be sure that the war will not be finished until we capture Lima."

From 1814 to 1821 San Martín's energies were devoted to the execution of this strategic plan. Before considering the measures which he took at Mendoza to carry out his project, brief mention should be made of the rise and fall of the patriot party in Chile.

The captaincy general of Chile included a narrow fringe of

territory between the cordillera and the ocean, extending from the Straits of Magellan to the desert of Atacama. In 1808 García Carrasco became its captain general: he was also the chief intendant and the president of the royal *audiencia*. Although reports of the deposition of Ferdinand VII. finally reached the city of Santiago, yet the news did not produce such a ferment there as in Buenos Aires. Many Chileans wished to conserve the rights of the idolized Ferdinand; some were apprehensive of the supposed designs of Carlota Joaquina, while others saw visions of independence from Spain.

In the city of Santiago on September 18, 1810, in the presence of a *cabildo abierto,* Captain General García Carrasco quietly laid down the baton of command. He was replaced by a provisional junta that made loud professions of loyalty to Ferdinand VII. Three months later, at the instance of the *cabildo* of Santiago, the junta issued a summons for the election of delegates to a congress which should form a new government for Chile. In the meantime, Camilo Henríquez, a learned monk who was steeped in the philosophy of Rousseau, published a pseudonymous pamphlet which advocated the establishment of an independent republic. The Chilean congress met at Santiago on July 4, 1811. Its members took an oath of fidelity to Ferdinand VII.; and they swore to support the constitution and the laws which congress might establish. José Miguel Carrera, an ambitious military officer who had served under the Spanish standard, soon became the leader of a faction which favored the independence of Chile from Spain. Soon after September 4, 1811, when, aided by his brothers Luis and Juan José, that leader overthrew the provisional government, the movement against Spanish rule in Chile became, in part, a struggle between the adherents of José Miguel Carrera and the followers of Bernardo O'Higgins. Ultimately the contending factions were compelled to bury their jealousies and to join hands against the common enemy. For, in 1813 and 1814, José de Abascal, viceroy of Peru, sent expeditions to re-conquer Chile. After several encounters between the royalist soldiers and the Chilean patriots, in October, 1814, the patriots led by Bernardo O'Higgins and the Carrera brothers were shamefully defeated at Rancagua by the royalists under General Mariano Osorio.

Bernardo O'Higgins, a protegé of Miranda, is the Chilean hero of the revolutionary epoch. The natural son of an adventurous Irishman who closed a career in the Spanish colonial service as viceroy of Peru, Bernardo was educated in South America and Europe. After the deposition of Carrasco, he organized a band of soldiers and offered his services to the new government. O'Higgins soon won a reputation for wisdom in council and impetuous bravery upon the field of battle. When, after the defeat at Rancagua many Chilean patriots were forced to seek a refuge beyond the frozen peaks of the Andes, O'Higgins led a group of Chilean *émigrés* to Mendoza, where they were cordially received by José de San Martín.

At that time the most important political problems confronting the inhabitants of la Plata provinces resembled those which had confronted Moreno in 1810. What should be their attitude toward the Spanish monarch? What form of government should they adopt? An interesting sidelight is cast upon the plans of Platean leaders by the fact that in 1814 Director Posadas commissioned Manuel Belgrano and Bernardino Rivadavia to negotiate with England, or with Spain, for the establishment of a constitutional monarchy in southern South America which might be ruled by a prince of Spain, of England, or of some other strong nation. It appears that when San Martín arrived in South America, he entertained the hope that he would find his compatriots disposed to establish a democratic form of government,—that is to say, a republic. An examination of his correspondence with Tomás Godoy Cruz, an intimate friend, furnishes some interesting suggestions in regard to the political organization which San Martín thought was most suitable for the Platean provinces. In February, 1816, he wrote to Cruz:

I feel as though I might die every time that I hear people speak of a federation. Would it not be more convenient to transfer the capital from Buenos Aires to some other place and thus to silence the just complaints of the provinces? A federation! How could this be established? If a country like the United States with an established government, well populated, artistic, agricultural, and commercial had so many difficulties under a federal system of government during the last war with England, what would happen if the provinces of la Plata became jealous of each other? If you consider also the rivalries and the clashing interests of various regions, you will agree that the United Provinces would become a den of beasts of which the royalists would be the masters.

Neither did San Martin believe in professions of loyalty to Ferdinand VII. On April 12, 1816, he wrote to Cruz, who then represented the province of Cuyo in a congress at Tucumán, "Does it not indeed appear ridiculous to coin money, to have a flag and a national cockade, and, lastly, to make war on a sovereign on whom it is believed that we are in a state of dependence?" In another letter dated May 24, 1816, San Martín said: "The inhabitants of the United Provinces have had no other object in their revolution than to emancipate themselves from Spanish rule and to establish a nation. Are we able to establish a republic without provoking the opposition of Brazil? A republic without arts, sciences, agriculture, inhabitants, and with a large extent of territory which may properly be called a desert, is not a good neighbor for a monarchy." Thus as early as 1816, San Martín—the republican at heart—had become convinced that the people of la Plata provinces were not ready for a republic. In other letters to Cruz he urged that the congress at Tucumán should make a public declaration of independence from Spain.

The delegates who assembled at Tucumán on March 24, 1816, were selected in accordance with a statute which had been issued by a junta at Buenos Aires. The congress was attended by delegates from various provinces of the former viceroyalty of la Plata; but Paraguay and *la Banda Oriental* were not represented, while only a few delegates of Upper Peru were present. In a short time the congress dispatched agents to Artigas and Francia to invite "the free peoples" and the Paraguayans to send delegates to the assembly. Vain was the invitation. This congress took other measures which indicated the assumption of governmental authority: it made provisions for the collection of forced loans; and, on May 3, it appointed Juan Martín de Pueyrredón, a delegate from San Luis, "the supreme director of the state." There appeared at Tucumán while congress was in session, Manuel Belgrano, who evidently reënforced the arguments of those delegates who favored a declaration of independence. The official act of that congress of July 9, 1816, declared that:

The ordinary session of the congress of the United Provinces having ended, it continued its former discussions concerning the grand object of the independence of the peoples represented therein. Although the opinion of the entire region in favor of emancipation from the despotic rule of the kings of Spain was general, constant, and decisive, yet the delegates devoted to this crucial question the profundity of their talents, and the rectitude of their intentions, which demanded a decision regarding their own fate, the fate of the peoples represented and of posterity. Finally, they were asked: if they wished that the provinces of the Union should form a nation free and independent of the kings of Spain and of her metropolis. At once, animated by a holy love of justice, each and every delegate successively announced his spontaneous decision in favor of the independence of the country, signing in consequence the following declaration. We, the representatives of the United Provinces in South America, assembled in a general congress, invoking the God who presides over the universe, in the name and by the authority of the people whom we represent, and proclaiming to heaven and to all nations and peoples of the earth the justice of our intentions, declare solemnly to the world that the unanimous wish of these provinces is to sever the oppressive bonds which connect them with the kings of Spain, to recover the rights of which they were deprived, and to assume the exalted position of a nation free and independent of Ferdinand VII., of his successors, and of the metropolis of Spain.

Thus certain provinces of la Plata adopted a declaration of independence. This declaration was the logical culmination of the action taken on May 25, 1810, in the city of Buenos Aires. Mariano Moreno's dream of Independence from Spain was thus partly fulfilled. The title of the new state, the United Provinces of South America, resembled the title proposed by Artigas in 1813. In practice, however, the name applied to that state was ordinarily the United Provinces of the Río de la Plata. In 1816 the prospect of independence from Spain was becoming brighter in the Platean provinces; but it had been darkened by royalist successes in many parts of South America. The royalist commander Morillo dominated New Granada and Venezuela. Captain General Marcó del Pont was the master of Chile. Yet down in the province of Cuyo the valiant José de San Martín was quietly recruiting the brave army of the Andes,—an army which was destined to eclipse in the New World the achievements of Hannibal. On hearing of the declaration of July 9, 1816, San Martín declared that this was "a masterly stroke." On August 8 he and his chief officers took a solemn oath to promote and defend the liberty and independence of the United Provinces of South America.

The congress of Tucumán also considered what type of government should be established in the United Provinces. At a secret session of congress on July 6, 1816, Belgrano urged that the most suitable form of government was a monarchy with a member of the Inca dynasty upon the throne. This project—which resembled Miranda's plan—apparently gained the approval of San Martín; for, on August 12, he wrote to Cruz declaring that "all judicious persons would be pleased with the plan concerning the dynasty of the Incas." In September, 1816, some members of the Platean congress were considering the establishment at Buenos Aires of a constitutional monarchy under a foreign prince. Two months later, Director Pueyrredón proposed to congress a scheme for the coronation of a prince of the house of Braganza as king of the United Provinces under a constitution. Early in the following year, the protean project was broached again. In a letter to San Martín on March 3, 1817, Pueyrredón declared: "I desire a monarch for our state; but I desire one worthy of the honor which he would receive in commanding us; that is to say, I wish a greater man than Prince John of Porugal; and I wish a monarch who would rule us only."

While Platetan publicists deliberated in regard to the frame of government for the United Provinces, San Martín was executing his military plans. His base of operations was at Mendoza. That city was located in an oasis that marked the line where the foothills of the lofty Cordillera sank into the broad pampas. On the west was "the snow-capped Andean range trending away towards distant Patagonia" till the farthest peaks sank belowe the horizon. With all possible secrecy San Martín prepared to attack the Spaniards in Chile. He formed from Chilean *émigrés* the nucleus of a regiment. He recruited soldiers and raised war revenues. He sent out spies to collect information concerning the Chilean royalists. San Martín solicited the impecunious government at Buenos Aires to aid him: he sent pleas to that city for muskets, sheepskins, mountain artillery, munitions, mules, horseshoes, anchors, clarinets, and money. Aware that the royalists would entertain apprehensions concerning his designs, he tried to lull their suspicions and to deceive them by various subterfuges. For example, messages bearing the similitude of truth were allowed to fall into the hands of Chilean royalists,—messages which contained false statements concerning San Martín's designs.

San Martín sent letter after letter to the Platean government urging that his plan of campaign was the wisest which could be adopted for the liberation of South America. On April 25, 1816, he declared: "Chile is the citadel of this part of America; her conquest will establish the basis of our political being. Peru will yield to her influence; and the continent will be free!"

In a letter to the supreme director on June 15, 1816, San Martín sketched his plan of operations. He maintained that the soldiers who were destined to invade Chile should cross the Andean range only by certain passes. The most fertile and populous provinces of Chile should be occupied at once. The great aim of the army should be utterly to overwhelm the royalists in the first action. Then Santiago should be captured. He declared that "upon the outcome of this expedition depended the liberty of South America." The difficulties which had to be surmounted in the projected march may be suggested by the statement that the Uspallata pass, the highest of the passes over the Andes from Mendoza, is about twelve thousand five hundred feet above sea level,—over four thousand feet higher than the pass of St. Bernard by which Napoleon crossed the Alps. San Martín did not underestimate the obstacles which confronted the expedition; for on June 14, 1816, he wrote to Tomás Guido, "It is not the opposition which the royalists can offer to my soldiers that disturbs my sleep but the passage of these immense mountains."

In the latter part of 1816 Director Pueyrredón took the final steps for the execution of San Martín's cherished design. On August 1, 1816, Pueyrredón appointed San Martín commander-in-chief of the army of the Andes; and on October 17, he made San Martín captain general of that army. On December 21 Pueyrredón signed the instructions for the expedition against Chile. These instruction declared that one purpose of the expedition was to acquire glory for the United Provinces,—which may have been merely a rhetorical flourish. The primary object of the campaign was to liberate Chile and thus to promote the independence of South America from the Spanish monarchy. San Martín was carefully instructed to remain at the head of the army: he was to engage in a pitched battle only when conditions favored a victory. In case the royalists were defeated, San Martín was cautioned never to agree that they should be allowed to retire to Lima, which was apparently regarded as his final objective point. Pueyrredón explicitly declared that the soldiers of the army of the Andes were neither to plunder nor to oppress the people of Chile. A design to acquire control of the liberated territory was expressly disclaimed. San Martín was authorized to make arrangements for a provisional government at Santiago. The hope was expressed that a government might be established in independent Chile which would resemble the government of the United Provinces. It was suggested that these two countries might even enter into "a constitutional alliance." San Martín was to try to persuade the Chileans to send delegates to a congress at Buenos Aires; in order that untimately Spanish South America might constitute one nation.

To deceive the Chilean royalists San Martín sent small detachments of soldiers against the enemy to the north and south of the passes through which he planned to send the main divisions of his army. By January, 1817, the army of the Andes was ready to march. That army was divided into three divisions, which were commanded by Colonel Gregorio de las Heras, General Miguel Soler, and General O'Higgins. General Soler commanded the vanguard of the army which was to proceed by the longer and more difficult route by Los Platos pass that wound around the northern side of Mount Aconcagua, General O'Higgins was to follow Soler with the reserve division, while Las Heras with a small body of infantry and the artillery was to lead his soldiers along the Uspallata road which traversed the mountains south of Mount Aconcagua. Each of these commanders received from San Martín an itinerary of the projected marches with topographical data and detailed instructions. The army of the Andes was composed of about two thousand six hundred infantry, seven hundred cavalry, and two hundred and fifty artillerymen. The procession started on January 18, when the soldiers of Las Heras left the camp near Mendoza and began to march up the trail leading toward the two passes. This division was supplied with carts and anchors and cables to aid in the transportation of the cannon over the crags and across the precipices of the Andes. About a week later San Martín left Mendoza to overtake his soldiers who were approaching the gloomy defiles of the cordillera. Twenty-one days after the expedition started, the soldiers of Soler, O'Higgins, and Las

Heras had passed the snowy summits of the Andes and were far down the valleys that converged toward the Chilean plains. On February 8, 1817, San Martín wrote to Pueyrredón from the valley of Aconcagua:

The passage of the Andes has been a triumph in itself. The soldiers of the army with supplies for almost a month, with armament, munitions of war, and baggage have marched a hundred leagues along a road which crossed craggy peaks, defiles, folds, and deep, narrow chasms,—a road intersected by four mountain ridges, where the cragginess of the soil competes with the asperity of the atmosphere. If to overcome these obstacles has been to gain a victory, it is no less a victory because it has frightened the enemy.

Physical geography made possible this marvelous march. In the execution of his daring design San Martín was favored by circumstances; the loyal support of Pueyrredón, the sacrificing spirit of the inhabitants of Cuyo, and the devotion of his soldiers. Nevertheless, his might have been foiled by Marcó del Pont, the captain general of Chile; but that commander, deceived by the false moves of San Martín, had guarded the Los Patos and Uspallata passes lightly. San Martín was a military genius. The student of history will search long in military annals to find a campaign more carefully matured, more systematically prepared for, and more successfully executed than his march over the Andean range. Although San Martín's army was much smaller than Napoleon's army which surmounted the Alps in 1800, yet it is hardly too much to say that the passage of the Andes had a more abiding influence upon history. The march of San Martín prepared the way for the establisment of the independence of Chile and Peru. This heroic march was San Martín's greatest achievement.

But when San Martín had reached the valley of Aconcagua, he had not yet set foot upon the plains of Chile. Royalist soldiers fled from the passes, while Spanish troops marched from Santiago toward the mountains. When San Martín heard of the movements of the royalists he decided to attack them at once, before they had an opportunity to concentrate their forces at the outlet of the passes. He divided his army into two parts: the right division was led by General Soler, and the left by General O'Higgins. Preparations were made for a night march in order to surprise the enemy. Early on the morning of February 12, San Martín's soldiers deployed from mountain paths and attacked the royalists, who were commanded by Colonel Rafael Maroto, in front and on the left flank. After a stubborn resistance, Maroto's soldiers were dislodged from their position near the village of Chacabuco and thrown into disorder. The decisive victory of Chacabuco opened the road to Santiago. Marcó del Pont fled precipitately from the capital; and two days later San Martín entered it in triumph. As the reports of this victory spread throughout Chile, the spirit of discontent with Spanish rule was stimulated, and the prestige of the Spanish arms was lowered. On February 28, 1817, José de San Martín wrote jubilantly to Pueyrredón saying that 'in twenty-four days his soldiers had completed the campaign, defeated the tyrants, and given liberty to Chile.' When the news of this victory was received in Buenos Aires great rejoicings took place: salvos were fired from the fortresses and from the ships in the river. The government of the United Provinces appointed the victorious commander brigadier general; it provided that he was to be presented with a pair of pistols and a sword. The *cabildo* of Buenos Aires provided that a gold medal should be struck off and a sword be forged for presentation to the victorious commander. The *cabildo* of Tucumán made him perpetual regidor. A *cabildo abierto* of Santiago unanimously selected the victor of Chacabuco to be the governor of Chile.

With characteristic devotion to his grand design, San Martín declined the appointment as brigadier general of the United Provinces; he also declined to accept the position of governor of Chile, for he considered it his duty to remain at the head of the army and to carry the war into Peru. Accordingly some prominent citizens of Santiago elected General O'Higgins Supreme Director of Chile: this act virtually made O'Higgins dictator of the liberated territory. O'Higgins soon selected a few secretaries to aid him in the government of Chile; he appointed Miguel Zañartu secretary of state, and José Ignacio Zenteno secretary of war. A little later Hipólito Villegas was placed in charge of Chile's treasury. Meanwhile Director O'Higgins issued decrees providing that the Chileans should take an oath of fidelity to the new government, that the property of the royalists should be confiscated, and that a Chilean army should be organized.

O'Higgins and San Martín soon discussed the plans for an

attack upon the royalists in Peru. Both leaders felt that to secure control of the Pacific Ocean a navy was necessary. To secure aid in this enterprise San Martín soon re-crossed the Andes, accompanied only by two companions, and proceeded to Buenos Aires. In the end of March he quietly entered that city, where he soon held conferences with Pueyrredón. In accordance with a resolution of the congress of Tucumán, Manuel de Aguirre, a merchant of Buenos Aires, was appointed by Pueyrredón agent from the United Provinces to the United States of North America. By an agreement between Pueyrredón and San Martín, who had been given the requisite authority by O'Higgins, Aguirre was also commissioned to act for Chile. That agent was instructed to enter into whaever negotiations might be necessary in the United States for the purchase of war vessels. He carried with him two hundred thousand pesos, and was authorized to borrow funds in the United States. Aguirre took with him a letter addressed by San Martín to the president of the United States which declared that the great object of the mission was to secure in that country a squadron of vessels to promote the liberation of Peru. Aguirre arrived in Washington in July, 1817; he soon attempted to execute his commission. He informed President Monroe of the declaration of independence of the United Provinces. In vain he pleaded with the secretary of state, John Quincy Adams, for the recognition of the United Provinces as a sovereign power and for the negotiation of a treaty of amity and commerce between that nation and the United States. At the same time Aguirre was bargaining with merchants and ship-owners for vessels and munitions for his struggling compatriots. As the United States government was pursuing a neutral policy in the struggle between Spain and her revolted colonies, after securing two vessels of war, Aguirre was arrested for violating the neutrality law. Finally he despatched two vessels, the *Curiaco* and the *Horiaco,* to Buenos Aires. In 1818 the *Curiaco,* rechristened the *Independencia,* joined Chile's squadron in the Pacific Ocean.

In the meantime the Chilean patriots were making progress. On June 9, 1817, shortly after the return of San Martín from Buenos Aires, Hilario de Quintana, who was acting as the director during the absence of O'Higgins from the capital, issued a decree providing for the coinage of money bearing the inscription "Liberty, Union, and Strength,—Independent Chile." The official declaration of Chilean independence purported to be signed at Concepción on January 1, 1818, by Director O'Higgins and his three ministers. The declaration asserted that the rule of Spain in America was based upon force, that the revolution of September 18, 1810, was the first step which Chile had taken to fulfill her high destiny, and that the ensuing war with Spain had inspired the inhabitants of Chile with the determination to separate from the motherland. It also declared that the citizens of Chile had decided in favor of an immediate declaration of independence from Spain. Hence the announcement was made that "the continental territory of Chile and the adjacent islands" formed "in fact and by right, a free, independent, and sovereign state, which will remain forever separated from the Spanish monarchy with full power to adopt a suitable system of government."

In his monumental history of Chile, Diago Barros Arana states that this declaration was drafted by Miguel Zañartu and revised by Bernardo O'Higgins. Barros Arana also declares that O'Higgins added to the clause declaring that Chile was to be forever independent of Spain, the words "and of any other state"—a phrase which was not inserted in the official declaration as printed. The Chilean historian also affirms that the document was subsequently antedated, for Bernardo O'Higgins actually signed the declaration of independence at Talca on January 2, 1818.

On February 7, 1818, a proclamation was issued by the government of Chile declaring that February 12 had been selected as the day when the independence of Chile from Spain was to be formally announced. The proclamation contained provisions concerning the arrangements for the ceremony. Accordingly on the forenoon of February 12—the first anniversary of the battle of Chacabuco—the tribunals and the corporations of Santiago, with the leading officials, including José de San Martín and Tomás Guido, the envoy of the government of the United Provinces, proceeded from the palace of government to a stage which had been erected in the great square. On that stage in the presence of an enthusiastic crowd of people, the declaration of independence was read; then José de San Martín and the chief governmental officials solemnly swore to sustain the absolute independence of the

Chilean state with their lives, their fortunes, and their honor. There were scattered among the populace medals of silver, bearing the Chilean coat of arms and an appropriate inscription. Copies of the declaration of independence were distributed among the people and also copies of a manifesto which stated the reason that justified the Chilean revolution. The people of many towns in Chile and the soldiers of the patriot army received the news of the declaration with joy.

Nevertheless the independence of Chile was not completely established. On the night of March 19, 1818, the united army of the Andes and of Chile was surprised on the plains of Cancha Rayada, north of Talca; and San Martín had to retreat with the loss of some artillery. But he gathered his soldiers together again, breathed into them his own indomitable spirit, and marched to the plains of Maipú, near Santiago. When the royalists under General Osorio forded the Maipú River and threatened Santiago, they found San Martín's army drawn up in battle array. On a beautiful day, April 5, 1818, San Martín attacked the enemy. After a stubborn conflict, the royalists were defeated and put to rout: San Martín had won the last important engagement which was fought for the independence of Chile. He and other patriot commanders were showered with decorations and medals. The battle upon the plains of Maipú instilled fresh courage into the soldiers of independence, while reports of the victory startled the viceroys of Peru and New Granada. This victory almost insured the independence of southern South America from Spain. Further, it enabled San Martín to use Chile as a naval base for his projected attack upon the last great stronghold of the Spaniards in Peru. In the meantime other patriots were driving the remaining royalists out of Chile.

In May, 1818, O'Higgins appointed a commission to frame a preject of a provisional constitution for the new state. The constitution thus formed was promulgated by the Supreme Director several months later and was known as the "constitution of the year 1818." It placed the executive authority of Chile, both civil and military, in the hands of Director O'Higgins, who was to be aided by secretaries of state, treasury, and war. It vested the legislative authority in a senate composed of five members chosen by O'Higgins, who had the right to veto legislation. It vested the supreme judicial authority in a supreme court composed of five members also selected by O'Higgins. For administrative purposes the territory of Chile was divided into three provinces which were to be managed by governor-intendants. Although this provisional constitution contained a promise that a constituent congress would be assembled, O'Higgins remained dictator of the Chilean people for several years. Not until 1828 was a constitution promulgated for the republic of Chile.

A few days after the battle of Maipú, San Martín started on another trip to Buenos Aires, where the congress of the United Provinces publicly thanked him for his services. His mission was to secure aid for the expedition against Peru. As a result of his representations, the government of the United Provinces promised to contribute five hundred thousand pesos for the army of the Andes,—a pledge which it found extremely difficult to fulfill. In July, 1818, from the city of Mendoza, where he had tarried on his return trip, San Martín sent to Bernardo O'Higgins and to General Balcarce a project for an expedition from Chile against Peru with an army of six thousand men. In April, 1819, San Martín accepted an appointment as brigadier general of Chile's army.

While San Martín was promoting the cause of independence at Buenos Aires, the Chileans were creating a navy. A number of vessels were purchased, mounted with guns, and placed under the command of a Chilean mariner named Blanco Encalada. The Chileans were soon pleased to hear that while their small squadron was cruising in the Pacific, it had captured a Spanish frigate. About the same time through the influence of an agent in London, José Antonio Álvarez Condarco, Chile secured a most valuable recruit; for Lord Cochrane, an able and resourceful naval officer who had fallen into disgrace in England, was induced to enlist in the cause of South-American independence. Soon after the arrival of Lord Cochrane at Valparaiso in November, 1818, he was made the commander of the Chilean navy. Shortly afterwards Admiral Cochrane engaged in some daring exploits. He attacked the fortified port of Callao, but without success; and, in February, 1820, he captured the port of Valdivia. The spectacular deeeds of Lord Cochrane under the Chilean flag soon frightened the Spaniards, who nicknamed him *El Diablo*.

There were some Platean leaders who still dreamed of

founding a monarchy at Buenos Aires. When he heard rumors of those designs, the ambassador of France in England, the Marquis of Osmond, sent Colonel le Moyne to that city on a secret mission. After arriving there, this agent held several conferences with Director Pueyrredón. On September 2, 1818, Le Moyne reported that Pueyrredón secretly favored the establishment of a monarchy in the United Provinces under French influence, while Belgrano and San Martín favored the establishment of a monarchy there under English influence. It is significant that in October, 1818, the government of the United Provinces sent José V. Gomez, an ecclesiastic, on a mission to Europe with instructions which directed him to enter into negotiations with the government of France. In May, 1819, Gómez had conferences with Marquis Dessolle, the French minister of foreign affairs, concerning the creation of an independent kingdom in the United Provinces with a European prince as its sovereign. Baron Desesolle evidently thought that the separation of the United Provinces from Spain was almost inevitable. The rôle which he wished to play was that of mediator between those provinces and Spain: he proposed a scheme for the coronation of Prince Charles Louis, Duke of Lucca, as king of the United Provinces. Gómez, however, did not favor the project because that duke was a prince of Spain. In the same month when these negotiations were pending, the congress of the United Provinces adopted a constitution which vested the supreme power of the state in a director, a native-born citizen who should swear to preserve the integrity and independence of the national territory. The legislative authority was vested in a senate and a house of representatives. In June, 1819, Pueyrredón renounced the position of supreme director: he was succeeded by General Rondeau. When Director Rondeau heard of the negotiations of Gómez, he sent a message to congress regarding the candidacy of the Duke of Lucca for the throne of the Unted Provinces. The aspirations of some Platean leaders are suggested by the surprising fact that the members of congress decided to accept that duke as their monarch upon certain conditions. But in the same month, the new French minister of foreign affairs, Baron Pasquier, informed Gómez that his government had withdrawn completely from the project of making a Spanish prince the king of the United Provinces. Thus the negotiations of 1819 for the establishment of a European dynasty in South America ended fruitlessly.

The discord and anarchy in the United Provinces, which made some leaders favor the establishment of a monarchy there, hindered the preparations for San Martín's expedition against Peru. The government at Buenos Aires even ordered San Martín to lead his soldiers back across the Andes. But instead of obeying that command, and thus, for the time being at least, relinquishing his long-cherished project, San Martín resigned his office as general of the army of the Andes, declaring that the director who had appointed him to the command was no longer in power. At the instance of San Martín, however, this resignation was referred to his army for consideration. At the town of Rancagua on April 2, 1820, a junta of his officers declared that San Martín was still the commander of the army of the Andes. The Platean soldiers of San Martín thus acted in defiance of their own government, while San Martín sanctioned their action by retaining the command of the army. In truth the so-called act of Rancagua was a revolutionary measure:—San Martín and his soldiers virtually renounced the governmental authority of the United Provinces.

About one month after the act of Rancagua, the Chilean government appointed San Martín commander-in-chief of the army of liberation. On July 22, 1820, General San Martín issued a proclamation from Valparaiso addressed to the people of the United Provinces of la Plata. In his farewell proclamation San Martín attributed the anarchy prevailing in those provinces to the attempt "to establish a federal government in a thinly-settled country where there were many jealousies and local antipathies, where the citizens were poorly acquainted with political affairs, and where revenues to pay the expenses of the national government were lacking." To justify his action in declining to return to Buenos Aires, he asserted that, if he had taken part in the dissensions of the United Provinces, he would have been force to relinquish his project for the liberation of Peru. "Provinces of the Río de la Plata," said General San Martín, "this proclamation will be my last response to my calumniators: I can do no more than to risk my life and my honor for the sake of my native land. Whatever may be my lot in the campaign against Peru, I shall demonstrate that ever since I returned to my native land, her independence has been my constant thought, and that I never entertained any other ambition than to merit the hatred of the ungrateful and the esteem of the virtuous."

In August, 1820, the expedition for the liberation of Peru gathered at Valparaiso. The fleet consisted of eight war vessels and sixteen transports which carried supplies for six months. The soldiers on board those vessels numbered over four thousand; more than one-half of them belonged ostensibly to the army of the Andes, while the remainder were mainly Chileans. There were about three hundred officers, most of whom were from the Platean provinces, or from Europe. A large number of the European military officers were from England. The seamen and marines in the expedition numbered about sixteen hundred: among the naval officers there were also a number of men of European birth. The flag of independent Chile flew from the masthead of the frigate *O'Higgins,* commanded by Lord Cochrane, which led the small squadron out of the harbor of Valparaiso on August 20, 1820. When Cochrane opened his sealed instructions, signed by O'Higgins and Zenteno, he read these words: "The object of the expedition is to free Peru from Spanish domination, to raise her to the rank of a free and sovereign power, and thus to complete the sublime task of establishing the independence of South America. Captain General José de San Martín is the chief to whom the government of the republic has given the entire charge of this great enterprise."

In secret instructions San Martín was informed that, if Admiral Cochrane disobeyed his commands, he was authorized to remove that admiral and to replace him by an officer who merited his entire confidence. In conferring these extensive powers upon San Martín, O'Higgins declared that the expedition was to liberate the Peruvian people, who should be organized in the political form which was best adapted to the circumstances of Peru and of South America. Director O'Higgins, to whose exertions the equipment of the expedition was largely due, had written a proclamation for distribution among the Peruvians in which he declared: "You shall be free and independent; you shall form your government and your laws according to the spontaneous wish of your own representatives. The soldiers of the army of liberation, your brothers, will exert no influence, military or civil, direct or

indirect, in your social system. Whenever it suits you, dismiss
the army which marches to protect you. A military force
should never occupy the territory of a free people unless invited by its legitimate magistrates."

The viceroyalty of Peru—the last important stronghold of
Spanish power on the American continent—stretched northward along the Pacific coast from the desert of Atacama to
the presidency of Quito. On the east it was bounded by
Brazil and the presidency of Charcas. Its chief port was the
fortified city of Callao. A short distance east of Callao was
the capital city of Lima, which Peruvians often designated as
the city of the kings. After 1810 there had been uprisings
against Spanish rule in Peru—notably the revolt of Pumaca-
hua at Cuzco in 1814—but no sustained movement such as
we have noticed in the basin of la Plata. A number of intellectual leaders had attempted to arouse the Peruvian people
against the motherland. Of these leaders we may only notice
Hipólito Unanue of the University of San Marcos, and José
de la Riva Agüero, a young lawyer who was the most able
and influential member of the revolutionary coteries. While
the army of the Andes was still at Mendoza, General Joaquin de Pezuela, who had commanded the royalist army in
Upper Peru, was appointed viceroy of Peru. When Pezuela
learned that San Martín was preparing an expedition against
his viceroyalty, he earnestly hoped that the Spanish government would send him reënforcements, but his hopes were
disappointed.

On September 8, 1820, the first division of the army of
liberation landed near Pisco, south of Callao. On that day
General San Martín issued an address to his soldiers declaring "that their main duty was to console South America, and
that they were not to make conquests but to free peoples."
He asked them "to respect the rights of their Peruvian brothers, as they had respected the rights of the Chileans after the
battle of Chacabuco." In an address to the people of Peru
he spoke of the triumph of the constitutionalists in the Spanish peninsula as follows: "The revolution in Spain is of the
same nature as our own revolution; both of these revolutions
were caused by oppression: the object of both revolutions is
to ensure liberty to the people. But Spanish America can
view the liberal constitution of Spain only as a fraudulent

attempt to conserve a colonial system which can no longer be maintained by force."

In accordance with instructions from the constitutional government of Spain, Viceroy Pezuela selected two commissioners, Count Villar de Fuente and Lieutenant Dionisio Capúz, to treat with San Martín regarding peace. San Martín sent as commissioners Colonel Tomás Guido, his aide-de-camp, and Juan García del Río, a cultured creole of New Granada who was acting as his secretary. On September 26 both parties agreed to observe an armistice during the negotiations. The commissioners held some conferences at Miraflores, near Lima. The agents of Pezuela asked that the constitution of 1812 should be accepted by the Chileans and by the army of San Martín, while the agents of San Martín asked that the independence of Peru should be recognized by Spain. In the course of the negotiations San Martín's agents evidently intimated that they might agree to a compromise which would provide for the coronation in South America of a European prince. According to the viceroy those agents even suggested that the prince might be selected from the ruling dynasty of Spain. However, the commissioners could not reach an agreement, evidently because Pezuela thought that to negotiate for the establishment of a European prince in South America was to exceed his authority. Pezuela also questioned the authority of San Martín to engage in such negotiations. In announcing to the people of Peru the outcome of the negotiations at Miraflores, San Martín declared that his functions as general of the army of liberation would cease upon the day when the Peruvians manifested their wishes concerning their governmental institutions.

When he decided to break off negotiations with Penzuela, San Martín sent a part of his army under General Arenáles toward the Andrean range, and meanwhile he feigned an attack upon Lima. Arenáles made a venturesome march northward; and on December 6, he defeated the royalists at Pasco, a short distance northwest of Lima. In the end of October, San Martín reëmbarked his army and sailed along the coast to Huaura, a point about seventy miles north of Lima, where, on January 8, 1821, he was joined by Arenáles.

In the same month the vacillating viceroy, who was in camp near Lima, was deposed by a junta of his officers led

by Generals Canterac and Valdez and replaced by General
José de la Serna, who had succeeded him as commander of
the army in Upper Peru. Soon afterwards La Serna, who
thus virtually became viceroy of Peru, invited San Martín to
enter into negotiations for reconciliation with Spain. Commissioners were again selected by the contending parties:
again no agreement was reached. The attempt was revived in
the following March, when Manuel Abreu, who had been commissioned by the Spanish government to negotiate with the
Chilean insurgents, arrived at Huaura. After Abreu and San
Martín met, La Serna appointed new commissioners to negotiate with San Martín for peace. The upshot of the negotiations was that an armistice was arranged at Punchauca
on May 23, 1821, which provided for an interview between
La Serna and San Martín. On June 2 this interview took
place at Punchauca in the presence of the peace commissioners and the generals of both armies. As a preliminary to
any negotiations, San Martín demanded the recognition of
Peruvian independence. Should this be granted, he proposed
that a governmental junta be established in Peru. To San
Martín the occasion seemed opportune for the presentation of
his favorite political project. Again he proposed the establishment of a constitutional monarchy in South America, suggesting that the king, or emperor, might be a prince of the
Spanish royal house. He even proposed to send envoys to
Spain to urge his project upon the government. After conferring with the officers of his army, La Serna declined to agree
to these proposals. It is noteworthy that this project bore
some resemblance to the Plan of Iguala, which unknown to
San Martín, had been proclaimed in Mexico three months before the armistice of Punchauca. When San Martín heard of
the progress of the Iturbidista movement in Mexico, he
broached his favorite design to General Canterac, but that
officer firmly replied that events in New Spain would in no
wise influence him to adopt a measure which was not in
harmony with the views of the Spanish nation. The interpretation which San Martín later gave to the negotiations with
the Spaniards should be noticed: namely, that his object
was to compromise the Spanish commanders by inducing
them virtually to recognize the independence of Spanish
America.

A short time after the failure of the negotiations between

Viceroy La Serna and General San Martín for the pacification of Peru, Captain Basil Hall, an English traveler, had an interview with the revolutionary leader on board a schooner which was anchored in the harbor of Callao. In his journal Captain Hall recorded his impressions of San Martín in these words:

There was little, at first sight, in his appearance to engage the attention; but when he rose up and began to speak, his great superiority over every other person I had seen in South America was sufficiently apparent. He received us in very homely style, on the deck of his vessel, dressed in a surtout coat, and a large fur cap, seated at a table made of a few loose planks laid along the top of two empty casks.

General San Martín is a tall, erect, well-proportioned handsome man, with a large aquiline nose, thick black hair, and immense bushy whiskers extending from ear to ear under the chin: his complexion is deep olive, and his eye, which is large, prominent, and piercing, jet black; his whole appearance being highly military. He is thoroughly well-bred, and unaffectedly simple in his manners; exceedingly cordial and engaging, and possessed evidently of great kindliness of disposition: in short, I have never seen any person, the enchantment of whose address was more irresistible. In conversation he goes at once to the strong points of the topic, disdaining, as it were, to trifle with its minor parts: he listens earnestly, and replies with distinctness and fairness, showing wonderful resources in argument, and a most happy fertility of illustration; the effect of which is to make his audience feel they are understood in the sense they wish. Yet there is nothing showy or ingenious in his discourse; and he certainly seems at all times perfectly in earnest, and deeply possessed with his subject. Several times during this interview his animation rose to a high pitch, and then the flash of his eye, and the whole turn of his expression, became so exceedingly energetic as to rivet the attention of his audience beyond the possibility of evading his arguments. This was most remarkably the case when the topic was politics. . . .

The contest in Peru, he said, was not of an ordinary description—not a war of conquest and glory, but entirely of opinion; it was a war of new and liberal principles against prejudice, bigotry, and tyranny. "People ask," said San Martín, "why I don't march to Lima at once; so I might, and instantly would, were it suitable to my views—which it is not. I do not want military renown—I have no ambition to be the conqueror of Peru—I want solely to liberate the country from oppression.

Of what use would Lima be to me, if the inhabitants were hostile in public sentiment? How could the cause of Independence be advanced by my holding Lima, or even the whole country, in military possession? Far different are my views. I wish to have all men thinking with me, and do not choose to advance a step beyond the gradual march of public opinion. The capital is now ripe for declaring its sentiments, and I shall give them the opportunity of doing so in safety. It was in sure expectation of this moment that I have hitherto deferred advancing; and to those who know the full extent of the means which have been put in action, a sufficient explanation is afforded of all the delays that have taken place. I have been gaining, indeed, day by day, fresh allies in the hearts of the people, the only certain allies in such a war. In the secondary point of military strength, I have been, from the same causes, equally successful in augmenting and improving the liberating army; while that of the Spaniards has been wasted by want and desertion. The country has now become sensible of its true interests, and it is right the inhabitants should have the means of expressing what they think. Public opinion is an engine newly introduced into this country; the Spaniards, who are utterly incapable of directing it, have prohibited its use; but they shall now experience its strength and importance."

Possibly it was partly because of the increasing sentiment in favor of independence in northern Peru that, early in July, the viceroy decided to evacuate the Peruvian coast. On July 6 the soldiers of La Serna marched out of that capital city toward the Andes, leaving a garrison in Callao. A deputation from the *cabildo* of Lima at once invited San Martín to enter the city. True to the policy which he had announced, San Martín declared that, if the citizens of Lima wished to declare themselves independent of Spain, he was ready to enter that capital. Captain Hall quoted him as saying: "All that I wish is, that this country should be managed by itself, and by itself alone. As to the manner in which it is to be governed, that belongs not at all to me. I propose simply to give the people the means of declaring themselves independent, and of establishing a suitable form of government; after which I shall consider that I have done enough, and leave them." Soon after the departure of the royalists, San Martín's soldiers occupied Lima. On July 12, Captain General San Martín quietly enterd that city. Captain Hall has left an interesting description of the reception of San Martín by the people.

A fine-looking woman offered him her sons for the Peruvian service. Five ladies wished to clasp his knees at once. A "tall raw-boned, pale-faced friar" praised the manner in which he had entered Lima. A "beautiful young woman . . . threw herself into the General's arms and lay there full half a minute without being able to utter more than, 'Oh mi General! mi General!' She then tried to disengage herself, but San Martín, who had been struck with her enthusiasim and beauty, drew her gently and respectfully back, and holding his head a little on one side, said with a smile, that he must be permitted to show his grateful sense of such good-will, by one affectionate salute."

By his addresses, proclamations, and letters San Martín had instilled the idea of independence from Spain into the minds of some Peruvians and stimulated it in the minds of others. In accordance with his suggestion, the *cabildo* of Lima now invited some prominent citizens to assemble in order to consider in an open council the question of Peruvian independence. On July 15 this *cabildo abierto* informed San Martín that the personages who attended the meeting had agreed that "the general wish was in favor of the independence of Peru from Spain, and from all other nations, and that measures should be taken to sanction the popular will by the proper oath." In a short time arrangements were made to declare Peru independent. On July 28, 1821, General San Martín, the chief officers of his army, representatives of the University of San Marchos, some prominent ecclesiastics, many nobles, the members of the *audiencia,* and the *cabildo,* accompanied by a military escort, proceeded from the former palace of the viceroy to the great square of Lima. There, on a spacious stage, General San Martín unfurled for the first time the flag of independent Peru. " *'From this moment,'* " he is reported to have said in the proclamation announcing the event, " *'Peru is free and independent, by the general wish of the people, and by the justice of her cause, which may God defend.'* Then, waving the flag, he exclaimed several times in a tone thrilling with the pure and celestial pleasure which only a beneficent personage could feel: *'Viva la patria! Viva la libertad! Viva la independencia!'*—expressions which, like a festive echo, resounded throughout the plaza, amid the noise of cannon, the ringing of all the bells of the city, and the exclamations of universal joy."

Thus the independence of Peru from Spain was proclaimed. Silver medals were scattered in the square. They bore upon one side the inscription, "Lima being liberated, avowed its independence on July 28, 1821"; and upon the other side, "Under the protection of the liberating army of Peru, commanded by San Martín." On the following day *Te Deum* was chanted and high mass performed in the cathedral of Lima. Then the leading inhabitants of the capital swore "to maintain and to defend with their opinions, persons, and properties the independence of Peru from the government of Spain and from any other foreign domination." In the evening a ball was given at the governmental palace, while the houses were decorated and illuminated. The consulate of Lima erected a triumphal arch which bore an equestrian statue of the liberator with saber in hand. The news of the ceremonies which marked the proclamation of Peruvian independence was published in Peru by the *Gaceta del Gobierno de Lima Independiente*. Meanwhile, San Martín had taken steps to make the people conform to the system of independence and to "the new institutions of Peru," or to leave Peruvian soil.

Then San Martín had to decide upon a system of government for the new state. This was a difficult task, for Peru was in a peculiar position. A large portion of her territory was still dominated by the royalists. There was no governmental nucleus around which a national organization might be formed. Instructions for the army of liberation which were framed by the Chilean senate had provided that, after the capture of Lima, a director, or a supreme junta, was to be elected there, with full power to govern Peru; but evidently these instructions were withheld from San Martín by O'Higgins. San Martín's administrative policy was embodied in a proclamation dated August 3, 1821. He announced that the supreme military and civil authority of the former viceroyalty of Peru was vested in himself with the title of protector. He declared that his object in taking this action was "to advance the sacred cause of America and to promote the happiness of the Peruvian people." He said that there still were enemies to combat in Peru; hence it was imperative that he should continue to exercise the civil and military authority. San Martín disclaimed any ambitious motives. The experience gained during ten years of revolution in South America, he said, had taught him the lesson that to convoke a congress while there still were royalists in a country was to produce serious evils. He argued that independence should first be secured and then liberty might be established firmly. Again he declared that, at the moment when he saw Peru free, he would relinquish his office to make way for the government which the Peruvians might wish to establish. "When I have the satisfaction of resigning the command and giving an account of my actions to the representatives of the people," said San Martín, "I am certain that they will not discover during the period of my administration those traces of venality, despotism, and corruption which have marked the administration of the Spanish government in America. To administer exact justice to all, to reward virtue and patriotism, and to punish vice and sedition wherever they may be found,—this is the ideal which will regulate my actions, while I am at the head of this nation."

The protector of Peru selected three secretaries to assist him in the administration of the government. Juan García del Río was made secretary of state and foreign relations; Bernardo Monteagudo was made secretary of war and the navy; and Hipólito Unanue was made secretary of the treasury. Wide differences of opinion have been expressed by various writers in regard to the wisdom of San Martín's proclamation declaring himself the protector of Peru. Perhaps the judgment of Captain Hall is the fairest: "It was more creditable to assume the full authority in a manly and open manner, than to mock the people with the semblance of a republic, and, at the same time, to visit them with the reality of a despotism." Unfortunately, however, the establishment of a protectorate, or rather a dictatorship, did not harmonize with the assurances which had been given to the Peruvians concerning a free and independent government. At a later time Lord Cochrane indignantly declared that San Martín had tried to induce him to accept the title of "First Admiral of Peru," that is, had virtually asked him to turn over Chile's squadron to the Peruvian government.

On October 8, 1821, the protector of Peru issued a provisional decree which was to be observed until a permanent constitution was promulgated. The decree provided that the laws of Spain which harmonized with it and with the declaration of independence were to remain in force. It vaguely defined the powers of the protector and provided a council of state to advise him in governmental affairs. It declared that the judicial department of government should be kept separate from the executive department. The precise form of government which was to be established in Peru, however, was tacitly left to the future. A short time after issuing this provisional decree San Martín founded a military fraternity, the Order of the Sun. His object was evidently to reward the warriors who had fought to establish Peruvian independence. The chief officers of his army were made members of the order; certain funds were assigned for its maintenance; and an academy was established for the education of the sons of its members. While the establishment of that order provided a reward for soldiers of merit, yet it also furnished a natural basis for a military aristocracy, it promoted jealousy among the Peruvians. In this particular the protectorate of San Martín resembled the rule of Emperor Agustín I. of Mexico. There is some significance in the fact that at a meeting of the patriotic society of Lima, which was founded under the auspices of San Martín, a member argued that Peru was not ready for a democratic government, and that a kingdom should be established there.

Several other decrees of San Martín the protector deserve attention. On August 4 he issued a decree warning the Spaniards who were secretly intriguing against the government that they would be made to feel all the rigors of the law and would be deprived of their properties. He declared that he was aware of what happened "in the most secluded corner" of their houses. On August 12 he issued another decree declaring that the children of slaves born in Peru after the proclamation of Peruvian independence should be free. Three days later the protector issued a decree which declared that every person who had left Valparaiso with his expedition should be considered as belonging to the Peruvian service and entitled to a pension. On August 27 the tribute which the Spaniards had levied upon the Indians was abolished. One of the most important decrees was that providing for the establishment of a national library at Lima.

But San Martín had passed the zenith of his power. The refusal to fight Canterac, who provokingly marched before the gates of Lima, although justified in September, 1821, by the surrender of Callao, nevertheless injured San Martín's military prestige. A bitter quarrel with the belligerent Lord

Cochrane respecting the payment of the officers and seamen of the Chilean squadron undermined the protector's authority, and resulted in the withdrawal from Peru of the squadron which had made her independence possible. In November, 1821, San Martín was attacked by a mysterious malady which confined him to his bed, convinced him of the precarious condition of his health, and made him desire private life. The wings of the "new Icarus," as Cochrane styled San Martín, would not support his lofty flight. Many of the revolutionary soldiers had become dissatisfied with the Fabian policy which their general had adopted. Grave dissensions appeared in the army of liberation. A jealous dislike of their austere chieftain spread among the military officers. A conspiracy against the authority, and perhaps even against the life, of San Martín was discovered. Furthermore, in 1822, the defeat of the soldiers whom he had sent south to the Ica Valley in charge of two Peruvians, Domingo Tristan and Colonel Gamarra, imperiled the cause of independence and damaged his military reputation. Lastly, suspicions were rife about the designs of San Martín regarding the government of independent Peru. Perhaps it was not simply by way of a jest that some of his military associates spoke of him as "King José."

The suspicions of San Martín's monarchical projects were strengthened by rumors in regard to agents who were sent abroad at the instance of the protector. In December, 1821, with the advice of his council of state, San Martín had chosen Juan García del Río and Diego Paroissien to proceed to the Old World on a secret mission. The ostensible objects of this mission were to solicit the recognition of the independence of Peru by European nations and to negotiate a loan of six million pesos. García del Río and Paroissien were instructed to negotiate a treaty of alliance with the government of England. In secret instructions the agents were directed to ask that a prince of the house of Brunswick should become the emperor of Peru under a constitution framed by representatives of the Peruvians. If the approaches of those emissaries to the court of London were unsuccessful, they were empowered to make similar proposals to Russia, Austria, France, and Portugal. They might even solicit the Duke of Lucca to occupy the throne of the Incas. San Martín attempted to secure the coöperation of Chile in his schemes; for he wrote to O'Higgins: "I am persuaded that my views will meet with your approval, for I believe that you will be convinced of the impossibility of erecting republics in these countries. In brief, I desire only the establishment of that form of government which is adapted to the existing circumstances, thus avoiding the horrors of anarchy." At that juncture, however, O'Higgins did not favor the establishment of a monarchy in Chile. In a memorandum which San Martín's agents wrote concerning their interview with Director O'Higgins, they recorded him as expressing the view that the monarchical plan was doubtless suitable for Peru, but that in Chile, where there was no definite opinion concerning the system of government, the best policy was to leave the government as it was. Apparently San Martín's emissaries never fully disclosed the monarchical project to a single chancellery of Europe. For after the middle of 1822, when, as will be shown in the following chapter, San Martín withdrew from the position of protector of Peru, his emissaries no longer felt authorized to negotiate with European nations for the creation of a monarchy in America.

The dramatic manner in which San Martín retired from public life, and the influence of that step upon the fortunes of the revolution against Spanish rule in Peru, can rightly be understood only after considering the career and the aspirations of his Colombian rival. For, although under the inspiration of San Martín's leadership, Chile had been re-conquered from the royalists and the city of the kings had been captured, yet the struggle for the establishment of South-American independence was not yet crowned with success. The narrative of that struggle is a serial story, which will be continued in the chapter devoted to Simón de Bolívar, who, after ten years of warfare, established the independence of northern South America.

Chapter 7

Simón de Bolívar

THE BOLÍVAR FAMILY, to name it with the mediæval spelling, was Spanish, and its ancestral home was at Marquina, a town in Vizcaya near Bilbao. Simón de Bolívar, the founder of the Bolívar family in northern South America, emigrated from Vizcaya to Santo Domingo in the middle of the sixteenth century. About 1588 he moved from Santo Domingo to South America, where his descendants figured prominently in the annals of Venezuela. They married into various noble families: de Rojas, de Rebolleda, de Villegas, de Ponte, de Narváez; and they served as judges, *alcaldes, corregidores,* and captains. In the eighteenth century, the Bolívar's accordingly held an enviable place in Venezuelan society. Nevertheless, it is suspected that in the veins of that aristocratic family there ran some Indian blood.

In 1772 Juan Vicente de Bolívar, the fifth lineal descendant of Simón, married María de la Concepción Palacios y Blanco, who, like himself, had been born in the city of Caracas. The ancestry of María Palacios y Blanco has been traced back to Juan de Palacios, who, in the seventeenth century, lived in the Spanish province of Burgos. Two daughters, María Antonia and Juana, and two sons sprang from this marriage. The elder son, Juan Vicente, figures dimly in the early revolution; for he was sent to the United States in 1810 as an envoy of the provisional junta of Venezuela, and apparently perished in a shipwreck on the homeward voyage. The second son, Simón de Bolívar, was born in the city of Caracas on July 24, 1783. His father was a wealthy and influential citizen of Caracas: he was a *regidor* of that city and a colonel of militia of the valleys of Aragua; he owned rich copper mines in the sierra de Aroa and various haciendas in the valleys of Venezuela.

On July 30, 1783, the second son of Juan de Bolívar was baptized Simón, José, Antonio, de la Santísima Trinidad. The child probably received the baptismal name "de la Santísima Trinidad" because his parents were accustomed to worship in a chapel of Caracas which a member of the Bolívar family had dedicated to the worship of the Holy Trinity,—a cult which Simón supported throughout his life. Only a few years of Simón's boyhood were spent in his father's house near the Plaza de San Jacinto; for he was left an orphan at an early age: his father died in 1786, and his mother died in 1792. Soon after the death of his father, the child was placed in charge of Miguel J. Saenz, a jurisconsult of Caracas, with whom he lived for about two years. After the death of his mother, the orphan was for a time under the guardianship of Esteban Palacios, his maternal uncle. According to traditions preserved in the Saenz family, the little boy was disobedient, talkative, and provocative, but mentally and physically alert.

For about eight years Bolívar was under the tutorship of Simón Rodríguez, an eccentric philosopher, who taught him the rudiments of Spanish grammar, Latin, arithmetic, and history. A younger tutor, Andrés Bello—who later became a famous Chilean scholar—strove to teach the youth geography and cosmography. Of his preceptors Bolívar liked Rodríguez the best; years afterwards he described that philosophic tutor as the wisest, most virtuous, and most extraordinary man: "he was the companion of my childhood, the confidant of all my joys and sorrows, the mentor whose advice and encouragement have influenced me greatly." In view of this intimate relationship it appears significant that in 1797 the favorite tutor of Bolívar was arrested for complicity in a revolutionary conspiracy. When he was released from prison the philosopher left South America. It is clear that Simón de Bolívar did not profit greatly by the admonitions of his tutors. In a biographical note one of his uncles declared that the boy read a little and wrote badly. In truth, a letter written when Simón was almost sixteen years of age shows that, in spite of his exceptional educational advantages, he did not spell some common Spanish words correctly.

At that time the youth displayed a passionate fondness for athletic exercise and outdoor life. It is likely that Simón spent many happy days on the haciendas which belonged to his family. At an early age he followed in his father's footsteps; for on January 14, 1797, he entered the Spanish military service as a volunteer in the battalion of white militia of the valleys of Aragua. The son of the deceased colonel of that battalion was soon promoted: on July 4, 1798, a royal order was issued which made him ensign of the sixth company of the Aragua militia. In the official reports of this company which have been printed, the officers of his battalion spoke hopefully in regard to Simón's ability and declared that his conduct was good. The youth evidently enjoyed militia service, but, as the occasion was lacking, he did not participate in any campaign.

According to a custom which prevailed among some aristocratic families of South America, Simón de Bolívar was sent abroad to complete his education. At the instance of his guardian, early in 1799 he sailed from La Guaira for Europe in the ship *San Illdefonso*. As the voyage was made by way of Vera Cruz, in March, 1799, Bolívar visited Mexico City. From Vera Cruz the *San Illdefonso* proceeded to the Iberian peninsula. For some time after arriving in Madrid, Simón de Bolívar lived again with Esteban Palacios, who was in favor at the Spanish court because he was an intimate friend of Manuel Mallo, a favorite of Queen María Luisa. Apparently the young South American also became one of Mallo's confidants. Years afterwards Bolívar declared that after winning a game of tennis from the Prince of Asturias, he audaciously declared that he would later deprive Ferdinand of the most precious jewel in his crown. It is possible that this story was an afterthought on Bolívar's part, for in later years his early life became enveloped in a romantic glamor.

While in Spain Bolívar met a relative of the Marquis of Toro named Bernardo Rodríguez del Toro. The young man soon became enamored of Toro's daughter, María Teresa. The youth of the lovers, however, made María's father wish that their marriage might be delayed. In September, 1800, Bolívar wrote to his guardian, Pedro Palacios, avowing a desire to marry María Teresa and asking his consent to the marriage. Meanwhile, for some reason or other, Bolívar incurred the displeasure of the Spanish government: in 1801 he left the peninsula in disgust. On that trip he made a visit to Paris, where he was much impressed with the achievements of the First Consul, Bonaparte, "the hero of the republic." His love affair soon drew him back to Spain, where on May 15, 1802, Charles IV. granted him a permit to marry María Teresa, a permit indispensable to officers of Bolívar's rank.

A short time afterwards the marriage of Simón de Bolívar and María Rodríguez del Toro was solemnized at Madrid.

Soon after the nuptials were celebrated Bolívar and his girl-bride sailed from Spain for South America. The bride-groom returned to his native land partly because of financial reasons. Before Simón was two years of age a relative named Juan Félix Jerez y Aristeguieta had conveyed to him an estate, which, at a conservative estimate, yielded an annual income of two thousand pesos. The fruits of that estate Bolívar could enjoy only by residing in Venezuela. Furthermore, he was interested in other properties, for he had been bequeathed a portion of the estate of Feliciano Palacios y Sojo, his maternal grandfather. Although kept in ignorance of the total amount of his fortune, yet Bolívar must have been aware that he was one of the wealthiest young aristocrats of Caracas.

If Simón de Bolívar had hoped to live quietly on a family hacienda at San Mateo in the beautiful valleys of Aragua—far from worldly strife—his idyllic dreams were rudely shattered. Soon after arriving in Venezuela, his young wife was stricken ill. On January 22, 1803, she died. Many years afterwards, when time had not effaced the impression made by his wife's death, Bolívar was quoted as saying that this bereavment greatly changed the current of his life:

I loved my wife much, and, at her death, I took an oath nevermore to marry. . . . If my wife had not died, I would not have made my second trip to Europe. It is probable that there would not have been born either at Caracas or at San Mateo the ideas which I acquired in my travels: in America I should not have gained the experience nor should I have made that study of the world, of men, and of affairs which has served me so well during the entire course of my political career. The death of my wife placed me at an early age in the road of politics: it caused me to follow the chariot of Mars instead of the plow of Ceres.

Soon after his wife's death, Bolívar made another trip to Europe. His second tour abroad lasted from 1804 to 1807. The young widower visited Spain, France, Austria, Italy, and England. On the voyage to Spain he spent some time reading Monesquieu, Voltaire, and Rousseau. Some of Bolívar's biographers declare—without presenting evidence to support the assertion—that, soon after disembarking at Cadiz, the South American was admitted into a secret society, which aimed to establish the independence of the Spanish colonies. From Cadiz Bolívar proceeded to Madrid, where he mourned the death of María Teresa with her father. Thence he went to Paris, where he apparently regretted the transformation of the first consul into the Emperor Napoleon. At Vienna he found his beloved preceptor Rodríguez engrossed in the study of science. Rodríguez seems to have feared that the melancholy young widower was falling into consumption. He told Bolívar that the total amount of the fortune which he had inherited was four million pesos. In a letter which he wrote in 1804 Bolívar extravagantly declared that, when the immense size of his fortune was thus revealed to him, the Spanish language could not express his emotion:

I went to London, where I spent one hundred and fifty thousand francs in three months. Then I went to Madrid, where I maintained the train of a prince. I did the same in Lisbon. In brief, I everywhere displayed the greatest luxury, and squandered wealth for the semblance of pleasure.

During this visit to the Old World, Bolívar indulged in speculations regarding the destiny of his native land. At Paris he discussed with Alexander von Humboldt the future of Spanish America. In the company of Rodríguez, who tried to arouse the ambition of his pupil and to interest him in the cause of science or of liberty, Bolívar visited many historic spots in Italy. According to the recollections of both master and pupil, in 1805 Bolívar took a solemn oath upon the Aventine Mount to dedicate himself to the task of liberating America from the yoke of Spain. Many years afterwards in a letter to Rodríguez, Bolívar mentioned the circumstance in these words, "You remember when we went to Monte Sacro at Rome to vow upon that holy spot the liberty of our fatherland." This romantic trip through Europe obviously had a great influence upon Bolívar. He strove to forget his bereavement in dissipation; he fell under the spell of Jean Jacques Rousseau; and his soul burned because of the enslavement of his native land. The rôle of the great Napoleon appears to have made a vivid impression upon him. José Gil Fortoul, the noted scholar and publicist of Venezuela, has appropriately said that Bolívar's second trip to Europe was in the nature of a parenthesis between two great passions.

After making a brief visit to the United States, Bolívar returned to South America in 1807. It seems likely that he sympathized with those fellow-countrymen who were secretly plotting to subvert Spanish rule in Venezuela. There is a tradition that, in 1809, he was compromised by participation in a conspiracy. Unmistakable evidence of Bolívar's revolutionary spirit was furnished after the creation of a provisional junta in April, 1810, for—as mentioned in the chapter concerning Miranda—that junta sent him on a mission to London. After returning to his native land Bolívar became a leader of the Venezuelan revolution. He made a stirring speech in favor of independence before the patriotic society, and served with distinction under Miranda in the campaign against the royalists of Valencia. In the second chapter Bolívar's part in the downfall of Miranda was discussed. After Miranda's betrayal General Monteverde allowed Bolívar to sail for Curacao. If, after the capitulation of San Mateo, Colonel Bolívar had actually harbored wild thoughts of enlisting under Sir Arthur Wellesley in the Spanish peninsula, those thoughts were dismissed when he became aware not only that the gold and silver which he had sent to Curacao had been sequestrated, but that Monteverde had confiscated his estates. Henceforth Simón de Bolívar was dedicated to the task of liberating his native land from Spanish domination. From the West Indies he soon proceeded to the city of Carthagena whare some revolutionists were entrenched.

At this point we must glance at the revolutionary movement in the viceroyalty of New Granada, which was, at times, the theater of Bolívar's activity. That viceroyalty extended from Venezuela to Peru. Its mountainous character made it well adapted to guerrilla warfare. Its capital, Bogotá, was styled by Humboldt "the Athens of South America." In 1810 reports of the governmental conditions in Spain made certain inhabitants of that capital, notably Camilo Torres, dream of a new régime which would ensure to the inhabitants of the viceroyalty the same rights as peninsular Spaniards.

Not until after the uprising of April, 1810, at Caracas, however, did a secessionist movement take place at Bogotá.

At that capital, on July 20, 1810, an extraordinary *cabildo,* which avowed allegiance to the Spanish regency, deposed Viceroy Antonio Amar and vested the government in a provisional junta. Shortly afterwards the deposed viceroy was deported to Europe. On November 27, 1811, delegates from several provinces who gathered at Bogotá adopted a confederate constitution for the "United Provinces of New Granada,"—a constitution which met with some opposition from a faction led by Antonio Nariño. On July 16, 1813, a congress of delegates from Cundinamarca—the central province of New Granada—which had assembled at Bogotá, adopted a declaration of independence from Spain. However, that declaration framed at the ancient capital of the viceroyalty was not the first which was made by the provinces of New Granada. On November 11, 1811, the members of a junta in the city of Carthagena—influenced by popular sentiment—framed a declaration of independence which contained an explanation of the motives that impelled them to decide upon a separation from the Spanish monarchy. The principal motives adduced were: the cession of the crown of Spain to Napoleon which had severed the bonds between the Spanish monarch and his people; the imprudent and provocative measures which the patriot government of Spain had taken in regard to the viceroyalty of New Granada; the inequality of representation which the American colonies had been granted in the Spanish *cortes;* and the lack of good government for the Spanish-Americans. The members of the junta declared that they were accordingly obliged to use those imprescriptible rights which they had acquired because of Napoleon's usurpations:

We, the representatives of the good people of the province of Carthagena de Indias, with their express and public consent, invoking the Supreme Being to witness the rectitude of our proceedings, and asking the impartial world to judge of the justice of our cause, declare solemnly in the face of the entire world, that the province of Carthagena de Indias is henceforth by fact and right a free, sovereign, and independent state; that it is absolved from the submission, vassalage, obedience, and relationship which previously bound it to the crown and government of Spain; and that as a free and absolutely independent state, it can do everything which free and independent nations can do. And, for the greater firmness and validity of this declaration, we solemnly pledge our lives and properties, vowing that we shall shed the last drop of our blood rather than fail to fulfill this sacred pact.

"I am, Granadians, a son of unhappy Caracas who, escaping miraculously from the midst of her physical and political ruins, is still faithful to the just and liberal system which my country proclaimed, and who comes here to follow the banners of independence which wave so gloriously in these states." Thus spoke Simón de Bolívar in a manifesto which he addressed at Carthagena to the inhabitants of New Granada on December 15, 1812. That manifesto contained a criticism of the policy which had been pursued by the revolutionary government of Venezuela and also a program of action for the revolutionists. In the first place Bolívar criticized the Venezuelans because of their humane treatment of the royalists: "The codes consulted by our magistrates were not those in which they might learn the practical science of government; but those which have been invented by certain benevolent visionaries, who, imagining chimerical republics, have thought it possible to attain political perfection, assuming the perfectibility of the human race. Thus it is that we have had philosophers in place of chiefs, philanthropy in place of legislation, dialectics in place of tactics, and sophists in place of soldiers." Bolívar denounced the spirit of faction as well as the opposition to the maintenance of a regular military force. He declared that a federal government was not adapted to the conditions existing in Venezuela. "Although the federal system of government is the most perfect system and the most apt to promote happiness of man in society, yet that system is the most antagonistic to the interests of our infant states. Generally speaking, not all of our citizens are in a position to exercise their political rights in the fullest measure, for they lack the political virtues which mark the true republican,—virtues which are not acquired under absolute governments that do not recognize the rights and duties of the citizen."

In the second place, Bolívar proposed, "as an indispensable measure for the security of New Granada, the re-conquest of Caracas." He said that a defensive war would be disastrous to the patriot cause; for Spain could use Venezuela as a base of operations against the entire continent of South America. He maintained that the people of New Granada should wage an offensive war against the royalists in western Venezuela; he exhorted them "to march swiftly to revenge the dead, to give life to the dying, to free the oppressed, and to give liberty to all." He declared that a government should adapt itself to circumstances, arguing that, in a turbulent age, the government should show itself terrible; that, without regard to constitutions or laws, it should arm itself with a firmness equal to the threatening perils. The glowing words of this manifesto were read with interest by patriotic leaders of New Granada.

A junta at Carthagena accepted the proffer of Bolívar's services, and directed him to serve under Colonel Labatut against the Spaniards. Early in 1813 by a daring campaign in which he disregarded the wishes of Labatut, Colonel Bolívar drove the royalists from the lower Magdalena and subsequently from the valleys of Cúcuta. Soon afterwards the congress of New Granada commissioned General Bolívar to attack the venezuelan royalists. On March 1, 1813, he issued a proclamation to his soldiers which fervently expressed his faith in their ability to expel the Spaniards, "From you, intrepid soldiers of Carthagena and the Union, the whole of America expects her liberty and salvation." In Bolívar's fertile mind the design to free Venezuela was apparently developing into a plan to liberate all of Spanish South America.

At Trujillo in the Venezuelan mountains, on June 15, 1813, Simón de Bolívar issued a proclamation of war to the death against the Spaniards,—a proclamation which he did not rescind until the middle of 1816. In that manifesto he denounced the Spaniards for the violation of the treaty of San Mateo and declared that their victims would be avenged. He invited the royalists to join the patriot cause, warning them that every Spaniard who did not support the patriots would be considered a traitor and put to death. "Spaniards and Canarians, count on death, even though you are neutral, if you do not work actively for the liberty of Venezuela! Americans, count on life, even though you are culpable!" Bolívar's bloody decree announcing a war of retaliation upon the Spaniards has been much discussed by students of the revolt against Spanish rule:—it divided the Venezuelans into two great camps, royalists and patriots, and presaged one of the darkest chapters of South-American history.

Early in August, 1813, after liberating several provinces of Venezuela, the implacable leader triumphantly entered the city of Caracas. Soon afterwards Monteverde sought refuge in La Guaira. The political ideas which Bolívar entertained at this time were suggested by a proclamation in which he declared that the liberating army intended not only to avenge the outraged dignity of the Americans but also to reëstablish "republican institutions." He suggested that "an assembly of wise and virtuous men" be convoked to decide upon the form of government which should be established. He disclaimed any desire for authority beyond that which was necessary to safeguard the country's welfare. On October 14, 1813, an extraordinary *cabildo* of the city of Caracas proclaimed that Bolívar was the captain general of the patriot soldiers: it gratefully bestowed upon him the title of "Liberator of Venezuela." At once the liberator acted as Venezuela's chief executive. He issued a decree declaring that natives of Venezuela and foreigners were to enjoy the same civil rights. On October 22, 1813, he issued another decree which created the order of Liberators of Venezuela. The professed object of that decree was to make known to the Venezuelans the valiant officers who had liberated them from Spanish domination. The badge of this military order was a star with seven radii—symbolizing the seven provinces of Venezuela—which was to bear on one side the name of the person who had been granted the honor, and on the other side the inscription "Liberator of Venezuela."

At that time Bolívar was virtually a dictator. Soon after driving the Spaniards from his native city, Bolívar chose three secretaries to aid him in the government: a secretary of state, a secretary of justice, and a secretary of war and the navy. He said that a congress should be assembled for the purpose of establishing a suitable government, but declared that the war which was being waged in Venezuela made the convocation of such a congress impracticable. On January 2, 1814, however, a *cabildo abierto* of the city of Caracas met to consider Bolívar's acts. The liberator informed this assembly that he had not bestowed freedom upon Venezuela: "You owe it to my fellow-soldiers. . . . I am not the sovereign. Your representatives should form your laws." After paying a compliment to Bolívar, Cristóbal de Mendoza suggested that the liberator should be entrusted with the task of joining New Granada and Venezuela in an indissoluble union. In a diplomatic reply Bolívar praised his brave lieutenants; he declared that a military despotism would not ensure the happiness of a people, and that a victorious soldier did not acquire the right to govern his own country. He told the assembly to select magistrates and to establish a just government; he said that the arms which had saved the republic would ever protect the liberty and glory of Venezuela. Juan Domínguez then spoke of the need of a dictatorship. Domingo Alzuru proposed that Bolívar should be acclaimed supreme magistrate of the republic and thus relieved of his dependent position as delegate of the congress of New Granada. Thereupon Bolívar spoke again. He suggested that, after the war for independence had terminated, General Mariño, the liberator of eastern Venezuela, ought to become the chief executive, and declared that he would merely accept the position of supreme magistrate of Venezuela until elections might be held. In this manner Bolívar bound Mariño to the revolutionary cause, strengthened his own prestige, and secured recognition as the supreme magistrate. The apparent reluctance of Bolívar to accept the supreme command was characteristic. It was displayed in a similar fashion on many subsequent occasions.

In 1813 a ferocious Spaniard, José Tomás Boves, at the head of reactionary royalists, committed many acts of cruelty against Venezuelans. The savage in Bolívar was aroused. On February 8, 1814, he ordered the patriot commanders at La Guaira and Caracas to shoot all the Spanish prisoners in their dungeons and hospitals. Accordingly over eight hundred royalists were killed in cold blood. The contagion of murder spread. Patriots and royalists vied with each other in sanguinary acts of vengeance. This is the period of Venezuelan history which most closely resembles the lurid age in Mexican history that was initiated by the revolt of Miguel Hidalgo.

On June 15, 1814, the fierce charges of Boves' cavalry routed the patriot soldiers at la Puerta. Bolívar and Mariño fled to Caracas, while Boves devastated the valleys of Aragua, captured Valencia and massacred its inhabitants in cold blood, despite his promises that their lives should be spared. Of the acts of Boves a royalist contemporary, José F. Hereida, said, "It seems impossible that these acts shou:d have been committed by civilized and Christian people under the banners of

Spain." On July 6 Bolívar evacuated the city of Caracas and marched toward Barcelona, while men, women, and children fled precipitately from Caracas to escape the wrath of Boves. In September Bolívar turned up in Tunja and made a report to the independent government of New Granada concerning the vicissitudes of his Venezuelan campaign. That government soon empowered him to lead a military expedition against Cundinamarca, which was maintaining a distinct government that did not act in harmony with other provinces in the confederation. After a brief and brilliant campaign, Bolívar forced the dictator of Bogotá to capitulate on December 12, 1814. Early in the following year the patriot government of New Granada was installed at Bogotá. In May, 1815, when he heard reports of the arrival of a strong royalist army in Venezuela, the liberator embarked at Carthagena for the English West Indies.

While sojourning in Jamaica, Bolívar addressed, on September 6, 1815, a remarkable letter to a gentleman who had displayed great interest in the independence of South America. In that letter, after surveying the Spanish conquest of America and the revolt against Spain, Bolívar expressed his thoughts respecting the Spanish-American peoples. He compared the empire of Spain in America with the Roman empire, which crumbled into states that formed governments suitable to their respective positions. He thought that the people of Spanish America needed the fostering care of paternal governments, which would heal "the sores and wounds of despotism and of war." Still, he declared that the project to establish one grand monarchical government in Spanish America was a dream, for a single monarchy would be "a clumsy colossus which would fall by its own weight at the least convulsion." He also expressed an opinion adverse to the establishment of a number of monarchical states declaring that he did "not believe in monarchies in America." His prophecy was that Spanish America would ultimately split into fifteen or seventeen independent states. With regard to the governments to be adopted by those states, Bolívar declared in favor of republics. He expressed the reasons why he preferred republics above monarchies as follows:

The well-understoood interest of a republic is concerned with its preservation, prosperity, and glory. . . . There is no stimulus which excites republicans to extend the boundaries of their territory to their own detriment in order that their neighbors may enjoy a liberal constitution. They obtain no right, they derive no advantage by conquering the neighboring states unless they make them colonies, conquests, or allies after the example of Rome. But such examples are in direct opposition to the just principles of republican systems; and, I may say further, in manifest opposition to the interests of their citizens. A state too extensive in itself, or by virtue of its dependencies, ultimately falls into decay; its free government is transformed into a tyranny; it disregards the principles which it should preserve, and finally degenerates into despotism. The distinguishing characteristic of small republics is stability: the character of large republics is mutability. Such republics always drift toward empire. Almost all of the small republics have lived long. Among the large republics only Rome sustained herself for several centuries. This happened because the capital city was a republic, while the rest of Rome's dominions were governed by different laws and institutions. . . . I think that the Spanish-Americans who are anxious for peace, arts, sciences, commerce, and agriculture would prefer republics to kingdoms. . . . Among the popular and representative systems of government I do not approve of the federal system: it is too perfect; and it requires virtues and political talents much superior to our own. For a similar reason I dislike the mixed monarchy formed of aristocracy and democracy, which has procured so much fortune and splendor to England. As it is not possible for us to select from republics and monarchies the most perfect form, let us not become demagogical anarchies or monocratic tyrannies. These opposite extremes would carry us to the same reefs,—unhappiness and dishonor; let us seek a mean between them!

Bolívar then made some remarkable predictions concerning the political destinies of the different sections of Spanish America. Mexico, he averred, would first establish a representative republic in which the chief executive would exercise great authority and perhaps hold office for life. He predicted that, if the dominant party in Mexico should be aristocratic or military, a constitutional monarchy would probably be established which would inevitably become absolute. He prophesied that the provinces of Central America would form a confederation. "Its canals will shorten the distances of the world; they will draw closer the commercial relations of Europe, America, and Asia, and will bring to that happy region the tribute of the four quarters of the globe. Some day the capital of the world may perhaps be located there—a capital which may occupy the place that Constantine wished to give Byzantium as the capital of the ancient hemisphere. At Buenos Aires there will appear a centralized government where the military class will predominate, as a result of internal divisions and external wars." He predicted that the government at Buenos Aires would necessarily "degenerate into an oligarchy or a monocracy." He declared that Chile was destined to be a republic, for her position, the customs of her inhabitants, and the example of the Araucanian Indians alike encouraged the formation of a democratic government.

I am inclined to believe that, if any republic endures long in America, it will be the Chilean. . . . On the contrary, Peru contains two elements which are inimical to any just and liberal rule: gold and slaves; gold corrupts everything; slaves are themselves corrupt. The soul of a slave rarely appreciates true liberty. A slave rushes furiously into tumult, or lives humiliated in chains. I suppose that in Lima the rich people will not tolerate the democracy, whle the slaves and the free negroes will not tolerate the aristocracy. . . . Peru will accomplish a great deal, if she secures her liberty. . . . New Granada will unite with Venezuela, if they agree to form a central republic, whose capital will be Maracaibo, or a new city, which, under the name of Las Casas —in honor of that hero of philanthropy—will be founded on the borders of the two countries in the magnificent harbor of Bahia Honda. . . . That nation should be called Colombia, as a sign of gratitude to the discoverer of the New World. Its government may imitate the English government, with the difference that, in place of a king, there will be an elective executive who should hold office at most for life, and should never be hereditary, if a republic is desired. There will be an upper house of the legislature composed of members elected under no other restrictions than those existing in regard to the lower house in England. I desire that this constitution should partake of the characteristics of all forms of government, but should not partake of all their vices. Colombia being my country, I have an incontestable right to wish for her that form of government which, in my opinion, is best.

Near the end of his prophetic letter, Bolívar mentioned the project to establish a confederate government in Spanish America. But he declared that differences of climate, geography, and interests would make it impossible to form there one great republic embracing all the revolted provinces. He suggested, however, that a Spanish-American congress should be assembled:

> How grand it would be if the Isthmus of Panama should be to us what the Isthmus of Corinth was to the Greeks! God grant that some day we may have the fortune to install there an august congress of representatives of republics, kingdoms, and empires to treat and discuss important subjects of peace and war with the nations of the other three-quarters of the world.

This letter suggests the liberator's design to assemble on the Isthmus of Panama an international American congress. Therein are expressed the views which he entertained in 1815 concerning the best type of government for the states which were destined to appear in Spanish America. His thoughts in regard to the political fortunes of those states—considered in the light of their subsequent history—give him a high place among political prophets.

While the exiled liberator was dreaming of an American state system, Spain's soldiers under the command of General Pablo Morillo, were completing the subjugation of northern South America. Morillo had fought bravely against the French invaders of Spain during the peninsular war. After the restoration of Ferdinand VII., he was made captain general of Venezuela, and was given charge of an expedition destined for South America. In elastic terms Morillo was instructed to pacify the captaincy general of Venezuela, to occupy the city of Carthagena, and to aid the royalists in New Granada. The soldiers in Morillo's expedition numbered about ten thousand: they were mostly infantry, who were veterans of the peninsular war. This was the most formidable expedition which Spain ever sent to subjugate her revolted colonists in America.

After gaining possession of the island of Margarita, Morillo disembarked on the mainland, and, on May 11, 1815, he entered the city of Caracas. There he issued a proclamation summoning the inhabitants to join his victorious banner and thus to ensure peace to their native land. He exacted a forced loan from the citizens of Caracas, replaced the *audiencia* of that city by other courts, and created a special junta to sequestrate the property of his enemies. In June, 1815, Morillo

left Salvador de Moxo temporarily in charge of the captaincy
general of Venezuela, and proceeded with the royalist army
to the seacoast. On December 6, after a siege of three months,
Morillo entered the desolate city of Carthagena. Early in
1816, he marched into the interior of New Granada: in the
end of May, he quietly entered Bogotá. Parties of royalist
soldiers sent from that city soon subjugated the outlying provinces. Thus, in the course of 1816, the authority of Ferdinand VII. was reëstablished throughout Venezuela and New
Granada. At first, the god of war was no more favorable to
Bolívar then he had been to Miranda.

Bolívar's career from 1815 to 1818 was extremely adventurous. From Jamaica he proceeded to Haiti, whence, in
March, 1816, he led a small expedition to Margarita. There
he issued a proclamation announcing that a new congress
would be convoked for Venezuela. His expedition was futile,
and he again took refuge in the West Indies. In December,
1816, he led an expedition to the continent of South America.
There he again announced his intention to convoke a congress.
He struggled against the sectional, or anarchical, designs of
Manuel Piar, who was eventually condemned by a military
court to be shot for insubordination and desertion. Bolívar
led his soldiers with varying success against the royalists. In
the words of the Spanish commander, Venezuela was "a vast
field of battle." Ultimately Bolívar secured control of a region
in the Orinoco Valley: there, at Angostura, the provisional
capital of Venezuela was established. Early in October, 1818,
Bolívar decided that a congress of delegates should be assembled to make laws for Venezuela. A revolutionary council
of state which he had established accordingly made rules for
the election of delegates to a congress that was to assemble
at Angostura. As only a small section of northern South
America was free from Spanish rule, the delegates were
chosen in an irregular fashion. In certain towns they were
chosen by the inhabitants; in some other places they were
apparently selected by the revolutionary soldiers.

In an interesting passage of his memoirs, Daniel F. O'Leary,
who joined Bolívar's followers as a private in a band of hus-
sars which was organized in England, described how Bolívar
was employed in the art of composition on a journey to Angostura. O'Leary said that while "reclining in a canoe on the
bosom of the Orinoco River, or lolling in a hammock under

the shade of the gigantic trees that fringed its banks, in the heat of the day, or in the cool hours of the night, as the mood seized him, with one hand on the lapel of his coat and a fore-finger upon his upper lip, Bolívar dictated the constitution which he was preparing for Venezuela and the famous address which has justly deserved the admiration of orators and statesmen." On February 15, 1819, Bolívar delivered an address to the congress of Angostura in which he again declared that he resigned the supreme command. With regard to one-man power in a republic, he made this interesting expression of sentiment:

The exercise of power by the same individual has often been the end of democratic government. Frequent elections are essential in popular governments; for nothing is more perilous than to allow power to remain in the hands of the same man. The people become accustomed to obey him, and he becomes accustomed to command them: from this originate usurpation and tyranny. A just jealousy is the guarantee of republican liberty. Our citizens ought rightly to fear that the magistrate who has governed them for a long time may govern them perpetually.

Bolívar again criticized the federal system of government:

As much as I admire the excellence of the federal Constitution of the United States, so much am I convinced that it is impossible to adopt that constitution in our state. To me it is a marvel that the Constitution of the United States has operated so successfully and has not been overthrown when the first embarrassments or perils appeared. But the United States is a singular example of political virtue and moral rectitude. That nation has been cradled in liberty, has been nurtured in liberty, and has been maintained by pure liberty. I will add that the people of the United States are unique in the history of the human race. And I repeat: it is a marvel that a government so weak and complicated as the federal system should have endured under such difficult and delicate circumstances as those which have existed in the United States. But whatever may be true in regard to the government, I must say with regard to the American people, that the idea never entered my head to consider as identical the characteristics of two peoples so different as the Anglo-American and the Spanish-American. Would it not be very difficult to apply to Spain the English system of political, civil, and religious liberty? It is even more difficult to

adopt the laws of the United States in Venezuela. Does not *l'Esprit
des lois* say that the laws should suit the people who make them?
That it is a mere chance if the laws of one nation suit another
nation? That laws should be adapted to the physiography of the
country, to the climate, to the soil, to the situation of the country,
to its extent, and to the manner of life of the inhabitants? That
laws should be adapted to the degree of liberty which the constitution can sanction, to the religion of the inhabitants, to their
inclinations, riches, numbers, commerce, and manners? This is the
code which we ought to consult and not the code of Washington.

Bolívar maintained that the Venezuelans who framed the
federal constitution of 1811 had failed to incorporate in their
fundamental law that provision in the constitution of the
United States which was most worthy of imitation, namely, a
single executive. Instead they had adopted a plural executive,
which necessarily lacked continuity and responsibility. He
affirmed that, when Venezuela declared her independence,
she was not ready for a federal republic: the operation of a
democratic government could be "sublime only when adopted
by a republic of saints." He pointed out that the Venezuelans
were neither Europeans nor Indians: white, black, and Indian
blood mingled in their veins. Among the prominent leaders
of the revolutionary era, Bolívar realized most acutely that
the Spanish-American peoples had not only battles to fight
and constitutions to form, but sociological problems to solve.

Despite the mixed character of the Venezuelan people, Bolívar thought that a republic would best suit them. "The government of Venezuela has been, is, and should be republican.
The bases of the Venezuelan government should be the sovereignty of the people, the division of powers, civil liberty,
the prohibition of slavery, the abolition of monarchy and of
privileges." He advocated, however, a political system modeled
rather upon the government of England than upon the government of the United States. He proposed that the legislature
of Venezuela should be composed of a house of representatives, the members of which were to be chosen by popular
election, and of a senate, the members of which were at first
to be chosen by congress from among the liberators. After the
first election, however, the senators were to hold their positions by hereditary right: thus the race of liberators—"virtuous, prudent, and valiant men"—might be preserved to the
republic:

It has been justly remarked that the house of lords is invaluable to the British nation because it forms a bulwark of liberty; and I dare to add that the senate of Venezuela will not only form a bulwark of liberty, but will be a means of rendering the republic perpetual. . . . The more thoroughly you examine the nature of the executive power in England, the more firmly will you be inclined to consider it as the most perfect model for a monarchy, an aristocracy, or a democracy. Let such an executive power be established in Venezuela in the person of a president chosen either by the people or by their representatives, and we shall then have taken a long step towards national felicity!

He urged that the powers of this executive should be analogous to the powers of the king of England:

Nothing is so perilous to a people as a weak executive; and, if it has been deemed necessary to endow the executive with so many powers in a monarchy, how infinitely more indispensable is a strong representative in a republic! . . . The chief executive of a republic is an individual isolated in the midst of society, charged at the same time to repress the tendency of the people toward license and the inclination of judges and administrators to abuse the laws. He is subject to the lower house of the legislature, to the senate, and to the people; he is a single individual resisting the combined attack of the opinions, interests, and passions which agitate society. As Carnot has said, he is a man who struggles unceasingly between the desire to dominate, and the desire to elude domination: in fine, he is an athlete struggling with a crowd. To correct this weakness the executive must be endowed with great energy,—energy corresponding to the resistance which he will encounter in the legislative and judicial departments as well as in the people. If the proper authority is not placed at his disposal, the executive department will inevitably become useless or be abused, which will be the death of government. It will have as heirs, anarchy, usurpation, and tyranny.

Bolívar suggested that the judicial department of government should be reformed by providing for the independence of the judges, by establishing the jury system, and by formulating wise civil and criminal codes. He also made some suggestive remarks about a government of laws:

Venezuelans love their country but they do not love its laws, because these laws are bad and the source of evil. . . . If a sacred respect does not exist for the country, for the laws, and for the constituted authorities, society is in a state of confusion; there is a singular conflict of man against man, hand-to-hand. . . . Our laws are the melancholy relics of ancient and modern despotisms. . . . Let us dictate a code of Venezuelan laws.

In the liberator's governmental scheme the judiciary was to be reënforced by a fourth department, or power, of government:

Let us give to our republic a fourth power with authority over the youth, the hearts of men, public spirit, habits, and republican morality. Let us establish this areopagus to watch over the education of the children, to supervise national education, to purify whatever may be corrupt in the republic, to denounce ingratitude, coldness in the country's service, egotism, sloth, idleness, and to pass judgment upon the first signs of corruption and pernicious example.

This moral power seems to be an elaboration of the provision for censors which was contained in the constitutional propects of Francisco de Miranda. The upshot of Bolívar's address to the congress of Angostura was the proposal that the Venezuelans should establish a centralized republic.

The liberator concluded his speech with an extravagant burst of oratory in which he pictured the future of the state which he thought should include New Granada as well as Venezuela:

When I contemplate this immense reunited country, my soul mounts to that height demanded by the colossal perspective of a picture so wonderful. My imagination takes flight toward future ages and admiringly observes from them the prosperity, the splendor, and the life which will exist within this vast territory. I am carried away; and I seem to behold it in the heart of the universe, stretching along its extensive coasts between two oceans which nature has separated; but which our fatherland has united by long and wide canals. I see it serve as the bond, as the center, as the emporium of the human race. I see it sending to the ends of the earth the treasures of gold and silver which its mountains contain. I see it, through the healing virtue of its plants, dispensing health and life to afflicted men of the Old World. I see it disclosing its precious secrets to the sages who know that the store of knowledge is more valuable than the store of riches which nature has so prodigally bestowed upon us.

I see it seated upon the throne of liberty, the scepter of justice in its hand, crowned by glory, showing to the Old World the majesty of the New World.

When asked by Bolívar to revise this discourse, the Venezuelan scholar, Manuel Palacio Fajardo, spoke of Bolívar's style in these words: "The discourse much resembles the gardens of painters where they love to place the pinks, the roses, the lilies, the hyacinths, and other beautiful flowers by the side of the borage and the scabious, that are also beautiful, but which are not worthy companions of the rose and the lily. . . . Your Spanish is not always pure; but it is always select, rhythmical, and elegant. There are audacious thoughts in your discourse; but their value depends upon the originality with which you judge of our political situation." The speech to the congress of Angostura contains the fullest statement of the political beliefs which Bolívar entertained early in 1819. As an exposition of his political gospel, this speech occupies an intermediate place between the prophetic letter which he wrote while sojourning in Jamaica and the constitution which, in 1826, he framed for the republic of Bolivia.

To the congress of Angostura Bolívar submitted an elaborate scheme for the fourth power,—the moral power. He proposed that the moral power should be vested in an areopagus composed of a president and forty members, who were to exercise a full and independent authority over the manners and the education of the Venezuelans. The jurisdiction of the areopagus was to extend to individuals, families, departments, provinces, tribunals, and even to the national government itself. Bolívar's proposal for the establishment of a moral power was viewed with interest by the congress of Angostura. That body finally decided not to adopt the proposal, but to publish it as an appendix to the constitution, in order that the wise men of all nations might pass judgment upon it. Eventually the liberator was induced to accept the presidency, while Francisco Antonio Zea, a citizen of New Granada, was made vice president. Bolívar selected three ministers to aid him in managing the government. The legislators of Angostura cast aside the federal constitution which had been adopted at Caracas, and, after several months of debate, they signed on August 15, 1819, a provisional constitution which embodied Bolívar's governmental scheme with some modifications. By that constitution the executive power was vested in a president who was to hold office for four years, while legislative authority was entrusted to a congress composed of a senate and a house of representatives. The constitution declared that the republic of Venezuela was "one and indivisible."

While the congress of Angostura was framing a constitution for a centralized republic, Bolívar was conceiving a plan for a campaign against the royalists in the central provinces of New Granada. In his memoirs General O'Leary declared that at a council of war held on May 23, 1819, during which Bolívar, and his chief lieutenants—Soublette, Anzoátegui, Briceño, Méndez, Carillo, Ibarren, Rangel, Rook, Plaza, and Manrique—sat on the bleached skulls of the cattle that had been slaughtered to supply their soldiers with meat, the momentous decision was reached to carry out the hazardous plan of a march against Bogotá. Early in June, 1819, Bolívar had decided to leave the patriot cavalry in the llanos of Venezuela to check Morillo's soldiers while he led the infantry to Casanare, where he would join the patriot soldiers of New Granada under their resolute general, Francisco de Paula Santander, who for some time had been coöperating with the Venezuelans. Thence by a daring march he planned suddenly to carry the war into the heart of New Granada by an unexpected route. He carried out this campaign by an achievement in mountain warfare which deserves to be chronicled with San Martín's heroic march across the Andean range. At the head of an army of about two thousand men, including those Englishmen who constituted the British legion, the liberator scaled the Granadian Andes and marched across the desolate plateau of Pisba, which is about thirteen thousand feet above the level of the sea. After terrible sufferings, on July 6, the weary soldiers of Bolívar reached Socha. To the royalists the sudden advent of Bolívar seemed like a terrible apparition. Inspiriting his soldiers, gathering supplies, and enrolling recruits, Bolívar prepared for a battle with the Spanish forces under General Barreiro. It seems ultimately to have been Barreiro's intention to effect a junction with the veteran soldiers under Sámano, the viceroy of New Granada, at Bogotá, before meeting Bolívar in a decisive conflict. But, on August 7, the patriot soldiers intercepted Barreiro's march toward the capital at a bridge across the River Boyacá. There the royalists were defeated. Sixteen hundred soldiers were captured, with

Barreiro and most of his officers, as well as a quantity of military supplies. Two days later the discomfited viceroy fled from Bogotá precipitately. In dispatches to the Spanish government General Morillo lamented the battle: in October, 1820, he confessed his inability to restore the king's authority in northern South America.

In the history of Colombia the battle of Boyacá was perhaps more important than the battle of Chacabuco in Chilean history. Boyacá freed the viceroyalty of New Granada from Spanish rule, with the exception of the presidency of Quito. This battle cleared the way for the conclusive combat in Venezuela. Further, the victory of Boyacá was of constitutional significance; for at the instance of Bolívar, on December 17, 1819, the congress of Angostura—which now included delegates from several provinces of New Granada—passed "a fundamental law" that proclaimed the union of the former viceroyalty of New Granada and the captaincy general of Venezuela into one state, the Republic of Colombia. The executive authority was to be entrusted to a president and a vice president elected by congress. The provisional capital of the extensive republic was located at Cúcuta. The republic was divided into three departments which were designated as Venezuela, Cundinamarca, and Quito. Each department was to have a vice president who should also be chosen by congress. Santander was made vice president of Cundinamarca; J. G. Roscio was made vice president of Venezuela; while Zea was made vice president and Bolívar the president of Colombia. In this manner there was faintly traced upon the map of northern South America the outlines of a new state that was destined to be known as Great Colombia.

Just as the revolution of 1820 in Spain affected her policy toward San Martín, so did it affect her policy toward Bolívar. Like the viceroy of Peru, Morillo was instructed to negotiate with the insurgents for peace on the condition that the constitution of 1812 should be accepted. Hence, in June, 1820, Morillo appointed commissioners, who, on November 25, signed at Trujillo with Bolívar's commissioners—one of whom was Antonio José de Sucre—a treaty providing for an armistice that was to last six months. That treaty delimited the zones which should be occupied by the opposing armies during the truce. It provided that the envoys whom Colombia might select to negotiate peace with Spain should be allowed freely to sail from South America. Bolívar and Morillo agreed to adopt a convention to regulate the war according to the law of nations. On November 26 the commissioners signed another treaty, which was apparently designed to check the horrible barbarities of war,—a treaty which Bolívar described as being "worthy of the soul of General Sucre." On November 26 and 27, Morillo approved the treaty for the regularization of the war and the treaty of armistice. By the treaty providing for an armistice the revolutionists clearly gained an advantage; because they were given time to prepare for the final struggle with the royalists,—a struggle, which, as Spain refused to recognize their independence, was inevitable. Years later Bolívar was reported to have said that he negotiated the armistice with Morillo merely in order that the world might see Spain negotiating with Colombia as with an independent nation. When speaking of an amicable meeting which he and Morillo held at Santa Ana on November 27, the liberator characterized that interview as "a diplomatic comedy." When Morillo informed his government of the treaty of Trujillo, he advised it either to send reënforcements to the royalists or to listen to the proposals of the revolutionists.

In accordance with the terms of the truce of Trujillo, in January, 1821, Bolívar appointed José R. Revenga and José Echeverría envoys to Madrid. The envoys were instructed to negotiate a treaty of peace with Spain acknowledging the independence of Colombia. Within that republic Venezuela, New Granada, and Quito should be included; but the envoys were authorized to arrange a treaty which might exclude from Colombia the Isthmus of Panama, or Quito, or both of those regions. Further, the envoys were authorized to offer Spain reciprocal commercial advantages. But they were to oppose any proposal for a confederation including Spain and America. At most, they might agree to a purely defensive alliance between Spain and Colombia. As it had at times "entered into the views of Spain to propose a prince of the house of Bourbon for king of Colombia"—so ran the instructions—the envoys were instructed to object to such a proposition. This protest was to be applied "not only to the Bourbons, but to every reigning house of Europe,—either princes, or sovereigns, or potentates. . . . Colombia will be independent, sovereign,

and free from all foreign domination, or will cease to exist."
After the envoys had departed Bolívar was haunted by the fear
that false rumors of reverses suffered by Colombian soldiers
might induce them to arrange a compromise with Spain: he
said that Colombia and not Spain "should dictate the terms
of peace and reconciliation." Nothing came of the negotiations of Revenga and Echeverría, however; for, in August,
1821, the government of Spain, alleging that Bolívar had
broken the armistice of Trujillo, ordered these emissaries to
leave the Spanish court.

Before this armistice had expired, with the aid of money,
supplies, and soldiers that were furnished by the former viceroyalty of New Granada, Bolívar prepared for a fresh attack
upon the royalists in Venezuela. In April, 1821, the revolutionary soldiers in northern South America were widely scattered. General Urdaneta with several thousand men was
encamped at San Cristóbal in New Granada. General Páez
with the soldiers of the llanos was near the Apure River.
General Bermúdez was at Barcelona, while Bolívar's headquarters were at Barínas. The royalists, commanded by General
La Torre—Morillo having sailed for Spain—were stationed
at Barlovento, San Carlos, Calabozo, Caracas, Guanare, and
Coro. La Torre's total available fighting force was about seven
thousand five hundred men. In March and April, 1821, Bolívar decided to bring the scattered divisions of the patriot
forces together at a central point, and there, with an equal, or
a superior force, to give battle to the enemy. Accordingly
General Bermúdez was ordered to attack the city of Caracas
as soon as the armistice of Trujillo had expired. The object
of that movement was to divert the enemy and thus to safeguard the march of the other divisions of the patriot army,
which were to move towards the point of concentration.
Colonel Carillo was sent with a column of soldiers to attack
the royalists at Valencia and San Felipe. While the royalists
were being thus misled, beginning on April 28, the soldiers of
Páez, Urdaneta, and Bolívar made slow marches toward the
rendezvous. At Tinaquillo, on June 23, the liberator reviewed
the united army of Colombia, which was about six thousand
five hundred strong. On the morning of June 24 Bolívar led
his army toward the royalist forces under La Torre. On reaching the heights of Buena Vista he could detect with a field
glass the royalist soldiers drawn up in battle array upon the

fields of Carabobo. According to his estimate—probably rather high—there were about six thousand soldiers in La Torre's army. It was while surveying the situation, said one of Bolívar's aides, that the liberator was told of a devious path leading to the rear of the enemy's right flank. He decided to send General Páez with a part of the army, including the British soldiers, along that path to attack the enemy. Those forces attacked the Spaniards in the rear, and the rest of Bolívar's army soon attacked the enemy in front. After a short but fierce conflict, in which the steadfastness of the British legion appears to have played no small part, the soldiers of La Torre fled from the field of battle pursued by the exultant soldiers of the revolution. La Torre took refuge in Puerto Cabello.

The battle of Carabobo was important, for it ensured the independence of the northern part of South America from Spain. This victory was more significant to New Granada and Venezuela than the battle of Maipú to Chile and the United Provinces. On June 25 Bolívar wrote to Santander: "Yesterday a splendid victory signalized the political birth of the republic of Colombia." The first congress of Colombia, which in accordance with the action of the congress at Angostura had assembled at Cúcuta, soon took measures to perfect the union between New Granada and Venezuela. On July 12 that congress passed a "fundamental law of union," which announced that the peoples of Venezuela and New Granada were united in the republic of Colombia with the understanding that its government should be democratic and representative. The Colombian nation should be free and independent of the Spanish monarchy and of any other foreign power; it should never become the patrimony of any family or of any person. This law declared that the supreme national authority should always be exercised through three distinct departments, executive, legislative, and judicial. The territory of the republic of Colombia was to comprise the regions included within the limits of the captaincy general of Venezuela and the viceroyalty of New Granada, reserving for a more convenient occasion an exact delimitation of its boundaries. The republic was to be divided into six or more departments. The law declared that this congress would act as a constituent assembly for the republic, a state which would assume all the debts that the two nations had contracted separately. Until the constituent congress should select the flag and the coat of arms for the new republic, it should continue to use the arms of New Granada and the standard of Venezuela.

A committee soon presented to congress a project of a constitution, which was adopted on August 30, 1821. This constitution vested the legislative authority in a senate and a house of representatives. It vested the chief executive authority in a president, who, in a critical period, was to have absolute power. The president was to hold his office for four years; he might be reëlected only once, without an intermission. In case of the death or disability of the president, or when he was commanding the army of the republic in person, his civil functions were to be exercised by the vice president. Provision was also made for five secretaries of state: foreign affairs, interior, treasury, war, and the navy. The supreme judicial power was vested in a high court of justice. Provision was made for an advisory council to the president which should be composed of the vice president, the secretaries of state, and a member of the supreme court. On September 7 the constituent congress selected the liberator as president. After a show of reluctance, Bolívar accepted the presidency on the express condition that he should be allowed to remain at the head of the army, while the chief civil authority should be exercised by Vice President Santander.

The congress of Cúcuta passed many decrees and laws of importance. Among these was a law providing that the city of Bogotá—"located in the heart of the republic, near rivers that afforded prompt communication with its coasts and with the departments of Venezuela"—should be the provisional capital. A decree was sanctioned which authorized the executive to negotiate a loan of three million pesos. On July 21 a law was enacted which prohibited the slave trade and which provided that the children of slaves born after the publication of that law should be free. Another law was enacted which provided that property belonging to the Spanish government in the provinces conquered by Colombian arms should be confiscated. The tribute which had been levied upon the aborigines was abolished—and it was declared that these people had the same status as other citizens of the republic. Stipulations were made concerning the process by which foreigners might become naturalized citizens of Columbia. In October a law was passed which divided the republic into departments, provinces, and cantons that should be governed by an administrative hierarchy composed mainly of intendants, governors, and "political judges." The former state of Venezuela was divided into three departments; New Granada was divided into four departments. These departments were subdivided into provinces. On October 4 congress enacted a law which provided that the arms of the Colombian republic should thenceforth be two cornucopias filled with flowers of the cold, temperate, and torrid regions—the symbol of abundance—and a sheaf of lances with a battle-axe and a bow and arrows—the symbol of force and union. The national standard was the tricolor first used by Miranda in 1806.

The constitution and the legislative enactments of the congress of Cúcuta are the most notable political achievements of the South-American republics in the first quarter of the nineteenth century. They embody the ideals cherished by many of Colombia's leaders during her age of gold. On October 14 the president of the first constituent congress of Colombia, José Ignacio Márquez, addressed to his countrymen an exposition describing the labors of that congress and conveying some wholesome advice: "Live in intimate and fraternal union, with reciprocal tolerance, and permit neither jealousies nor rivalries to enter your hearts. These are the arms which your enemies have always used to sow discord. Union will make you strong and will put an end to the revolutionary war. Dissension will deprive you of repose and of the true blessings of society. United, you are invincible: disunion is the only enemy which you should fear. Obey the laws which are your work; for they have been adopted by your representatives, and respect the magistrates elected by your votes. Think only of Colombia!" The student of South-American history cannot but pause to conjecture what might have been the destiny of Great Colombia if her people had followed this sage advice!

The complete expulsion of the Spanish soldiers from the former viceroyalty of New Granada took place shortly after the adoption of the constitution of Cúcuta. In November, 1823, Puerto Cabello, the last stronghold of the Spaniards in northern South America, fell into the hands of the Colombians. As early as November 28, 1821, a junta on the Isthmus of Panama had declared that the isthmus belonged to Colombia. Accordingly, early in the following year, Vice President Santander issued a decree providing for the administration of the isthmus as a department of the Colombian state. In the meantime, Colombians were subverting the rule of Spain in the presidency of Quito. For although Quito was not specifically mentioned in the constitution of Cúcuta as belonging to the republic of Colombia, yet some Colombians considered it as an integral part of that republic as provided by the fundamental law of 1819.

In the presidency of Quito the revolutionary cause had suffered many vicissitudes of fortune. As early as August 10, 1809, the people of the city of Quito had established a junta to govern on behalf of Ferdinand VII. But soldiers of the viceroy of New Granada soon overthrew that provisional government. In September, 1810, another junta was estabilshed at Quito, which was swept away by Toribio Montes, who had been made president of Quito by the Spanish regency. In October, 1820, the inhabitants of Guayaquil revolted against the Spanish government, and established a governmental junta composed of three persons of whom a poet, José de Olmedo, was the chief.

When, shorlty afterwards, Bolívar felt that it was inexpedient for him to lead his soldiers into the presidency of Quito at once, he decided to send General Sucre as his substitute. In January, 1821, the liberator ordered General Sucre to take command of an expedition of one thousand soldiers which was to proceed to Guayaquil. Antonio Sucre was thus made the lieutenant of the liberator in the execution of his long-meditated and ambitious plan to extend the revolution down the Pacific shores. On April 4, 1821, the Colombian expedition destined for the presidency of Quito left Buenaventura in the corvette *Alejandro,* two brigantines, and several transports. According to statements made by General Sucre, he did not have one thousand soldiers on board those vessels. After a voyage of twenty-eight days the vessels reached Point St. Helena, which was about thirty-five leagues from Guayaquil; at that point Sucre's soldiers disembarked, while the *Alejandro* proceeded to Guayaquil with the munitions. Sucre reached that port with his forces on May 6. As his soldiers were in poor condition, he wisely decided to postpone a campaign against the royalists: instead he sent a request to Bogotá for reënforcements. In the meanwhile he was not idle; for on May 25, 1821, he signed a convention with the revolutionary junta of Guayaquil. According to this convention, the province of Guayaquil placed itself under the protection of Colombia; that province conferred upon Bolívar the powers which were necessary for the preservation of its independence; it promised to coöperate in Colombia's plans; and it conferred upon Sucre the power to negotiate with the Spanish officials in the city of Quito. The agreement between General Sucre and the provisional junta of Guayaquil helped to thwart the designs of José de San Martín.

In August and September, 1821, Sucre had engagements with the royalists. The most important of those conflicts took place in the valley of Ambato where the royalists disputed the march of Sucre's soldiers toward the city of Quito. Although Sucre did not feel ready to fight the enemy, he yielded to the importunities of his companions and suffered a bloody repulse. In a letter to Bolívar on September 18, 1821, Sucre lamented his defeat as an "imprudent act," which had misused "the best opportunity to liberate Quito," and had destroyed a division of his army. As the news of that defeat reached Bolívar soon after the victory at Carabobo, it probably made him hasten his preparations to march to Quito. On October 9, 1821, President Bolívar left Cúcuta to carry the conquering banner of Colombia southward. Vice President Santander, who possessed much ability as a civil executive, was entrusted with the political functions of the president. Before the liberator departed, the Colombian congress passed a law authorizing him to organize as he deemed best the provinces which he liberated from Spanish rule. On December 15 Bolívar left Bogotá on the long march overland to Quito. He led his soldiers up the beautiful Cauca valley, and tried in vain to avoid marching through the province of Pasto, which was controlled by devoted royalists. On April 7, 1822, his march was disputed by two thousand soldiers, who, under Colonel García, occupied a strong position near the plateau of Bombaná. After a desperate conflict the royalists retired. But the battle of Bombaná was "a costly and barren victory": Bolívar was compelled to send to Bogotá for reënforcements.

It was while the liberator was still maneuvering against García that he received reports of a battle which Sucre had won in the presidency of Quito.

While the liberator was making the hazardous march south from Bogotá, Sucre, who had received reënforcements from San Martín which were commanded by a Peruvian, Colonel Andrés Santa Cruz, led his soldiers across the Andes to Cuenca. He evaded the royalists by a flank march, and on May 17, 1822, he reached the valley of Chillo, a few leagues south of Quito. Meanwhile the royalist army under General Aymerich, who was now acting as the Spanish commander in the ancient viceroyalty of New Granada, took possession of the capital city. After some maneuvering, Sucre marched by a difficult route to the volcano of Pichincha, west of that city. Early on the morning of May 24, the soldiers of Sucre gazed down upon the capital of the presidency.

General Aymerich soon accepted the challenge. On May 24 a battle, lasting about three hours, in which, said O'Leary, Colombian dragoons and Platean grenadiers vied with each other in bravery, was fought between Aymerich and Sucre on the slopes of Mount Pichincha. The royalists were decisively defeated. As a result of this battle, eleven hundred soldiers, one hundred and sixty officers, fourteen pieces of artillery, and seventeen hundred muskets, besides standards and munitions of war, were surrendered to General Sucre. The capitulation which followed the battle of Pichincha provided that the city of Quito and also the territory under Spanish domination north and south of that city were to be given up by the royalists; the soldiers of Spain were to march out of the capital with the honors of war; they were to be allowed freely to leave the country; and the officers were generally to be allowed to keep their arms and their horses. When, on the afternoon of May 25, Sucre entered the capital city at the head of his victorious columns, he was given a cordial reception by the Quiteños. The news of the victory of Pichincha caused Bolívar to rejoice; on June 8, he issued the following proclamation to his soldiers:

Colombians! All your beauteous fatherland is now free. The victories of Bomboná and Pichincha have completed the work of your heroism. From the banks of the Orinoco River to the Peruvian Andes the army of liberation, marching triumphantly, has covered all the territory of Colombia with its protecting arms. . . . Colombians of the South! The blood of your brothers has redeemed you from the horrors of war. . . . The constitution of Colombia is the model of a representative, republican, and strong government. You need not expect to find a better government among the political institutions of the earth, unless it should be this constitution made more perfect. . . . Colombians! share with me the ocean of joy which floods my heart; and in your own hearts erect altars to the liberating army which has given you glory, peace, and liberty!

On May 29, the *cabildo* of Quito proclaimed that the provinces of the presidency were incorporated into Colombia. It provided that a medal celebrating the victory of Pichincha should be presented to the soldiers of the liberating army, and that a pyramid should be built upon the field of battle bearing an inscription to the effect that it was erected "by the sons of the equator to Simón Bolívar, the angel of peace and Colombian liberty." On this monument there was also to be inscribed the name of Sucre with these words: "Quito free on May 24, 1822." The busts of Bolívar and Sucre were to be placed in the hall of the *cabildo* as well as in the palace of government. The victory of Pichincha was indeed a milestone on the road to South-American independence. It had a beneficial influence upon Bolívar's fortunes, for the royalists of Pasto soon capitulated: on June 16 Bolívar entered the city of Quito amid the plaudits of the inhabitants. He soon proclaimed that the liberated territory was incorporated with Colombia.

Even before the battle of Pichincha took place, Bolívar had kept a watchful eye upon the protector of Peru. A friend of the liberator in San Martín's camp had kept him informed of the jealousy which the protector's officers entertained of their leader and of their dislike for his monarchical schemes. After he received reports of the negotiations of Punchauca, Bolívar directed his secretary, Colonel O'Leary, to instruct Colonel Ibarra, a Columbian in San Martín's army, to induce that leader to desist from his project of establishing a throne in Peru. Bolívar argued that such a scandalous project would produce new dissensions among the patriots and would stimulate the Spaniards to continue the war. He declared that Colombia would not agree to such a scheme, for it harmonized neither with her institutions nor with her desires for liberty. The liberator's apprehensions regarding San Martín's plan for the establishment of a European prince in South America became more acute when he heard of the progress of the Mexican revolution under Agustín de Iturbide. On November 15, 1821, after he heard of the treaty of Córdoba, Bolívar wrote to San Martín announcing that he would soon march to complete the liberation of southern Colombia.

At present the liberty of the southern provinces of Colombia and the complete expulsion of the enemies who remain in South America is of increasing importance, because events in Mexico will give a new aspect to the American revolution. This new order of things gives me reason to believe that, if the Spanish cabinet accepts the treaty which Generals Iturbide and O'Donojú have agreed to in Mexico, and, if Ferdinand VII., or some other European prince goes to that country, Spain will entertain similar designs in regard to all the other independent governments of Spanish America: she will desire to terminate her differences with them upon the same principles accepted in regard to Mexico. The transfer of European princes to the New World and their support by the monarchs of the Old World may produce important alterations in the policy adopted by the government of America. Accordingly I am more than ever of opinion that it is indispensable to complete the expulsion of the Spaniards from the entire continent. We should draw closer together and agree to engage with the new enemies and with the new means which they can employ.

Evidently San Martín was also of opinion that Peru and Colombia should coöperate in the war for independence. In January, 1822, he made public in Lima his intention of meeting the liberator of Colombia at Guayaquil. The protector of Peru declared that an interview with Bolívar was necessary in order to promote the interests of both Peru and Colombia, to prosecute the war with energy, and to ensure a stable destiny for Spanish America. "The course of events," said he, had made them "in a high degree responsible for the outcome" of their "sublime enterprise." On June 17, 1822, Bolívar wrote a letter to San Martín from Quito expression a desire to furnish effectual aid to Peru in the campaign against the royalists. On July 13, 1822, the protector replied:

Peru is the only field of battle which remains in America: there those men should unite who wish to share the honor of the last triumph over the forces which have been vanquished in the rest of the continent. To promote the success of this campaign and to leave nothing to the fluctuations of fortune, I accept the generous offer which you made to me in your letter of June 17. Peru will receive with enthusiasm and gratitude all the troops that your Excellency can spare.

Temporarily delegating his power to the Marquis of Torre Tagle, San Martín embarked on board the *Macedonia,* and sailed towards the former presidency of Quito. When the protector of Peru reached Guayaquil, he found the liberator of Columbia had already taken possession of that port. Bolívar feigned surprise at the arrival of San Martín, but effusively welcomed him to "Columbian soil."

San Martín spent July 26 and 27 at Guayaquil. The meeting of San Martín and Bolívar at that port was enveloped in a cloud of mystery, which has not been completely lifted. For no unprejudiced third party witnessed their conferences:—the only descriptions of their conversations are those which emanated directly or indirectly from Bolívar or San Martín. Shortly after the mysterious interview, both participants admitted that they had there discussed the fortunes of Spanish America; and each leader left on record his impressions of his great antagonist. Among the correspondence of Bolívar there are found some brief characterizations of his rival. On September 26, 1822, he wrote to Fernando Peñalver, "General San Martín came to see me at Guayaquil: he appeared to me the same that he seemed to those persons who have judged him in the most favorable manner." On July 29, he wrote to Santander concerning San Martín: "His character appeared to me to be decidedly military; he appeared to be active, prompt, and not obtuse." A little later Bolívar wrote to Sucre:

General San Martín had the respect of the army which was accustomed to obey him, while the people of Peru considered him as their liberator. Besides, he had been fortunate, and you know that illusions lent by fortune are at times worth more than merit. In fine, my friend, Peru has lost a good captain and a benefactor.

From expressions which escape from San Martín upon various occasions, it is clear that he was disappointed with the personality and the designs of his Colombian antagonist.

Many years later, the French traveler, LaFond, recorded San Martín's opinion of General Bolívar in these words:

> He appeared to possess much pride, which hardly harmonized with his habit of never looking into the face of the person whom he addressed,—at least unless that person was greatly his inferior. I was able to convince myself of his lack of frankness in the conferences which I had with him at Guayaquil, for he never responded in a positive manner to my propositions but always in evasive terms. I perceived—and Bolívar himself told me—that those officers in whom he had most confidence were the Englishmen who served in his army. To touch upon another trait, his manners were *distingué* and showed the good education which he had received. His language was at times somewhat trivial, but it seemed to me that this was not a natural defect, and that he only sought in this manner to assume a most martial air. Public opinion accused him of excessive ambition and an ardent thirst for command—a reproach which he himself has completely justified. People credited him with great disinterestedness, and that justly, for he died in poverty. Bolívar was very popular with his soldiers, for he permitted them a license which military laws did not authorize; but he was much less popular with his officers, whom he often treated in a fashion that was most humiliating.

Not until after the death of Bolívar, however, did San Martín give to the world a letter which he had written to that commander from Lima one month after the conferences at Guayaquil. This letter is worth quoting at length.

> The results of our interview have not been those which, as I promised myself, would promote the speedy termination of the war. Unfortunately, I am fully convinced either that you did not believe that the offer which I made to serve under your orders was sincere, or that else you felt that my presence in your army would be an impediment to your success. Permit me to say that the two reasons which you expressed to me: first, that your delicacy would not permit you to command me; and, second, that even if this difficulty were overcome, you were certain that the congress of Colombia would not consent to your departure from that republic, do not appear plausible to me. The first reason refutes itself. In respect to the second reason, I am strongly of the opinion that the slightest suggestion from you to the congress of Colombia would be received with unanimous approval,

provided that it was concerned with the coöperation of yourself
and your army in the struggle in which we are engaged. The
high honor of terminating the struggle for independence would
reflect as much credit upon you as upon the republic over which
you preside.

General, do not delude yourself. The reports which you have
received of the royalist forces are misleading: in Upper and
Lower Peru they amount to over nineteen thousand veteran soldiers who can be united within two months. The patriot army is
decimated by sickness: there cannot be placed in battle array
more than eight thousand five hundred men of whom the greater
number are recruits. . . . The division of fourteen hundred Colombian soldiers that you might send would be necessary to
maintain the garrison of Callao and to preserve order in Lima. . . .
Thus the struggle will be prolonged for an indefinite period.
I say an indefinite period; for I am profoundly convinced that,
whatever the vicissitudes of the present war, the independence
of America is inevitable. I am convinced, however, that the pro-
longation of the war will cause the ruin of her people; hence
it is a sacred duty of those men to whom America's destinies
are confided to prevent the continuation of great evils.

Lastly, general, my decision has been irrevocably made. I have
convened the first congress of Peru for the twentieth of next
month: on the day following that on which congress convenes,
I shall embark for Chile, for I am convinced that my presence
is the only obstacle which prevents you from marching to Peru
with your army. It would have been the acme of happiness for
me to have terminated the war of independence under the orders
of a general to whom America owes her liberty. Fate decreed
otherwise. . . .

I will say nothing to you regarding the reunion of Guayaquil
to the republic of Colombia. Permit me, however, to suggest that,
in my opinion, we were not called upon to decide that important
affair. After the war had terminated, the respective governments
could have adjusted this question without causing results which
may now prejudice the interests of the new South-American states.

I have spoken to you, general, with frankness, but the sentiments which this letter contains will remain buried in the most
profound silence: if they were to become public, our enemies
might profit by them and injure the cause of liberty, while ambitious and intriguing persons might use them to foment discord.

With Commander Delgado, the bearer of this letter, I send
to you a gun and a pair of pistols, as well as a pacer which I
offered to you in Guayaquil. Accept this remembrance from the
first of your admirers.

In conclusion San Martín expressed the wish that the glory of terminating the South-American war for independence might belong to Bolívar alone. Inferences drawn from this important document—which does not appear to have been found among Bolívar's papers—indicates what took place at secret conferences between Bolívar and San Martín. The decision was evidently reached that Guayaquil, the key to the former presidency of Quito, should remain in Bolívar's possession. San Martín deemed that the liberator did not offer to furnish a sufficient number of Colombian soldiers to co-operate in the war for Peruvian independence, because the projected campaign against the royalists was confronted with immense difficulties; while Bolívar diplomatically but firmly declined to accept the generous offer of San Martín to serve under him against the Spaniards. As a consequence, the protector of Peru decided to withdraw from public life. Obviously, he hoped that the ambitious liberator of Colombia would then bring his army to Peru and lead in person the last struggle against Spain. While the writer admires the spirit of self-abnegation that animated San Martín, he must commend the decision which entrusted the struggle in the debatable land to his resourceful rival. For his veteran soldiers, his able lieutenants, and his genuine powers of leadership, seemed to make Bolívar the man of destiny, who, if unhampered by rivalries and jealousies, might bring the war for independence to a successful termination.

It should be noticed, however, that, according to sources emanating from Bolívar, there was another side to the famous interview. In Bolívar's letter to Santander of July 29, 1822, the liberator stated that San Martín had declared that he neither desired to become king of Peru nor did he desire a democracy there, for he wished that a prince should come from Europe to rule that state. In this letter Bolívar mentioned a memorandum of his conversations with San Martín which he was transmitting to Bogotá. That memorandum was evidently a letter written to the secretary of state of Colombia from Guayaquil on July 29, 1822, by J. G. Pérez, Bolívar's general secretary,—a letter the original of which the writer has seen in the Colombian archives with his own eyes. Pérez reported San Martín as saying that before he retired from public life, he wished to see the foundations of government well established: "that the government should not be democratic in Peru, for such a system did not suit that country; and that there should come from Europe a prince who would take complete charge of the state. His excellency, Bolívar, replied that the introduction of European princes would not suit America or Colombia, for they were so different from our peoples: that, for his part, he would oppose this, so far as he was able; but that he would not object to the particular form of government which each state wished to adopt for itself. On this point, Bolívar added his thoughts in regard to the character of governments, making a reference to his discourse to the congress of Angostura. The protector of Peru replied that the European prince would arrive later. Whereupon, Bolívar responded that he would never agree to allow such princes to be enthroned in America; that he would prefer to invite General Iturbide to accept the throne; in order that no Bourbons, or Austrians, or other European dynasty should come to America."

If we accept this version of the interview as supplementary to the account of San Martín, it is clear that at Guayaquil his design to enthrone European princes in South America was buried beyond resurrection. It is certain that the triumph of Bolívar over his rival in the mysterious conferences near the equator made him the dominant personality of the South-American revolution. An anecdote has come down to us that, at a banquet which followed the last conference, Bolívar gave a toast. "To the two greatest men of South America: General San Martín and myself," and that San Martín made the response, "For the speedy termination of the war, the organization of the different republics of the continent, and the health of the liberator of Colombia." In the record of this incident, which may be partly apocryphal, we may read the judgment which posterity has passed upon the character and the aspirations of these two men. That story rightly suggests how they drew a veil over their negotiations and tacitly presented to the world an appearance of harmony and friendship.

The mood of the protector of Peru at this juncture is revealed in a letter which he wrote to O'Higgins on August 25, 1822.

Believe me, my friend, I am tired of being called tyrant, and of having it said in all quarters that I wish to become a king, an emperor, or even the devil. Further, my health has become much poorer: the climate of this country is bringing me to my grave. Lastly, as my youth was sacrificed in the service of Spain and my middle age in the service of my native land, I believe that I have the right to dispose of my old age.

Step by step San Martín retired from the scene. From Guayaquil he returned to Lima. There the delegates who had been chosen to the first Peruvian congress met on September 29, 1822. San Martín at once resigned his position as protector of Peru. The constituent congress thanked "the first soldier of liberty" for his services; it appointed him generalissimo of the army and navy, and granted him a pension of twelve thousand pesos per annum during his lifetime. San Martín firmly declined to exercise the functions of commander-in-chief, declaring that his presence in Peru would be inconsistent with the continued existence of congress. He declared that, if the liberty of Peru were ever attacked, he would spring to her defense. On September 20, 1822, he issued a farewell address to the Peruvians which breathes his admirable spirit and furnishes his answer to the charge that he desired to become king of Peru.

I have witnessed the declarations of the independence of the states of Chile and Peru; I have in my hand the standard which Pizarro brought to enslave the empire of the Incas; and I have ceased to be a public man. Thus am I recompensed with usury for ten years employed in revolution and in war. My promises to the countries for which I have fought are fulfilled: to secure their independence, and to leave them to select their own governments. The presence of a fortunate soldier, however disinterested he may be, is dangerous to newly-established states. Then, too, I am weary of hearing people say that I wish to make myself a monarch. Nevertheless, I shall always be ready to make the last sacrifice for the liberty of this country, but only in the capacity of a private citizen. With regard to my public conduct, my compatriots, as in most affairs, will be divided in opinion:—their children will give a just verdict.

The remaining years of San Martín's life were spent as an exile from Peru. From Lima he proceeded to Santiago.

Thence he soon departed to seek repose on an estate near his ever-beloved Mendoza. Here he received the mournful news of the death of his wife in the city of Buenos Aires. In 1824 he departed from that city for Europe, with his little daughter María Mercedes. After paying a brief visit to England, which he reached at the same time as Agustín de Iturbide, San Martín took up his residence in Brussels, where he supervised his daughter's education. Although the hero of San Lorenzo had been treated with indifference and neglect on his return to Buenos Aires, yet he displayed a lively interest in South-American affairs, corresponding with Guido, O'Higgins, and General Miller—an Englishman who had served in the wars for independence. When, in April, 1826, General Miller wrote to San Martín and intimated that Bolívar had declared that the mysterious interview at Guayaquil was chiefly concerned with San Martín's design to crown himself emperor of Peru, San Martín replied that, if he entertained such a design, he would have merited the appellation of impostor. "I can assure you that, if this had been my design, Bolívar could not have made me change my plan." In 1829 San Martín sailed from Europe for South America: his intention was to live a secluded life at Mendoza. Before disembarking at Buenos Aires, however, he became convinced that political conditions were so unsettled that he could not live in his native land without becoming involved in factional strife. In consequence he sadly returned to Europe. Sometimes the voluntary exile was ill; and he was often in financial straits: these circumstances at times made him speak with bitterness of the ingratitude of the republics of South America toward himself. Ultimately, however, through the generosity of a former comrade-in-arms in Spain, the financial condition of San Martín was improved. After living for a short time in Paris, he secured a comfortable home near that capital. In 1848 the precarious state of his health caused him to transfer his residence to Boulogne, where he died on August 17, 1850. Three days later he was buried in the cathedral of that city. In 1880, in accordance with his last wishes, the remains of San Martín were disinterred, and transported to Argentina. There, on May 29, they were reinterred with much ceremony in the cathedral of Buenos Aires. The sword which General San Martín had carried in the revolutionary wars, he bequeathed to General Rosas of the Argentine republic, because the latter had upheld the honor of that state against the pretensions of foreign powers.

While the personality of San Martín ordinarily made a favorable impression upon foreigners who met him, yet it appears that his associates sometimes saw only the less agreeable traits of his disposition. For the most part, San Martín disdained to leave behind him documents which might explain or interpret his changing moods. We may safely judge that certain idiosyncrasies were probably due to constitutional infirmities. Intimations may indeed be found in his private papers, as well as among the dispatches from English naval officers on the Pacific coast to their government, that San Martín occasionally resorted to the use of morphine to alleviate his sufferings. At rare moments, San Martín's pen revealed his attitude toward contemporaries; witness the inscription, which, at his direction, was carved on his wife's mausoleum in the city of Buenos Aires, "Here lies Remedios Escalada, the wife and friend of General San Martín." His conception of a woman's role in the world is suggested in the statement which he made concerning the object of his daughter's education: namely, that it was not to fashion her into a dame after the grand mode, but "to make her a tender mother and a good spouse." The conduct of San Martín, who remained an exile from his native land in order that he might not encourage a factional spirit there, furnishes a contrast with Iturbide's conduct. Among the remarks made by San Martín while living in exile, one, in particular, deserves to be mentioned; he sagely said that, in regard to contemporary affairs, men were accustomed to judge according to their prejudices, but that history would record the truth.

San Martín was not endowed in a high degree with the art of a politician, the finesse of a diplomat, or the administrative ability of a statesman. Never did he take the people, seldom did he take his associates, completely into his confidence. Nor did he make a consistent and well-sustained effort to appear to do so. But San Martín had an organizing brain; he had a prophetic vision, for he saw in the liberation of Chile and Peru the best guarantee of South-American independence; and he possessed an indomitable will that triumphed over great and numberless obstacles. So little confidence did he entertain in the capacity of South America for self-government, that he preferred a monarchical form of government to a democracy. Conscious that a strong spirit of sectionalism existed in some provinces of the former viceroyalty of la Plata, he decried proposals for the establishment of a federal republic at Buenos Aires. After reaching Peru, this high-minded patriot unfortunately lost the confidence of his jealous comrades. What was said of Miranda may almost be said of San Martín: namely, that the separation of South America from Spain eventually became the ruling purpose of his life. But San Martín would deliberately have made the Spanish-American states appanages of Europe.

Fame has been gracious to San Martín. The name of Simón de Bolívar is not more deeply graven upon the hearts of his fellow-countrymen than the name of San Martín upon the hearts of the citizens of southern South America. Misjudged by his associates, with no true apologist among his contemporaries, José de San Martín, silent and reserved, is revealed in history as one of the founders of Argentina, a liberator of Chile and Peru,—the warrior whose valiant leadership helped to ensure the ultimate triumph of Bolívar. The writer indeed hardly knows which to admire the more, the heroic march of San Martín across the Andes, or the remarkable spirit of self-abnegation with which he relinquished the position of protector of Peru, in order to promote the liberty and welfare of South America.

Upon José de San Martín widely different judgments have been passed, depending upon the prejudice or the viewpoint of the writer. Here only a few estimates of South-American writers may be noticed. The Venezuelan, C. A. Villanueva, grudgingly declared that, although San Martín was a great general, yet he lacked the qualities of a great leader. The Argentine writer, Manuel F. Montilla, extravagantly eulogized San Martín as a master of the art of war, a pure liberator, a most magnanimous and noble statesman, a humble and disinterested patriot,—the greatest man whom the New World has produced. Many and diverse are the parallels which have been made between San Martín and Bolívar. A unique comparison was made by the Chilean publicist, Domingo Santa María, who declared that San Martín was a fox, while Bolívar was an eagle.

Let us turn again to Simón de Bolívar,—the greatest personality of the heroic age of South America. Simón de Bolívar was about five feet six inches in height, lean of limb and body. His cheek bones stood out prominently in an oval-shaped face, which tapered sharply towards the chin. His countenance was vivacious; but his skin was furrowed with wrinkles, and tanned by exposure to a tropical sun. The curly black hair that once covered Bolívar's head in luxuriant profusion, began to turn white about 1821: thenceforth, he was accustomed to wear his hair short. His nose was long and aquiline. Flexible, sensual lips were often shaded by a thick mustache, while whiskers covered a part of his face. In 1822 Bolívar's large, black, penetrating eyes, "with the glance of an eagle," were losing their remarkable brilliancy. At that time Bolívar had also lost some of the animation, energy, and extraordinary agility which had distinguished him in youth and early manhood: even the casual observer judged him to be many years older than he really was, so sick and weary did he appear. Ordinarily, Bolívar's address was pleasant and his manners were graceful. Gifted with conversational ability of no mean order, at leisure moments he was accustomed to tell anecdotes concerning his romantic career. He could harangue his soldiers or address a congress in eloquent words. When in good humor, his manner was pleasing and attractive; but when impatient, irritated, or contradicted, unless he was anxious to appear otherwise, he became disagreeable, and at times appeared to act like a madman. A man of many moods, jovial, talkative, taciturn, gloomy, he changed swiftly from sunshine to storm. When in a meditative mood, the liberator sometimes assumed a pose that was statuesque.

The personality of the liberator was indeed so complex that it is not easily described. Prodigal in his youth, when he became dictator of Colombia he scattered his own silver with open hand. He was extremely sensitive to criticism, particularly did he detest the criticism of the press. So nervous was his disposition, that, even when resting from the strife of battle, or the labors of the cabinet, he was seldom in complete repose. His slumbers were short and light:—a habit to which, on at least one occasion, he owed his life. He was very fond of physical exercise, especially did he like horseback riding and dancing. Bolívar was passionately fond of the female sex.

Certain South-American historical writers speak of his different mistresses and of his many amorous escapades with a frankness that is amazing—at least to an Anglo-Saxon. At the table the liberator's habits varied according to circumstances; when necessary, he lived upon a soldier's scanty fare; at other times, he had upon his table rich viands and sparkling wines. Bolívar was a skillful horseman. There is a tradition that, in the use of the sword, he was ambidextrous. Speaking of Bolívar as a warrior, Páez said: "In the camp Bolívar showed his good humor by jests and jokes; but when on the march, he always became somewhat fidgety and to relieve his impatience he hummed a patriotic song. A lover of combat—perchance he was too fond of it—while a battle was being fought, he showed the utmost serenity. To rally soldiers who had been routed, he did not spare example, voice, or sword." Defeat left Bolívar undismayed. Said O'Leary, who served for a time as an aide-de-camp of the liberator: "Always great, he was greatest in adversity. His enemies had a saying that 'when vanquished Bolívar is more terrible than when he conquers.' "

Chapter 8

Antonio José de Sucre

"IF GOD should give to men the right to select the members of their own family, I should select . . . for a son General Sucre." Thus, according to his secretary, spoke Simón de Bolívar of that comrade whose career was closely interwoven with his own. Although not so well known as the house of Bolívar, yet the members of Sucre's family had gained distinction in the Spanish service in the Indies, where they had lived for several generations. The founder of the Sucre family in northern South America was Carlos de Sucre, apparently a native of Flanders, who faithfully served the Spanish king in important offices at Carthagena and Havana. On December 22, 1729, Carlos de Sucre was made governor of the province of New Andalusia in eastern Venezuela. For many years after leaving Cuba, Governor Sucre made his home at Cumaná, the capital of New Andalusia. His children intermarried with prominent families of Venezuela: his son Antonio, who seems to have been born in Cuba, married Josefa Margarita de Urbaneja, whose ancestors apparently fought under the *conquistadores*. In 1792 by a royal decree Antonio de Sucre was appointed colonel of infantry. One of Antonio's sons was Vicente Sucre, who married twice. The first wife of Vicente Sucre was María Manuela de Alcalá, who bore him numerous progeny. On February 20, 1795, in a church at Cumaná, the seventh son of this marriage was baptized Antonio José Francisco: the brief entry in the register of the church indicates that the child was born at Cumaná on February 3, 1795.

There are very few contemporary documents available which throw light upon the early career of Antonio José de Sucre. However, it is clear that he did not enjoy such educational advantages as Simón de Bolívar. A part of Sucre's education was evidently obtained in Caracas. In later life Sucre often expressed regret that he had not received the proper training for a political career. "It is no disgrace to confess," said he, "that I grew up in the midst of revolution and of war; that my education was in the school of the sol-

250

dier; and that I know little concerning political affairs." Moreover, Sucre's family encouraged his predilection for the military profession. According to a statement of Sucre, a paternal uncle encouraged him to take up arms for the provisional junta of Caracas. An official list of the engineers employed by that junta bearing date of April, 1811, contains the following item, "In Margarita, Lieutenant Don Antonio Sucre Alcalá, commandant of his department in that island." Evidently Antonio, who was only sixteen years of age, had been placed in charge of the engineers in Margarita. Another fragment of evidence shows that in July, 1812, this lad was acting as lieutenant of the engineers and artillerymen of the revolutionary soldiers who were stationed at Barcelona. After General Miranda capitulated at San Mateo, Lieutenant Sucre sought an asylum in the West Indies. From 1813 to 1817 he bravely participated in campaigns which were waged against the royalists in northern South America. O'Leary declares that in 1819 Francisco A. Zea, Vice President of Venezuela, appointed Colonel Sucre general. Sucre had accordingly risen to the rank of revolutionary general at the early age of twenty-three.

Fragments of evidence which convey suggestions of Sucre's personality indicate that in stature he was somewhat below the medium height. Sucre was an alert and vigorous man with a vivacious countenance and pleasing manners. Friend and foe alike testify to his gentlemanly demeanor. The best portrait of General Sucre is probably that painted by the Venezuelan artist Tovar, which depicts this general as a man of dignified mien with a thoughtful aspect. In his memoirs O'Leary describes the first meeting of General Sucre and General Bolívar in an entertaining fashion. He declares that, while proceeding down the Orinoco River after the battle of Boyacá, the liberator's boat met a canoe going up the river. In a peremptory manner, Bolívar hailed the boat and asked, "Who goes in this canoe?" The reply was "General Sucre." With anger, Bolívar exclaimed, "There is no such general"; and he thereupon commanded that both crafts should make for the river bank. Then the youthful Sucre explained that although he had been named general because his military services merited such promotion, yet he had not thought of accepting the title without the acquiescence of the liberator. Even though this explanation conveyed a rebuke, the liberator deigned to accept it. Thenceforth Bolívar and Sucre were loyal friends, who with some truth have been characterized as the Achilles and Patroclus of the American *Iliad*.

O'Leary declared that upon a certain occasion, when Bolívar made his entrance into Cúcuta, General Sucre rode out to meet him. "When I beheld Sucre," said O'Leary, "I asked the liberator who was the horseman who approached us. 'That,' he responded, 'is one of the best officials of the army; he combines the professional knowledge of Soublette, the generous character of Briceño, the talent of Santander, and the activity of Salom. . . . I am resolved to bring him into the foreground, for I am convinced that some day he will rival me.'" As was shown in the last chapter, early in 1821, the liberator sent General Sucre as his substitute into the presidency of Quito,—a mission that was justified by the victory at Pichincha, an operation which evoked words of praise from José de San Martín. After the fateful interview of Bolívar and San Martín at Guayaquil, which determined that the equatorial coast of South America should be under the suzerainty of Colombia, a subject of much anxiety to Bolívar and Sucre was the condition of Peru.

In September, 1822, the constituent congress of Peru, which San Martín had mistakenly convoked, placed the executive power of the state in the hands of a governmental junta, a triumvirate composed of its own members. On December 6, 1822, that congress promulgated a provisional constitution. In Utopian terms the constitution declared that all the provinces of Peru united into one organization composed the Peruvian nation; that sovereignty resided in the nation which was independent of all foreign powers,—a nation which could not become the patrimony of any person or family. This new nation was designated the *República Peruana;* its government should be democratic and representative; and its religion should be exclusively Roman Catholicism. The separation of the executive, the legislative, and the judicial departments was declared to be a fundamental principle of government. There was a stipulation that the executive power should never be held for life. Besides a congress of one house, provision was made for a senate which should watch over the execution of the laws as well as the conduct of the republic's magistrates and citizens. Judges were to hold office for life. It was provided that the future constitution of the Peruvian republic should acknowledge Peru's debts, should provide for public education, and should contain some guarantees of individual rights.

In February, 1823, the Peruvian congress abolished the inefficient governmental junta and entrusted the executive authority to Colonel José de la Riva Agüero with the title of president. The first president of the republic of Peru was granted by congress the rank of grand marshal. In March, 1823, President Riva Agüero instructed General Mariano Portocarrero to proceed as an envoy to Bolívar in order to solicit four thousand soldiers, money, and munitions. Bolívar promptly decided to send three thousand Colombian soldiers to Peru. On March 18, 1823, representatives of Colombia and Peru signed at Guayaquil a convention by which Bolívar agreed to aid the Peruvian patriots with six thousand soldiers, and Peru agreed to pay the cost of transporting and maintaining those troops. About a month later General Sucre was sent to Lima as Colombia's commissioner. On May 22, 1823, Sucre informed the Peruvian congress at Lima that the auxiliary Colombian division under his command offered its services to Peru for the preservation of her liberty. Bolívar's instructions directed Sucre to take such steps as were necessary to promote the independence of Peru and the safety of his soldiers. He was urged to beware of a pitched battle with the royalists, for anything was better than the loss of a battle. The army of liberation was not to risk a conflict with the royalists unless the chances of victory were in its favor. In supplementary instructions which Bolívar sent to Sucre on May 25, 1823, the latter was directed not to engage in any military operations without carefully studying the plan of campaign. In elastic clauses General Sucre was authorized to take whatever steps might seem necessary or prudent for the liberation of Peru and the preservation of Colombia's army. In reality the mission of Sucre to Lima was a reconnaissance. Shortly after his arrival in the Peruvian capital, Sucre wrote to the secretary of Bolívar to inform the latter of the plots against Riva Agüero, and declared, "According to my instructions, and guided by the dictates of prudence, I am observing and shall continue to observe a perfect neutrality so long as no attempt is made to disturb the public order and so long as the government is not attacked by factions."

Sucre's arrival in the city of the kings was followed by a steady decline in the power and prestige of President Riva

Agüero. Certain historical writers have attributed that decline to the intrigues of Sucre who was secretly preparing the way for his master. It should be borne in mind, however, that, after San Martín vanished from the scene, the advent of Bolívar was almost inevitable; indeed a Peruvian faction soon advocated that the liberator should be brought to Lima. On June 20, 1823, the Peruvian congress sent two emissaries to Guayaquil to invite Bolívar to Peru. When the royalist army threatened the Peruvian capital, congress transferred its meetings to Callao, where, on June 23, 1823, it decreed that Riva Agüero was no longer to exercise his functions within the theater of hostilities, while on the contrary, it informed Sucre that the fate of Peru was in his hands. This step was taken in the presence of the enemy, for when General Canterac marched upon Lima with an army of about seven thousand men, Sucre had reluctantly evacuated the capital and occupied Callao. Thus, for the time being, he lost Lima, but saved the army. In July Riva Agüero, who did not renounce his post in spite of the growing opposition in congress, arbitrarily dissolved that assembly, which had transferred its residence to Trujillo; but a number of its members reassembled at Lima —again evacuated by the Spaniards—where in August they declared Riva Agüero to be a traitor, and appointed the Marquis of Torre Tagle president of Peru. The writer has not found evidence to substantiate the view that these grave civil dissensions in the Peruvian republic were due mainly to Sucre's influence. In truth, it was in accordance with a secret agreement between Riva Agüero and Sucre dated June 22, 1823, that the latter prepared for an expedition against the royalists in southern Peru. There Sucre found it impossible to coöperate with General Andrés Santa Cruz, who was subsequently defeated by the Spaniards. Enough has been said of the tumultuous events in Peru to indicate that the talented, unfortunate, and misunderstood Riva Agüero,—who is viewed by his great-grandson as the champion of Peruvian nationality against the imperialistic hero of Colombia—was impotent to control the situation. Conditions were indeed ripe for the advent of Bolívar.

In response to the liberator's request, early in June, 1823, the congress of Colombia granted Bolívar permission to leave Colombian soil, in order that he might personally direct the war for Peruvian independence. On September 1 Bolívar landed at Callao; he proceeded immediately to Lima, where he was given a flattering reception. Amid the acclamations of the populace he was escorted to the mansion designated for his residence. The *Gaceta de Lima* compared the liberator with General Washington; it characterized him as "the first soldier of America." At a banquet which was given in Bolívar's honor in the former viceregal palace certain Peruvian leaders toasted the Colombian hero. In response Bolívar expressed the hope that the Spanish-Americans might never consent "to the erection of a throne in their territory, that just as Napoleon was swallowed up in the ocean, and as the new Emperor, Iturbide, was driven from the throne of Mexico, thus might the usurpers of the rights of the American people be humbled until not one remained triumphant in the New World." The Peruvian congress received the liberator of Colombia with enthusiasm, while he apparently promised to liberate Peru, or to die in the attempt. On September 10, 1823, congress decreed that there should be deposited in the hands of Simón de Bolívar, who was given the title of liberator, the supreme military authority of Peru and the political authority, so far as was necessary for the prosecution of the war. The news of Bolívar's arrival on Peruvian soil made Sucre rejoice. At Arequipa, on October 7, he issued a proclamation to his soldiers announcing that he transferred the command of the united army to Bolívar, "the son of liberty." Soon after Bolívar was declared liberator of Peru, he attempted to initiate negotiations to terminate the dissentions between congress and Riva Agüero, but in vain: a short time afterwards that leader was exiled from his native land, nursing in his heart a bitter hatred of the Colombian commanders.

Months before he reached Lima, Bolívar had sketched plans for a campaign against General Canterac. In a plan which he presented to General Sucre in May, 1823, the liberator argued that the Colombian soldiers should keep possession of Peru, but that they should rather remain inactive than be defeated by the royalists. Bolívar took the view that the patriot forces were not ready to take the offensive against the disciplined and experienced soldiers of Spain. "Canterac and Valdez are not terrible; still their resources, their positions, and their victories give them a decided superiority which cannot be overcome suddenly but only slowly and progressively." To this view Bolívar wisely adhered despite the pugnacious advice of Sucre, who wished to take the offensive at once. Near the end of 1823 Sucre took charge of the Colombian soldiers who were stationed north of Lima; in December of that year Bolívar advised Sucre to take preparatory steps for a campaign against the royalists. The impetuous liberator of Colombia had become the cautious dictator of Peru.

Early in 1824, even Bolívar saw clearly that his extraordinary activity had sapped his constitution. He felt deeply hurt at the intrigues which were being carried on against him in Colombia. A letter which he wrote to Sucre on January 16, 1824, will suggest the despondent mood into which the liberator sometimes fell when contemplating the affairs of South America.

I have asked for my dismissal by the Colombian congress and have displayed much disgust at the ingratitude of the people. This action will certainly produce a favorable result at Bogotá, as well as at Lima. If it does not, I shall take the occasion to leave public life completely; for I am resolved that Colombia shall not be lost in my hands. Neither will I liberate her a second time. Such a task should not be performed twice. I felt ready to give battle to the Spaniards, in order to terminate the war in America; but I feel ready no longer. I feel tired; I am old; and I have nothing more to expect from fortune. On the contrary, I feel like an avaricious rich man who is always afraid that someone will steal his money. Everything causes me fear and alarm. It appears to me that, from moment to moment, I am losing my reputation, which is the reward and the fortune that I have obtained for my immense sacrifices. A similar fate will befall you. Nevertheless, I ought to say that you are still very young, and that a brilliant prospect is before you. Would that I might be in your position; so that I need not tremble for my own fortune: at least I would have desires; I would have hopes to caress me!

Thus wrote Bolívar the liberator,—who was old at forty years—partly because of excesses that this history had rather not name. Fortunate was it for the cause of South-American independence that, in the hour of need, his comrade Sucre could grasp the baton of command.

On January 26, 1824, Bolívar wrote to Sucre recommending that cattle should be gathered for the use of the army, that arrangements be made to store provisions for the projected campaign, and that the soldiers be compelled to march regularly in the mountains, in order that they might become hardened and accustomed to the altitude. On February 4 Bolívar again wrote to Sucre; he again declared that the secret of their success in the war lay in the preservation of the Colombian army:

> This army is the safeguard of Peru, the vanguard of Colombia, and the military agent of South America. If we expose it to defeat without having previously arranged for new forces and new reserves, we shall be inconsiderate and imprudent. Time will procure for us new truces and new political successes. . . . Your spirit is fertile in coöperative expedients; there is no limit to your efficiency, zeal, and activity. I expect much of time.

The cause of Peruvian independence was seriously injured, when, early in February, 1824, the garrison of Callao, which was composed partly of soldiers from the Platean provinces, mutinied and gave up that stronghold to the royalists. The loss of that port was followed by the re-occupation of Lima by royalist soldiers. Thus the Spaniards held the center and the south of Peru, as well as the highlands, General Canterac being encamped at Jauja on the elevated Andean plateau. On February 10, 1824, the Peruvian congress conferred upon Bolívar the supreme political power of the state. A few days later the dictator of Peru—who was still the titular president of Colombia—informed General Sucre that the latter was to act as the commander-in-chief of the united army of liberation.

Bolívar and Sucre spent months quietly preparing for the arduous campaign against General Canterac. For a time the center of Bolívar's activity was the town of Trujillo, while Sucre was located at Huaraz, and General José de La Mar, a native of Cuenca, was in charge of the Peruvian soldiers at Cajamarca. At that juncture Bolívar demonstrated that his residence in Peru had not destroyed his talent for organization. He tried to secure thousands of additional soldiers from Colombia; he sent instructions and queries to Sucre in regard to roads, horses, and cattle. For example, he advised Sucre that the soldiers' horses were to be shod only with shoes of Vizcayan iron. To paraphrase O'Leary, Trujillo was "an immense arsenal, where no one was idle." General Sucre was "the right arm of the liberator": he studied the topography of the Andean range; tirelessly did he explore the mountains, surveying the roads, spying upon the royalists, and secreting barley and wood in caverns. Thousands of ounces of silver were collected from the churches of Peru for the support of the expedition. Forced contributions were levied upon the inhabitants, and many Peruvians were induced to enlist in the army of liberation. After describing the liberator's preparations for this campaign, O'Leary said that it would seem "as though from the head of a new Jupiter there had sprung not a new Pallas armed from head to foot, but eight thousand soldiers equipped for battle."

About the middle of June the divisions of the army broke camp, and detachments of soldiers proceeded towards the appointed rendezvous by different routes along dangerous Andean paths. After marching about two hundred leagues, in the end of July, soldiers from Colombia, la Plata, and Peru bivouacked at the rendezvous on the plateau north of Lake Reyes, twelve thousand feet above the level of the sea. There Bolívar assembled his united army, which numbered about nine thousand men. To the soldiers of his army the titular president of Colombia and dictator of Peru addressed an inspiring proclamation. "You are about to complete the greatest task which Heaven has entrusted to men,—the emancipation of an entire world from slavery. . . . Peru and America expect from you peace,—the daughter of victory. Even liberal Europe contemplates you in enchantment; for the liberty of the New World is the hope of the universe."

In command of this army, under Bolívar, was placed General Sucre. General José María Córdoba, a Colombian, was placed in charge of the vanguard; the division of the center was commanded by General La Mar; and the rearguard was commanded by General Jacinto Lara. General Nechochea was made commander of the cavalry; Colonel Carvajal was placed in immediate charge of the Colombian cavalry; and General Miller was given charge of the Peruvian cavalry. Among the cavalry, as well as the infantry, there were some soldiers who had followed José de San Martín from Chile and even from the United Provinces. The picturesque scene which took place upon the Andean plateau is thus described in the memoirs of General Miller:

Nothing could exceed the excitement felt upon that occasion. Every circumstance tended to impart a most romantic interest to

the scene. Near the same spot, four years before, the royalists had
been defeated by General Arenales. The view from the table land,
upon which the troops were reviewed, and which is at an elevation
of more than twelve thousand feet above the level of the sea, is
perhaps the most magnificent in the world. On the west arose the
Andes, which had just been surmounted with so much toil. On the
east were enormous ramifications of the Cordillera stretching towards the Brazils. North and south, the view was bounded by
mountains whose tops were hidden in the clouds. On that plain,
surrounded by such sublime scenery, and on the margin of the
magnificent lake of Reyes, the principal source of the Amazon, the
mightiest of rivers, were now assembled men from Caracas, Panama, Quito, Lima, and Buenos Aires; men who had fought at Maypo
in Chile; at San Lorenzo, on the banks of the Parana; at Carabobo
in Venezuela; and at Pichincha at the foot of the Chimborazo.
Amidst these devoted Americans were a few foreigners, still firm
and faithful to the cause, in support of which so many of their
countrymen had fallen. Amongst those few survivors were men
who had fought on the banks of the Guadiana and of the Rhine;
who had witnessed the conflagration of Moscow, and the capitulation of Paris. . . . Americans or European, they were all animated
by one sole spirit, that of assuring the political existence of a vast
continent.

In the end of July reports of the unexpected march of
Bolívar's soldiers rudely awoke Canterac from his fancied security. At the head of an army of about eight thousand men,
he marched north from Jauja, and proceeded along the eastern shores of Lake Reyes. But meanwhile the soldiers of
Bolívar were marching south along the western shores of that
lake. When the royalist commander learned where Bolívar's
army was, he suddenly faced his army about, and marched
back toward his encampment. In the afternoon of August 6,
on the plains of Junín, a part of the eager patriot cavalry
under General Nechochea encountered the royalist forces. At
once General Canterac led his cavalry in a spirited charge
against Nechochea's troops, which, being attacked at a disadvantage, were thrown into disorder. But a squadron of
Peruvian huzzars under the brave Colonel Suarez led a
counter-attack. "The terrible silence was interrupted only by
the strident voice of the clarinets, the clash of sabers and
lances, the galloping and stamping of horses, the maledictions
of the vanquished, and the lamentations of the wounded."

After a fierce hand-to-hand conflict which lasted scarcely an hour, the Spanish cavalry fled hastily from the plains of Junín. In a dejected mood General Canterac led his soldiers toward Cuzco.

In a poem composed in honor of the victory of Junín, Olmedo compared Bolívar's sword to the sun which obscured the stars. But it does not appear that Bolívar took part in the cavalry engagement at Junín except to direct the patriots in the opening struggle. Yet he undoubtedly deserved a large share of the credit for the management of the campaign which culminated in a victory that lowered the prestige of the soldiers of Spain and gave the patriots possession of several provinces in the Peruvian highlands. Sucre's was the honor of acting as Bolívar's chief commander. When the royalists at Lima heard of the battle of Junín, they evacuated that city for the last time.

After the victory at Junín, Bolívar slowly led his soldiers southward across the elevated plateau of the Andes toward Huamanga. General Sucre was placed in command of the rearguard,—a position which much disgusted him. On August 28, 1824, he wrote to Bolívar in these words:

I have been deprived of the command of the army to execute a commission which would ordinarily be entrusted to an officer of no higher rank than an aide-de-camp, and have been sent to the rearguard when the army is advancing upon the enemy. Thus the impression has been publicly given that I am considered incapable of active operations: my companions in arms have been given reason to consider me as either a useless person or a fool.

On September 4 Bolívar made a reply to his sensitive friend.

I respond to the letter which Escalona brought me with an expression that Rousseau used when the lover of Julia complained of the offense which she had committed by sending him money: "This is the only tactless action which you have performed in the course of your life." I believe that you committed an error of judgment when you thought that I wished to offend you. I am full of regret, because of your sorrow; but I do not feel in the least guilty of an intentional offense. I gave you a commission which I did not wish to undertake myself; for I believed that you were better able to perform it because of your extraordinary agility. I gave you that commission rather as an indication of my favor than as a proof of humiliation.

Near the end of August the soldiers of Bolívar encamped at the Indian hamlet of Huamanga, which was west of the Apurimac River on the road leading from Cuzco to Lima. About a month later Bolívar decided to leave the army and to proceed to the coast, evidently intending to await there the arrival of the reënforcements which he expected from Colombia. Apparently his plan was to join Sucre with those reenforcements, and then to engage the royalists in the last great battle, which would decide the fate of South America. When the liberator journeyed to the Peruvian coast, General Sucre remained in charge of the soldiers who had been victorious on the plains of Junín. Before he departed Bolívar carefully instructed Sucre to encamp with the army for a month; in order that the men and horses might get a much-needed rest. After he thus became the commander of the patriot army, Sucre stationed his soldiers at points which extended over leagues of territory,—the center of his line was at Lambrana. On hearing of this disposal of the troops Bolívar instructed Sucre that he was not to divide the army, and that he was to preserve it at any cost; for to weaken the army was to risk the loss of a battle and to jeopardize the interests of Spanish America. "The liberty of Peru will not be achieved by the occupation of territory unless that territory is the very region where we gain a victory over the enemy."

In October, General Valdez, who had been pacifying Upper Peru, joined forces with General Canterac at Cuzco. Viceroy La Serna, the former antagonist of San Martín, took command of the united royalist army which numbered about ten thousand men. La Serna soon led the royalist soldiers through deep valleys and across rugged mountains in search of the patriots, who were near the capital of the ancient empire of the Incas. Early in November General Sucre was suddenly warned that the combined royalist forces were advancing against him,—news which he declared gave him mingled feelings of surprise, disgust, and pleasure. He consequently prepared to concentrate his soldiers; in order that, as a military disciple of Bolívar, he might meet the enemy under the most favorable conditions possible. A very remarkable series of maneuvers then took place: at time the hostile armies moved on parallel lines, separated only by a precipitous ravine or a mountain torrent; they marched and counter-marched: La Serna frequently attempted to take his opponent at a disadvantage, while Sucre, in accordance with Bolívar's advice, acted ordinarily on the defensive. On November 16 the royalist soldiers occupied Huamanga; thus Sucre was cut off from his base of supplies on the Pacific coast. By December 1 he was tired of a retreat from the enemy with soldiers who were sighing for a battle: he declared that, under no circumstances, would he retire beyond Huamanga. On December 3, while Sucre's soldiers were on the march, they were attacked by the royalists and suffered a loss of men, munitions, and artillery. Incited by the royalists, the neighboring Indians rose against the patriots. At this critical juncture the patriot commander received a letter from Bolívar which authorized him to offer battle to the royalists in the Peruvian highlands, while the liberator sustained the cause of independence upon the seacoast.

At last, Sucre was in supreme command of the patriot army. Convinced that he should not act upon the defensive, he decided to offer battle to the enemy at the first favorable opportunity, even though his forces were numerically inferior. Sucre's army numbered about six thousand men; whereas the viceroy had over nine thousand men. While the soldiers of Spain were led by generals who did not always act in harmony, the revolutionary soldiers were commanded by an able and inspiring general who appeared confident of victory. It seems that to offset the numerical superiority of the enemy, Sucre sought an arena for the conflict which might afford him a strategic advantage.

Sucre's aide-de-camp, Colonel López, asserted that Generals Sucre and La Mar deliberately selected for the field of battle the small secluded plain of Ayacucho, "the corner of death," which, according to tradition, was an ancient Inca battle-field. On December 6 the army of Sucre paused near the Indian village of Quinua, which was located on the western side of Ayacucho. When arrayed on this plain, the flanks of Sucre's army were protected by ravines, while the rear was guarded by a valley. To the east, the field of battle was bordered by the craggy, wooded heights of Condorkanki. On the afternoon of December 8 the soldiers of La Serna climbed the heights of Condorkanki, which seemed to dominate the plain of Ayacucho:—at last, the patriot soldiers appeared to be at bay. As his chief of staff Sucre had chosen General Agustín Gamarra, a native of Cuzco. The patriot army was arranged in three main divisions under experienced leaders. The left was composed largely of Peruvian soldiers under General La Mar; the right was made up mainly of Colombians under General Córdova; the center was composed of cavalry under General Miller; while the reserve was in charge of General Lara. At a critical moment during the forenoon of December 9, when the royalist files were slowly descending the heights and forming into columns upon the plain of Ayacucho, General Sucre rode along his battle-line and inspirited his followers. According to his aide, he exclaimed, "Upon the efforts of today the destiny of South America depends," and, pointing towards the royalist columns, he assured his soldiers that their admirable constancy would soon be rewarded by another day of glory.

When only a part of the royalist army had formed in battle array, Sucre ordered the gallant Córdova to begin the attack. While the Spanish soldiers were engaged in a desperate hand-to-hand struggle with the Colombian soldiers upon the plain, Sucre sent a detachment of cavalry to charge the royalists who were descending from the heights. The Spanish soldiers were soon routed, and, in part, driven to the heights of Condorkanki. A brilliant charge by the patriot cavalry upon a division of the royalist army under General Valdez which attacked Sucre's left wing, drove it into flight. After a struggle which lasted only about an hour, the royalists were driven from the plain of Ayacucho. The Spanish soldiers who sought a refuge upon the heights were fiercely pursued; and there the wounded viceroy was captured. To quote again from the memoirs of General Miller: "The battle of Ayacucho was the most brilliant ever fought in South America. . . . It was not a victory of mere chance, but the result of the most determined bravery and an irresistible onset conceived and executed at the proper moment." In one of those rare moments when General Sucre mentioned his own military achievements, he wrote to a friend concerning the battle upon the plain of Ayacucho, "A proud Spanish army was there put to rout; but this was done so skillfully that the battle can scarcely be described."

The victory of Ayacucho gave the *coup de grâce* to the royalist army in Lower Peru. Late in the afternoon of December 9, General Canterac appeared before Sucre's tent to propose a capitulation. Of that proposal the magnanimous victor said, "Although the condition of the enemy made possible a surrender at our discretion, I believed it worthy of American generosity to concede some honors to the vanquished soldiers, who had been victorious in Peru for fourteen years. The capitulation was arranged upon the field of

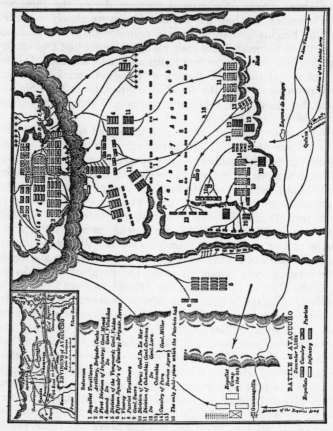

PLAN OF THE BATTLE OF AYACUCHO
(From the "Memoirs of General Miller")

battle." The treaty which was signed by Sucre and Canterac shortly afterwards provided that Lower Peru should be relinquished to the victors. The vanquished soldiers were to be allowed freely to proceed to Spain, on the condition that they were not to return to the New World to take up arms against the Spanish-American states. It was provided that they might be admitted into the army of Peru. No person should be disturbed because of his political opinions or because he had served under the Spanish banner, provided that he observed the laws. Any persons might emigrate from Peru with their families and properties within one year; those persons who chose to remain in the country should be considered as Peruvians. The property held in Peru by non-resident Spaniards was to be respected, provided that those Spaniards did not oppose the independence of that state. Subject to the approval of congress, Peru was to assume the responsibility for the debts which Spain had incurred in the liberated territory. If Peru approved, viceregal officers might even retain their positions. Obviously both Sucre and Canterac felt that this capitulation determined the destinies of other states than Peru; for a clause in the treaty provided that certain patriot and royalist commanders should be sent to the Platean provinces in order that the archives, munitions, and garrisons might be promptly transferred to the independent government. Spanish merchant vessels and war ships were to be allowed to secure provisions in Peruvian ports for six months after the publication of the treaty; but such war vessels were to leave the Pacific Ocean promptly; and they were not to touch at any port which was still held by the Spaniards. The Spanish officers who had been captured at Ayacucho, including fourteen generals, were to be set at liberty. The prisoners who had been captured in other engagements between the patriots and the royalists were also to be released. The generals and other officers of Spain were to be allowed to keep their swords and uniforms. The defeated soldiers might move about freely in order to arrange their affairs without being embarrassed by the actions of any independent state. The last article of the capitulations provided that "any question which might arise in regard to any article of this treaty" should be interpreted "in favor of the soldiers of the Spanish army." Such generous treatment of a vanquished enemy by the victor should have influenced the government of Spain to ratify the treaty which was signed upon the plain of Ayacucho.

In Miller's memoirs a pathetic picture is drawn of La Serna, the captive viceroy of Peru, leaning against the mud wall of an Indian hut near Ayacucho, his white hair clotted with blood from a wound received in the battle. That picture symbolizes the end of the Spanish empire in continental America. In the former capital of the Peruvian viceroys the battle of Ayacucho was rightly believed to signalize the destruction of Spanish rule in Peru. This victory was indeed significant not only to Peru but also to other states of South America: on one side, it completed the achievements of José de San Martín; on the other side, it almost concluded the labors of Simón de Bolívar. The glowing tribute of the liberator to the hero of Ayacucho will furnish his estimate of the significance of the battle: it will furnish another illustration of the occasional exuberance of Bolívar's style.

The battle of Ayacucho is the climax of American glory, and the work of General Sucre. The arrangement for this battle was perfect, and the execution divine. In one hour rapid and masterly maneuvers routed the victors of fourteen years,—an army perfectly constituted and ably led. . . . Just as the battle of Waterloo decided the destinies of European nations, so did the battle of Ayacucho decide the fate of the nations of Spanish America. . . . General Sucre is the father of Ayacucho: he is the redeemer of the sons of the sun; he has broken the chains with which Pizarro bound the empire of the Incas. Posterity will represent Sucre with one foot at Pichincha and the other foot at Potosí, holding in his hands the cradle of Manco Capac, and contemplating the chains of Peru broken by his sword.

In truth, Sucre's victory exercised a decisive influence upon the fortunes of the dissident provinces of Spain in America from the Río de la Plata to the Río Grande. Nevertheless, the court of Madrid did not sanction the treaty of Ayacucho. Ferdinand VII.—unfettered by a constitution—would not recognize the independence of the rising states of Spanish America. The achievements of Bolívar and Sucre, however, were appreciated in South America. On February 12, 1825, the Peruvian congress decreed that a medal should be struck off in honor of the liberator, Simón de Bolívar, and that henceforth General Sucre should be dignified with the title of Grand Marshal of Ayacucho. It also provided that an equestrian statue of Bolívar should be erected at Lima. About the same time the Colombian congress passed a law providing that a medal of platinum should be presented to Bolívar, the liberator of Colombia and Peru, and that a sword of gold should be presented to Sucre, the victor of Ayacucho. From the ancient capital of the Inca empire, Sucre wrote to Bolívar,

"I shall forward to you the banner which Pizarro carried to Cuzco three hundred years ago."

General Sucre soon led the army of liberation into the presidency of Charcas—Upper Peru—that extensive region which, during the last years of Spanish rule, was under the jurisdiction of the *audiencia* of Chuquisaca and also of the viceroy of Buenos Aires. Early in 1825 Sucre terminated successfully the war for the liberation of that region. The political status of Upper Peru presented a thorny problem to Marshal Sucre. In certain particulars he occupied a position similar to that which San Martín had held in 1821 with regard to Lower Peru. In other particulars his position was different. Upper Peru had been liberated by soldiers from Colombia, la Plata, and Lower Peru; the republic of Peru wished to establish jurisdiction over Upper Peru; it was far from the former seat of government at Buenos Aires; and some of its people wished to found an independent state. Further, Sucre was acting under Bolívar's ægis. Marshal Sucre soon decided that it would be wise to avoid a military dictatorship and also to abstain from any interference in the domestic affairs of this section. As early as February 9, 1825, he issued a significant proclamation. Declaring that the former viceroyalty of Buenos Aires lacked a central government, he announced that Upper Peru would remain under the control of the liberating army until delegates of the provinces should assemble. He proposed that the delegates should meet in April, 1825, to deliberate freely in regard to a provisional government and to consider the political destinies of Upper Peru. Sucre also suggested that the decision reached by this assembly should be sanctioned by the governments at Buenos Aires and Lima. When Bolívar heard of the proclamation, he sent a letter to Marshal Sucre which was couched in these words:

Neither you, nor I, nor the congress of Peru, nor of Colombia, can break and violate the basis of public law which we have recognized in Spanish America. This basis is: that republican governments are being founded within the limits of the former viceroyalties, captaincy generals, or presidencies, for example, Chile. Upper Peru is a dependency of the viceroyalty of Buenos Aires, just as Quito is a contiguous dependency of Bogotá. Although Chile was a dependency of Peru, yet it was in reality separated from Peru some time before the revolution began, just as Guatemala was separated from New Spain. Thus both of these presidencies might rightly become independent of their ancient viceroyalties; but neither Quito nor Charcas can rightly become independent except by an agreement embodied in a treaty resulting from a war between the parties, or resulting from the deliberations of a congress.

This protest embodied the idea which, consciously or unconsciously, influenced some leaders of the revolutionary epoch in South America: namely, that the boundaries of the independent states should coincide with the boundaries of those colonial divisions which had been under the control of a viceroy, a captain general, or a president. In other words, this was Bolívar's statement of a doctrine which is commonly known in the international law of Spanish America as the *uti possidetis* of 1810.

In the case of Upper Peru, however, the scruples of Bolívar were outweighed by Sucre's arguments and actions. On May 16, after the meeting of the delegates summoned by Sucre had been postponed, Bolívar the dictator of Peru, reluctantly sanctioned the assembly and decreed that, in the meantime, Upper Peru should be subject to Sucre's authority. During the interregnum Marshal Sucre busied himself with reforms concerning justice and finance. Soon after the delegates of Upper Peru assembled at Chuquisaca, on July 19, 1825, they wrote to Bolívar declaring that they placed themselves under his protection; the liberator responded that he felt honored by this announcement made at a time when those delegates were entering upon their new career. After considerable debate, on August 6, the anniversary of the battle of Junín, delegates from the provinces of Charcas, La Paz, Cochabamba, Potosí, and Santa Cruz proclaimed the independence of Upper Peru from Spain. The justification which they presented for this act was the misgovernment and oppression of the motherland. They declared that both Peru and the United Provinces had expressed their intentions to allow Upper Peru to determine her own political destiny. They proclaimed that the rule of Ferdinand VII. had ceased and expressed their desire to establish a sovereign state which would be independent alike of the nations of the Old World and the New,—a state that should be governed by a constitution and laws formed by its own citizens.

On August 11, 1825, the assembly of Upper Peru decreed that the new state should be designated the *República Bolívar*. It provided that Bolívar was the father and protector of this state, as well as the first president. It also decreed that the future capital of the republic should be named Sucre. A few days later it adopted a national flag, as well as a coat of arms, and made provision for a national coinage. On August 31 it declared that the new nation was to have "a representative republican" government. Apparently the Bolivians did not feel able to maintain their independence without foreign aid, for, on October 4, the assembly expressed a desire that two thousand Colombian soldiers should be allowed to remain in the republic so long as its legislators might deem necessary. In regard to the provisional government of the new republic, on October 3, 1825, the assembly passed a decree providing that Marshal Sucre should be the supreme ruler of the state when Bolívar was not upon Bolivian soil.

While Bolivian legislators were thus laying the foundations of a new state, Bolívar—who had delegated his power as dictator of Peru to a council—was making a triumphal tour through the liberated provinces of Lower and Upper Peru. On August 18 he reached La Paz, where he met a delegation from the Bolivian assembly that asked him to promote the independence of their state, whereupon Bolívar apparently gave it assurances that he would use his influence with the Peruvian congress to secure such recognition. On November 1 Bolívar reached Chuquisaca, where he acted as the chief executive of the state. During the few months when Bolívar was actually the dictator-president of Bolivia he inaugurated some political and administrative reforms: by various decrees he insisted upon economy in the administration of the government; he provided that the tribute which had been levied upon the Indians should be replaced by a head-tax; he took various measures to promote education, making his old tutor, Rodríguez, director of public instruction; he provided for the establishment of new judicial tribunals; and he ordered that wagon-roads should be constructed between the different sections of the republic. On December 29 Bolívar issued a decree announcing that the constituent congress of Bolivia would assemble on May 25, 1836. On the same day he transferred his executive authority to Sucre.

Early in 1826—while again acting as the chief executive of the nascent state—Sucre took measures to carry out several orders or decrees of the liberator. In addition, he initiated some administrative reforms. He soon entrusted the management of such matters as internal affairs, war, and the finances to distinct ministries. On January 23, 1826, he issued an important decree which laid the basis of Bolivia's administrative system. That decree provided that her territory should be divided into five departments; these departments were to be subdivided into provinces, and the provinces were to be divided into cantons. As the chief executive of Bolivia, Sucre ardently desired to secure control of the district of Tarija, but that district became a bone of contention between Bolivia and the United Provinces. In vain did Sucre hope to secure from Peru a strip of territory upon the Pacific Ocean which would include the port of Arica and thus furnish Bolivia a good outlet to the sea. Still, he made certain of an outlet further south; for, as early as March, 1826, he exercised jurisdiction over the district of Atacama, which later became the debatable land between Bolivia and Chile. The territory of the new state which was thus being hewn out of the side of the United Provinces included, roughly speaking, the region which had been subject to the *audiencia* of Chuquisaca. On May 25 Sucre resigned his extraordinary authority to the constituent congress which had gathered at Chuquisaca; but that congress at once elected him provisional president of the republic, a position which he finally accepted with much reluctance.

What of the first constitution of the republic of Bolivia? It was while residing in Chuquisaca that Bolívar fulfilled the request of Bolivia's first assembly to frame a constitution for the new state. Accordingly, when he was not enjoying the felicitations of the inhabitants, or receiving the commissioners who had been sent from the Platean provinces to congratulate him, or issuing reformatory decrees, Bolívar was framing a constitution for the republic which bore his name. When he discussed the motives which impelled Bolívar again to essay the rôle of maker of constitutions, O'Leary said:

I do not consider myself competent to pass upon the merits or the defects of this constitution; but it is my duty—a duty imposed alike by honor and justice—to give testimony to the purity of the motives which animated its illustrious author to propose changes in the political system which was so popular in America. Profoundly versed in the history of the human race and well instructed in the theories of political science, he was not ignorant of the institutions which, in ancient and modern times, had raised nations to prosperity and glory, or had promoted their decadence and ruin. Bolívar possessed another qualification even more essential. He had a perfect knowledge of the world, and, interested as he was in the study of the human heart, few individuals possessed a keener intuition, or a more delicate tact. The peculiar circumstances of his adventurous life and the extraordinary events of his public career, had brought him into contact with all classes of society and enabled him to observe men in all phases and conditions. More than any other person did he understand his fellow-patriots of South America. . . . The political condition of Spanish America did not gratify the observant and penetrating eyes of Bolívar, who had played the principal rôle in the revolutionary drama, and who was aware of America's most hidden secrets. . . . Full of fear, he contemplated the terrible picture, and proposed to derive wise lessons from the spectacle. Although he knew that the easiest method to preserve his ascendancy was to cajole popular prepossessions, yet he had too much patriotism to traffic with the fortunes of his country for personal advantage. So great was his soul that he would not sacrifice his convictions, which were sustained by reason and experience, upon the altar of popularity. Thus he reached his decision without any vacillation. He sought a system which would be strong enough to curb revolutions and not theories which would foment them.

By the end of February, 1826, Bolívar had completed his task. When he saw that political conditions in Lima would not permit him to be present at the opening of the Bolivian constituent congress, the liberator composed a discourse to explain the constitution which he had framed for the "Republic of Bolivia." In June, 1826, Sucre presented the project to the constituent congress and read to it Bolívar's discourse.

In this constitution the executive power was vested in a president chosen by congress, who was to serve for life. If the president died, or was disabled, he was to be succeeded by the vice president, who ordinarily presided over the meetings of the cabinet. That body was to be composed of three secretaries: a secretary of the interior and foreign relations, a secretary of finance, and a secretary of war and the navy. The president was vested with powers which were analogous to the powers of the President of the United States. In his discourse Bolívar compared the position of the president in his plan to the position of the sun in the solar system. "This supreme authority should be perpetual; for governments without hierarchies, in particular, need a fixed point around which magistrates and citizens, men and things, may revolve: 'Give me a fixed point,' said an ancient sage, 'and I will move the world.' To Bolivia a president holding office for life will be such a point. Though not endowed with action, he will support the entire system. His head has been removed, in order that no person may fear his intentions; and his hands have been tied that he may injure no one." Bolívar argued that as America was largely unsettled, it would be difficult to establish a monarchy there. "Deserts are favorable to independence. In America we have no grandees, either civil or ecclesiastical. . . . There is no power more difficult to maintain than that of a new prince. Bonaparte, who vanquished so many armies, could not overcome this rule, which is stronger than empires." Thus, apparently, did Bolívar conceive the rôle of president under his constitution. Nevertheless, it appears that a president for life, as proposed by him, would have meant in practice a constitutional monarch.

The legislative authority of Bolivia was to be vested in three houses: the house of tribunes, the house of senators, and the house of censors. Each house was to be composed of thirty members. The tribunes, whose special powers were largely concerned with financial affairs, the army, the navy, and foreign affairs, were to hold office for four years. The senators, whose special powers were concerned chiefly with judicial, ecclesiastical, and constitutional matters, were to hold office for eight years. The censors were to hold office for life: they should watch that the constitution, laws, and treaties of Bolivia were faithfully observed. The censors were also given the exclusive right to propose all laws concerning education and the press. They were to protect the liberty of the press, to encourage arts and sciences, to distribute honors and rewards, and to condemn to "eternal opprobium the usurpers of public authority, notorious traitors, and atrocious criminals." In his discourse Bolívar compared "the political and moral power" of the censors to the power exercised by "the areopagus of Athens and the censors of Rome." The censors of the Bolivian constitution—"the high priests of the laws"—illustrate the idea of a moral power, which Bolívar proposed to the congress of Angostura.

The judicial power was to be vested in a supreme court and certain inferior courts. The supreme court should be composed of a president and six other judges. Only some of the cases in which that court had jurisdiction may here be named: it was to take cognizance of cases relating to ambassadors, other diplomatic agents, and consuls, of criminal cases involving certain important officers of the republic, and of matters relating to the patronage. It was to examine papal bulls, briefs, and rescripts relating to civil affairs. Provisions were also made for inferior courts in judicial districts which were to be carved out of the provinces. In every town of one hundred inhabitants there were to be judges, or justices, who were to promote the reconciliation of contending parties. The use of torture or the extortion of confessions was prohibited. In his discourse Bolívar praised the judicial system because of its "absolute independence. The people present the candidates, while the legislature selects the individuals who are to be the members of the courts."

The selective process which Bolívar thus suggested was provided by what he styled "the electoral power." In reality that so-called power was an arrangement for the choice of certain officers by means of electoral colleges in the provinces. The citizens who had the right to vote should choose electors that were to hold their offices for four years. The electors were to meet annually in the capitals of their respective provinces to receive the reports of elections, to petition the legislature for reforms, to elect members of the legislature and certain other officers, and to nominate candidates for such offices as prefects, *alcaldes,* and curates. The suggestions for a so-called electoral power were probably adapted from the Constitution of the United States. In Bolívar's discourse he praised this power which constituted a new weight cast into the balance against the authority of the executive. To paraphrase the words which the author used in a circular extolling his constitution: it entrusted the exercise of important acts of sovereignty to electoral bodies. This elaborate electoral power was probably the liberator's most distinctive contribution to political science.

Bolívar stipulated that the republic was to be composed of departments which were to be divided into provinces. Those provinces were to be subdivided into cantons. The head of each deparment was to be a prefect. In each province a governor was to be the chief authority. The political affairs of each canton were to be managed by a *corregidor.* Provision was made for a navy as well as an army. In his discourse Bolívar maintained that the constitution should contain no prescription in regard to religious faith; but the constituent congress of Bolivia did not accept this view.

The monarchical constitution framed for the republic of Bolivia embodied the ideas of the "liberator of Colombia, Peru, and Bolivia" in regard to the type of government which was most suitable for an independent state in the existing condition of Spanish America. In an address which he later made in Peru, Bolívar is reported to have said in regard to the framing of the constitution: "This constitution is the work of ages. To form it I have consulted every ancient and modern authority. It combines the lessons of experience with the counsels and opinions of the wise." In all likelihood in framing his constitution, Bolívar tried to imitate in some respects the government of France under General Bonaparte, the First Consul. An agent of France in South America quoted Bolívar as having said that by this constitution he established a mixed government which utilized the best principles of monarchy, aristocracy, and democracy. According to an inedited note of Tomás de Heres found in the archives of the liberator at Caracas, the wise men whom Bolívar consulted were certain of his associates—as Tomás de Heres—who were asked to furnish him in writing with their reflections upon his draft of the constitution. It would appear that Bolívar's main intention was to ingraft a monarchical custom into the republican system. Unwittingly, perhaps, Bolívar made the executive authority in the Bolívian system somewhat weaker than in the constitution which he presented in 1819 to the congress of Angostura. When he sent copies of his constitution and discourse to General Páez, the liberator declared that it was not possible for him to present any other plan of government to a state which was named after himself. In letters to prominent Colombians he expressed the hope that conditions in Colombia might alter so as to make possible the adoption there of the Bolivian constitution. To synchronize our story, it should be noticed that at the very time when the Bolivians were considering the liberator's constitution, a constituent assembly at the former capital of the viceroyalty of la Plata was adopting a centralistic constitution for the Argentine republic.

Bolívar's constitution was referred to a committee of the congress of Bolivia which suggested some changes. After several months of debate, with some modifications—the most important being that article which provided that Roman Catholicism should be the state religion—congress adopted this constitution. In October, 1826, General Sucre was elected the president of Bolivia. This office he was reluctant to accept; because he had an inherent dislike for the position of civil magistrate which he felt unfitted to fill, and he apprehended that it might be difficult to preserve Bolivia as a buffer state between Peru and the Argentine republic. Nevertheless he waived his personal desires in order that the rule of law might be established in Bolivia. On December 9, 1826, he took a solemn oath to observe the Bolivian constitution. He made a short address to congress announcing his fixed determination to retire from the presidency on August 2, 1828, the day set for the convocation of the first congress of Bolivia under the constitution. Bolívar did not share his friend's opinion with regard to the presidency of Bolivia; for he urged Sucre to accept that token of the republic's gratitude to its founder. About the time of Sucre's inauguration, the Peruvians adopted the Bolivian constitution, slightly modified, as the constitution for their state upon the condition that Bolívar should be their president. But in September, 1826, Bolívar had relinquished the supreme authority in Peru and had started on the long journey for Bogotá. In the following year his beloved constitution was discarded by the Peruvians and they promulgated—with some modifications—a constitution for the republic of Peru which had been adopted in 1823, but which had been practically suspended during Bolívar's dictatorship.

The Marshal of Ayacucho often regretted that he had become the president of Bolivia. In spite of Bolívar's advice and despite the constitutional provision for a life president, Sucre steadfastly adhered to his resolution to relinquish the presidency. To judge by letters which he wrote in 1827, Sucre believed that the people of Bolivia were tranquil under his rule. But he felt that the Peruvians viewed Bolivia as "a battery of the liberator" which might some day destroy their freedom and independence. Aware that there was some dissatisfaction with his administration, he felt that the Bolivians were ungrateful to him. On June 4, 1827, he wrote to Bolívar declaring that the anarchy, the confusion, and the ingratitude which prevailed among the Spanish-Americans had convinced him that, if the leaders who had figured prominently in the wars for independence did not relinquish their positions, they would soon lose their heads,—a remarkable prophecy which almost came true in his own case. For, on April 18, 1828, at Chuquisaca, or Sucre, the discontented soldiers in the garrison tumultuously rebelled. While quelling the insurrection President Sucre was badly wounded in the arm; in a letter to Bolívar about a week later he exclaimed: "I, who came through the wars of independence without a wound, carry a mark of the ingratitude of men in a shattered arm!" The mutiny at the capital was followed by a Peruvian invasion, which was finally repelled by President Sucre. In his last message to congress on August 2, 1828, he denounced the dangerous policy of intervention which Peru had thus adopted. A few extracts from this message of Sucre to the Bolivians will serve to depict the man:—

I shall not conclude my message without asking of the nation's representatives a reward for my services, which—great or small— have given existence to Bolivia,—services which consequently deserve some requital. The constitution makes me inviolable: I cannot be held responsible for the acts of my government. I ask, then, that I should be deprived of this prerogative, and that all my conduct should be examined minutely. If, by April 18, it is shown that I have violated a single law; if the constitutional chambers judge that there is occasion for the presentation of a case to the ministry, I shall return from Colombia and submit to the judgment of the law. I ask this reward with so much more reason, for I solemnly declare that, during my administration, I have governed: the good or the evil which has been done, I have done. . . . I ask another reward from the people of Bolivia and their administrators: that they should not destroy the work of my creation; that they should preserve amid every peril the independence of Bolivia. . . .

For the rest, gentlemen, it is sufficient remuneration for my services to return to my native land after six years of absence, having gloriously served the friends of Colombia. Although as a result of foreign intrigues, I bear this arm withered—the arm which at Ayacucho terminated the war for American independence, destroyed the chains of Peru, and brought Bolivia into existence—yet I am content. In the midst of trying circumstances, I have kept my conscience free from all crime. When I crossed the Desaguadero River, I beheld a group of men: assassins and victims, slaves and tyrants, devoured by rancor and thirsting for vengeance. I have pacified men's minds; I have formed a nation that has its own laws; that is transforming its education and its colonial habits; that is recognized by its neighbors; that is free from foreign indebtedness; that has only a small and advantageous domestic debt; and, that, if directed by a prudent government, will be happy. When the general assembly invited me to take charge of Bolivia, I declared that the independence and the organization of the state would rest upon my labors. Although I have lived in the midst of parties which have been active for fifteen years, and in a desolated country, yet to secure these benefits I have not made a single Bolivian grieve: I have made no widow or orphan mourn; I have pardoned some of the wretches who were condemned by law. My government has been distinguished by clemency, tolerance, and kindness. Perhaps it will be alleged that this clemency was the cause of my own wounds. But I shall not regret them, if my successors with equal lenity shall accustom the Bolivian people to be guided by the laws, without the need of noisy bayonets perennially threatening men's lives and endangering liberty. In my retirement I shall see my scars; but I shall never regret that I carry them, when I recollect that to found Bolivia, I chose to rule by the empire of law rather than by the actions of a tyrant or an executioner, who constantly holds a sword suspended over the heads of the citizens.

In Sucre's farewell address to the Bolivians, he expressed his opinion that the constitution which had been framed by Bolívar should be amended. He said that he was "not a partisan of the Bolivian constitution"; for although it appeared to give "stability to the government," in fact it deprived the government "of the means to make itself respected." He declared that under this constitution the president had "neither the vigor nor the force necessary to support himself"; hence his rights amounted to nothing. Under such conditions he said that upheavals were bound to occur frequently. In particular was President Sucre dissatisfied with the constitutional provisions concerning the presidency. "I am persuaded," he said, "that one feature of this constitution, a weak executive, will encourage disturbances, for an executive who is so weakly supported cannot act as a curb." Thus, according to the judgment of Bolívar's dearest friend, this cherished constitution was defective.

In Sucre's letters to Bolívar he at times suggested that the liberator's political designs were over-ambitious. As early as 1823 Sucre had writtten to Bolívar arguing that they ought to confine themselves to a Colombian policy, and that they should not adopt a policy which would view all the Spanish-

Americans as brothers, for they were not such. At a later period with regard to Bolívar's design for a federation of Colombia, Peru, and Bolivia, Sucre expressed the opinion that a federal system might remedy some of the existing evils, but that such a system would unite those states too closely. Above all, Sucre was anxious that Bolívar should preserve for himself the title of liberator, for he considered that title unique. In 1826 when General Páez proposed that Bolívar should be crowned king of Colombia, Sucre advised the liberator against the project, urging in particular that as Bolívar had no sons this Napoleonic project would ultimately involve the fatherland in destruction. He frankly stated his views to Bolívar in these words:

For, after your death, each advocate of the project would think that he had a right to the succession: each would seize a piece of territory, in order that he might rule over it despotically. I agree with your sister that either you ought to be the liberator, or you ought to be dead—as liberator you will live with glory during the coming centuries. . . . The concentration of the powers of government and the maintenance of the liberty and independence of the nation should be the object of every Colombian who labors for the welfare of his country. I think that if you constantly retain the support of popular ideas, you will retain your ascendancy; so that under all circumstances you ought to be the ark of the covenant of the Colombian people and of the people of America,—the lifeboat that rescues them from shipwreck during political tempests.

When Sucre relinquished the presidency of Bolivia, a romantic motive which had impelled him to withdraw from public life became apparent. Soon after the battle of Pichincha he had become enamored of Mariana Carcelén y Larrea, Marchioness of Solanda, an heiress of Quito. Frequent meetings were followed by mutual pledges. Forced to leave the city of Quito in order to fight for independence, induced to remain away from that city by exacting official duties, it was not strange that Sucre frequently lamented his inability to retire to private life. While president of Bolivia, he arranged to be married by proxy to the marchioness: that ceremony took place at Quito just a few days after Sucre had been wounded at Chuquisaca. Some time after relinquishing the presidency of Bolivia, Sucre appeared in the city of Quito.

There for a short period he lived the quiet life of a private citizen. He superintended his wife's estates, directed the cultivation of the fields, and lamented the decadence of Colombia. At times Marshal Sucre was ill, and depressed in spirit. On October 9, 1829, he wrote to Bolívar from Quito: "I am not ashamed to say that there are days when I do not have a single *real;* but nevertheless I live by the mercy of God, and sometimes by the mercy of my wife. Such is this unhappy world."

The plan of this book precludes an attempt to describe in detail the public career of Bolívar from 1825 to 1829. Here only such events will be considered as are intimately concerned with Spanish-American independence. From this viewpoint the most significant problem which confronted Bolívar during those troublous years was the identical problem which had perplexed San Martín, namely, the establishment of monarchies in Spanish America. The available evidence upon that subject, emanating directly or indirectly from Bolívar, is conflicting and difficult to evaluate. In part it consists of reports sent to England by her agents in South America. From these only one pertinent example will be taken. Three months after the victory of Ayacucho, Bolívar had a conference at Lima with Captain Malling of the English frigate *Cambridge*. According to that captain's report to his government, Bolívar expressed the idea that if the English cabinet ever proposed to promote the establishment of a monarchy in Spanish America, such a proposal would meet with his approval, for he would steadily support the prince whom England might wish to place upon the South-American throne. Further, Bolívar seems to have suggested that instead of the name king the name Inca should be used,—a title for which the Indians had a predilection. "If we are to have a new Government," Bolívar is also reported to have said, "let it be modeled on yours, and I am ready to give my support to any sovereign England may give us." Similar reports respecting Bolívar's designs were made at a later date by other English agents. Possibly the dispatch of Captain Malling did not rightly represent the views of the liberator. Even if the reports of English agents correctly described the conversation of the volatile Colombian, it seems likely that Bolívar, the diplomat, was merely toying with them.

For when General Páez proposed to Bolívar, who was acting as dictator of Peru, that he should return to Colombia to assume the rôle which Napoleon had played in France after his Egyptian campaign, the liberator replied in March, 1826, that Colombia was not France, nor was he Napoleon; and that he did not desire to imitate such unworthy personages as Cæsar or Iturbide. But the idea of a vast monarchy in northern South America seemed destined to bloom perennially. For, when Vice President Santander responded to Bolívar's letters regarding the adoption of the Bolivian constitution in Colombia, on July 6, 1826, he expressed the belief that "an empire stretching from Potosí to the Orinoco River would be very strong and influential," but that it would be "a perpetual cause of war between monarchists and democrats." Santander also declared that, after having striven for sixteen years for "the establishment of a legal régime under republican forms," he could not betray his principles and accept a foreign prince. He asserted that he would gladly obey Bolívar as emperor; but he raised an insuperable obstacle to this project when he stated that after the death of Bolívar, he would never accept Páez, or any other Colombian leader, as "supreme and crowned chief for life." These excerpts will suggest how persistent was the idea that an unmasked monarchy might be established in northern South America.

The views of Bolívar—the president of Colombia—were again suggested when, in 1828, a periodical of Cuenca proposed that a monarchy should be founded in northern South America with its capital at Lima. At that time Bolívar openly disclaimed any connection with the scheme. A little later President Bolívar argued strongly against such a project upon an occasion when his secretaries favored the establishment of a monarchy in Colombia under a European prince in order to provide a successor to his power. A luminous statement of Bolívar's views was made on July 14, 1829, in a letter to Estanislao Vergara, the Colombian secretary of foreign affairs.

Although the project to invite a foreign prince to succeed me in the command might produce some good results, yet I see a thousand obstacles which it would encounter. No foreign prince would accept as his patrimony an anarchical principality without any guarantees. Colombia's debts and the poverty of the people do not ensure the revenues which are necessary for the support of a prince and a court,—even in a miserable fashion. The lower classes would become alarmed, fearing the effects of aristocracy and inequality. The generals of the revolution and ambitious personages of every stamp could never tolerate a government which would deprive them of the supreme power. I have not spoken of the obstacles in Europe: to suppose that there were none would be to imagine a rare combination of favoring circumstances.

As Bolívar grew older he seems to have become more and more pessimistic regarding democratic government in Spanish America. Obviously, he expressed different views at different times concerning the establishment of a monarchy, or of monarchies, in South America. It is hardly too much to suggest that he was all things to all men. The puzzling question as to what Bolívar actually believed regarding governmental systems during his last years is essentially psychological. Who can say with certainty what political ideals were cherished in the recesses of the liberator-president's mind? Still, it is an indisputable fact, that the fullest, the most mature, and the most authentic expression of Bolívar's political creed, remains the constitution which he framed for the republic of Bolivia,— a constitution which apparently made provision for a masked constitutional monarchy.

From 1826 to 1830 Great Colombia was disturbed by factions whose quarrels presaged the disruption of the state. Generals La Mar and Córdova led unsuccessful revolts against Bolívar's domination. General Páez became the leader of a faction which favored the secession of Venezuela. In Bogotá Vice President Santander, "the champion of the constitution," directed a party which opposed the dictatorial policy of Bolívar. In an attempt to allay that partisan strife the Colombian congress summoned delegates to meet at Ocaña early in 1828 to reform the constitution of 1821. At the convention of Ocaña Bolívar's supporters could make no compromise with the followers of Santander; some delegates even walked out of the convention, which soon dissolved. Subsequently, certain Colombian leaders at Bogotá proclaimed that Bolívar was dictator. Whereupon daring conspirators planned to enter the palace of the dictator, who now styled himself liberator-president, in order to secure his person, living or dead. An attempt to seize him which was made on the night of September 25, 1828, was unsuccessful; for, while his favorite mistress, Mrs. Thorne, or, as she is commonly known, Manuela Saenz, parleyed with the conspirators, the hero of many battles jumped out of a window, and thus escaped the assassin's dagger. Bolívar was now thoroughly disgusted with his compatriots; in a letter to Sucre on October 28, 1828, he said: "You are the only man of integrity in this heroic and unfortunate country." And in a rare pamphlet attributed to Bolívar, which was published in the city of Quito in 1829, this statement was made: "There is no faith in America; neither among men, nor among nations: their treaties are paper; their constitutions are books, their elections are combats: liberty is anarchy; and life is a torment."

Thus, in the sere and yellow leaf, Bolívar bewailed the anarchy of "Great Colombia." In the south, the Peruvians under Riva Agüero invaded Colombian territory. They were only repelled after Marshal Sucre was placed at the head of an army, which in February, 1829, defeated them at the battle of Tarqui. The secession movement in Venezuela finally became so strong that on November 26, 1829, an assembly of prominent citizens in Caracas decided upon the separation of Venezuela from Colombia. General Páez was naturally selected as the Venezuelan executive. In January, 1830, the constituent congress of Colombia, which Bolívar had convoked, made a last effort to save the republic from dissolution. It appointed a commission to treat for peace and union with the secessionists of Venezuela. General Sucre, who had been serving as the president of this congress, was selected as one of the commissioners. But even Sucre's efforts at reconciliation were futile. Thereupon Bolívar renounced, for the last time, the office of chief magistrate. In his last message to the Colombian congress, he declared despairingly, "Independence is the only blessing which we have acquired at the expense of everything else." The renunciation of his power by the liberator-president sealed the doom of Great Colombia. In an inedited letter of Sucre to Colonel Andrade, May 10, 1830, the former declared that Bolívar had said that Colombia was about to be dissevered; that in whatever section he might live, the inhabitants would ask him to become their *caudillo;* and that neither his position nor his dignity would permit him to become the chief of a faction.

After the conferences with the Venezuelan commissioners had failed, Sucre wrote a farewell letter to Bolívar, and then started on the long and tiresome trip overland to Quito. This was the last journey of the Marshal of Ayacucho. On June 4, 1830, while riding through the lonely forest of Berruecos, not far from the town of Pasto, he was shot in a cowardly manner by hired assassins. The odium for Sucre's mysterious assassination fell largely upon General Ovando, the military commander in the department of Cauca, who may have instigated the murder. The melancholy news of the untimely death of Sucre shocked his friends. When his widow wrote to Bolívar, informing him that the sword presented to Sucre by the Colombian congress to celebrate the battle of Ayacucho had been bequeathed to the liberator, she said: "You lost a loyal friend who knew your merits. I lost a companion. The sad memories of this event will embitter the remaining days of my life." The news of the assassination must have confirmed Bolívar's belief that "those who had served the cause of the revolution had plowed the sea." On July 1 he wrote to his compatriot, General Juan Flores: "This news has produced so deep an impression upon me that I judge it impossible to live in a country where they cruelly and barbarously assassinate the most illustrious generals whose labors have ensured the liberty of America. . . . The immaculate Sucre has not been able to escape the ambuscades of these monsters. . . . I believe that the object of this crime was to deprive the country of a successor to me."

The ingratitude of Colombia seemed to Bolívar sharper than a serpent's tooth. His plan to sail from South America to Europe was frustrated, for he could not sell the mines of Aroa because of the litigious opposition of his political enemies in Venezuela. In his extremity he again thought of an asylum in the West Indies. On May 11 in a letter to an intimate friend Bolívar expressed his intention to leave Colombia in any event: "I have decided nevermore to return to Colombia,—nevermore to serve my ungrateful compatriots." The former dictator resisted the supplications of friends who wished him to assume the supreme power again. He avowed that he had never looked with favor upon insurrections, declaring that he now regretted the revolutions which he had led against Spanish rule. Sick and steadily declining in health, he said that rather than take medicine, he preferred to die. Early in December, accompanied by a few of his military comrades, "the liberator of Colombia, Peru, and Bolivia," was carried on a litter into the town of Santa Marta. On December 17, 1830, he died near that place of pulmonary tuberculosis. A proclamation which he had signed on December 10 was his political testament:—

Colombians! You have witnessed my attempts to establish liberty where tyranny had reigned. I have labored disinterestedly, relinquishing my fortune, and even my peace of mind. I gave up the supreme command when I became convinced that you doubted my disinterestedness. My enemies abused your credulity and trampled upon my most sacred possession,—my reputation and my love for liberty. Although I am the victim of my persecutors, who have driven me to the gates of the tomb, yet I forgive them. About to leave this world, my affection tells me that I ought to make known to you my last wishes: I do not aspire to any other glory than to consolidate Colombia. All of you should labor for the inestimable boon of union. The people should obey the existing government in order to free themselves from anarchy. The priests of the Church should direct the progress of the people toward heaven. And the soldiers should employ their swords to defend the social guarantees. Colombians! My last wishes are for the happiness of my native land. If my death helps to check the growth of factions and to consolidate the union, I shall rest tranquilly in the sepulcher!

On January 12, 1830, the dying man had signed his last will. Bolívar provided that the medal which had been granted to him by the Bolivian congress should be returned to that body as a testimonial of the sincere affection which he entertained for Bolívia. To the University of Caracas he bequeathed two books which had belonged to Napoleon: Rousseau's "Social Contract," and Montecuccoli's "Art of War." The sword which Sucre had bequeathed to Bolívar was to be returned to the marshal's widow; in order that she might preserve it as a token of the love which the liberator had cherished for the hero of Ayacucho. Bolívar expressed a wish that his remains should be buried in his native city. He provided that, after the payment of a legacy to a faithful servant, the remnant of his wealth, his debts, and his rights were to be the heritage of his two sisters and of the children of his deceased brother. Bolívar ordered that his voluminous papers, which were stored in ten boxes, should be burned. Fortunately for the student of the South-American wars for independence, this order was not observed. These documents, which were later placed at the disposal of Bolívar's former secretary, form a large part of the collection known as the *Memorias del general O'Leary* that constitutes a valuable record of the career of the liberator-president, who exercised so profound an influence upon the fortunes of northern South America during the heroic age.

Bolívar's hopes regarding the political existence of the state which had been created by his genius were vain. Even before the hero of Colombia expired at Santa Marta, Great Colombia had split into three parts. In September, 1830, a convention of delegates from the former captaincy general of Venezuela which had assembled at Valencia adopted a constitution for the republic of Venezuela. In the same month a constitutional convention composed of delegates from the provinces of the former presidency of Quito which had assembled at Riobamba adopted a republican constitution for the state of Ecuador. In November, 1831 a convention which had assembled at Bogotá, announced that the provinces which had composed the central part of Colombia formed the state of New Granada—at a later time again designated as Colombia—and a short time afterwards a republican constitution was adopted which had been framed by the constituent congress in May, 1830.

The sanity of Bolívar's judgment was well illustrated by the selection of Antonio José de Sucre to be the commander of the army of liberation upon the Pacific coast. Many of the letters which passed between Bolívar and Sucre contained evidence of their mutual affection. Sucre frequently gave expression to the tender love and genuine admiration which he cherished for the liberator. "If I could be sure of your friendship," wrote Sucre to Bolívar in 1825, "I would be satisfied in a corner of Quito." In truth, it would be difficult to find in the chronicles of history two other leaders who, in an atmosphere of jealousy and suspicion, preserved their friendship more hallowed, or maintained their loyalty to a common cause more unsullied, than these two Venezuelans.

Antonío José de Sucre was not without faults. His greatest fault was perhaps his pride and sensitiveness which occasionally made him interpret actions as slights to himself. By a somewhat unusual combination of qualities, Sucre was not only proud, but also modest. At times he ascribed all the credit for his military successes to his master. It would indeed seem that Sucre possessed the spirit of self-abnegation to almost as great a degree as San Martín. Marshal Sucre was an honest man; for although he served South America for many years in a public capacity, and doubtless had opportunities to line his own purse, yet at his death he owned very little property. He even declined to accept the monies which were granted him by Peru and Bolivia as a reward for his services as liberator, while his salary as a soldier of Columbia was partly used to relieve the needs of his relatives at Cumaná. Other incidents in Sucre's career demonstrate his deep attachment for the numerous family of his father. Nor did the valiant general forget his birth-place: after the battle of Pichincha, Sucre sent to the city of Cumaná a wreath of gold which had been presented to him by the city of Cochabamba. Obscured for a time by the over-shadowing figure of the liberator-president, with every passing year the hero of Ayacucho rises higher in the esteem of Venezuelans who now reverence him as one of their revolutionary trinity,—Miranda, Bolívar, and Sucre. And, in the vast mediterranean state of South America, the memory of Sucre is revered as that of the true founder of Bolivia.

A remarkable diary which was apparently written in 1828 by Peru de la Croix, a companion in arms of Bolívar, preserves some illuminating remarks made by the liberator while sojourning at Bucaramanga. If the words which La Croix attributed to Bolívar concerning the Bayard of South America do not preserve the liberator's precise sentiments, at least they contain a suggestive contemporary opinion of Bolívar's favorite general:—

Sucre is always a gentleman; he has the best intellect in Colombia; he is methodical; he is capable of the most lofty conceptions; he is the best general of the republic, and her first statesman. His ideas are excellent and definite; his morality is exemplary; his soul is grand and strong. He knows how to persuade and how to lead men. He knows also how to judge them: and, if in political affairs, it is not a defect to consider men as worse than they really are, General Sucre is able to demonstrate in an extreme fashion the unfavorable judgments which he has formed of them. Another defect of General Sucre is that he wishes to make it appear that he is extremely ingenuous and popular, while he is not able to conceal that in reality he is not so. But these are only slight defects, which are found among so many merits and virtues that a very observant eye is needed to detect them. To all this it may be added that the Grand Marshal of Ayacucho is brave among the brave, loyal among the loyal, a lover of laws and not of despotism, a partisan of order, an enemy of anarchy, and finally, a true liberal.

Of particular interest are the statements which La Croix attributes to Bolívar in regard to politics and revolution. The diary of Bucaramanga records the words of the liberator to the effect that only a despot could rightly govern Colombia. With respect to himself, Bolívar affirmed that he had not acted as a despot, for the Colombian people had chosen him to serve as their dictator. He even appears to have ironically asserted that a theocratic form of government would be best adapted to the people of Spanish America. In 1828, Bolívar evidently felt that there were some defects in the constitution which he had framed for Bolivia. The honied words of praise which fell from the liberator's lips at Bucaramanga indicate that in his heart of hearts Bolívar admired and emulated the great Frenchman as administrator, statesman, and soldier. The truth of the matter seems to be that Napoleon was Bolívar's inimitable model.

According to Peru de la Croix, the liberator sententiously said that the art of politics was rightly to judge men and affairs. If indeed Bolívar made that remark, he certainly practiced what he preached. Almost unerring in his judgment of men, he intuitively recognized the strength as well as the weakness of his political and military associates. Perhaps as a necessary consequence, Bolívar was able to secure good service from available men. This service he secured partly because he carefully selected the man best fitted for the particular position, partly because he wisely instructed his agents, and partly because he made each agent feel the cardinal importance of his assigned task. Then, too, until near the end of his remarkable career Bolívar had a sublime faith in his mission as liberator—a faith that could move mountains. Still, he did not over-estimate his own achievements; nor did he, like some great men, consider himself as being charged with a divine mission, which no one else could have performed. It is indeed not given to all statesmen or warriors to judge of the part which they have played in history so justly as Bolívar, the warrior-statesman, seems to have judged of his rôle. La Croix records a remarkable conversation between Bolívar and himself in which the liberator stated his views concerning the rôle which he had played in the struggle for the independence of the Spanish-American republics. " 'I have not been the sole author of the revolution,' " said Bolívar. " 'If I had not been present during the crisis of the revolution and during the protracted struggle between the Spanish troops and the patriots, some other champion of independence would have appeared: the penumbra of my fortune would not have overshadowed other patriots, who have been kept in an orbit inferior to my own. Superstitious people may believe, if they wish, that a kind Providence destined me for the redemption of Colombia: —the truth is that circumstances, my genius, my character, and my passions, placed me on the road which led to independence; my ambition, my constancy, and my lively imagination caused me to follow that road. . . .' "

Thus did Bolívar answer the question of the Sphinx which guards the highway of history as to the influence of a masterful personality upon the movements of his age. As extracts from his letters and speeches have indicated, Bolívar has some claim to consideration as a literary man. The large collection of letters which he left behind attests his far-reaching interests, as well as his unresting energy, when in his prime. With his own hand Bolívar wrote letters only to relatives or intimate friends. To the letters which were ordinarily taken from dictation by his secretary, he occasionally added a few words of greeting in his own handwriting. Official letters and memorials were read to the liberator by his secretary or by a clerk. The replies were often dictated while Bolívar was swinging in a hammock or pacing a room with a book in his hand. In a passage of his invaluable memoirs, O'Leary thus describes the mode in which the liberator conducted his correspondence.

He dictated the official dispatches and letters to as many as three amanuenses at once. No matter how humble the station of the writer, never did he lay aside a letter without making a reply. Although he was sometimes interrupted while engaged in dictation, never did I hear him make a mistake, never did I see him at a loss to pick up the phrase. When he was not acquainted with the correspondent or the petitioner, he would ask one or two questions. This occurred very rarely, however, for, as Bolívar was endowed with a marvelous memory, he remembered not only all the officers of the army but also the officials of the government and the notable personages of the country.

The picturesque and imaginative style of Bolívar, ordinarily limpid and lucid, but at times obscure, has led Gil Fortoul to say that the liberator thought in French and expressed himself in Spanish.

Simón de Bolívar has been characterized as the Napoleon of the South-American revolution. Endowed with unusual power to discipline, to organize, and to inspirit his compatriots, he led his devoted soldiers from Caracas to Lima,—soldiers whose valor and constancy were largely responsible for the victories of Junín and Ayacucho. Bolívar's mission was to free from the heavy yoke of Spain the inhabitants of two viceroyalties and to lay the foundations of several independent states. His biographer, De Schryver, has said that "besides establishing the independence of five nations, the achievement of Bolívar consisted in the fact that he thrust half a million of slaves into struggles for republican government and democracy." Bolívar's chief defects as a publicist may be thus briefly enumerated: a fondness for personal and autocratic rule; a pretorian spirit; and a tendency toward imperialism. These were the defects of his good qualities. From the military as well as the political point of view, Bolívar towered above most of his contemporaries in South America; for with the exception of San Martín, their gaze seldom left their own native provinces, while Bolívar's comprehensive vision embraced all the rising Spanish-American republics. This distinguished son of Caracas looked beyond the boundaries of Venezuela and beheld a liberated and a confederated Spanish America. After the lapse of many generations in which Bolívar's alluring dream of a confederation of the Spanish-American states has remained unfulfilled, it is easy to say that his ideal of a confederated state in northern South America was impracticable. For his ideal ignored these facts: that even the peoples of New Granada, Quito, and Venezuela were separated by vast wildernesses and lofty mountain ranges; that they did not possess a real national spirit; and that, on the contrary, they were obsessed with a fierce spirit of particularism. Nevertheless, it was this idealism which swept Bolívar beyond the ken of his contemporaries, that helped to make him—in words attributed to San Martín while in exile—"the most extraordinary personage that South America has produced." What wonder that his personality has been obscured by legends, while his fame has been sung by poets, and his figure depicted by painters and sculptors! A few stanzas from a poem inscribed to "the father of Colombia and liberator of Peru" by a Colombian contemporary, José Fernández Madrid, as done into English by A. C. Luthman, will furnish the reader with a noteworthy appreciation of Bolívar by a citizen of northern South America.

Once lit the fire of patriot feeling ran
From heart to heart, and brighter, stronger grew;
Each doff'd the slave—proclaim'd himself a man—
And to the camp of brave Bolívar flew.
Full well they knew their long and dark career
Through fields of blood, and fire, and peril lay,
They heeded not—the voice in their ear,
That promised deathless palms and victory!

* * * * * * *

Thy high heroic deeds shall bear thy name,
Renown'd Bolívar through the shades of time;
And men who live for virtue, freedom, fame,
Must copy thee—no model more sublime.
Ye mighty rivers that through ocean flow,
To distant lands his patriot story bear;
Ye Andes glittering in eternal snow,
Show ye the footprints of his glory here!
The unfading laurel for his brow prepare
Who push'd the bark of freedom from the shore,
And steered her through the ocean of despair,
Nor left the helm until the storm was o'er.

Chapter 9

Conclusion

THERE IS NO DOUBT that the leaders whose revolutionary careers have been sketched were exceptional men. By ancestry, by training, and by ability they were much superior to the average creole. By the same tokens they were immeasurably superior to the members of the lower classes in Spanish America. Possibly it is significant that the ancestry of several of the leaders can be traced to natives of northern Spain. It is noteworthy that all of those leaders came from the middle or upper strata of society in their respective colonies: they were often members of an intellectual or property-holding aristocracy. Several of the 'liberators' had enjoyed the advantages of study and travel in Europe. From Miranda to Sucre, with the possible exception of Iturbide, they had been better educated than the ordinary creole of their generation. A strange fate decreed that several of these men should meet a tragic death. Miranda expired in a lonely dungeon near Cadiz; Hidalgo was shot as a traitor by the Spaniards; Iturbide was shot as an outlaw by the Mexicans whom he had liberated; Moreno perished while crossing the Atlantic; San Martín died a voluntary exile in France; Sucre was treacherously assassinated; and Bolívar lived long enough to regret his achievements as founder of Colombia, Peru, and Bolivia. The seven narratives have shown that the ultimate success of the revolution against Spanish rule in America was in large measure due to the example, the achievements, and the influence of the liberators and their companions. In the South-American wars for independence, Venezuelan warriors played the most notable part: besides liberating their own state, they aided effectively to liberate the territories within the present republics of Colombia, Ecuador, Peru, and Bolivia. Although when measured by the great wars of Europe, the military achievements of the liberators shrink in magnitude, yet their long-sustained struggle moulded the history of rising states.

This is a convenient point at which to summarize the causes

for the revolt against Spanish domination in America. Careful students of the history of Spanish America are not able to explain that movement, as chemists explain a reaction, by a formula. At present little more can be done than to mention some of the obvious causes of the revolution. It is clear that among the conditions which made the revolution in Spanish America possible was a conviction entertained by some colonists that the burdens of the colonial régime were unendurable: —the oppressive fiscal system of Spain was particularly detested. Then, too, the Spanish officials often displayed a shocking disregard for the humane provisions of the antiquated laws of the Indies,—a behavior on the part of colonial officials which encouraged among the people a spirit of contempt for the motherland's authority. In certain sections of the Indies the belief that the Spanish laws lacked sanction was promoted by Spain's attempts to reform her colonial administration. As in the case of the English colonies in North America, the revolution in Spanish America was partly due to the lack of a well-managed colonial system. The secret spread of philosophic, revolutionary doctrines emanating from France constituted an intellectual cause of the Spanish-American revolution, as did also a desire among certain leaders to emulate the revolutionists who separated the English colonies in North America from the motherland. As a moral cause of the revolution may be characterized the fact that, because of his traditions, training, and environment, the creole of Spanish America was a different type of man than the Spaniard overseas. The historian of the future may indeed seek a partial explanation of this uprising in the psychology of a "race." But, although because of certain economic, religious, and political conditions a spirit of discontent was present in various sections of Spanish America, yet this was not enough to provoke a general rebellion. It was the usurpation of Napoleon in the Iberian peninsula that precipitated the movements which developed into the protracted revolution. The inflammable tinder that lay scattered throughout the vast dominions of Spain in America was lighted by Napoleon's hand.

Let us contrast the revolution which culminated in the separation from Spain of her continental American colonies with the revolution that separated the English colonies in North America from their motherland. The Spanish-American revolution affected a more extensive territory than the revolution in the thirteen colonies. The territory which became free as a result of the wars between Spain and her colonies was about seven times as large as the territory conceded to the United States by the treaty of 1783. From this it is obvious that in the struggle with her revolted colonists Spain had, in some respects, a more difficult task than England. Spain's far-flung battle line extended from the Sabine River to the Río de la Plata: in more accurate terms, Spain had in America a number of detached battle lines which fronted the alert enemy. Again, because of the nature and extent of the arena of combat, the Spanish-Americans could not coöperate as did the North Americans. Between Mexico and South America, to take an extreme illustration, there was absolutely no coöperation and scarcely any sympathy. Although revolts broke out contemporaneously in several sections of South America, yet these uprisings were sometimes sporadic or local. It seems like a truism to say that no military commander in South America ever held a position like that conferred by the continental congress upon George Washington. In truth the strongest links between the widely-separated sections of South America were the activities of the revolutionary soldiers led by the liberators San Martín, Bolívar, and Sucre. Unlike the North-American revolutionists, the South Americans received no aid, material or moral, through an alliance with a foreign state. For them there was no such agreement as the treaty with France of February, 1778, which, like a sunburst after a troubled dawn, gladdened the hearts of Washington's followers. The South Americans had no wise old Franklin, no Beaumarchais! They received little encouragement from foreign lands beyond surreptitious loans of money from sympathizers in England and the aid of filibusters from England and the United States.

The South-American revolution differed from the North-American in another particular: namely, it was neither accompanied nor followed by the establishment of a general government. During the early revolution the local juntas indeed played a part comparable with the rôle of committees of correspondence in the English colonies; but no union of the revolutionary colonies in Spanish America was formed. Certain leaders at Buenos Aires, Caracas, and Santiago de Chile indeed suggested that the people in Spanish South America should join hands against the peninsular Spaniards. But, with the exception of the congress of Panama, no assemblage of representatives of different regions was held. The reasons for the failure of the Spanish-American revolutionists to form a union are not far to seek: they are found partly in the sparsity of the population, and partly in the absence of preëxisting institutions of self-government. It was largely because the colonists lived in isolated groups that, in the sections which later became independent nations, they successively framed separate and distinct declarations of independence.

There were indeed some features in which the Spanish-American revolution was analogous to the Anglo-American revolution. Perhaps the most striking analogy was the fact that a considerable number of the Spanish colonists—the Tories of the Indies—opposed the revolution. It must never be forgotten that there were many devoted loyalists who followed the Spanish standard on many widely-separated battlefields. In certain sections of the Indies the revolution which separated those regions from the motherland was, in some stages at least, the work of a capable, vigorous, and determined minority. Probably it is not an exaggeration to say that the spirit of loyalty to the motherland was stronger and more enduring in the Spanish colonies in America than in the thirteen English colonies in North America. Spain's banner of blood and gold waved so long in South America largely because so many colonists were at heart loyal to Ferdinand VII. and to their motherland. The extreme statement has recently been hazarded by a Colombian writer that, if La Serna had triumphed upon the plain of Ayacucho, the absolute king would have reëstablished his authority throughout Spanish America. As in the case of the revolt against George III., there was some sympathy for the revolutionary colonists in the mother country. This sentiment was particularly significant during the years from 1820 to 1823 when Spain was a constitutional monarchy. The liberal government actually commissioned envoys who were instructed to negotiate with the insurgent provinces from Mexico to Patagonia with a view to the pacification of America. But, after Ferdinand VII. was restored to absolute power, the proceedings of those envoys were formally repudiated. That monarch announced that a preliminary convention of peace which the commissioners of the constitutional government had signed on July 4, 1823, with the revolutionary government at Buenos Aires, was void.

No treaty of peace recognizing the triumph of the revolutionists—like the treaty of 1783 between England and the United States—terminated the Spanish-American wars for independence. Neither were they terminated by contemporaneous conventions which acknowledged the independence of all the Spanish-American nations. The government of Spain disavowed the treaty of Córdoba and ignored the treaty of Ayacucho:—the pride of the Spaniard dreaded the independence of the alienated colonists. Long after the Spanish-American republics had indisputably established their independence, the Spaniards tenaciously cherished their dream of a colonial empire.

This leads to another suggestion concerning the circumstances which affected the outcome of the revolution: namely, that to some extent the achievements of the partisans of independence in America were made possible by the governmental fluctuations in Spain,—fluctuations which rendered a firm and consistent policy toward the revolutionists well-nigh impossible. At war with Napoleon, successively governed by a junta, by the regency and a *cortes,* by an absolute king, by a constitutional ministry and a *cortes,* and again by her misguided and illiberal monarch, Spain was heavily handicapped in her long struggle to win back the disaffected colonists to their allegiance. Those fluctuations coupled with the fact that the Holy Alliance cautiously refrained from any attempt to restore Spain's authority over her revolted colonies, help to explain why the Spanish navy played such an unimportant part in the revolution. In truth, at the battle of Trafalgar Spain's naval power had been shattered, and it seems likely that after 1823 any attempt by the Holy Alliance to furnish soldiers for the subjugation of the American revolutionists would have provoked the intervention of the English navy. The only occasions when a fleet played a very important rôle were in transporting Morillo's expedition to Venezuela, and in conveying San Martín's soldiers to Peru. In the main, the struggle was fought upon the land.

But the great revolution, or, as some Spanish-American writers prefer to designate it, the movement for emancipation, which disrupted the largest colonial empire that the world had ever known and reconstructed the map of the Three Americas, was not followed by the establishment of stable governments. Under the influence of lofty and mistaken ideals, the Spanish-Americans adopted democratic forms of government which were unsuited to their training and temperament. These ideals were at times mirrored in the governmental projects of the liberators. Moreno, the republican, wished to establish democracies in South America. San Martín discarded the thought of establishing republics upon that continent and dreamed of founding monarchies there. The liberator Iturbide audaciously crowned himself emperor of Mexico only to be overthrown largely because of republican intrigues. And Bolívar, under the forms of a republic, moved toward a thinly-veiled monarchy upon the Napoleonic model. It was only natural that statesmen who had been nurtured under a paternalistic monarchy and who keenly felt that their compatriots were not fitted for republican government, should have imagined that the establishment of a monarchical régime would solve some political problems. To North-American readers, who are acquainted with the proposals of Colonel Nicola to crown General Washington king, the projects of Bolívar and his contemporaries will not seem altogether fanciful. Animated by a somewhat different spirit than that of George Washington, Simón de Bolívar coquetted with the monarchists but refrained from placing the tiara upon his own head.

The protracted struggle for the emancipation of Spanish America furnished a stern school for her citizens. Many Spanish-American publicists of the national era received their preliminary training in those wars which resulted in the political, as well as the military, triumph of the creole aristocracy. After the downfall of Iturbide, Guadeloupe Victoria, Vicente Guerrero, and Antonio Santa Anna successively became presidents of Mexico. Early in 1823, when O'Higgins abdicated his office as dictator of Chile, he was succeeded by General Ramón Freire, another soldier of the revolution, who, became the supreme director of that state. In 1826 Bernardino Rivadavia became the first president of the Argentine republic. Shortly after Bolívar's death General Santander became the political chieftain, as well as the president, of the republic of New Granada. So great an influence did General Páez exert in Venezuelan politics that the period from 1831 to 1863 has been designated as the age of Páez. In Ecuador General Flores vainly strove to keep the reins of government from Vicente Rocafuerte, who had played an obscure rôle in the Mexican revolution. General La Mar became the president of Peru in

1827. A few years after Bolívar's death, as chief executive of Bolivia, General Santa Cruz tried to unite Peru and Bolivia into a confederation. In 1831 Francia, the mysterious dictator, still dominated the destinies of Paraguay.

The secession of the American colonies from Spain entailed much economic and social re-adjustment. That movement was often accompanied by a guerrilla warfare. Sometimes the war was a fratricidal contest. Occasionally it resembled a struggle between bands of banditti. This struggle devastated vast areas, incited factions, and encouraged the formation of revolutionary habits. During the war for independence thousands of lives were sacrificed; wherever the revolutionists were victorious, some of the loyalists emigrated to other countries. Thus in one way or another the sparse population of Spanish America was considerably reduced. In many sections of the Indies agriculture and cattle-raising were interrupted, commerce was destroyed, and public administration was more or less demoralized. The Spanish mercantile system was steadily undermined, for much colonial commerce fell into the eager hands of foreign merchants. In general, wherever an independent state was founded, its ports were opened to the commerce of the world, commercial relations with neutral states were formed, and coastwise trade with other revolted colonies was allowed. With the progress of the revolution, the ancient bars to emigration were taken down; foreigners—who had hitherto been excluded—soon formed another class in the population of Spanish America and furnished another element for that vast melting-pot of peoples. A new phase in the industrial development of Spanish America is suggested by the fact that, from 1811 to 1830, consuls of the United States were sent to towns and cities in Mexico, Central America, Great Colombia, Peru, Chile, Uruguay, and Argentina.

After the disruption of Great Colombia in 1831, there existed in Spanish America eleven independent states. On the north of these new nations, the boundary line between Mexico and the United States was the line which had been drawn by the treaty of 1819 between the United States and Spain,—a line that had not been surveyed, and which was unsatisfactory to some citizens of the United States. The subsequent history of the Spanish-American states demonstrated that their boundaries in 1831 were more or less uncertain, largely because the *uti posseditus* of 1810 upon which by tacit consent those boundaries depended, was based upon Spanish laws and orders which, dealing as they sometimes did with extensive areas that were unexplored, were often vague or conflicting in regard to the metes and bounds of the colonial divisions. The heirs of presidencies, as Bolivia and Ecuador, were most unfortunate: here an illustration will be taken from Ecuadorian history; in 1802 a royal decree had been issued commanding that an extensive region in the interior of the presidency of Quito should be transferred to the jurisdiction of Peruvian authorities:—after the dissolution of Great Colombia that decree furnished the basis for a controversy between Ecuador and Peru which remains unsettled to the present day.

Although some colonial evils, as negro slavery, had been swept away by revolutionary reformers, yet many Spanish manners and customs prevailed, especially in the towns and cities. The mode of procedure which was followed in the administration of justice was essentially Spanish. The transactions of merchants were often regulated by the ordinances of Bilbao. The legal codes of Spain still remained influential, for the new states sometimes enacted statutes providing that the Spanish laws which harmonized with their laws were still to be considered in force. Throughout the Spanish-American republics the capital cities—in whose streets and plazas many stirring scenes had been enacted during the revolution—continued to play a most important rôle in politics. In some capitals the governmental offices were located in the "palace of government" which had sheltered the colonial officials during the old régime. That régime left its impress upon the governmental systems of the new nations, which sometimes borrowed Spanish names and functionaries. The early Spanish-American constitutions often presented a curious mingling of ancient ideals, colonial customs, and French revolutionary philosophy. In form they were ordinarily republican, more or less in imitation of the Constitution of the United States. According to these constitutions, the provinces which had existed in colonial days were sometimes dignified with the names or invested with the attributes of states. Thus artificially created, the states did not function as organic parts of the systems to which they belonged. In truth, many conditions still favored the establishment of strongly centralized governments,—governments where the chief executive bearing the name of president had some monarchical attributes. Accordingly political parties were sometimes composed of persons who were in favor of quasi-monarchical, or centralized, governments; on the other hand, there were parties composed of such persons as wished to entrust a large share of governmental power to the officials of important administrative subdivisions. Sometimes a political party was composed mainly of the adherents of a prominent political leader. Some publicists of the South-American republics harbored fears of monarchical aggressions, for along the borders of their states stretched the colossal empire of Brazil, which seemed to menace their political ideals as well as their territorial integrity.

The founding of republics in Spanish America necessarily involved the formation of new international relations. From the very beginning of the secessionist movement some insurrectionary provinces in South America attempted to enter into closer relations with neighboring provinces. In the course of time, if not at once, certain nascent states adopted the policy of treating their neighbors as political entities which were vested with sovereign rights. Some Spanish-American states which had declared their independence of Spain, sent diplomatic missions to the capitals of other states, while several of the rising states recognized the independence of their neighbors. For example, in August, 1823, the United Provinces of Central America appointed a diplomatic agent to Mexico, while in the same month the Mexican congress recognized the independence of Central America. The most notable event in the relations of the Hispanic-American states during the third decade of the nineteenth century was the attempt of Simón de Bolívar to realize his dream of a congress composed of representatives of these states.

On December 7, 1824, Bolívar issued from Lima an invitation to the governments of la Plata, Brazil, Chile, Guatemala, Colombia, and Mexico, to send delegates to a congress on the Isthmus of Panama. He proposed that the congress should serve those nations as a council in great danger, as a faithful interpreter of treaties, and as an umpire and conciliator when disputes arose. Appealing to the spirit of the Spanish-American peoples, Bolívar declared that a common basis should be found for the protection of their independent governments. Anxious to find a *point d'appui* for common action against Spain, he declared that the congress should establish a supreme authority to direct the policies of the Spanish-American states. The replies to Bolívar's invitation differed. La Plata disliked the plan, while Chile, Colombia, and Mexico praised the proposal for a league directed against their common enemy, Spain, or against European intervention in America. The instructions of Bolívar to the Peruvian envoys to this congress dated May 15, 1825, suggested that the Spanish-American states should make a concerted attack upon the coasts of Spain. He urged that these states should solemnly agree not to cease the war until Spain should formally recognize their independence. He proposed that certain principles of American international law should be formulated, and that a declaration against European intervention in America should be promulgated similar to the announcement contained in President Monroe's message to congress of December 2, 1823. In connection with his project for an international congress, Bolívar even dreamed of a league of American nations which should be sanctioned by Great Britain.

In the end of 1825 and early in 1826, the delegates from Colombia and Peru held some preliminary conferences on the Isthmus of Panama. The delegates of Central America arrived on the isthmus in March, 1826, and the Mexican delegates arrived in June. The formal meetings of the Panama congress, which was composed of eight delegates, were held in June and July, 1826. The concrete results of the congress were a treaty of perpetual union, league, and confederation, and two other treaties, which dealt with the contingents of ships, soldiers, and monies that the states concerned were to furnish to the projected confederation. Although these treaties were ratified only by the government of Colombia, yet the amphictyonic council was not without significance. It symbolized a unity of spirit among the Spanish-Americans. It evoked expressions of opinion from prominent states of Spanish America upon matters of common interest. It was the first of a series of international congresses which served to crystallize the ideas of American publicists concerning the relations of independent states. Negatively, the congress of Panama indicated that Bolívar's dream of a league composed of the nations of Spanish America was Utopian.

About the time when the Panama congress was being convoked, the United States and the leading nations of Spanish America were interchanging diplomatic missions. As indicated in the preceding chapters, at various stages in the revolt against Spain the Spanish-Americans sent emissaries to the United States to plead for aid and for the recognition of their independence. At first the government of the United States did not receive those envoys officially: it strove to remain neutral in the protracted struggle between Spain and her colonies. Not until 1822—the year when Iturbide was crowned emperor of Mexico—did the United States decide to recognize the independence of the *de facto* states. On March 8, 1822, President Monroe sent to congress a special message recommending that five Spanish-American states, Colombia, Chile, Peru, la Plata, and Mexico, should be recognized as independent nations. On May 4 of the same year, the president signed a law which made an appropriation for diplomatic missions to "the independent nations of the American continent." By this act the United States announced her intention to acknowledge the independence of the revolted colonies of Spain in America which stretched from the parallel of forty-two degrees, north latitude, to Cape Horn. With the exception of the Portuguese monarchy seated at Rio de Janeiro, the North-American Republic was the first member of the society of nations to extend the hand of fellowship to the new family of states. The announcement of the United States concerning her foreign policy caused great dissatisfaction to the Spanish ministry, which sent to the leading nations of Europe a manifesto protesting against the acknowledgment of Spanish-American independence. Ignorant of the excitement which the policy of recognition by the United States provoked in the chancelleries of continental Europe, the significance of that policy was not sufficiently appreciated by statesmen throughout the Spanish-American republics.

The act of May 4, 1822, was not completely carried out for several years. The first Spanish-American nation formally recognized by the United States was Columbia. On June 19, 1822, Secretary Adams presented Manuel Tórres, as *chargé d'affaires* from Colombia, to President Monroe. On December 12 following, José Manuel Zozaya, envoy extraordinary and minister plenipotentiary from Mexico, was officially presented by Adams to Monroe: that ceremony constituted the recognition of the independence of the Mexican empire by the United States. The recognition of the independence of other Spanish-American nations by the United States during the revolutionary epoch of their history was consummated by the appointment of diplomatic agents to these countries. On January 27, 1823, the senate of the United States confirmed the appointment of ministers to Colombia, la Plata, and Chile. Richard C. Anderson, the first minister of the United States to serve in a Spanish-American state, was formally received in the capital of Colombia on December 16, 1823. Later in the same month Minister Rodney was received by the government of la Plata. In April, 1824, Heman Allen was formally received at Santiago de Chile as minister of the United States. In May, 1826, James Cooley was received as *charge d'affaires* of the United States at Lima. Thus did diplomatic action by the Great Republic of the North crown the victories which had been won by the swords of Bolívar and Sucre. In December, 1825, John Williams was received as *chargé d'affaires* of the United States by the government of Central America. Joel R. Poinsett, the first envoy extraordinary and minister plenipotentiary of the United States to serve in Mexico, was formally received in the Mexican capital on June 1, 1825. During a critical period in Hispanic history, the United States accordingly established legations in six capitals of Spanish America. From 1822 to 1830, four Spanish-American states, Mexico, Central America, Colombia, and Argentina accredited envoys to Washington. In this reciprocal fashion the governments of the Three Americas laid the foundations for Pan-Americanism.

Whatever influence the decision by the United States to acknowledge the independence of the Spanish-American nations may have exerted upon the fortunes of those nations was reënforced by the President's message to congress of December 2, 1823, announcing the Monroe Doctrine. The original Monroe Doctrine was given a cordial reception by journalists and publicists in Bogotá and Buenos Aires. In the United Provinces of la Plata it was mentioned with approval in certain state papers of 1824 by Bernardino Rivadavia and General las Heras. In a message to the congress of la Plata on December 16, 1824, Las Heras said that the United States had assumed that the Platean provinces could struggle single-handed against Spain, but had "constituted herself the guardian of the field of battle in order that no foreign power" might interfere. In a message to the Colombian congress on April 6, 1824, Vice President Santander declared that the announcement of President Monroe was "an act eminently just,—an

act worthy of the classic land of American liberty." Shortly
before the battle of Junín, Bolívar read about Monroe's message in the columns of a Jamaica gazette which reprinted the

THE HISPANIC AMERICAN STATES IN 1831

news from the *London Courier*. On April 28, 1824, he made
the following comment upon the news: "The United States
of North America have solemnly declared that they will view

as an act of hostility toward themselves whatever measures the powers of the European continent may take against Spanish America and in favor of Spain." Bolívar associated this declaration of policy by the United States with the policy of opposition to European intervention in Spanish America which England had avowed; and hence he believed that those nations would protect the Spanish-Americans against an attack by the Holy Alliance. During the third decade of the nineteenth century, Colombia and la Plata actually invited the United States to guard their respective national interests against foreign aggression by enforcing the Doctrine of Monroe. Upon these proposals the United States did not consider it necessary to take action. As was suggested by Bolívar's comment upon Monroe's message, the influence which the United States exercised by its foreign policy upon the fortunes of the Spanish-American states was sometimes inextricably associated with the influence of England, which sprang from "the dear-bought glories of Trafalgar's day."

During the revolutionary epoch the foundations were also laid of diplomatic and commercial relations between the Spanish-American states and European nations. Here only Spain and England may be noticed. In June, 1822, Lord Castlereagh, the English secretary for foreign affairs, intimated to Spain that his government was contemplating the recognition of the Spanish-American states. From time to time divers English merchants petitioned their government to take such a step. In October, 1823, George Canning, who had succeeded Castlereagh as foreign secretary, wrote instructions for agents to Mexico City, Bogotá, and Buenos Aires, who were to make reports concerning the conditions in Spanish America. In January, 1825, the English government formally notified the diplomatic corps in London of its intention to recognize the independence of certain Spanish-American states. That announcement evoked a protest from Spain, Austria, Prussia, and Russia. Still, early in 1825, England negotiated treaties with la Plata and Colombia; late in the following year, she negotiated a treaty with Mexico. In thus acknowledging the independence of those states, Canning was animated by the notion that this policy would aid England to counterbalance the growing influence of the United States in the New World. It was during this epoch that several Spanish-American states borrowed money from English financiers in order to promote the revolution. The basis was thus gradually laid for the financial dependence of those states upon England. According to an estimate which was published in the *Times,* Central America, Chile, Colombia, Mexico, and Peru had incurred in England, as the price of liberty, a bonded indebtedness which in 1833 with the arrears of interest, exceeded twenty-two million pounds.

Not until long after the revolutionary period, *par excellence,* had terminated, did the Spanish government deign to recognize her former colonies as sovereign nations. For Ferdinand VII. persistently strove to prevent or to retard such action by other nations. From time to time the ambassadors of Spain at various European courts were instructed formally to protest against the acknowledgment of the independence of her revolted colonies either by the reception of diplomatic agents or by other acts. The Spanish-American republics—whose independence was acknowledged by important nations in America and Europe—accordingly occupied an anomalous position for many, many years. Although they had established their independence *de facto,* their motherland had not recognized them as independent *de jure.* It was not until after Isabella II. became queen of Spain, on December 4, 1836, that the *cortes* reluctantly passed a decree which authorized the government to negotiate treaties with the Spanish-American states acknowledging their independence. In accordance with that decree, José M. Calatrava, Spain's secretary of state, and Miguel Santa María, envoy extraordinary from Mexico, signed a treaty at Madrid on December 28, 1836, which recognized Mexico as "a free, sovereign, and independent nation." By that treaty Isabella II. renounced all pretensions to the government, property, and territory of Mexico. Article five declared that an immediate result of the treaty of peace would be to open commercial relations between the contracting parties upon the reciprocal basis of the treatment accorded to the most favored nation. The treaty with Mexico was the first treaty which Spain ratified with a state that had been carved out of her former American dominions. In the same manner, during the period from 1836 to 1895, by conventions of recognition, peace, and amity—which were sometimes preceded by the establishment of commercial relations between the contracting parties—the court of Spain tardily recognized the independence of Ecuador, Chile, Venezuela, Bolivia, Argentina, Peru, Colombia, Paraguay, Uruguay, and also of five other states that had formerly been members of the Central-American Federation.

During the period from 1808 to 1831, Cuba, Porto Rico, and the Philippine Islands remained subject to Spain, while upon the American continent, viceroyalties, captaincies general, and presidencies had been transformed into independent republics. But although a new family of states had appeared upon the map of America, yet the tumult and the shouting did not die away. Some abuses had indeed disappeared in the maëlstrom of revolution, but there were still many reforms to be accomplished. Against the motherland some Spanish-Americans had a grievance because she was loath to recognize their independence—a grievance that might encourage or provoke war. The citizens of the new republics had not only to heal the grievous wounds of war, but they had also to adjust their economic and social life to altered conditions. The publicists of the Spanish-American states had to handle the delicate problems arising out of unsettled boundaries between neighboring states, they had to solve the difficult problems of fiscal readjustment, and they had to grapple again and again with the problem of their political organization. For the newborn statesmen had still to climb the long and painful road of governmental inexperience in search of political wisdom.

SELECT BIBLIOGRAPHY

Select Bibliography

A. Bibliographical Aids

BANCROFT, H. H., The Works of Hubert Howe Bancroft: volume eight, The History of Central America, 1801-1887; volumes twelve and thirteen, The History of Mexico, 1803-1861, San Francisco, 1885-1887.

These volumes contain useful bibliographical notes on Spanish North America.

MEDINA, J. T., Biblioteca Hispano-Americana (1493-1810), especially volume seven, Santiago de Chile, 1907.

Only the last volume of this great work touches the Spanish-American revolution directly.

—————— "Museo Mitre": Catálogo de Biblioteca, Buenos Aires, 1907.

This catalogue contains a list of the books collected by the Argentine historian and publicist, General Bartolomé Mitre, when preparing to write his volumes on Manuel Belgrano and José de San Martín.

PAZ SOLDÁN, M. T., Historia del Perú Independiente, primer período, 1819-1822; segundo período, 1822-1827, three volumes, Lima, 1868-1874.

Valuable bibliographies of the revolution in Peru are found in these volumes.

ROBERTSON, W. S., Francisco de Miranda and the Revolutionizing of Spanish America, in the Annual Report of the American Historical Association, 1907, volume one, Washington, 1909.

In this work, pages 491-509, there is a select, annotated bibliography of the early revolution, with special reference to Venezuela.

SALAS, C. J., Bibliografía del general don José de San Martín y de la Emancipacíon Sudamaricana, 1778-1910, five volumes, Buenos Aires, 1910.

A very useful bibliography of the movement for the emancipation of southern and western South America, which contains extensive annotations, some documents, and fine illustrations.

SÁNCHEZ, M. S., Bibliografía Venezolanista, contribución al conocimiento de los libros extranjeros relativos á Venezuela y sus grandes hombres, publicados ó reimpresos desde el siglo XIX, Caracas, 1914.

This scholarly bibliography is devoted mainly to books and studies concerning Miranda, Bolívar and Sucre.

B. Atlases

BIEDMA, J. J., and BEYER, C., Atlas Histórico de la República Argentina, Buenos Aires, 1909.

CODAZZI, A., Atlas Fisico y Político de la República de Venezuela, Caracas, 1840.

———— Atlas Geográfico é Histórico de la República de Colombia (antigua Nueva Granada) el cual comprende las Repúblicas de Venezuela y Ecuador, Paris, 1889.

Based as they are upon personal study and investigation, the atlases of Codazzi are very useful for the student of the history and geography of northern South America. Several maps show the routes of the revolutionary armies.

DEMERSAY, L. A., Histoire physique, économique du Paraguay et des établissements des Jesuites. Atlas, Paris, 1860.

PAZ SOLDÁN, M. F., Atlas Geográfico del Perú, Paris 1865.

RESTREPO, J. M., Historia de la Revolución de la República de Colombia. Atlas, Paris, 1827.

This atlas contains detailed maps of Great Colombia and its departments about 1827.

SHEPHERD, W. R., Historical Atlas, New York, 1911.

Among the maps in this atlas are a few that are useful on Spanish America.

C. Secondary Accounts

1. Books and Pamphlets

ACEVEDO, L., José Artigas, Jefe de los Orientales y Protector de los Pueblos Libres, three volumes, Montevideo, 1909, 1910.

The author quotes in his commentary the most important sources which have been published in regard to the career of the enigmatical Artigas.

ALTAMIRA Y CREVEA, R., Historia de España y de la Civilización Española, volumes three and four, Barcelona, 1906, 1911.

The fourth volume of this scholarly work contains a select bibliography of Spanish history.

ALTAMIRA Y CREVEA, R., Resumen Histórico de la Independencia de la América Española, Buenos Aires, 1910.

ÁLVAREZ, A., Rasgos generales de la Historia diplomática de Chile (1810-1910), primera época, la Emancipación, Santiago de Chile, 1911.

A very suggestive volume by an eminent Chilean scholar.

AMUNÁTEGUI, M. L., Camilo Henríquez, two volumes, Santiago de Chile, 1889.

—————— La dictadura de O'Higgins, Santiago de Chile, 1882.

—————— Los Precursores de la Independencia de Chile, three volumes, Santiago de Chile, 1870.

—————— Vida de Don Andrés Bello, Santiago de Chile, 1882.

ANTEQUERA, J. M., Historia de la Legislación Española, desde los tiempos más remotas hasta nuestros dias, Madrid, 1895.

AZPURUA, R., Biografías de Hombres Notables de Hispano-América, four volumes, Caracas, 1877.

These volumes contain useful, although not always accurate, accounts of many Spanish-Americans.

BÁEZ, C., Ensayo sobre el Doctor Francia y la Dictadura en Sud-América, Asunción, 1910.

The best biography of Francia.

BANCROFT, H. H., The Works of Hubert Howe Bancroft: volume eight, The History of Central America, 1801-1887; volumes twelve and thirteen, The History of Mexico, 1803-1861, San Francisco, 1885-1887.

Bancroft's volumes are still very useful.

BARALT, R. M., and DÍAZ, R., Resumen de la Historia de Venezuela desde el año 1797 hasta el de 1830, two volumes, Paris, 1841.

BARBAGELATA, H. D., Artigas y la Revolución Americana, Paris, 1914.

BARROS ARANA, D., Historia Jeneral de Chile, volumes eight to fourteen, Santiago de Chile, 1854.

This standard history of Chile ranks among the finest historical products of Spanish Americans.

—————— Historia General de la Independencia de Chile, four volumes, Santiago de Chile, 1854.

BAUZÁ, F., Historia de la Dominación Española en el Uruguay, volume three, Montevideo, 1897.

Useful on the closing years of the Spanish régime in la Plata.

BECERRA, R., Ensayo Histórico Documentado de la Vida de Don Francisco de Miranda, two volumes, Caracas, 1896.

The best appreciation of Miranda which has been written by a South American.

BERTLING, H., Estudio sobre el Paso de la Cordillera de los Andes efectuado por el general San Martín en los meses de enero i febrero de 1817 (campaña de Chacabuco), Santiago de Chile, 1917.

BINGHAM, H., The Journal of an Expedition across Venezuela and Colombia, 1906-1907, New York, 1909.

BULNES, G., Historia de la Expedición Libertadora del Perú (1817-1822), two volumes, Santiago de Chile, 1887-1888.

———— Últimas Campañas de la Independencia del Perú (1822-1826), Santiago de Chile, 1897.

CARRANZA, A. P., La Junta Gubernativa de 1810, Buenos Aires, 1910.

CEVALLOS, P. F., Resumen de la Historia del Ecuador desde su origen hasta 1845, volumes three, four, and five, Lima, 1870.

CHISHOLM, A. S. M., The Independence of Chile, Boston, 1911.

ESPEJO, G., El Paso de los Andes, crónica histórica de las operaciónes del ejercito de los Andes para la restauración de Chile en 1817, Buenos Aires, 1882.

FLAIROTO, M. T., Mariano Moreno: estudio de su personalidad, y de su obra, Buenos Aires, 1916.

A biography of Moreno which hardly does justice to the subject.

FUENTE, J. M. DE LA, Hidalgo Íntimo, apuntes y documentos para una biografía del benemérito cura de Dolores, d. Miguel Hidalgo y Costilla, Mexico, 1910.

A useful biography of Hidalgo which contains some sources.

GARAY, B., La Revolución de la Independencia del Paraguay, Madrid, 1897.

The most scientific account of the early revolutionary movement in Paraguay.

GARCÍA CALDERON, F., Les démocraties latines de l'Amérique, Paris, 1912.

A sparkling and suggestive volume by a Peruvian scholar.

GERVINIUS, G. G., Geschichte des neunzehnten Jahrhunderts seit den Wiener Vertragen, volumes three and four, Leipsic, 1858, 1859.

GIL FOURTOUL, J., Historia Constitucional de Venezuela, volumes one and two, Berlin, 1907, 1909.

Within its limits, the most useful history of Venezuela.

GOENAGA, J. M., La Entrevista de Guayaquil (Bolívar y San Martín), Rome, 1915.

This pamphlet is the most important contribution to the literature concerning the famous interview.

GROUSSAC, P., Santiago de Liniers, Conde de Buenos Aires, 1753-1810, Buenos Aires, 1907.

GUINAN, F. G., Historia Contemporánea de Venezuela, volume one, Caracas, 1909.

GUTIERREZ, J. R., Revolución del 16 de Julio de 1809 y Biografía de don Pedro Domingo Murillo, La Paz, 1878.

HISPANO, C. (pseudonym of López, I.), Colombia en la Guerra de Independencia. La Cuestion Venezolana, Bogotá, 1914.

Emphasis is here laid upon Colombia's sacrifices in the revolution and some inedited documents are printed.

Historia de la Vida y Reinado de Fernando VII de España, con documentos justificativos, ordenes reservados y numerosas cartas del mismo monarca, three volumes, Madrid, 1842.

A manuscript note by Pascual de Guayangos in the first volume of this useful work which is in the National Library at Madrid, states that its author was Costa Bayo, who lived in Valencia.

HUBBARD [N.] G., Histoire contemporaine de l'Espagne, volumes one, two, and three, Paris, 1868-1878.

HUMBERT, J., Les origines Venézuéliennes, essai sur la colonization Espagnol au Venezuela, Paris, 1905.

IRISARRI, A. J., Historia Crítica del Asesinato cometido en la Persona del gran mariscal de Ayacucho, Caracas, 1846.

One of the most important productions in the long controversy concerning the murder of Sucre.

IZCUE, J. A., de, Los Peruanos y su Independencia, Lima, 1906.

LAFUENTE, M., y Valera, J., Historia General de España, desde los tiempos primitivos hasta la muerte de Fernando VII, continuada desde dicha época hasta nuestros días, volumes sixteen to twenty-two, Barcelona, 1889, 1890.

In these volumes the revolt in the colonies is discussed from a Spanish viewpoint and some inedited documents are printed.

LARRAZÁBAL, F., Vida y Correspondencia General del Libertador Simón Bolívar, enriquecida con la inserción de los manifestos, mensages, exposiciónes, proclamas, etc., two volumes, New York, 1901.

Although eulogistic in tone, this is a useful biography based, in part, upon documents which were subsequently lost.

LARRAZÁBAL, F., The Life of Simón Bolívar, Liberator of Colombia and Peru, Father and Founder of Bolivia, volume one, New York, 1866.

LEA, H. C., The Inquisition in the Spanish Dependencies: Sicily, Naples, Sardinia, Milan, The Canaries, Mexico, Peru, New Granada,—New York, 1908.

LICEAGA, J. M., Adiciónes y Rectificaciónes á la Historia de México que escribió D. Lucas Alamán, Guanajuato, 1868.

LLANOS, J., El Dr. Francia, Buenos Aires, 1907.

LOPEZ, V. F., Historia de la República Argentina, su origen, su revolución, y su desarrolle político hasta 1852, ten volumes, Buenos Aires, 1911.

A detailed history of Argentina which furnishes much material upon the revolution.

Lozano y Lozano, F., El Maestro del Libertador, Paris (1914).

Maeso, J., Artigas y su Época. Apuntes documentados para la historia oriental, two volumes, Montevideo, 1885.

———— Los Primeros Patriotas Orientales de 1811, Montevideo, 1888.

Mancini, J., Bolivar et l'emancipation des colonies espagnoles des origines à 1815, Paris, 1912.
   The most careful and sympathetic biography of Bolívar. Unfortunately the author died before completing the work.

Mantilla, V. F., San Martín, Buenos Aires, 1913.

Markham, C. R., A History of Peru, Chicago, 1892.

Marure, A., Bosquejo Histórico de las Revolución es de Centro-América, desde 1811 hasta 1834, volume one, Guatemala, 1877.

Medina, J. T., Historia del Tribunal del Santo Oficio de la Inquisición en México, Santiago de Chile, 1908.

Mendiburu, M. de, Diccionario Histórico-Biográfico del Perú, parte primera que correspondé á la época de la dominación española, eight volumes, Lima, 1874-1890.
   A monumental and encyclopedic work, which, however, needs revision.

Michelena, T., Resumen de la Vida Militar y Política del Ciudadano esclarecido general José Antonio Páez. Caracas, 1890.

Mitre, B., Las Cuentas del Gran Capitán (en el centenario de San Martín), Buenos Aires, 1878.

Mitre, B., The Emancipation of South America. Being a condensed translation by William Pilling of the history of San Martín by General Don Bartolomé Mitre, London, 1893.
   A survey of the South-American revolution, with special attention to the career of San Martín.

———— Historia de Belgrano, two volumes, Buenos Aires, 1859.
   A detailed account of Belgrano's rôle in the revolution, with documents in the appendices.

———— Historia de San Martín y de la Emancipación Sud-Americana, three volumes, Buenos Aires, 1887, 1888.
   Written from the Argentine viewpoint, this is the classic work on San Martín's rôle in the revolution.

Molinari, D. L., La 'Representación de los Hacendados' de Mariano Moreno, su ninguna influencia en la vida económica del pais y en los sucesos de mayo de 1810, Buenos Aires, 1914.
   A critical study of the influence of Moreno's famous memorial.

Moreno, F. R., Estudio sobre la Independencia del Paraguay, volume one, Asunción, 1911.

Moses, B., South America on the Eve of Emancipation, New York and London, 1908.

NOLL, A. H., and MCMAHON, A. P., The Life and Times of Miguel Hidalgo y Costilla, Chicago, 1910.

Ó KELLY DE GALWAY, A. C., Francisco de Miranda. . . . Biographie et Iconographie, Paris, 1913.
A documented biographical sketch which is serviceable for Miranda's iconography.

OLAVARRÍA Y FERRARI, E., México Independiente, 1821-1855 (volume four in México á través de los siglos), Barcelona (c. 1880).

OMAN, C., A History of the Peninsular war, volume one, Oxford, 1902.

PAXSON, F. L., The Independence of the South-American Republics, a study in recognition and foreign policy, Philadelphia, 1903.

PAZ SOLDÁN, M. F., Historia del Perú Independiente, primer período, 1819-1822, segundo período, 1822-27, three volumes, Lima, 1868-1874.
This standard work contains some inedited documents.

PEREIRA DA SILVA, J. M., Historia da Fundaçao do Imperio Brazileiro, three volumes, Rio de Janeiro, 1870, 1871.

PESQUERA VALENILLA, V., Rasgos Biográficos del general en jefe Antonio José de Sucre, gran mariscal de Ayacucho, Caracas, 1894.

PETRE, F. L., Simón Bolívar, "El Libertador," a life of the chief leader in the revolt against Spain in Venezuela, New Granada, and Peru, London and New York, 1909.
The most detailed biography of Bolívar in English: emphasis is laid upon military events.

PI Y MARGALL, F., and PI Y ARSUGA, F., Historia de España en el Siglo XIX, volumes one, two, three, Barcelona, 1902.

PINILLA, S., La Creación de Bolivia (volume seventeen in Biblioteca Ayacucho, edited by R. Blanco-Fombona), Madrid (1917).
A helpful volume upon an obscure period.

QUESADA, E., Las Reliquias de San Martín, Buenos Aires, 1900.

QUESADA, V. G., Vireinato del Río de la Plata, 1778-1810, apuntamientos críticos-históricos para servir en la cuestion de límites entre la república Argentina y Chile, Buenos Aires, 1881.
Important for the study of colonial boundaries in southern South America.

RENÉ-MORENO, G., Bolivia y Perú. Notas Históricas y Bibliográficas, Santiago de Chile, 1905.

——— Bolivia y Perú. Más Notas Históricas y Bibliográficas, Santiago de Chile, 1905.

——— Nuevas Notas Históricas y Bibliográficas, Santiago de Chile, 1907.

—— Últimas Días Coloniales en el Alto-Perú: narración; documentos inéditos de 1808 y 1809, two volumes, Santiago de Chile, 1896, 1901.

ROBERTSON, W. S., Francisco de Miranda and the Revolutionizing of Spanish America, in Annual Report of the American Historical Association, 1907, volume one, pages 189-540, Washington, 1909.

A scientific monograph which is based largely upon archival investigations.

—— The Life of Miranda, two volumes, Chapel Hill, North Carolina, 1929.

RODRÍGUEZ, G. F., Historia de Alvéar con la Acción de Artigas en el Periodo Evolutivo de la Revolución Argentina de 1812 á 1816, volumes one and two, Buenos Aires, 1913.

—— El General Soler, contribución histórica, documentos inéditos, 1783-1849, Buenos-Aires, 1909.

RODRÍGUEZ VILLA, A., El teniente general don Pablo Morillo, Primer Conde de Cartagena, Marqués de la Puerta (1778-1837), estudio biográfico documentado, four volumes, Madrid, 1908, 1910.

This set contains much material concerning the revolt in northern South America.

ROJAS, A., Los Hombres de la Revolución, 1810-1826. El canónigo José Cortes Madariaga, El general Emparan, Caracas, 1878.

—— Historia Patria, estudios históricos, origines Venezolanos, volume one, Caracas, 1891.

ROJAS, EL MARQUÉS DE, Simón Bolívar, Paris, 1883.

A documented study.

—— Tiempo Perdido, colección de escritos sobre literatura y hacienda pública, Paris, 1905.

ROSSEEUW ST.-HILAIRE [E. F. A.], Histoire d'Espagne depuis les premiers temps historiques jusqu'à la mort de Ferdinand VII, volumes thirteen and fourteen, Paris, 1878, 1879.

SAAVEDRA, A. Z., Don Cornelio de Saavedra, presidente de la junta de gobierno de 1810, Buenos Aires, 1909.

SALDÍAS, A., La Evolución Republicana durante la Revolución Argentina, Buenos Aires, 1896.

SÁNCHEZ, M. S., Apuntes para la Iconografía del Libertador, Caracas, 1916.

An illustrated study of Bolívar as depicted by artists and sculptors.

SASSENAY, LE MARQUIS DE, Napoleon Ier. et la fondation de la republique Argentine, Paris, 1892.

SCHRYVER, S. DE, Esquisse de la vie de Bolivar, Brussels, 1898.

Unsurpassed as a presentation of Bolívar's career in one volume.

TEMPERLEY, H. W. V., Life of Canning, London, 1905.
Useful for the study of English policy toward Spanish America.

URQUINAONA Y PARDO, P., Resumen de las causas principales que preparon y dieron impulso á la Emancipación de la América Española, Madrid, 1835.

VARELA, L. V., Historia Constitucional de la República Argentina, four volumes, La Plata, 1910.

(VICUNA MACKENNA, B.), La Corona del Héroe, recopilación de datos i documentos para perpetuar la memoria del jeneral don Bernardo O'Higgins, Santiago de Chile, 1872.
A biographical account of O'Higgins which is accompanied by many important documents.

VICUNA MACKENNA, B., and others, Historia Jeneral de la República de Chile desde su independencia hasta nuestros días, five volumes, Santiago de Chile, 1886-1882.
This coöperative history contains special studies of various phases of the Chilean revolution.

VICUNA MACKENNA, B., El jeneral d. José de San Martín, considerado según documentos enteramente inéditos, Santiago de Chile, 1863.

——— El Ostracismo del jeneral d. Bernardo O'Higgins, escrito sobre documentos inéditos i noticias auténticas, Valparaiso, 1860.

——— La Revolución de la Independencia del Perú desde 1809 á 1819, Lima, 1860.

——— Vida del capitán jeneral de Chile, don Bernardo O'Higgins, escrito sobre documentos inéditos i noticias auténticas, Valparaiso, 1860.

——— El Washington del Sur, cuadros de la vida militar del jeneral Antonio José de Sucre, Santiago de Chile, 1893.

VILLANUEVA, C. A., Historia y Diplomacia, Napoleón y la independencia de América, Paris, 1911.
A study of Napoleon's influence upon the Spanish-American revolt which supplements De Sassenay.

——— La Monarquía en América: Bolívar y el general San Martín; Fernando VII y los nuevos estados; La santa alianza; El imperio de los Andes, four volumes, Paris (1911-1914).
These volumes print—in Spanish—many documents from European archives concerning the Spanish-American revolution. The author's thesis is that Bolívar was a monarchist.

VILLANUEVA, L., Vida del gran mariscal de Ayacucho, Caracas, 1895.

The best life of Sucre.

WASHBURN, C. A., The History of Paraguay, with notes of personal observations and reminiscences of diplomacy under difficulties, volume one, Boston, 1871.

This volume transmits some Paraguayan reminiscences and traditions of Francia.

ZÁRATE, J., La Guerra de Independencia (volume three in México á través de los siglos), Barcelona (c. 1880).

A volume by a scholar of Mexico upon her struggle for independence.

ZINNY, A., Historia de los Gobernantes del Paraguay, 1535-1887, Buenos Aires, 1887.

2. Articles in Periodicals, etc.

ANCÍZAR, M., "Antonio José de Sucre," in the Boletín de la Academia Nacional de la Historia, volume two, pages 52-80, 107-139, Caracas, 1913.

BÁEZ, C., "Historia del Paraguay: las leyes de extrangería," in the Revista del Instituto Paraguayo, año IX, pages 385-417, Asunción, 1908.

DESDÉVISES DU DEZERT, G., "Vice-rois et capitaines généraux des Indes espagnoles à la fin du XVIIIᵉ siècle," in Revue Historique, volume one hundred and twenty-five, pages 225 ff., Paris, 1917.

FRANCIA, F., "Genealogía de la Familia del Libertador Simón Bolívar," in the Gaceta de los Museos Nacionales, volume one, pages 33 ff., Caracas, 1912.

FUENTE, J. M. DE LA, "Apuntes y Documentos sobre las Familias Hidalgo y Costilla, Gallega Mandarte y Villaseñor," in the Anales del Museo Nacional de Arqueología, Historia, y Etnología, volume one, pages 531-552, Mexico, 1909.

—— "Arbol Genealógico del Benemérito Cura de Dolores, D. Miguel Hidalgo y Costilla . . ." in the Anales del Museo Nacional de Arqueología, Historia, y Etnología, volume one, page 232, Mexico, 1909.

GARCÍA, G., "Leona Vicario, heroína insurgente," in the Anales del Museo Nacional de Arqueología, Historia, y Etnología, volume one, pages 255-457, Mexico, 1909.

HUMBERT, J., "Los Bolívar de Vizcaya, los antepasados del Libertador de la América del Sur," in the Anales de la Universidad Central de Venezuela, volume eleven, pages 53-63, Caracas, 1910.

A valuable study of Bolívar's ancestors in Spain.

LEA, H. C., "Hidalgo and Morelos," in the American Historical Review, volume four, pages 636-651, New York, 1899.

LECUNA, V., "La campaña de Carabobo y la diversión de Bermúdez," in *El Cojo Ilustrado,* December 15, 1912, pages 663-669, Caracas, 1912.

A scientific study by a student of military history.

MENDOZA C. A., "Sucre," in the Memorias de la Academia Nacional de la Historia, volume one, pages 16-40, Caracas, 1890.

PONTE, A. F., "Arbol genealógico del Libertador Simón Bolívar," in *El Universal,* July 5, 1911, Caracas, 1911.

A careful study of Bolívar's ancestry.

RAMOS, J., "Origenes del Mariscal de Ayacucho," in the Boletín de la Academia Nacional de Historia, volume three, pages 125-144, Caracas, 1914.

A documented study of Sucre's ancestry.

ROBERTSON, W. S., "The Beginnings of Spanish-American Diplomacy," in the *Turner Essays in American History,* pages 231-267, New York, 1910.

——— "The First Legations of the United States in Latin America" in the *Mississippi Valley Historical Review,* volume two, pages 183-212, Cedar Rapids, 1915.

——— "The Juntas of 1808 and the Spanish Colonies," in the *English Historical Review,* volume thirty-one, pages 573-585, London, 1916.

——— "The Recognition of the Spanish Colonies by the Motherland," in the *Hispania American Historical Review,* volume one, pages 70-91, Baltimore, 1918.

——— "South America and the Monroe Doctrine, 1824-1828," in the *Political Science Quarterly,* volume thirty, pages 82-105, New York, 1915.

——— "The United States and Spain in 1822," in the *American Historical Review,* volume twenty, pages 781-800, New York, 1915.

The six above-mentioned studies, by the author of the present volume, are mainly concerned with the international relations of the American states during the revolutionary epoch. They utilize considerable archival material.

SAMPER, S. A. DE, " Sucre," in the Memorias de la Academia Nacional de la Historia, volume one, pages 41-320, Caracas, 1890.

WEBSTER, C. K., "Castlereagh and the Spanish Colonies," in the *English Historical Review,* volume twenty-seven, pages 78-85, and volume thirty, pages 631-644, London, 1912, 1915.

This study utilizes archival material and supplements Temperley's volume.

WITZKE, C. F., "Bosquejo de la Vida de Simón Bolívar desde su Nacimiento hasta el Año de 1810," in the *Gaceta de los Museos Nacionales,* volume one, pages 147 ff., Caracas, 1912.—

The most useful study of Bolívar's early career.

D. Sources

1. Books and Pamphlets

ADAMS, J. Q., Memoirs of John Quincy Adams, comprising portions of his diary from 1797 to 1848. Edited by C. F. Adams, volumes four to eight, Philadelphia, 1875, 1876.
—— The Writings of John Quincy Adams. Edited by W. C. Ford, volumes five and following, New York, 1915.—
ALAMÁN, L., Historia de México, con una noticia preliminar del sistéma de gobierno que regía en 1808 y del estado en que se hallaba el pais en el mismo año, five volumes, Mexico, 1883-1885.
> These volumes contain a detailed history of the Mexican revolution which is written from the royalist viewpoint.

American State Papers: Foreign Relations, volumes three to six, Washington, 1832-1859.
Annals of the Congress of the United States, eleventh, twelfth, thirteenth, fourteenth, fifteenth, sixteenth, and seventeenth Congresses, Washington, 1853-1856.
The Annual Register, or a view of the history, politics, and literature for the year 1808, for the year 1809, etc., London, 1820.—
Archivo general de la Nación: Partes oficiales y Documentos relativos á la Guerra de la Independencia Argentina, four volumes, Buenos Aires, 1900-1903.
> An important collection of documents for the study of the revolution in the Platean provinces, 1808-1828.

ARTIGAS (J.), Artigas: Estudio histórico, Documentos justificativos. Edited by C. L. Fregeiro, Montevideo, 1886.
> A collection of documents dealing with conditions in the Platean basin, 1803-1814, and especially with Artigas.

AUSTRIA, J. DE, Bosquejo de la Historia Militar de Venezuela en la guerra de su Independencia, volume one, Caracas, 1885.
BELGRANO (M.), . . . Documentos del Archivo de Belgrano, five volumes, Buenos Aires, 1913.—
> Important for the investigation of Belgrano's career.

BENESKI, C. DE, A Narrative of the last moments of the Life of Don Augustin de Iturbide, ex-emperor of Mexico, New York, 1825.
BERTLING, H., Editor. Documentos históricos referentes al Paso de los Andes efectuado en 1817 por el general San Martín, Concepción, 1908.
[BIGGS, J.], The History of Don Francisco de Miranda's attempt to effect a Revolution in South America, in a series of letters

by a gentleman who was an officer under that general, to his friend in the United States. To which are annexed sketches of the life of Miranda and geographical notices of Caracas, Boston, 1810.

The most useful published source on Miranda's expedition of 1806.

BLANCO, J. F., and AZPURUA, R., Editors. Documentos para la Historia de la Vida pública del Libertador de Colombia, Peru, y Bolivia, publicados por disposición del general Guzmán Blanco, fourteen volumes, Caracas, 1875-1877.

This is probably the most useful collection of documents concerning the revolution in Spanish America.

BOCANEGRA, J. M., Memorias para la Historia de México Independiente, 1822-1846, two volumes, Mexico, 1892.

BOLÍVAR (S.), Papeles de Bolívar, publicados por Vicente Lecuna, Caracas, 1917.

Carefully selected from inedited manuscripts in the archives of the liberator at Caracas, this volume contains documents which supplement the O'Leary collection at many points.

BRACKENRIDGE, H. M., Voyage to South America in the years 1817 and 1818, in the frigate Congress, two volumes, London, 1820.

British and Foreign State Papers, volumes one to twenty-five, London, 1841-1853.

Scattered through this collection are many documents on the Spanish-American revolution.

BUSTAMANTE, C. M. DE, Campañas del general d. Félix María Calleja, comandante en gefe del ejercito real de operaciones llamado del centro, Mexico, 1828.

———— Continuación del Cuadro Histórico. Historia del Emperador d. Agustín de Iturbide hasta su muerte, y sus consecuencias, y establecimiento de la república popular federal, Mexico, 1846.

Important for the career of Iturbide as emperor.

———— Cuadro Histórico de la Revolución Mexicana, comenzada en 15 de Septiembre de 1810 por el ciudadano Miguel Hidalgo y Costilla, cura dey pueblo de los Dolores, en el obispado de Michoacán, five volumes, Mexico, 1843-1846.

One of the most important sources on the Mexican revolution.

[BUSTAMANTE, C. M. DE], Historia militar del General Don José María Morelos, sacado en lo conducente á ella de sus declaraciónes recibidas de orden del virey de México, cuando estuvo arrestado en la ciudadela de esta capital, Mexico, 1825.

CALVO, C., Recueil historique complet des traités, conventions, capitulations, armistices et autres actes diplomatiques de tous les états de l'Amérique Latine, 1re. période, 2de. période, fifteen volumes, Paris, 1863-1867.

Scattered through these volumes are documents which concern particularly the diplomatic history of the revolution.

CAMBA [A. G.], Memorias para la Historia de las Armas Españolas en el Perú, two volumes, Buenos Aires, 1895-1899.

CARRANZA, A. P., Editor. Archivo general de la República Argentina, segunda série, fourteen volumes, Buenos Aires, 1894-1899.

Catástrophe de don Agustín de Yturbide, aclamado emperador de Méjico, el 18 de Mayo del año 1822, ó relación exacta de las circunstancias que han acompañado el desembarco y la muerte de este hombre célebre, Paris, 1825.

Causa criminal seguida contra el coronel graduado Apolinar Morillo, y demás autores y cómplices del asesinato perpetrado en la persona del señor Jeneral Antonio José de Sucre, Bogotá, 1843.

Original documents concerning the trial of those persons accused of Sucre's murder.

[CAVIA, P. C.], El Protector nominal de los Pueblos libres, d. José Artigas, clasificado por el amigo del órden, Buenos Aires, 1818.

This booklet contains some much-disputed statements concerning the early career of Artigas.

COCHRANE, C. S., Journal of a Residence and Travels in Colombia during the years 1823 and 1824, two volumes, London, 1825.

COCHRANE, T. B., and BOURNE, R. F. H., The Life of Thomas, Lord Cochrane, tenth Earl of Dundonald, G. C. B., two volumes, London, 1869.

Colección de Historiadores i de Documentos relativos á la Independencia de Chile, volumes one to twenty-two, Santiago de Chile, 1900.—

A most important collection on the Chilean revolution.

Colección de leyes, decretos y ordenes publicados en el Perú desde el año de 1821 hasta 31 de diciembre de 1859, reimpresa por orden de materias por el dr. d. Juan Oviedo, abogado de los tribunales de la república, especially volume one, Lima, 1861.

This volume contains the earliest constitutional statutes of Peru.

Colección de ordenes y decretos de la soberano junta provisional gubernativa, y soberanos congresos generales de la nación mexicana, four volumes, Mexico, 1829.

A collection of orders and decrees of the first empire of Mexico and of the republic which followed.

Colección de los decretos y ordenes que han expedido las Cortes generales y extraordinarias desde su instalación . . . 1810, ten volumes, Madrid, 1813-1823.

(Colección legislativa de España):
Decretos del Rey Don Fernando VII, volumes one to eighteen, Madrid, 1818-1834.

Decretos de la Reina nuestra señora doña Isabel II, dados en su real nombre por su augusta madre la reina gobernadora y reales ordenes, resoluciónes y reglamentos generales expedidos por las secretarías del despacho universal desde 1⁰ de enero . . . de 1834, volumes nineteen to twenty-one, Madrid, 1835-1837.

Colección de las leyes, decretos, y declaraciónes de las Cortes, y de los reales decretos, ordenes, resoluciónes, y reglamentos generales expedidos pod las secretarías del despacho desde 1⁰ de enero . . . de 1837 . . . volumes twenty-two to thirty-five, Madrid, 1837-1846.

Colección legislativa de España (continuación de la colección de decretos), volumes thirty-six to one hundred and thirty, Madrid, 1848.

Among the above collections of laws and decrees are many documents concerning Spain's policy toward her colonies.

Colección oficial de leyes, decretos, ordenes y resoluciónes vigentes de la República Boliviana, volumes one to five, Sucre, 1846, 1847.

This collection contains many administrative and legislative provisions of Bolivia, 1825-1830.

Colección legislativa de la República Oriental del Uruguay, volume one, Montevideo, 1900.

The first statutes of the Uruguayan republic.

Cuerpo de leyes de la República de Colombia, three volumes, London, 1825.

These volumes contain important legislative material in regard to the founding of Great Colombia.

DEPONS, F., Voyage à la partie oriental de la Terra-ferme, dans l'Amérique méridionale, fait pendant les années 1801, 1802, 1803, et 1804: contenant la description de la capitainerie générale de Caracas, . . . three volumes, Paris, 1806.

A valuable source concerning conditions in northern South America on the eve of the revolution.

Diario de las actas y discusiónes de las Cortes, legislatura de los años de 1820 y 1821, twenty-three volumes, and three volumes of appendices, Madrid, 1820-1821.

Diario de las actas y discusiónes de las Cortes extraordinarias del año de 1821, six volumes, Madrid, 1821.

Diario de las sesiones de Cortes: legislatura extraordinaria (esta legislatura dió principio el día 22 de setiembre de 1821 y terminó el 14 de febrero de 1822), three volumes, Madrid, 1871.

Diario de las actas y discusiónes de las Cortes extraordinarias del año de 1822, six volumes, Madrid, 1822, 1823.

Diario de las sesiones de Cortes, estamento de ilustres próceres, legislatura de 1835 á 1836, Madrid, 1869.

Diario de sesiones de las Cortes constituyentes, dieron principio el 17 de octubre de 1836, terminaron el 4 de noviembre de 1837, volume one, Madrid, 1870.

In the above six collections of the debates in the *cortes* may be found many documents respecting the policy of Spain's statesmen towards the American colonies.

Dias del Mayo: actas del cabildo de Buenos Aires, 1810, Buenos Aires, 1910.

Documentos para los Anales de Venezuela desde el movimiento separatista de la unión Colombiana hasta nuestros días, primer período, seven volumes, Caracas, 1889-1891; segundo período, volume four, Caracas, 1912.

Documentos relativos á los Antecedentes de la Independencia de la República Argentina, Buenos Aires, 1912.

Documentos en honor del Gran Mariscal de Ayacucho coordinados por la comisión, que nombro de su seno la Academia Nacional de la Historia, Caracas, 1890.

Documentos para la Historia de la Provincia de Cartagena de Indias, hoy estado sobrano de Bolívar en la unión Colombiana, two volumes, Bogotá, 1883.

DUCOUDRAY HOLSTEIN, H. L. V., Memoirs of Simon Bolivar, President Liberator of the Republic of Columbia, and of his principal generals, secret history of the revolution, and of the events which preceded it from 1807 to the present time, Boston, 1829.

DUNDONALD, THOMAS, Earl of, Narrative of Services in the Liberation of Chile, Peru, and Brazil, from Spanish and Portuguese domination, two volumes, London, 1859.

FILISOLA, V., La Cooperación de México en la Independencia de Centro América (volumes thirty-five and thirty-six in Documentos inéditos ó muy raros para la historia de México, edited by G. García), Mexico, 1911.

GARCÍA, G., Editor. Documentos Históricos Mexicanos: obra conmemorativa del primer centenario de la independencia de México, seven volumes, Mexico, 1910.

This important collection supplements Hernández y Dávalos.

HACKETT, J., Narrative of the Expedition which sailed from England in 1817 to join the South American patriots, comprising every particular connected with its formation, history, and fate; with observations and authentic information elucidating the real character of the contest, mode of warfare, state of the armies, etc., London, 1818.

HALL, B., Extracts from a Journal written on the coasts of Chile, Peru, and Mexico, in the years 1820, 1821, 1822, part I, part II, London, 1840.

This contains interesting commentaries upon the revolutionary movement.

HAMILTON, J. P., Travels through the interior provinces of Colombia, two volumes, London, 1827.

HEREIDA, J. F., Memorias sobre las Revoluciónes de Venezuela, Paris, 1895.

HERNÁNDEZ Y DÁVALOS, J. E., Editor. Colección de Documentos para la Historia dé la guerra de Independencia de México de 1808 á 1821, six volumes, Mexico, 1877-1882.

In general this is the most useful collection of documents upon the revolution in Mexico.

HERRARA, J. H., Editor. El Album de Ayacucho: colección de los principales documentos de la guerra de la independencia del Perú y de los cantos de victoria y poesías relativas á ella, Lima, 1862.

Prose and poems concerning the revolution in Peru.

HIPPISLEY, G., A Narrative of the Expedition to the Rivers Orinoco and Apuré in South America, which sailed from England in November, 1817, and joined the patriotic forces in Venezuela and Caracas,—London, 1819.

HUMBOLDT, A. DE, and BONPLAND, A., Personal Narrative of travels to the equinoctial regions of the new continent during the years 1799-1804. Translated by H. M. Williams, six volumes, London, 1818-1829.

HUMBOLDT, A., Essai politique sur le royaume de la Nouvelle Espagne, five volumes, Paris, 1811.

Humboldt's writings contain much valuable material on colonial conditions.

(ITURBIDE, A. DE), A Statement of some of the Principal Events in the Public Life of Augustin de Iturbide, written by himself, with a preface by the translator, and an appendix of documents, London, 1824.

Iturbide's *memoirs* done into English by M. J. Quin.

——— Breve diseño crítico de la emancipación y libertad de la nación Mexicana, y de las causas que influyeron en sus más ruidosos sucesos, acaecidos desde el grito de Iguala hasta la espantosa muerte del Libertador en la villa de Padilla, Mexico, 1827.

A Spanish translation of Iturbide's above-mentioned memoirs, accompanied by some other documents.

LABARRIETA, A., Informe del Dr. Don Antonio Labarrieta, cura de la ciudad de Guanajuato, sobre la conducta que observó Iturbide siendo comandante general del Bajío, Mexico, 1821.

LACROIX, L., Perú de, Diario de Bucaramanga, ó vida pública y privada del Libertador Simón Bolívar, publicada por primera vez con una introducción y notas por Cornelio Hispano (pseudonym of I. López), Paris (1912).

This much-discussed diary purports to contain Bolivar's confidential remarks in 1828 concerning his career and his companions.

LAFOND (DE LURCY), G., Voyages autour du Monde et naufrages célebres, volumes one, two, and three, Paris, 1870.

Leyes promulgadas en Chile desde 1810 hasta el Iº de Junio de 1912. Edited by R. Anguita, volume one, Santiago de Chile, 1912.

This volume contains the earliest constitutional statutes of Chile.

El Libro nacional de los Venezolanos, actas del congreso constituyente de Venezuela en 1811, origenes de la república, Caracas, 1811.

LONDONDERRY, R. S., Memoirs and Correspondence of Viscount Castlereagh, second Marquess of Londonderry. Edited by Charles Vane, Marquess of Londonderry, twelve volumes, London, 1850-1853.

LOPEZ, M. A., Campaña del Perú por el Ejército Unido Libertador de Colombia, Perú, B. Aires, y Chile, á las ordenes del immortal Bolívar, en los años de 1823, 24 y 25 con mapas de los campos de batalla que dieron libertad á aquella república y aseguraron la independencia del nuevo mundo, Caracas, 1843.

MALO, J. R., Apuntes históricos sobre el destierro, vuelta al territorio Mexicana y muerte del Libertador d. Agustín de Iturbide, Mexico, 1869.

MEDINA, J. T., Biblioteca Hispano-Chilena (1523-1817), volume three, Santiago de Chile, 1899.

Memorias de los Vireyes que han gobernado el Perú durante el tiempo del coloniaje Español, six volumes, Lima, 1859.

Valuable upon the colonial régime in the Peruvian viceroyalty.

MENDIBIL, P. DE, Resumen histórico de la Revolución de los Estados Unidos Mejicanos, sacado del "Cuadro Histórico," que en forma de cartas escribió el Lic. d. Carlos María Bustamante, London, 1828.

MILLER, J., Memoirs of General Miller in the service of the Republic of Peru, two volumes, London, 1828.

Based as these memoirs are upon the correspondence and notes of General William Miller, a participant in the revolutionary war, they constitute a valuable source on the South-American revolt.

MIRANDA, F., Miranda dans la révolution Française: recueil de documents authentiques relative à l'histoire du Général Francisco de Miranda pendant son séjour en France de 1792 à 1798. Edited by A. Rojas, Caracas, 1889.

Documents concerning Miranda's career in the French revolution.

MIRANDA (F.), El general Miranda. Edited by El Marqués de Rojas. Paris, 1884.

Documents concerning various phases of Miranda's career.

—— South American Emancipation, documents historical and explanatory, shewing the designs which have been in progress, and the exertions made by General Miranda for the attainment of that object during the last twenty-five years. Edited by J. M. Antepara, London, 1810.

This contains documents which were edited under Miranda's direction.

MOLAS, M. A., Descripción histórica de la antigua provincia del Paraguay, correjida, aumentada y anotada por el Doctor Angel Justiniano Carranza, Buenos Aires, 1868.

MONROE, J., The Writings of James Monroe, including a collection of his public and private papers and correspondence now for the first time printed. Edited by S. M. Hamilton, volumes five to seven, New York and London, 1901-1903.

MOORE, J. B., Editor. A Digest of International Law as embodied in diplomatic discussions, treaties, and other international agreements . . . , especially volume one, Washington, 1906.

MORENO, MARIANO, Colección de Arengas en el foro y Escritos del doctor dn. Mariano Moreno, abogado de Buenos Aires, y secretario del primer gobierno en la revolución de aquel estado, volume one, London, 1836.

The only volume published, which was presumably edited by Manuel Moreno.

—— Escritos de Mariano Moreno, con un prólogo por Norberto Piñero, Buenos Aires, 1896.

The most complete edition of Moreno's writings: it includes the memorial of 1809.

—— Representación que el apoderado de los hacendados de ias campañas del Río de la Plata dirigió al excelentísimo señor virey don Baltasar Hidalgo de Cisneros en el expediente promovido sobre propocionar ingresos al erario por medio de un franco comercio con la nación Inglesa. La escribió el doctor don Mariano Moreno, Buenos Aires, 1810.

An edition of the famous memorial by which Mariano Moreno acknowledged its authorship.

MORENO, MANUEL, Vida y Memorias del dr. dn. Mariano Moreno, secretario de la junta de Buenos Aires, capital de las provincias del Río de la Plata, con una idea de su revolución y de la México, Caracas,—London, 1812.

A biography of Mariano Moreno by his brother.

MOSQUERA, T. C. DE, Memorias sobre la Vida del Libertador Simón Bolívar, New York, 1853.

Novísima recopilación de las leyes de España, mandada formar por el Señor Don Carlos IV, edición publicada por don Vicente Salvá, five volumes, Paris, 1854.

O'DONOJU, J., Modelo de virtud y filantropía, loor eterno al exmo. señor capitán general don Juan O'Donojú, carta de remision al gobierno Español del tratado celebrado en la villa de Córdoba, por el exmo. señor don Juan O'Donojú, Mexico, 1822.

O'HIGGINS, B., Epistolario de d. Bernardo O'Higgins, capitán general y director supremo de Chile, gran mariscal del Perú y brigadier de las Provincias Unidas del Río de la Plata, anotado por Ernesto de la Cruz, first volume, Santiago de Chile, 1916.

This volume of O'Higgins' papers contains many inedited documents.

O'LEARY, D. F., Memorias del General O'Leary, publicados por su hijo Simón B. O'Leary, thirty-two volumes, Caracas, 1879-1888.

Under this misleading title, was published the most valuable collection of sources for the life of Bolívar: it also contains a large amount of material concerning his comrades.

OLIVART, MARQUÉS DE, Colección de los tratados, convenios, y documentos internacionales celebrados por nuestro gobiernos con los estados extranjeros desde el reinado de doña Isabel hasta nuestros días, volumes one to eleven, Madrid, 1890-1902.

Indispensable upon the recognition of the Spanish colonies by the motherland.

PÁEZ, J. A., Autobiografía del general José Antonio Páez, two volumes, Caracas, 1888.

[PALACIO FAJARDO, M.], Outline of the Revolution in Spanish America, or an account of the origin, progress, and actual state of the war carried on between Spain and Spanish America containing the principal facts which have marked the struggle. By a South American, New York, 1817.

PARISH, W., Buenos Aires and the Provinces of the Río de la Plata from their discovery and conquest by the Spaniards to the establishment of their political independence, London, 1852.

POINSETT, J. R., Notes on Mexico, made in the autumn of 1822, accompanied by an historical sketch of the revolution and translations of official reports on the present state of that country, London, 1825.

An interesting account of conditions in Mexico under Iturbide.

POSADA, E., and IBANEZ, P. M., Editors. Biblioteca de Historia Nacional; especially volumes one, two, four, six, eight, and thirteen, Bogotá, 1902-1914.

A meritorious series—coöperative in type—published under the direction of the National Academy of History of Colombia. Many of its volumes contain much source material concerning conditions in northern South America during the revolutionary era.

POUDENX, H., and MAYER, F., Mémoire pour servir à l'histoire de la révolution de la capitainerie générale de Caracas, depuis l'abdication de Charles IV, jusqu'au mois d'aout 1814, Paris, 1815.

The proceedings of a general court martial held at Chelsea hospital on Thursday, January 28, 1808, and continued by adjournment till Tuesday, March 15, for the trial of Lieut. Gen. Whitelocke, two volumes, London, 1808.

PROCTER, R., Narrative of a journey across the cordillera of the Andes and of a residence in Lima and other parts of Peru in the years 1823 and 1824, London, 1825.

Publicaciones del archivo general de la nación, Estados Unidos Mexicanos, secretaría de relaciones exteriores, volumes three and four, La Constitución de 1812 en la Nueva España, Mexico, 1912.

PUEYRREDON, J. M. DE, . . . Documentos del Archivo de Pueyrredón, four volumes, Buenos Aires, 1912.

Important for the rôle of Pueyrredón in the revolution.

Recopilación de leyes de los reinos de las Indias, mandada imprimir y publicar por la magestad católica del rey don Carlos II nuestro señor, two volumes, Madrid, 1841.

Registro oficial de la República Argentina que comprende los documentos espedidos desde 1810 hasta 1873, volumes one, two, three, Buenos Aires, 1879-1882.

An important collection for the history of Argentina.

RENGGER [J. R.], and LONGCHAMP [M.], Essai historique sur la révolution du Paraguay, et le gouvernement dictatorial du docteur Francia, Paris, 1827.

One of the most useful accounts of Francia's rule by a foreign visitor.

——— Ensayo histórico sobre la Revolución del Paraguay por Rengger y Longchamp. Edición especial precedida de la biografía del Tirano Francia, y continuada con algunos documentos y observaciones históricas por M. A. Pelliza, Buenos Aires, 1883.

RESTREPO, J. M., Historia de la Revolución de la República de Colombia en la América Meridional, five volumes, Besançon, 1858.

The best edition of the classic history of the Colombian revolution, written by a contemporary publicist.

REY DE CASTRO, J. M., Recuerdos del Tiempo Heróico, pájinas de la vida militar i política del gran mariscal de Ayacucho,— Guayaquil, 1883.

La Revolución de la Paz en 1809, documentos históricos, Buenos Aires, 1897.

[RIVA AGÜERO, J. DE LA], Memorias y documentos para la historia de la independencia del Perú y causas del mal éxito que ha tenido esta. Obra póstuma de P. Pruvoneva, two volumes, Paris, 1858.

Riva Agüero's apology, edited with the aid of certain priests.

ROBERTSON, J. P., and ROBERTSON, W. P., Letters on Paraguay: comprising an account of four years' residence in that republic under the government of the Dictator Francia, two volumes, London, 1838.

——— Francia's Reign of Terror, being the continuation of letters on Paraguay, London, 1839.

ROBINSON, W. D., Memoirs of the Mexican Revolution, including a narrative of the expedition of General Xavier Mina, . . . Philadelphia, 1820.

[ROCAFUERTE, V.], Bosquejo ligerisimo de la Revolución de Mégico, desde el grito de Iguala hasta la proclamación imperial de Iturbide. Por un verdadero Americano, Philadelphia, 1822.

An Ecuadorian's views concerning Iturbide's revolution, with some illustrative documents.

RODNEY (C. A.), and GRAHAM (J.), The Reports on the Present State of the United Provinces of South America, London, 1819.

SAN MARTÍN, J., . . . Documentos del Archivo de San Martín, twelve volumes, Buenos Aires, 1910, 1911.

These useful documents were selected from the manuscripts collected by General Mitre for his life of San Martín,— documents preserved in the Mitre Museum under whose auspices these volumes and also those concerning Belgrano and Pueyrredón were published.

——— . . . San Martín, su correspondencia, 1823-1850, Buenos Aires, 1911.

Material on San Martín's life during his retirement and some after-thoughts concerning the revolution.

SANTA ANNA, A. L. DE, Mi historia militar y política, 1810-1874 (volume two in Documentos inéditos ó muy raros para la historia de México, edited by G. García), Mexico, 1905.

SANTANDER, F. DE P., Archivo Santander. Publicación hecha por una comisión de la academia de la historia, bajo la dirección de don Ernesto Restrepo Tirado, volumes one to nine, Bogotá (1913-).

Containing as it does numerous inedited documents concerning Bolívar's great rival, this work promises to be one of the most important sources for the history of northern South America.

SMITH, M., History of the Adventures and Sufferings of Moses Smith during five years of his life, from the beginning of the year 1806, when he was betrayed into the Miranda expedition until June, 1811, when he was non-suited in an action at law which lasted three years and a half, to which is added a biographical sketch of General Miranda, Brooklyn, 1812.

STEVENSON, W. H., Historical and descriptive Narrative of twenty years' residence in South America, three volumes, London, 1829.

TORATA, EL CONDE DE, Editor. Documentos para la Historia de la Guerra separatista del Perú, five volumes, Madrid, 1894-1898.

These volumes contain material of value concerning the last period of the Peruvian war for independence.

TORENO, EL CONDE DE, Historia del levantamiento, guerra, y revolución de España, seven volumes, Madrid, 1848.

TORRENTE, M., Historia de la Revolución Hispano-Americana, three volumes, Madrid, 1829, 1830.

A royalist view of the Spanish-American revolution.

TORRES LANZAS, P., Independencia de América, fuentes para su estudio, catálogo de documentos conservados en el archivo general de Indias de Sevilla, primera serie, six volumes, Madrid, 1912.

A catalogue of inedited documents in the Spanish archives which, at some points, is detailed enough so that it can be used as a source.

Tratados celebrados en la villa de Córdoba el 24 del presente entre los señores d. Juan O'Donojú, teniente general de los ejercitos de España, y d. Augustín de Iturbide, primer gefe del ejército imperial Mejicano de las tres garantías, Córdoba, 24 de Agosto de 1821,—Mexico, 1821.

Ultimos instantes de los primeros caudillos de la independencia. Narración de un testigo ocular. Edited by L. G. Obregón, Mexico, 1896.

[VISCARDO Y GUZMÁN, P.], Lettre aux Espagnols-Américains. Par un de leurs compatriots, Philadelphia, 1799.

A rare pamphlet which indicts Spanish rule in America.

WALTON, W., Present State of the Spanish Colonies, including a particular report of Hispaniola, London, 1810.

WARD, H. G., Mexico in 1827, London, 1828.

WELLINGTON, A., Supplementary despatches, correspondence, and memoranda of Field Marshal, Arthur, Duke of Wellington, K.G., volumes six and twelve, London, 1860-1865.

ZERCERO, A., Memorias para la Historia de las Revoluciónes en México, volume one, Mexico, 1869.

2. Newspapers, etc.

Aurora de Chile, 1812-1813. Reimpresión paleográfica á plana y renglón con una introducción por Julio Vicuña Cifuentes, Santiago de Chile, 1903.

Gaceta de Buenos Aires (1810-1821). Reimpresión facsimilar, dirigida por la junta de historia y numismática Americana . . . , five volumes, Buenos Aires, 1910-1914.

Of great value upon the revolution in the viceroyalty of la Plata.

Gaceta de Madrid, Madrid, 1821-1825.

Gaceta Imperial de México, Mexico, 1821, 1822.

Invaluable upon the Iturbidista revolution.

The Courier, London, 1822-1824.

The Daily National Intelligencer, Washington, 1822, 1823.

The Political Herald and Review, or, a survey of domestic and foreign politics . . . , London, 1785.

El Tiempo, Caracas, 1910.

The Times, London, 1822-1824.

El Universal, Caracas, 1915.

The Weekly Register, edited by H. Niles, volumes one to thirty-seven, Baltimore, 1811-1830.

Some useful documents concerning Spanish America found their way into this newspaper.

3. Periodicals, etc.

"Bolívar y Sucre, E. Martinez y T. Guido; Preciosas cartas para servir á la historia de las campañas de la independencia de Perú," in La Revista de Buenos Aires, volume eighteen, pages 3-16, Buenos Aires, 1869.

"Cartas del Libertador que no están en las Memorias de O'Leary," in the Gaceta de los Museos Nacionales, volume one, pages 43 ff., Caracas, 1912-

"Centenario del Libertador," in Anales de la Instrucción pública en los Estados Unidos de Colombia, volume six, pages 3-64, Bogotá, 1883.

"La Diplomacia de la Revolución: misionés de Mariano Moreno

al Brazil y á Inglaterra," in *La Revista de la Universidad de Buenos Aires,* volume fifteen, pages 502-514, Buenos Aires, 1911.

This contains some inedited documents on Moreno's mission.

"Documents concerning the consular service of the United States in Latin America, with introductory note, in the *Mississippi Valley Historical Review,* volume two, pages 561-568, Cedar Rapids, 1916.

"Documentos Inéditos," in the Boletín de la Academia Nacional de Historia, volume two, pages 139-175, Caracas, 1913.

Some inedited letters of Sucre, Santander, and others.

"English Policy toward America in 1790-1791," in the *American Historical Review,* volume seven, pages 706-735, New York, 1902.

"Entrevista en Guayaquil (1822) de los generales San Martín y Bolívar," in the *Revista de Buenos Aires,* volume fifteen, pages 66-75, Buenos Aires, 1868.

GÉRARD, A., "Le Général José de San Martín," from *L'Impartial de Boulogne-sur-mer,* Boulogne-sur-mer, 1850.

"Miranda and the British Admiralty," in the *American Historical Review,* volume six pages 500-530, New York, 1901.

"South American Emancipation," in the *Edinburgh Review, or Critical Journal,* volume thirteen, pages 277-312, Edinburgh, 1809.

This is a review of "Lettre aux Espagnols-Américains": as Miranda evidently aided in preparing it, it partakes of the character of autobiographical material concerning his career.

"Sucre Íntimo," in the Boletín de la Academia Nacional de la Historia, volume three, pages 1-30, Caracas, 1914.

4. Manuscript Collections

There is an enormous amount of manuscript material concerning Spanish America during the revolutionary period preserved in archival repositories. The writer utilized some of this material while preparing his "Francisco de Miranda": a complete list of the archives then consulted will be found on pages 507-511 of that work. Since that work was published, he has used other inedited materials upon certain phases of the Spanish-American revolution. There are collections of unexploited material in the archives of England, France, and the United States; this material is frequently most useful because it furnishes the impressions and the viewpoints of foreign observers. Helpful suggestions concerning the material in some of these archives relating to Spanish-American history may be found in the Carnegie Institution guides to materials in foreign archives relating to the history of the United

States. As yet, the historical archives—public and private—of South America, are virtually unknown in North America. Many of those collections are in the possession of the respective governments; other collections are in the control of learned societies; while some collections are, at least in part, in the hands of private individuals. For the present purpose, the writer has confined his statements concerning archival material to a briefly annotated list of the main collections which he has actually found useful upon one phase or another of the movement for the emancipation of Spanish America.

Archivo Diplomático y Consular de Colombia, Bogotá.

Through the courtesy of Señor Antonio Gómez Restrepo the writer was allowed to view in these archives the original of the letter written by Bolívar's general secretary concerning the fateful interview between Bolívar and San Martín at Guayaquil.

Archives of the English Government: Public Record Office, London.

A vast amount of useful material concerning Spanish-American affairs is found among the reports of English officials in America which are in the various groups of manuscripts found in this repository.

Archivo del general José E. Andrade, Caracas.

By the courtesy of Señor V. Lecuna the writer secured from this collection some inedited letters of José E. Andrade concerning the period from 1826-1830.

The Library of Congress: Division of Manuscripts.

"Iturbide Papers."

This important collection is concerned rather with Iturbide's career as a royalist commander and his rôle as emperor of Mexico than with his career as liberator.

Archives of the Mexican Government: Archivo General de la Nación, Mexico City.

The writer has used inedited papers in this archive which concern Iturbide's revolution.

Archivo del Libertador (Simón de Bolívar), Caracas.

By the courtesy and aid of Señor Lecuna, the writer secured copies of certain inedited papers of Bolívar which still remain in this archive.

Archives of the Spanish Government:

Archivo General de Simancas, Simancas.

From Simancas material was secured relating to the military services of Iturbide, as well as to the early career of Miranda.

Archivo General de Indias, Seville.

This is, of course, the great repository of material concerning the Spanish Indies. Many papers found here are concerned with the revolution; they are especially useful on diplomatic problems.

Archives of the United States Government, Washington, D. C. Bureau of Indexes and Archives.

There is a large amount of unpublished material concerning the Spanish-American revolution, 1810-1830, reposing in this bureau of the American department of state.

INDEX

Index